THE
LOYALISTS
OF
NEW BRUNSWICK

by

ESTHER CLARK WRIGHT

Available from
E. C. Wright,
P. O. Box 710,
Wolfville, N. S., Canada
B0P 1X0

All Rights Reserved

First Edition May 1955
Second Printing February 1972
Third Printing February 1977
Fourth Printing March 1981

PRINTED BY LANCELOT PRESS

087123   Hantsport, N. S.

CONTENTS

CHAPTER ONE

TORY INTO LOYALIST

HE WAS KNOWN FOR HIS LOYALTY TO HIS KING IN 1775

The words are graven on the large stone which covers the resting place in the churchyard at Gagetown, New Brunswick, of Thomas Gilbert, formerly of Taunton, Massachusetts. They might have been carved many hundreds of times in burying grounds up and down the St. John River, and in other parts of New Brunswick as well. In brief summing up they tell the story of years of gathering suspicion and division, of years of active persecution, of exile from home, of imprisonment, of loss of property, of proscription and attainder. Who were these people whose loyalty to their king brought such dire consequences? When and why and how did they come to New Brunswick? What did they find upon arrival? What happened to them in their new home?

The Loyalists have been vilified by those who forsook their allegiance to their king; they have, sometimes, been worshipped with fanatic pride by their descendants; for the most part, they have been contemptuously dismissed by historians of the American Revolution, or, rarely, accorded sympathetic but cursory treatment; they have not been studied as a group whose existence, whose movements, and whose consequences, raise problems which need investigation. The attempt to analyze the origins of the Loyalists who came to New Brunswick and to set forth the circumstances of their coming necessitated an examination of the whole obscure subject of the gathering together and the exodus from the thirteen colonies of these followers of a losing cause and a not impossible loyalty.

I

Loyalty to the king and desire to preserve the connection with Britain had not been obnoxious attitudes before 1775. "Nothing is more earnestly our wish," declared the *Circular Letter* of the Boston Sons of Liberty, under date of February 3, 1766, "than that the most happy perfect union may be preserved betwixt Great Britain and her Colonies." In May, 1769, the Virginia House of Burgesses, although setting forth that the sole right of levying taxes was vested in the legislature of the province of Virginia, and protesting against the subjection of Americans to English tribunals, nevertheless assured the king of "our inviolable attachment to his sacred person and government." Even in 1774, the Continental Congress addressed the king as their "Most Gracious Sovereign", and assured him that if he would but turn his royal indignation upon those "designing and dangerous men" in the Ministry, who were prosecuting "the most desperate and irritating projects of oppression," all would be well within the empire.[1]

The Continental Congress of 1774, however, in spite of its protestations of loyalty, and in spite of having completed its sessions without committing the colonies to a policy of independence, had widened the cleavage between the radicals or Whigs, and the conservatives or Tories. It had passed the Nonimportation, Nonexportation, and Nonconsumption Agreements, which were adopted under the name of the Continental Association. Tories who refused to subscribe to the Association were proclaimed as violators, and were sometimes subjected to tarring and feathering. The clashes between the British troops stationed in Boston and the American militiamen, at Lexington, in April, and at Bunker Hill, in June, 1775, and the violent propaganda which followed those clashes, widened still further the rift between Whig and Tory. The publication, in January, 1776, of Tom Paine's *Common Sense*, with its bold demand for independence, openly declared in a

2

manner in which Sam Adams and the radicals had not yet dared proclaim it in the Continental Congress, jolted Whig and Tory further apart.

The experience of that Thomas Gilbert who was known for his loyalty to his king in 1775 shows what this widening cleavage between Whig and Tory meant to a Massachusetts Tory. Gilbert, whose previous military experience had included serving as captain in the attack on Louisbourg, in 1745, and as lieutenant-colonel, in succession to Ephraim Williams, at Crown Point ten years later, had been asked by General Gage, the British Commander-in-Chief at Boston, to rally the Tories in Bristol County. In answer to this call, Gilbert had gathered a force of three hundred. The General Court of Massachusetts, in session at Freetown, thereupon proclaimed him as an "inveterate enemy to his country, to reason, to justice and the common rights of mankind." He and his followers deserved "to be instantly cut off from the benefit of commerce with, or countenance of any friend of virtue, America or the human race." In consequence of this proclamation, Gilbert was forced to flee from his home and take refuge on the *Rose*, a British warship stationed at Newport. Thence he made his way to Boston, from which place, on May 4, 1775, he wrote his sons urging them to meet him at Boston. When the British troops, and their inglorious commander, General Gage, evacuated Boston, in March, 1776, Thomas Gilbert and his brother Samuel were among the nine hundred and twenty-six evacuees who sailed with them.[2]

The evacuation of Boston was a shadow of things to come. In the long process of making Tories into Loyalists, a process which was to reach its culmination in the evacuation of New York in 1783, the evacuation of Boston was the beginning. From March, 1776, there was in existence a group of refugees who had been driven from their homes and their occupations because they had

3

refused to renounce their allegiance to their king. To escape the fury of the mob, they had been forced to take their departure when the British troops were withdrawn to Halifax. Fourteen members of the Governor's Council, thirty-nine employees of the Customs, and two hundred and twenty-six "refugees", with their families, made up the nine hundred and twenty-six civilian evacuees who went to Halifax. Of this number, only a few remained in Halifax; several set sail as soon as possible for England; others attempted to return to their homes in Boston and elsewhere in Massachusetts, where they were thrown into gaol, unless, as happened in a few cases, they were able to reinstate themselves in favour by forswearing their allegiance and paying large fines; the remainder accompanied the army to New York after that city had been occupied by the British forces under Howe.[3]

From the autumn of 1776 until the autumn of 1783, New York and Long Island were occupied by the British and were the place of refuge for those who were known for their loyalty to their king. To the Massachusetts refugees were added refugees from other parts of New York province, from Connecticut, from Rhode Island, from New Jersey, and from Pennsylvania. Successive British commanders wrestled with the problem of the dispossessed Tories, a problem which was not made any easier by the incompetence of those same commanders and by their withdrawal from one colony after another.

In some respects the plight of refugees in the eighteenth century was not as serious as in the twentieth century. In the less complex civilization of the 1770's, the basic needs of shelter, food and clothing could be more readily provided than under the elaborately organized and highly mechanized economy of the 1940's. The refugees of the earlier age were more independent than their modern brothers and sisters, more used to coping with the wilderness, more used to living on the

4

country. Many of the Tory refugees purchased or rented, or without such formalities took possession of, houses and farms left vacant by the Whigs who had fled at the advance of the British army. For a few years, they were the most fortunate of the evacuees, but when, in 1783, they had to pull up stakes again, and leave, generally without any compensation, the improvements they had made in the course of several years' expenditure of money and toil, they considered themselves twice dispossessed.

The refugees who carried on their normal occupations, in a different place, were few in number compared with those who were drawn, in one way or another, into employment in connection with hostilities. In the more or less regularly embodied corps of provincial troops—the British Legion, DeLancey's Brigade, Emerick's Chasseurs, Ferguson's Corps, the Guides and Pioneers, Hierlihy's Corps, the King's American Dragoons, the King's American Regiment, the King's Orange Rangers, the Loyal American Legion, the Loyal American Regiment, the Maryland Loyalists, the New Jersey Volunteers (Skinner's), the New York Volunteers, the Pennsylvania Loyalists, the Prince of Wales' American Regiment, the Queen's Rangers—some 8000 officers and men served, many of them from the very beginning of the conflict. Thus, Lieutenant-Colonel George Turnbull, on April 11, 1783, writing on behalf of the New York Volunteers, said that "this Corps was imbodied so Early as 1775 that we had a Share in the Dangers of the Actions of 27th August 1776 on Long Island". The first battalion of the New Jersey Volunteers was commissioned on July 1, 1776, four more battalions in November of that year, and the sixth in December, 1776. All three battalions of DeLancey's Brigade were commissioned in August, 1776, and the King's American Regiment and the King's Orange Rangers before the close of the same year. In addition to these corps, the Royal Highland Regiment, the 84th, and the Royal Fencible Americans were also recruited in America. There were also several

5

other groups, such as the South Carolina Royalists, Loyal New Englanders, the North Carolina Volunteers, the King's Carolina Rangers, the North Carolina Highlanders, the Westchester Loyalists, and perhaps others, which aided the British armies more or less spasmodically, and acted in a more or less voluntary capacity, that is without regular pay or provisions, sometimes without any pay or subsistence. The Westchester Loyalists, for instance, were largely concerned with supplying forage and provisions for the garrison in New York (wherefore they were known by the opposing forces as "cattle rustlers"), and in repelling raids by American forces who were engaged in similar activities in the no-man's-land between the two armies.[4]

In addition to service in the provincial regiments, there were other opportunities of employment in and around New York, in Ordnance, Engineering, the Barrackmaster-General's Department, the Commissary-General's, the Paymaster-General's, and the Hospital. Other refugees, not regularly employed in these Civil Departments of the army, were more or less regularly employed in bringing in supplies of various kinds: wood, hay, cattle, fish, and other provisions. Some of these men were contractors, others speculators, still others were employed by the day or week, when and as their services were needed.

And then, as always, there were the unemployables: men of too exalted a station to accept any ordinary employment in the army or the subsidiary services; the aged and the invalids, including men wounded in fighting, men whose health had been impaired by long imprisonment in the Simsbury salt mines and other unhealthy places of detention, and men incapacitated by illness—this was the eighteenth century when lack of sanitation and medical ignorance meant that towns were breeding places of disease and epidemics; men with too large a family, their own or a brother's; and widows, particularly widows with families. A quarterly allowance

6

varying according to the importance of the recipient, or the size of his family, was paid to such "distressed loyalists". From the 1st of January, 1779, to the 31st of March, 1783, the payments were handled by Colonel Roger Morris, a former British army officer, who had married Mary, daughter of Frederick Philipse, one of the large landowners of the Hudson valley. On December 25, 1781, about three hundred and fifty of those who were receiving "Rations as Loyal Refugees and sufferers by Rebellion" protested against the "Ill Usage that the said Colonel R. Morris daily practices towards his Majestys Loyal and distressed Subjects Committed to his Care," and "his total Ignorance of the Characters of the Refugees and his Austere manners." At the time, the petition was ignored, but it probably had some effect later in affecting Sir Guy Carleton's decision to appoint a Board to consider the circumstances and claims of distressed Loyalists. Two reports of this Board exist for the period from April to June, 1783. The "List of Persons recommended by the Board" contains 452 names, 208 from New York, three from New Hampshire, 81 from New Jersey, 22 from Massachusetts Bay, 40 from Connecticut, 21 from Rhode Island, 33 from Pennsylvania, 15 from Virginia, 14 from Maryland, 10 from North and South Carolina, Georgia and Florida, six from the Wentworth Volunteers, one from Canada. Since about a third of the names on this list appear among the New Brunswick Loyalists, the distribution of these refugees among the provinces is of interest and foreshadows the proportions found by the study of origins of the New Brunswick Loyalists. The second report of the Board, containing 275 names, is denoted, "An alphabetical list of distressed loyalists recommended for an allowance for their support". This list of lesser persons shows a larger proportion of New Brunswick settlers than the other list, which is also significant and prophetic.[5]

It was hardly to be expected that the unemployables would achieve very much in the way of an organization

7

of the loyal refugees. The petition of protest against the austerity of Colonel Morris affords evidence of a rudimentary organization of companies with captains and lieutenants. There was apparently some kind of a committee of representatives from the different provinces. Sabine's *American Loyalists* quotes a letter of Christopher Sower, a printer from Pennsylvania, who spent a few years quarrelling with other Loyalists in New Brunswick, in which Sower mentions that the deputies of the refugees from the different provinces were accustomed to meet once a week, and that, on December 5, 1779, Daniel Cox, of Trenton, New Jersey, was appointed to the chair, to deprive him of the opportunity of speaking, as he had the "gift of saying little with many words."[6] The paucity of references to this committee of deputies suggests that it remained an unimportant and uninfluential group until after the arrival of the New Englanders, who had had a longer experience of refugee organization and of harassing the enemy. Again, we return to Boston for the beginnings of the story.

On October 28, 1775, William Howe had issued a proclamation in which he pointed out that it had become the "indispensable duty of every loyal and faithful citizen to contribute all in his power for the preservation of order and good government within the Town of Boston", and called upon the citizens to "associate themselves to be formed into Companies, under proper officers." Their employment would be solely within the precincts of the town, and General Howe himself would choose the officers from among the associators. The association was to be opened in the Council Chamber, under the direction of the Hon. Peter Oliver, Foster Hutchinson, and William Brown, Esquires, on Monday, October 30, and continue for four days, that "No one may plead ignorance of the same." Those who were able to discharge the duty required of them were to be properly armed, and those who required allowance of fuel and provisions should have one equal to that issued

8

His Majesty's troops within the garrison. The orders of the day, on November 17, 1775, listed three companies, with Hon. Timothy Ruggles, who had attained the rank of Brigadier-General during the French war, as commanding officer, and Abijah Willard, of Lancaster, Massachusetts, James Putnam, of Worcester, a lawyer and graduate of Harvard, and Francis Green, a Boston merchant and graduate of Harvard, as captains of the three companies. The companies were to be called the Loyal American Associators, and the members were to be distinguished by a white sash around the left arm.[7]

The evacuation of Boston, in the spring of 1776, brought to an end this phase of the organization which was concerned with the preservation of order and good government within the town of Boston. All but four or five of the nineteen officers named in the November 17 orders sailed to Halifax with the army, and were thenceforth refugees. The more energetic of those who returned from Halifax found their way to the British headquarters at Newport, Rhode Island, and assisted the British troops in various capacities. Among these was George Leonard, a native of Plymouth, who had been a merchant and shipowner in Boston, and had been named as one of the first lieutenants of the first company of the Loyal American Associators. In a printed Memorial to the Right Honourable Lord George Germaine, one of his Majesty's Principal Secretaries of State, Leonard gives a vivid account of his considerable part in various forays:

That there having been at New-York and Rhode-Island great numbers of Loyalists, who had left their All to follow the Royal standard; zealous to become useful, but destitute of the means of putting their zeal in practice; owners of large property in the several provinces and generally of a rank in life superiour to the class from which the common seaman and soldier are taken, they were averse to entering into the service, as such, and still more so to remaining idle spectators of the contest.

9

With a view to prevent persons of that description from becoming burthensome to Government, and to enable them to co-operate with his Majesty's forces in suppressing the rebellion, your Lordships' Memorialist, with others, under the sanction and authority of Sir Henry Clinton, the Commander-in-Chief in America, concerted and undertook a service, which at the same time that it gave employment and subsistence to many hundred Loyalists, was very distressing and alarming to the Rebels; afforded supplies of fresh provisions for the hospitals and garrison at Rhode-Island; and in other respects aided and promoted his Majesty's service.

The Loyalists in general were unable to contribute anything more than their services; but the Memorialist having been so fortunate as to bring from Boston the greater part of his property, cheerfully devoted the whole, together with all the credit he could obtain, to the undertaking; and purchased, fitted for sea, and manned the following vessels, viz.

The Frigate ship Restoration,
     of 20 nine pounders, ...   150 men.
   Sloop General Prescot,
     10 nine and six pounders, ...   50 men.
   Schooner Charlotte,
     10 six and four pounders, ...   40 men.
   ———— General Leslie,
     10 four pounders, ...   40 men.
   ———— General Garth,
     10 four pounders, ...   40 men.
   Armed schooner Hazard, ⎫
     Sloop George, and   ⎬ . . . .   60 men.
     Sloop Harriet,   ⎭
   Transport brig Lucy, ...   9 men.
   Transport schooner Sally, ...   9 men.
     Besides several armed boats.

The undertaking was entered upon not only with the entire approbation of Sir Henry Clinton, but the Memorialist gratefully acknowledges the unceasing patronage given him by General Prescot, under whose more immediate command he was. To them he is indebted for the greater part of the ammunition and military stores, as well as for a donation of 550 guineas.

Sir George Collier, then the Commander of his Majesty's fleet in North America, was pleased to give the Memorialist a commission authorizing him to perform the intended services.

With the above force, the Memorialist and his associates annoyed the enemy, obtained supplies of fresh provisions, and were at all times a faithful band of guides and pilots to the King's army and navy, having made it their invariable practice to desist from private pursuits, to give convoy and protection to transports, victuallers, etc. as well as to co-operate with the army in making descents on the coast, whenever called upon; which services occupied the greater part of their time.

The Memorialist begs leave to mention the following services, in which no private emolument accrued to him or his associates.

He was called upon to cruise, or to take particular stations, when Rhode-Island was destitute of naval force, and insults from the Rebels were apprehended; which services were always cheerfully performed.

One of his principal vessels was employed six weeks, with his Majesty's frigate Thames, in blocking up the harbour of New-London, at the request of Sir George Collier.

Four of the Memorialist's vessels, at the request of Captain Grant of his Majesty's ship the Lioness, were employed thirty days as station-vessels at the different harbours on Long-Island Sound; the Rebel privateers having, not long before, captured a number of wood-vessels, and done other damage on Long-Island.

At the request of General Prescot, he assisted in the convoy of three regiments from Rhode-Island to New York.

Upon his arrival at New-York, the Memorialist and his associates were employed in the descent upon Connecticut, under General Tryon; which service occupied fifteen days, and wherein the Memorialist's armed vessels were of signal utility in assisting to cover the landing of the troops.

After that expedition, as none of the King's ships could then be spared, the Memorialist took charge of twenty-four vessels belonging to his Majesty's service, which had lain inactive at Huntington above a month for want of convoy, and conducted them safe to Rhode-Island.

At the evacuation of Rhode-Island, the Memorialist assisted in covering the embarkation of the garrison, in convoying them, and in transporting the friends of Government, their families and effects, to New York; in which service his whole squadron, then consisting of nine armed vessels, besides six others, were employed above a fortnight.

In these and several other instances, no private benefit accrued to the Memorialist, but on the contrary, the whole expense of the vessels and seamen fell on him, the former being his property, and the latter in his pay, at certain stated wages.

To the above instances of public services, the Memorialist begs leave to add, the destruction of the enemy's coasting vessels and other craft, as well as the taking of great numbers of the enemy prisoners, he and his associates having been so fortunate as to take off several guards from different parts of the coast.

The Memorialist and his associates, in company with seven other armed vessels under his direction, made a descent upon Nantucket, took and destroyed all the vessels there that could be serviceable to the Rebels, and induced the inhabitants to discontinue their practice of supplying the Rebels with West-India goods and military stores, and to send their submission to Sir Henry Clinton and Sir George Collier.[8]

From another native of Plymouth, Edward Winslow, who had not been listed among the officers of the Loyal American Associators, but had been a Boston evacuee and had come to the fore during the Rhode Island period, come additional details regarding refugee activities. According to instructions issued by General Prescott from his Newport Headquarters, on March 31, 1779, Winslow was appointed to command a detachment of "Provincial Forces and Refugees ordered on a Secret Expedition", and very strict orders were given that the Refugees were to be in the centre at debarkation and embarkation. Those orders and the rather ominous sentence that the "future reputation and dearest interests of the Refugees depending on the success of this exertion it is not doubted that regularity, sobriety and the most implicit obedience will invariably be observed", illuminate a later remark of Winslow's that he and his friends, Joshua Upham and Daniel Murray, "every day risqued our reputation as well as our lives", by engaging with a party of refugees from Rhode Island. Several days afterward, in his report concerning the expedition he commanded, Winslow says that the attempt on Bedford failed of success by want of wind to carry the vessels into the harbour and because the rebels had gathered in force to oppose the landing. Since General Prescott had "so pointedly ordered me not to contend with superior force and suggested that in the infant state of our party 'easy conquest ought to be our object',"

Winslow carried out his instructions to alarm and harass the enemy as much as possible by proceeding down the Sound as far as Falmouth, "against which Mr. Leonard drew up the Privateers in a line, while Capt. DePeyster of the King's American Regiment and Capt. Murray of Governor Wentworth's Vols . . . made a show of landing." Winslow expressed himself as exceedingly gratified at being able to testify "that every individual of the party discovered the most extreme ardor," and was convinced that it would be more his duty to "check than to encourage them in their future operations." After expressing indebtedness to Major Upham for his advice and assistance, Winslow stated that he had left the command of the Refugees with Captain Murray, "who has already exhibited most convincing proofs of a spirit of enterprize and sound judgment."

The *Winslow Papers* show also that on April 11, 1779, the "Regimental Orders of the Corps of Loyal Associated Refugees" carried instructions for Captains Murray, Goldsbury, and Martin to embark their companies, taking with them blankets and provisions for two days, and sixty rounds of ammunition which would be furnished. After embarkation, orders would be given by Colonel Fanning (Edmund Fanning of the King's American Regiment, later Lieutenant-Governor of Nova Scotia), who is described as the "Commandant of the Corps of Refugees." The transport and armed vessels for this expedition were to be furnished by Mr. Leonard, "the navy agent and contractor for the Associated Refugees." On such excursions the Associated Refugees had, by June 10, 1779, captured two brigs, two schooners, one sloop, ten boats with a considerable quantity of goods of various kinds, and 35 prisoners, 134 horses, 138 cattle, 1843 sheep, 11 hogs, 642 lambs, 38 calves. On September 16, 1779, Winslow reported that, in the subsequent excursions, the Refugee vessels had taken thirteen prizes, three of them armed vessels, and that

14

the account of sales of property taken from the Rebels, by the Agent's certificate, amounted to the sum of £23,427/18s/6d.[9]

Both Leonard and Winslow hint at the dismay of these refugee groups when the Commander-in-Chief, Sir Henry Clinton, withdrew the British troops from Newport in preparation for his expedition against Charleston, South Carolina. Leonard was particularly annoyed at the withdrawal, because he had paid for 1500 cords of wood cut by the inhabitants of Martha's Vineyard for the use of the garrison at Newport during the ensuing winter. After the retreat from Newport, the two men pursued very different policies. Winslow, who had been appointed Muster-Master-General of the Provincial Forces on July 15, 1776, and had put out most of the actual duties to deputies, endeavoured to get an increase in pay from the Commander-in-Chief. When that application failed, he asked for leave to go to England, but had an unfavourable answer to that request likewise. He also joined with his friends Upham and Murray, first under the patronage of General Ruggles and then in hopes of support from Sir John Wentworth, the last royal governor of New Hampshire, in trying to raise a New England brigade. The only result of this ambitious scheme was the commissioning of the King's American Dragoons, with Benjamin Thompson of Rumford, Massachusetts, as Commanding Officer, and first Upham and then Murray as Major. Leonard spent his time to more effect. He drew up the Memorial, which, after reviewing his services and giving the details of the firewood project, went on to make a "Proposal for reviving the Association of the Loyalists in North America, and making that respectable Body essentially useful to the public service."

That five Commissioners be appointed by Government to superintend the affairs of the Association, and direct all their operations.

15

That the Commissioners have authority to embody such of the American Loyalists as shall be willing to associate for the above purposes, in such manner as they shall think most conducive to his Majesty's service; and to grant commissions to as many persons as shall be thought necessary for carrying the design of the Association into effective execution.

That the Commander in Chief be authorised to furnish arms, ammunition, and rations of provision, to as many Loyalists as shall associate under the direction of the Commissioners.

That this associated body, or any part of them, be permitted to carry on such offensive operations against his Majesty's Colonies in America, as the Commissioners (or the major part of them) shall direct, and the Commander in Chief not disapprove.

That all captures that shall be made from his Majesty's rebellious subjects, or others his enemies, by sea or by land, by this associated body, or any part of them, shall be distributed among them, in such shares or proportions as shall be settled by the Commissioners. And that each person who shall continue in the Association, during the rebellion, upon the recommendation of the Commissioners, shall be entitled to Two hundred Acres of Land in America, when the rebellion shall be suppressed.

And, in order to enable them to carry on their operations upon the sea-coasts of his Majesty's rebellious Colonies, where it is imagined they will be most essentially useful in distressing the enemy, and keeping the country in continual alarms, it is proposed that the Commander in Chief of his Majesty's forces shall be authorized to furnish this body, or any detachment of them, with such a quantity of shipping, upon the requisition of the

16

Commissioners, as shall be necessary to transport them from place to place; and also to afford such other assistance as may be necessary to give vigour and effect to their operations.

And, for the protection of such expeditions by sea as may be undertaken, and to enable them more effectually to annoy the enemy, it is proposed that the Commander in Chief be authorised to furnish sufficient armed vessels, properly equipped for sea; to be manned by the Association, without any expense to the Public: Also that the Commander in Chief be authorised to furnish such gun-boats and field-pieces, as may be deemed necessary for the service.

And, to prevent the delays that would be otherwise unavoidable, it is proposed, that in case of the absence of the Commander in Chief from the post or place where the Commissioners shall reside, the Officer commanding such post or place should be invested with similar authority respecting the Association, during the absence, and subject to the control of the Commander in Chief.

That the mariners employed in this service shall not be impressed into any other service whatever.

By adopting this proposal, it is humbly apprehended, that Government may, at a very moderate expence, be served with a very considerable number of men, well acquainted with the country and coast, and whose interest and principles unite in attaching them to his Majesty's cause. [10]

Leonard's plan commended itself to the authorities in London, and on April 21, 1780, Lord George Germaine sent a printed copy of the Memorial to Clinton and said that the proposals contained therein appeared to His

Majesty "a proper ground upon which a Plan may be formed for employing the Zeal of His Majesty's faithful Subjects in North America in annoying the Sea Coasts of the revolted Provinces, and distressing their Trade". As Board of Directors for the conduct and management of the affair, the King approved of William Franklin Esquire, Governor of New Jersey, Josiah Martin Esquire, Governor of North Carolina, Timothy Ruggles of Massachusetts, Joseph Wanton of Rhode Island, Daniel Cox of New Jersey, George Duncan Ludlow, Edward Lutwyche, and George Rome of New York, and George Leonard. These were probably the provincial representatives of the refugees who had been accustomed to meet once a week, or such of them as were known to Germaine, with the author of the proposal added to their number. Germaine's letter indicated also the King's approval of the granting of commissions for commanding the Loyalists, "but without Pay or Rank in the Army or Command over other Corps"; of the furnishing of ordnance and stores, small arms and ammunition, rations of provisions for the expeditions, and of shipping as it could be spared; of the captures made by the Associators "when not acting in conjunction with any of His Majesty's Land or Sea Forces," being their own property; and of the gratuitous grant of two hundred acres of land in North America.

What with delays and wrangling over the details of the scheme, it was not until December, 1780, that the Board was finally commissioned and arrangements completed. On receipt of Germaine's letter, Clinton asked the intended Board of Associated Loyalists to prepare a plan for carrying into execution the proposals approved. When he wrote on October 28, 1780, William Franklin explained that the "Absence and Avocations of some of the Gentlemen nominated" delayed their meeting. Since Governor Martin and Mr. Ro(o)me were absent, Mr. Wanton had died, and General Ruggles and

18

Mr. Ludlow lived at a distance, Franklin suggested that Anthony Stewart and Robert Alexander, Esquires, of Maryland, might be added to the board. The Commission and Instructions sent by Franklin were not acceptable to Sir Henry Clinton; in consequence, he sent the Board a Commission along with the Regulations he thought advisable. This action evoked a lengthy letter of protest, on December 1, 1780, that the regulations were in several respects different from those the Board had proposed, and from "what we conceive to have been the Intention of His Majesty". The principal objections of the Board were to a clause making them subject to "New Instructions" from the Commander-in-Chief, or his successor; to the Board's not having control over the treatment and confinement of the prisoners taken by the Loyalists as well as over their exchange; to the requirement that the Board were "to direct the Associators in *all* their Excursions to *obey* such *Commands* as may be given from *Head Quarters* as to their *Conduct* and *Duration*"; and to the whole body of Associated Loyalists being made liable, on an order of the Commander-in-Chief, to repay the damage done to loyal and inoffensive inhabitants within the rebel lines, by any particular party of Associators.

To this lengthy protest—although it was signed by all the Board, it was written by William Franklin, who was as fond of words as his father Benjamin—Sir Henry Clinton answered that the Commission he sent was, "upon the most mature Deliberation, framed not only with the strictest Regard to the Minister's Letter, but as nearly conformable to the Plan you laid before me, as the Spirit of it would admit", and that he had himself added the benefits of His Majesty's hospitals. He intimated that it would be well if they got on with the job and discovered whether the Commission did not work out satisfactorily.[10] This communication was dated December 10, and the Honourable Board of Directors was at once set up, with William Franklin as president, and Sampson Salter Blowers, a Boston lawyer, graduate of Harvard in 1763, as secretary. On the 28th of the month, the Board issued a declaration, which, after a lengthy preamble, set forth the Benefits and Rewards, such as provision of ordnance, rations, shipping, hospital privileges, and the two hundred acres of land, which would be available to encourage the Associators. "It will also be an Object of their immediate Care to put a Stop to those distinguished Cruelties with which the Colonial Loyalists are generally treated, when they have the Misfortune of falling into the Hands of the Rebels," the Proclamation continued. "Should these hereafter, to answer their malignant Purposes, endeavour to avail themselves of their usual Distinction of Prisoners of State from Prisoners of War, by which so many worthy Loyalists have already suffered the most ignominious Deaths, the Directors pledge themselves to the Associators, to omit nothing in their Power, to make the Enemy feel the just Vengeance due to such Enormities."[11]

This section of the declaration by the Board of Directors of the Associated Loyalists touched upon an aspect of the Revolutionary War which has been largely ignored, the barbarous treatment of those who refused to join in the rebellion. The histories of individual Loyalists provide many accounts of tarring, feathering, riding on rails, imprisonment in chains, execution, or of threats of death escaped only because the Loyalists fled to the surrounding woods or broke out of an insufficiently guarded gaol. The violent propaganda which was used to cover these excesses has come to be believed as a justification for them. The furor which one incident connected with the Associated Loyalists called forth is in itself evidence that they generally avoided what their articles of Association called, "Excesses, Barbarities or Irregularities, contrary to the acknowledged Laws of War as practised by civilized Nations". The refugees from New Jersey had been incensed by the ill-treatment accorded prisoners and Loyalists in that province, and had seized upon an opportunity to take revenge by seizing a Captain Huddy, who had been ordered exchanged, and hanging him. On the body was pinned the notice:

> We the Reffugees having with Grief Long beheld the Cruel Murders of our Brethren and finding Nothing but Such Measures Daily Carrying into Execution.
>
> We therefore Determine not to Suffer without taking Vengeance for numerous Cruelties and thus begin and have made use of— Captain Huddy as the first Object to present to your Views, and further *Determine* to Hang Man for Man as Long as a Reffugee is left Existing.
>
> Up goes Huddy for Phillip White.

This gave the Americans an opportunity to protest. Washington wrote to Sir Guy Carleton, who had replaced Sir Henry Clinton as Commander-in-Chief, and the incident was made the subject of representations to the British Government, who wrote Sir Guy for an explanation. Sir Guy asked for certified copies of the minutes of the Board of Directors of the Associated Loyalists, and for their account of the affair. The Loyalists produced a list of twelve men, in addition to Philip White, who had been put to death by the New Jersey rebels, and claimed, in further justification of the hanging, that Huddy had assisted in murdering a Loyalist by the name of Edwards.[12]

In the absence of any record of the number of associates or of the number of expeditions undertaken, it is difficult to assess the activities of the Associated

Loyalists. The formal minutes of the Board report on exchange of prisoners, the fitting and chartering of a sloop or two, the occasional arrival of new associators, for instance, Northrup Marple with twenty men, the distribution of prize money from expeditions not otherwise mentioned. One expedition noted was into Connecticut under the leadership of Major Hubbill, who collected cattle and horses, killed three rebels and took seven prisoners. In June, 1781, a request to the Associated Loyalists to undertake the garrisoning of the fort at Lloyd's Neck, Long Island, elicited from the Board a lengthy list of conditions, that Colonel Upham be granted a lieutenant-colonel's commission and Captain Hubbill a major's commission; that two 18-pounders and four long 12-pounders be provided; that, since part of the garrison would be on constant actual service and the other part employed in making excursions with armed vessels, a constant supply of provisions, arms, and ammunition, be granted, "in the manner as heretofore usual at that Post when garrisoned by the King's Troops"; and that they be given entire possession of the fortifications, barracks, military stores, as well as of the rebel lands on the Neck, with the privilege of cutting wood for fuel for the Barracks and for the use of themselves and families. A much worn paper, found among the *Ontario Land Papers* in the Public Archives of Canada, contains "Instructions from the Board of Directors of Associated Loyalists to Captain Gideon Vernon Commanding a Whaleboat and a Party intending an Excursion to Delaware." This evidence of one expedition not mentioned in the minutes of the Board suggests that there may have been many such undertakings. The eleven paragraphs of the Instructions, probably drawn up by S. S. Blowers, the secretary of the Board (afterwards Attorney-General of Nova Scotia), embody the principles laid down in the Board's Proclamation and Articles of Association, and appear to have been part of a routine procedure.[13]

22

It was a not unimportant contribution of the Associated Loyalists that they brought into general use the term Loyalist, to supersede Tory, King's man, British adherent, Royalist, Loyal Associator, Loyal Refugee, and other names. One of the earliest uses of the term seems to have been on Long Island, at Oyster Bay. At the Town Meeting, on the first Tuesday in April, 1775, many of the townsmen had objected to "having Anything to do with Deputys or Congresses", and the minute to that effect was signed by Thomas Smith, John Hewlett, and John Townsend, Justices, and by John Cock, Town Clerk. The entry was later ordered erased, but was re-entered on March 24, 1778, because it was first put on record to perpetuate to distant ages "What a Large Majority of Loyellist the Township Contained," and if it were not put on the record again, the rising generations might be led to believe "that the Great Majority of Loyellist that Voated against Deputys to form Congresses at the Anual Town Meeting April 1775 Changed there Sentiments Before the Anual Town Meeting April 1776."[14] It was most fitting that the Associated Loyalists, whose stronghold was on Long Island, should continue and perpetuate the name of Loyalist.

The Huddy affair, coming as it did at the end of hostilities, was unfortunate for the reputation of the Associated Loyalists. There was no opportunity to retrieve their good name by their zeal in prosecuting the war, and the business had embarrassed the new Commander-in-Chief. Beamish Murdoch, the historian of early Nova Scotia, says that Sir Guy Carleton broke up the Board of Directors.[15] The Carleton Papers contain no evidence to support the charge, except that William Franklin drops out of the picture, and that the Associated Loyalists, as an organization, were not entrusted with the responsibility of arrangements for the embarkation of the Loyalists for Nova Scotia and elsewhere, in the autumn of 1782 and the spring of 1783. It seems probable that circumstances relieved Sir Guy of the necessity of breaking up the Board, a supposition which is borne out by a letter from George Leonard, under date of September 10, 1782, in which he begs to tender his resignation, "the late Resolution of the House of Commons against offensive measures, having in my humble opinion entirely done away with the utility of the Board".[16] Once again, George Leonard had shown his acumen in sizing up the situation.

The resolution of the House of Commons, which had induced George Leonard to tender his resignation from the Board of Directors of the organization which he had proposed, was part of the expression of the growing dissatisfaction in England with the war, its conduct, its conception, its disasters. The surrender of Cornwallis at Yorktown, Virginia, on October 19, 1781, was the final reverse which induced the Commons to adopt a resolution suggesting a desire for a "happy Reconciliation" with America. Sir Guy Carleton, who as governor of Quebec had shown himself an able administrator in North America, was sent out as Commander-in-Chief and Commissioner of Peace, with instructions for withdrawing the troops from the South and from New York, making provisions for the civilians within the lines, and safeguarding British property and interests.

To the Loyalists at New York, the news of the surrender of Cornwallis, which was many months in reaching them, was a bitter blow. When details of the articles of capitulation were received, the Loyalists' dismay was increased by apprehensions regarding their own future. Cornwallis had asked, in Article 10, that natives or inhabitants of the different parts of the country presently in Yorktown and Gloucester should not be punished for having joined the English army, and the American authorities had refused consent to the article, saying that this was a civil matter. Although Sir Henry

Clinton, on March 16, 1782, wrote Franklin that the Minister had signified to him the "King's most gracious approbation of my Intentions to give the loyal Subjects on this Continent who have borne Arms in Support of the Constitution the strongest Assurances that no Post, Place or Garrison, in which Loyalists are joined with the King's Troops, should be surrendered on any Terms which might discriminate between them and put one on a worse Footing than the other", the apprehensions of the Loyalists were not allayed. On March 23, Franklin wrote Lord Shelburne concerning the necessity of giving assurances to the Provincials serving with His Majesty's troops, by which their minds be relieved from the alarm they had taken from the consequence of the 10th Article of Lord Cornwallis' Capitulation at Yorktown. Shelburne enjoined Carleton to repeat to the Loyalists "that their Interests and security shou'd be considered."[17]

One of Carleton's early acts, after his arrival at New York in May, 1782, was to write, in conjunction with Admiral Digby, to General Washington, to inform him that negotiations for general peace had commenced at Paris, and that the independency of the thirteen provinces should be proposed in the first instance, instead of making it a condition of a general treaty, "however, not without the highest Confidence that the Loyalists should be restored to their Possessions, or a full Compensation made them for whatever Confiscations may have taken place." When this letter was laid before Congress, that body considered it as "mere matter of Information", and counselled the States to carry on the war with vigour. A copy of the letter, sent to the principal persons among the Loyalists, was their first intimation of the change of temper of the people and authorities in London. Their reply, signed "on behalf of the Loyal Inhabitants and Refugees within the British Lines at New York" by Robert Alexander, Daniel Coxe, Edward G. Lutwyche, (significantly only three of the Board of

25

Directors of the Associated Loyalists) Isaac Low, Samuel Seabury, Charles Inglis, Elias Hardy, and Christopher Billopp, after stating that it was impossible to express the consternation with which they were struck, "even on the probability of so calamitous an Event taking place," went on to state their firm belief that "there yet exists a Majority of the People throughout the Provinces, who are ardently desirous to be again reunited under His Majesty's just Authority and Government", that this spirit of reunion was now actually operating in several quarters, that the time when "his Majesty's Naval Superiority" had been gloriously asserted and regained, when his arms were victorious in the East, the "Hour of Victory and Success", was not the proper hour to dismember the empire. If, however, the independency of the thirteen colonies was determined, they had only to "entreat Your Excellencies' Interposition with His Majesty, by every consideration of Humanity, to secure, if possible, beyond the mere form of Treaty, our Persons and Properties; that Such, as think they cannot safely remain here, may be enabled to seek Refuge elsewhere."[18]

The dismay of the Loyalists at the turn of events found its way into a book of *Hymns for the Nation*, published in London in 1782:

> The men who dared their King revere,
>   And faithful to their Oaths abide,
> Midst perjur'd Hypocrites sincere,
>   Harass'd, oppress'd on every side;
> Gaul'd by the Tyrant's iron yoke,
> By Britain's faithless sons forsook.

CHAPTER TWO

THE DECISION

A "very general Affliction" was produced among the Loyalists when they were informed of the proposal of independence which Mr. Grenville had been directed to make at Paris. Some of the gentlemen, Sir Guy Carleton reported to Earl Shelburne, on August 17, 1782, would make overtures to the Americans, but others seemed determined "to abide any Extremity rather than submit either to the Domination or Principles of their domestic Foes." "The Passions of these" Sir Guy added, "I have endeavoured to moderate by turning their Views to other Settlements, if the most reasonable Expectations should fail them here." The reactions of the Loyalists in other parts of the country, he thought, would be similar, and everywhere there would be much exultation on the part of the victorious Americans. "But what Course the Passions of Men will ultimately take in this Country, where they will have so free a Scope," Sir Guy felt it was difficult to predict.[1]

There had already been notice from one group calling themselves Loyalists that they were going to make terms with the ruling powers. In a "Humble Address", dated May 30, 1782, the Associated Loyalists in the Provinces of Pennsylvania and Maryland and the Three Lower Counties of New Castle, Kent and Sussex on Delaware, announced that they would assist "in restoring the King's Authority in these Provinces and Counties, as repeatedly offered, to the last drop of their Blood," but if Great Britain, "from an inglorious and dishonest despondency", should withdraw her right and claim to the sovereignty over these colonies, they

27

would consider themselves "as a deserted People, left in a State of Nature and a Liberty to become the Subjects" of the local governments.[2]

Loyalists without the lines had some chance of making their peace with the American authorities, but those who had taken refuge within the British lines had little hope that such a solution would be possible for them. It was clear to the Loyalists in and around New York that the offer of independence would mean the withdrawal of the British forces from New York. That eventuality and its consequences had to be considered. When the British forces had been withdrawn from Boston, in March, 1776, the troops and those who depended on them for protection had sailed for Halifax, and Halifax, not for the last time in its history, had not inclined its involuntary visitors to think well of Nova Scotia. Nevertheless, Nova Scotia offered one overwhelming advantage, it was the nearest British territory to New York. Canada was far distant, unknown, and inhabited by French settlers, whose language, religion and customs were different from those of the majority of the Loyalists. Moreover, the parent country of the Canadians had been an ally of the "revolted colonies". Florida and the islands in the West Indies were other possible places of refuge, but they were also far away, unknown, and peopled with alien races. The climatic difference and the danger of tropical diseases, especially yellow fever, presented further obstacles to using the West Indies as destination. Nova Scotia, in spite of Halifax, might be the most desirable refuge for the Loyalists, and surely on the long coast line and in the interior valleys, such as the Annapolis and the St. John, favourable sites for settlement might be found.

At any rate, Sir Guy Carleton thought it advisable to send with Major-General Paterson, who was taking over command of the Halifax military district, a copy of the letter he and Admiral Digby had sent to General

28

Washington, and to include in his letter to Sir Andrew Snape Hamond, the acting governor of Nova Scotia, a suggestion that many refugees would need and would have a just claim to establishments outside the thirteen provinces, and that it would therefore be "an act of necessary caution" for the governor of Nova Scotia to reserve as much land as possible in the province "to answer demands which are so likely to press, both on the generosity and good faith of the public."[3]

Meanwhile, Sir Guy's endeavours to "turn their Views to other Settlements" were bearing fruit in the Loyalist communities on Long Island and on the Jersey shore. Meetings of refugees were held and agents were chosen, "for the Loyalists who purpose to settle in Nova Scotia as well those who go this Autumn as those who are to follow in the Spring." For the Lloyd's Neck group, the agents named were Benjamin Thompson of Rumford, Massachusetts, who had recently been gazetted lieutenant-colonel of the King's American Dragoons, Edward Winslow of Plymouth, Massachusetts, Muster-Master-General of the Provincial forces, and closely associated with refugee activities in Rhode Island in previous years, Sampson Salter Blowers, attorney of Boston, who had been secretary of the Board of Directors of the Associated Loyalists, Reverend John Sayre, formerly Rector of Trinity Church, Fairfield, Connecticut, Captain John Moseley, shipbuilder, and Amos Botsford, Esquire, attorney of Newton, Connecticut. The refugees living in Queen's County, Long Island, chose Joshua Chandler, Esquire, of New Haven, Connecticut, and Samuel Cummings, Esquire, of New Hampshire. The agents for the Bergen Loyalists were Dr. Samuel Seabury, formerly Rector in Westchester, New York, Chaplain of the King's American Regiment, Major Thomas Ward, of Newark, New Jersey, Captain George Harding, Captain Frederick Hauser, a surveyor, William Harding of Ulster County, New York, and Joshua Pell of New

York, probably of Westchester County. A Board of Agents was set up, with Dr. Seabury as president and S. S. Blowers as secretary. "Articles of Settlement in Nova Scotia" were drawn up, and Dr. Seabury and Lieutenant-Colonel Thompson were appointed by the Board of Agents to wait on his Excellency, Sir Guy Carleton, on behalf of the Loyalists desirous of emigrating to Nova Scotia, and to present their proposals.[4]

Their first request was for vessels, and convoy, to carry the intending settlers, their horses and cattle, as near as possible to the place where they were to settle; their next, for provisions for the voyage, one year's provision after that, or money to enable them to purchase food, for warm clothing, for medicines. After that, they requested pairs of mill-stones, the iron necessary for grist mills, saws, and so forth, nails and spikes, hoes and axes, spades and shovels, plough irons and other necessary farming utensils, and window glass. The land, they suggested, should be free from disputed titles and as conveniently situated as may be; the tracts should be granted, surveyed, and divided at the public cost "so as to afford from 300 to 600 acres of useful land to each family"; 2,000 acres in every township should be allowed for the support of a clergyman, and 1,000 acres for the support of a school, these lands to be inalienable for ever. They asked also good muskets and cannon, with powder and balls, "to enable them to defend themselves against any hostile invasion", and also a proportion of powder and lead for hunting.

It is to be presumed that Sir Guy Carleton gave some sort of approval to these proposals, for the "Articles of Settlement" were presented to the Loyalists by the agents, papers were signed by those who were willing to emigrate with their families to Nova Scotia upon the terms and assurances given, approval was given to the appointment of agents to represent each group, and lists were made of those who were willing to go to Nova

Scotia in the autumn of 1782. The Lloyd's Neck list, dated September 20, 1782, contained the names of thirty-six men and women, with eighty-five dependents, but most of those who signed did not get away until the spring of 1783. Each group chose one agent to go to Nova Scotia with the fall fleet—Lloyd's Neck picked Amos Botsford, Queen's County, Samuel Cummings, and Bergen, Frederick Hauser—and Blowers, presumably, drew up instructions for them. They were to discover whether there was a tract, or tracts, of land sufficient to accommodate the Loyalists and their families, whether the land was free from all disputed titles, either with the Indians or former grantees; they were to examine the soil, timber, game, limestone, the rivers, bays, creeks, harbours, streams and ponds of water, and their possibilities for mills, fishing, trade, and so forth; they were to inquire what lands in the neighbourhood were granted, to whom, and on what terms they might be purchased; they were to consider the difficulties and obstacles to forming new settlements, the probable advantages, the distances from the principal settlements in existence, from the rivers and harbours, the difficulties of transportation; they were to keep a journal and make reports from time to time to the secretary in New York; they were to see that "such Lands as may be obtained, be distributed and divided among the proposed Adventurers, in as just and equitable a manner as the nature of the Case will admit of." With these careful and exacting instructions, and with a recommendation from Sir Guy Carleton to Sir Andrew Snape Hamond that he extend to them his favour and protection, and a request that he give them the necessary assistance in exploring the country, including just and proper access to the records of the province, the agents embarked with the fall fleet.[5]

In his letter, which is dated September 22, Sir Guy enclosed the lists of those who, "relinquishing all Hope

31

of repossessing their former Property in the revolted Provinces," desired to emigrate to Nova Scotia and accept such grants of lands as could be allowed them. Since such grants, Sir Guy suggested, were to be "considered as well founded Claims of Justice rather than of mere Favor, it is their very reasonable Expectation" that the grants should be made without payment of fees, or any reservation of quit rents, or any pecuniary obligations whatever. From his experience of colonial administration, Sir Guy undoubtedly knew the necessity of making such a suggestion as this one regarding the granting of land without the customary fees, quit rents, and other payments which had become the perquisites of colonial officials, but he could hardly have foreseen what a storm this issue was to raise in Nova Scotia and how nearly the determination of the officials to receive their customary fees was to wreck the whole project of Loyalist settlement in Nova Scotia.[6]

The letter to Hamond mentioned also the expectations of the Loyalists that families would receive six hundred acres and single men three hundred acres of land, and that Church and School grants would be asked. Sir Guy hoped that for these "real efficient Settlers", who had skill and ability and would be provided with tools from the stores at New York, the authorities in Nova Scotia would make available the materials they would require and the labour. Unfortunately for Carleton's well meant efforts to smooth the way for the Loyalists, there had been a change in the administration in Nova Scotia before his letter arrived. Hamond, who had expected the governorship after his year as lieutenant governor and acting governor, had been annoyed at being superseded by a new appointee and had resigned.

The new governor of Nova Scotia was John Parr, the son of an impoverished Irish officer. Before his retirement from the active list, Parr had had long and arduous service with the 20th regiment and had risen to the command of the regiment. Two letters which he wrote, shortly after assuming the governorship of Nova Scotia, are indicative of the character of the man and his attitude toward his new duties. The first, dated October 9, 1782, was to Carleton, to notify the Commander-in-Chief of his arrival and to acknowledge receipt of the letter to Hamond.

> ... I am to assure you, Sir, that no assistance which can possibly be derived from this Government, shall be wanting to those who have made so great a Sacrifice to their Loyalty, and that they shall receive every accommodation that I can afford them.

> At the same time Sir I must inform you, that it will only be in my power to provide them with Lands, and that there is not any Houses or Cover to put them under shelter, this Town is already so crouded that a considerable Body of the Recruits for the Army are Hutted in the Woods for want of Houses to Convert into Barracks. And when I add the Scarcity and difficulty of providing fuel, and Lumber for building which is still greater, the many inconveniences and great distress these people must suffer, if any of them come into this Province this Winter, will sufficiently appear unto your Excellency; and I am to add that what I have said of this Town may be applied to any other part of the Province; therefore I hope Sir that no necessity will compel these people to further suffering and Calamities.[7]

Two weeks later, Parr wrote to a friend in England:

> I have found everything here to exceed my expectation, have met with the greatest civility and attention from all Ranks of People, a most excellent

33

house and Garden, a small farm close to the Town, another of 70 or 80 Acres at the distance of two Miles, where I propose passing two or three months in Summer a snugg little farm house upon it, a beautifull prospect, with good fishing, plenty of Provision of all sorts except Flower, with a very good French Cook to dress them, a Cellar well stock'd with Port, Claret, Madeira, Rum, Brandy, Bowood Strong Beer & a neat income (including a Regim^t of Provincials of which I am Colonel) of £2200 Ster^g p Annum, an income far beyond my expectations, plenty of Coals & Wood against the severity of the Winter, a house well furnish'd, and warm Cloths, that upon the whole my Dear Grey, your friend Parr is as happy and comfortably seated, as you could wish an old friend to be . . . I am determined to be happy and to make everyone so who comes within my line.[8]

This was the man to whom the destinies of 30,000 Loyalists were shortly to be committed. Is it any wonder that difficulties ensued? The time called for a broad vision, and this man's was focussed on himself and his consequence and comfort; it called for a worker of miracles, and here was a maker of difficulties. Sir Guy Carleton sent a propitiatory note from New York on November 7, and noted that he had just heard of the safe arrival of the Loyalists who had gone to Annapolis Royal in the fall fleet. To Townshend, who had succeeded Shelburne as Minister, Carleton reported that the refugees had arrived in Nova Scotia, that they had been "kindly received there by the Inhabitants, as well as countenanced & protected by the Governor"—a nicely ambiguous phrase—and that they expressed "great Satisfaction in the change & in the prospects which open before them". The Commander-in-Chief noted with satisfaction that the Assemblies had taken alarm at a measure, "which while it affords a refuge and

34

reward to men persecuted for their Loyalty & some compensation for their losses, promises at the same time a rapid increase of strength to a province, which, should it become a frontier, will find men of distinguished valor to joyn in its defence if necessary." The possibility that those who settled in Nova Scotia would have to defend themselves against their neighbours to the south was evidently very much in the minds of the British at New York. The Loyalists, it will be remembered, had asked for guns and cannon and the necessary ammunition so that they might be able to defend themselves. Sir Guy mentioned the matter again, in a letter of December 22 to Parr, on behalf of the Loyalists, "who have sacrificed their properties and exposed themselves to hazards of every kind in supporting the union of the empire" and particularly on behalf of Joseph Pynchon and James Dole, agents for upwards of 120 families who were interested in getting grants adjoining Port Roseway, for the purpose of carrying on the fisheries, "and establishing a commerce in that advantageous situation, which may be made as it appears easily defensible, and which they profess themselves ready and will probably be numerous enough, to defend." It might be noted here, that although Sir Guy had expressed the hope that no impediment would stand in the way of this settlement, which would bring a great accession of strength and wealth to Nova Scotia, "and give it suddenly that importance which it is now of the highest consequence that it should obtain," in a very few months spokesmen returned from Port Roseway [Shelburne], with bitter complaints about the treatment they had received and the obstacles placed in the way of the settlement.[9]

After the arrival of the fall fleet at Annapolis, on October 19, 1782, the three agents of the Loyalists, Messrs. Botsford, Cummings, and Hauser, had proceeded to carry out their instructions for investigating the possibilities for settlement. On January 14, 1783, they wrote to the Board of Agents in New York that they had looked at the country from Annapolis to St. Mary's Bay and considered that it had very good soil and was favourable for the fisheries. They had then proceeded to the St. John River, at the latter end of November, and found there too much ice for boats, but not enough for travel over the ice. As a result, they steered through the woods by compass, making camp for several nights, until they reached the Oromocto, where they found a block-house, "a British post." The St. John they thought a fine river, equal in magnitude to the Connecticut or Hudson, with a fine harbour at the mouth, accessible at all seasons of the year, never frozen or obstructed by the ice, which was broken in passing over the falls, and guarded by Fort Howe.

Since it was probably this report which turned the attention of so many of the Loyalists to the St. John and Kennebecasis rivers, it is worth quoting their description:

... Half a mile above the mouth, at a narrow place in the river, the falls are very curious, and deserve a particular description. At low water the descent is several feet down the stream, and at high water several feet up stream. The tides in the Bay of Fundy rise and fall from thirty to sixty feet; were it not for the falls the whole country up the river would be deluged by the tides. The falls obstruct the tides up the river to such a degree that the water rises but one foot and a half above the falls, and rises about as high as that seventy or eighty miles up; it is navigable for vessels of seventy or eighty tons burthen, for about eighty miles up the river, and for boats much farther, extending, as we are told, three hundred miles, its course being for a considerable distance parallel to the river St. Lawrence; this route is frequently taken to Quebec across the country; it is about five hundred miles from Fort Howe.

There are many settlers along this river upon the interval land. They are chiefly poor people, who come here and get their living easily. The interval lies on the river, and is a most fertile soil, annually matured by the overflowings of the river, and produces crops of all kinds with little labour; and vegetables in the greatest perfection; parsnips of great length, &c. They cut down the trees, burn the tops, put in a crop of wheat or Indian corn, which yields a plentiful increase. These intervals would make the finest meadows. The up lands produce wheat both of the summer and winter kinds, as well as Indian corn. Here are some wealthy farmers, having flocks of cattle. The greater part of the people, excepting the township of Maugerville, are tenants, or seated on the bank without leave or licence, merely to get their living. For this reason they have not made such improvements as might otherwise have been expected, or as thoro' farmers would have done.

Some of our people chuse Conway [now Digby], others give the preference to St. John's. Our people who came with us are settled here for the winter; some at the fort, some in the town, and others extend up the Annapolis river near 20 miles, having made terms with the inhabitants; some are doing well, others are living on their provisions; their behaviour is as orderly and regular as we could expect.

Immense quantities of lime stone are found at Fort Howe, and at the mouth of the river. We also went up the Kennebecasis, a large branch of St. John's river, where is a large tract of interval and up-land, which has never been granted; it is under a reserve; but we can have it. Major Studholm and capt. Baxter, who explored the country, chose this place, and obtained a grant of 9000 acres. On

37

each side of this grant are large tracts of good land, convenient for navigation. A title for these lands may be procured sooner than for such as have already been granted, such as Gage, Conway, &c., which must be obtained by a regular process in the Court of Escheats. The lands on the river St. John are also sufficiently near the cod fishery in Fundy Bay, and perfectly secure against the Indians and Americans. The inhabitants are computed to be near one thousand men, able to bear arms. Here is a county and court established, and the inhabitants at peace, and seem to experience no inconveniency from the war.[10]

This report must have been eagerly scanned by the Loyalists who were spending their last and most unhappy winter in New York and its environs. The favourable prospects for settlement in Nova Scotia (the St. John River, and all the territory north of the Bay of Fundy, which later became New Brunswick, was then part of Nova Scotia, be it noted), and the British victories in the West Indies were the only encouraging features in their situation. They were surrounded by victorious enemies, who, while exulting in their successful bid for independence, were nevertheless so fearful that the victory might not be permanent that they were constantly indulging in vehement denunciation of the British sympathizers. The Loyalists were aware that negotiations for peace were being carried on in Paris, but whether the terms of the peace would improve or worsen their situation they did not know.

The articles of peace, for submission to the governments concerned, were signed on November 30, 1782, but in those days the world could not stand by to hear the scratch of the pens as a treaty was signed. Copies of the articles were sent from Whitehall on December 31, 1782, and reached the Commander-in-Chief at New York on March 19, 1783. Copies had then to be sent to

Congress for their signatures before the terms could be made public. Articles 5, 6 and 7 were of particular concern to the Loyalists. According to Article 5, it was agreed that the Congress should "earnestly recommend to the Legislatures of the respective States, to provide for the Restitution of all Estates, Rights and Properties which have been confiscated", of real British subjects and of persons "resident in Districts in the possession of His Majesty's arms, and who have not borne Arms against the said United States". "Persons of any other Description", Congress was to recommend to the States, were to have "free Liberty to go to any part or parts, of any of the Thirteen United States, and therein to remain unmolested in their endeavours to obtain the restitution of such of their Estates, Rights and Properties as may have been confiscated". Congress was also to recommend "a Reconsideration and Revision of all Acts or Laws regarding the premises" so as to make them perfectly consistent, not only with Justice and Equity, but with "that spirit of Conciliation, which on the return of the Blessings of Peace should universally prevail". Restoration of property was also recommended, on condition that the former owner refunded to the person now in possession the "bona fide price" paid for purchasing it. It was also agreed that "all persons who have any Interest in confiscated Lands, either by debts, Marriage Settlements, or otherwise, shall meet with no lawful Impediment in the prosecution of their just Rights."[11]

To the plentipotentiary of Great Britain it may have seemed sufficient that Congress should "earnestly recommend to the Legislature of the respective States" that they take these measures to restore the property of British subjects and Loyalists, but the Loyalists had little hope that the intentions of Article 5 would be carried out. Those who had lived in America knew that the States paid attention to Congress only when they wished

39

to heed the orders of that body, and that the phrases of Article 5 were mere expressions of pious hopes which would never be fulfilled. The dismay of the Loyalists was expressed by Edward Winslow's sister Sarah, in a letter to her cousin, Benjamin Marston, under date of April 10, 1783:

> ... our fate seems now decreed and we left to mourn out our days in wretchedness. No other resource for millions but to submit to the tyranny of exulting enemys or settle a new country. I am one of the number that gladly would embark for Nova Scotia was it either prudent or proper, but I am told it will not do for me at present. What is to become of us, God only can tell. In all our former sufferings we had hope to support us—being deprived of that is too much.

> Was there ever an instance, my dear Cousin, can any history produce one, where such a number of the best of human beings were deserted by the government they have sacrificed their all for?

> The open enemys of Great Britain have gained their point, and more than ever they could have had impudence to have asked for—while their brave persevering Noble Friends, who have suffered and toiled for years, and whom they were bound by every tie of honour and gratitude to assist, are left without friends, without fortune, without prospect of support but from that Being who has hitherto supported us, and upon whom we must rely for further protection ...[12]

Article 6 of the treaty stated that no future confiscations would be made, "nor any prosecutions commenced against any person or persons, for or by reason of the part which he or they may have taken in the present War," no one was to suffer any "future loss or damage either in his Person, Liberty or Property," any

40

persons in confinement on such charges were to be set at liberty immediately and the prosecutions discontinued. During the spring and summer of 1783, as will be shown in the next chapter, the Loyalists were to find out how little attention was paid to Article 6.

Article 7 stated that there was to be a "firm and Perpetual Peace between his Britannic Majesty and the said States, and between the Subjects of the one, and the Citizens of the other," that all hostilities were to cease, that all prisoners on both sides were to be set at liberty, and "His Britannic Majesty shall with all convenient speed, & without causing any Destruction, or carrying any Negroes, or other Property of the American Inhabitants, withdraw all His Armies, Garrisons and Fleets from the said United States". A final clause provided for the restoration of all archives, records, deeds and papers belonging to any of the States or their Citizens.

Whether there was advance notice of the terms of the treaty, or whether it so happened that the officers of the provincial corps were able to get together a few days before the official receipt of the articles of peace is not clear. At any rate, on March 14, 1783, a memorial was drawn up and presented on behalf of the Provincial Regiments by "B. Thompson, Lt. Col., Commandant Kings American Dragoons, Gab. D'Veber, Lt. Col., Comg. Prince of Wales American Regiment, John Coffin, Major, Kings American Regiment, Thos. Menzies, Major, American Legion, Ed. Winslow, Muster-Master-general of Provincial Forces, Gabriel G. Ludlow, Coll., 2d. Battn. Delancey's Brigade, Bev. Robinson Coll., Loyal American Regiment, Stephen DeLancey, Lt. Col. 1 Battn. New Jersey Volrs., J. H. Cruger, Colo. 1st. Bat. Br. Genl. DeLancey's, Abrm. VanBuskirk, Lt. Col. 3d. Batt. Newjersey volrs., Geo. Turnbull, Lt. Col., Commr. New York Volunteers, Beverley Robinson Junr, Lt. Col., Loyal American Regt., William Allen, Lt. Col. Commdt, Pennsylvania Loyalists, I. Allen, Lt. Col.,

Commdt, 2. Batt., N.J. Volunteers". The memorial, which was probably largely the work of Benjamin Thompson and Edward Winslow, who had been concerned with similar memorials from the Loyalists, pointed out that the offer of independence to the American colonies, and the probability of separation of Great Britain and the colonies as a result of the war, filled their minds with the most alarming apprehensions. From the "purest principles of Loyalty, and attachment to the British-Government, their Sovereign and the British Nation", they had "persevered with unabated zeal through all the vicissitudes of a calamitous and unfortunate war, their hearts still glowed with Loyalty, their detestation to the republican system was unconquerable." Whatever stipulation might be made at a peace for the restoration of the property of the Loyalists, and whatever permission might be given for them to return home, they were certain that it would be utterly impossible for those who had served His Majesty in arms in this war to remain in the country. "The personal animosities that arose from civil dissenssions have been so heightened by the Blood that has been shed in the Contest, that the Parties can never be reconciled." The officers had sacrificed their property, their lucrative professions or their expectations, many of them had wives, who were unaccustomed to want, and children for whose education they were concerned. There were many "respectable yeomen of good connections" in the regiments, many men suffering from wounds and illness contracted during their service, widows and orphans of officers and soldiers. They asked grants of land in some of His Majesty's American Provinces and assistance in making settlements, pensions for the disabled, the widows and orphans, permanent rank in America for the officers and half-pay when the regiments were reduced.[13]

Eventually all these requests were granted, although not without some difficulties in getting the assent of

42

Parliament to the allowing of permanent rank to the officers. As far as settlement was concerned, the campaign thus initiated was to culminate in the removal to the St. John River not only of the thirteen regiments represented by the signers of this petition, but of several other corps as well. From this time, there were two groups, the refugees and the officers and men of the regiments, the Loyalists and the Provincials, two aspects to every situation, two strands which sometimes went side by side in the weaving of the design and sometimes crossed each other. It is impossible to gain an understanding of the story of the New Brunswick Loyalists without recognizing this duality. The refugees had been first in proposals to go to Nova Scotia, and first in sending agents. They had been first, also, in engaging Winslow's interest, which may have had some influence on later developments.

The memorial from the officers suggests that they had a fairly good idea of the terms of the peace treaty. It is possible that the principal points of the petition had been discussed with the Commander-in-Chief before it was formally presented: it is even possible that he suggested some such move. A memorandum, which appears to be in Edward Winslow's handwriting, and which is dated March 15, 1783, the day following the signing of the memorial, says that the commanding officers of Provincial Corps who met to take into consideration the proposals of Carleton relative to the granting of Crown Lands "to such of His Majesty's Provincial Forces as shall be willing to remove to Nova Scotia or any other part of His Majesty's American Dominions for the purpose of making a Settlement", suggested 300 acres for a private soldier, 350 for a corporal, 400 for each serjeant, with the same allowances to commissioned officers and staff officers as was granted after the last war. In addition, the commanding officers suggested that the non-commissioned officers and privates

43

be allowed provisions, pay, and clothing for three years, that they be furnished with arms and ammunition for the defence of the settlement and a proportion of ammunition for hunting, and a proportion of farming utensils, tools and materials for building and for erecting mills.[14]

Carleton sent the memorial of the officers to Townshend, on March 15, 1783, and begged the serious consideration of His Majesty's Ministers to it "as a measure I think necessary both for the dignity of the Crown and the interest of Great Britain." The most cordial connection should be established with the provinces which have preserved their allegiance, he felt, and not only should all grievances be done away with, but "every source of jealousy, or suspicion, should be done away for ever." Quit rents and fees of office should be dispensed with, taxes should not be imposed in future by Great Britain, nor any permitted "but for their own benefit, and for their provincial defence and security, till their strength becomes respectable, and their wealth will readily enable them to contribute to the general support of the empire". "I entertain the most sanguine hope," Sir Guy's letter continued, "that the provinces which are to remain under His Majesty's dominion will suddenly become powerful, and objects of envy to those who in the present moment, madly renounce the most equitable and wise system of government, for anarchy and distraction". Meantime, the provinces should be protected by a naval force, at least until the new arrangements were completed and the troops had arrived at their destinations.[15]

This was but one of many letters sent by Sir Guy Carleton to the home authorities in order to persuade them to pursue an enlightened policy with regard to the colonies which remained. How much of the detail of the policies suggested and how much of the actual wording was Sir Guy's is a debatable point. There is a definitely colonial tinge in the letter from which the above extracts are quoted, and in other letters. Probably William Smith, formerly chief justice of New York, was in part responsible for the ideas, the urgency with which they were sent forward, and the actual wording of the letters. Sir Guy Carleton had other duties and there were many urgent practical problems to which his attention must be given during the remainder of his stay in New York. He had been successful in his endeavour to turn the views of the Loyalists, and the Provincial Troops, to other settlements, and he had to supervise their departure for their places of refuge, as well as the forwarding to Europe of the British and Hessian troops under his command.

CHAPTER THREE

THE DEPARTURE

One part of Sir Guy Carleton's task had been accomplished: the Loyalists had been persuaded to move to Nova Scotia, and an advance party of three hundred had actually been sent forward in the autumn of 1782. Before the Commander-in-Chief could turn over to the Americans New York and the other territory in British possession, the main body of British sympathizers had still to be dispatched to some haven. When Sir Guy wrote Sir Andrew Snape Hamond on September 22, 1782, he said that he was given to understand that upwards of six hundred persons, women and children included, wished to embark in the autumn, and a much larger number the ensuing spring. There was no indication at that time that the "much larger number" would be one hundred times the number who sailed in the fall fleet to Annapolis.

The first spring fleet was slow in getting away. On March 10, 1783, forty-four ships were victualled and waiting.[1] On March 23, a "Humble address of ALL who intend settling at Port Roseway" solicited that His Excellency would be pleased, "(previous to his declining the Command) to issue the necessary orders, for the Conveniency of Embarkation and Settlement of Port Roseway".[2] Sir Guy, who had been hoping for permission to return home, had written Townshend, in December, 1782, that he recommended to the consideration of his successor the proposition he had received from over 120 families of Refugees for the settlement of "Rosway Harbour about ten leagues from Cape Sable".[3] Since the king had particularly wished that Sir Guy remain at his

46

post, the Commander-in-Chief was now faced with the necessity of carrying out his own recommendations.

Although Carleton's correspondence mentions only the Port Roseway Associates, there were by this time two other groups, the Annapolis or Digby or Conway Associates, and the St. John's River Associates. Presumably they had been formed upon receipt of the report of their agents, Messrs. Botsford, Cummings, and Hauser; certainly the St. John's River Associates were not as ready for embarkation as the Port Roseway group. On April 2, 1783, Samuel Seabury and John Sayre sent a note to the Commissary-General to say that with their utmost application it was impossible to give an exact return of the men, women, and children to come from Lloyd's Neck and Eaton's Neck, on Long Island.[4] As the Commissary-General had to have precise information as to the number in each class for the victualling arrangements (which are explained more fully in Chapter V), this was one delaying factor. Another was the necessity of picking up the Loyalists in these scattered hamlets on Long Island and elsewhere around New York, and bringing them to some centre for final embarkation for Nova Scotia. This process sometimes took seven days, and involved much shifting of passengers from one vessel to another. According to the account given by Walter Bates, a Loyalist who settled in Kingston, New Brunswick, the Loyalist colonies at Huntington, Lloyd's Neck, Eaton's Neck, and Oyster Bay, were visited in April by Reverend John Sayre and informed that those who were willing to go to Nova Scotia would be given two hundred acres of land for each family [a scaling down of amounts formerly suggested], two years' provisions, and free passage.[5] Embarkation of the *Union*, the ship on which Walter Bates and other Kingston Loyalists sailed, was begun at Huntington April 11, and completed on April 16, 1783. A document signed by James Peters, Agent for the Associated Loyalists, shows that the vessel

47

left Huntington Bay on April 16 for New York, where forty-three of the passengers were disembarked on April 23. With the remaining one hundred and sixty-four passengers, the *Union* left New York on April 24. The *Aurora*, embarking her passengers at New York on April 15, sailed to Staten Island, where she remained until April 23, when she set sail for St. John. The *Hope* picked up passengers at Lloyd's Neck on April 12, but discharged thirty-four of them at New York on the 24th.[6]

The note from Seabury and Sayre asked that "for the sake of the Emigrants," vessels for the transportation of eighty or one hundred horses and neat cattle be provided, and that one or two of the vessels go to Lloyd's Neck to take on board the horses, etc., that were there. The owners, they thought, would have hay enough for the voyage. It was impossible to find any record as to whether this request was granted or not. Some horses may have been sent up; cattle were largely obtained from the pre-Loyalist settlers who had, according to the agents, "large flocks". It was apparently possible to carry a considerable quantity of household furniture and family effects in the vessels. In addition, numerous sloops and schooners were cleared from New York for Nova Scotia, during the summer and autumn of 1783, with cargoes of "Family Effects".[7] The Commander-in-Chief had already directed the Superintendent of Imports and Exports to grant to persons embarking for Nova Scotia permission for the shipping of every article they might find necessary to carry with them, and to give a general clearance conformable to the enclosed form [which has disappeared], since enumerating the variety of articles necessary for family uses would give "the Adventurers" much trouble, and perhaps bring them into difficulties should there be any omissions.[8]

Sir Guy Carleton and his staff were certainly taking great pains to smooth the way for the Loyalists. On April 11, 1783, for instance, Brook Watson, the Commissary-

General, suggested that the Loyal Refugees going to Nova Scotia would stand in want of immediate shelter for the women and children, and as there were in the King's Stores a great number of halfworn tents, with a very large quantity of new camp equipment, the Commander-in-Chief might be induced to order the Storekeeper to issue two of the tents to every family going to settle in that province. Brook Watson, who had spent nine years in Nova Scotia, would appreciate the necessity for shelter from the inclement weather of early spring in that area. His suggestion was approved and each family received two tents, in addition to other supplies. Damaged blankets were doled out, about one and a half for each individual. Each man received a spade, an axe, four yards of woollen cloth, seven yards of linen cloth, two pairs of shoes, two pairs of stockings, one pair of mittens, each woman three yards of woollen cloth, six yards of linen, one pair of shoes, one pair of stockings [fortunately not nylons], and one pair of mittens; each child over the age of ten, three yards of woollen cloth, six of linen, one pair of stockings and one pair of mittens; each child under ten, one and a half yards of wool and three yards of linen. On special orders of the Commander-in-Chief, some families received extra supplies. Colonel Thomas Gilbert, for example, and his family, eight in all, two men, two women, two children over ten, and two servants, were supplied with thirty yards of legging cloth, eight pairs of shoes, eight pairs of hose, eight pairs of mittens, eight good blankets, eight frilled shirts, two camp kettles [the juxtaposition is presumably accidental], two hatchets, two axes, and two spades.[9]

On April 12, 1783, Sir Guy Carleton wrote Townshend that about four or five thousand of the Refugees who were going to Nova Scotia would embark the next day, and sail in a few days for Port Roseway and St. John's River, and that probably many more would follow. "A considerable increase of shipping", he pointed out, "will be necessary to accomplish the entire evacuation of this place in the course of the Summer as you will be more particularly informed by Rear-Admiral Digby."[10] Meantime, new difficulties and delays prevented the embarkation and sailing of the first fleet. Although an American agent must always be present to superintend all embarkations, in order to see, as Article 7 of the treaty required, that no negroes or other property of Americans were carried away, Congress had not as yet authorized "proper Persons", and Captain Chads of the Royal Navy, who was in charge of Transports, took it upon himself to request two gentlemen to act. On April 15, the Adjutant-General, Oliver DeLancey, issued instructions that the Refugees themselves and the masters of the vessels were to take care that no person who had not resided twelve months within the British Lines be permitted to embark as a Refugee, unless he had a special Passport from the Commandant. The Refugees were also recommended to take care that no person of bad character was suffered to embark with them.[11]

Finally, on April 26, the convoy was assembled and sailed from Sandy Hook. It was known as the Spring Fleet, or sometimes, ignoring the small migration to Annapolis in the autumn of 1782, as the First Fleet. A few years later, when the Admiralty was endeavouring to compute the cost of transporting the Loyalists, a list furnished by Captain Chads showed thirty-two vessels bound for Port Roseway and St. John River. The Storekeeper, tidying up his accounts on April 27, 1783, revealed that he had issued 10,181 yards of Shirting Linnen, 4,767 yards of Legging Cloth, 1,283 pairs of shoes, 2,252 pairs of hose, 1,394 pairs of mittens, 1,387 damaged blankets, 790 axes, 790 spades, 425 tents, to the 790 men, 433 women, 536 children ten years of age and over, 464 children under ten, and 211 servants going to St. John's River. The Commissary General's return of October 10, 1783, reduced slightly the numbers in each class, and produced a total of 2,383 instead of 2,434 for St. John's River. In addition, 267 men, of the King's American Dragoons, 45 women, 52 children under ten, 40 servants, a total of 404, sailed with the Spring Fleet, in the *Lady's Adventure*, 705 tons, Robert Gibson, Master.[12]

On April 26, the day on which the fleet sailed, the Commander-in-Chief wrote General Paterson, who was in charge of the military district of Nova Scotia, enclosing embarkation returns of the troops and refugees going to different parts of Nova Scotia, together with returns of artillery, ordnance stores and provisions. He added that the King's American Dragoons [Benjamin Thompson's regiment], who were dismounted, had desired to be sent to St. John's River, Bay of Fundy, and were to proceed thither directly, to encamp, and do duty for the present. As the period of their stay at the St. John River was uncertain, General Paterson was advised not to withdraw the troops actually posted there. Many officers of the provincial regiments had taken this opportunity of going to Nova Scotia to look for places for future settlements and were recommended to General Paterson for every assistance in his power.[13]

The embarkation returns were likewise enclosed in a communication to Governor Parr, together with a list of persons to whom Sir Guy had granted commissions, such commissions to be in force only until the governor of Nova Scotia should make further, or other, regulations concerning them. The commissions covered sixteen companies of militia. Sir Guy suggested that the provisions ought to be made commensurate with the absolute necessities of the settlers, and that it might therefore become indispensable that they should be further supplied in Nova Scotia and orders would be given accordingly. Sir Guy again recommended the whole expedition to his Excellency's protection, and expressed his satisfaction, "that we are able to give these deserving people some refuge, which I trust they will amply repay by that increase of wealth, and commerce and power which they may give in future to a greatly diminished Empire."[14]

Along with this official letter from Sir Guy Carleton, went another communication to Governor Parr, the text of which suggests that it might have been composed by Benjamin Thompson, who was at the time engaged in exploring in many directions openings for future employment and renown:

The establishments which are now forming in your province I conceive to be 'of the highest importance to the British Empire, and very much will depend on the present arrangements, which should have in view both advantages and security, and settlements be now made with such wisdom and foresight as that the whole may take permanent root, and grow up together into the most desirable System. I cannot therefore excuse myself, on occasion of sending thither the Provincial Regiment which is now embarked, from recommending to your Excellency the consideration of establishing a strong frontier on the river St. Croix, and reserving land for a strong military post at the mouth of that river; this front line might be strengthened by establishments in its rear, and on St. John's river, with reservations likewise, which security and the civil uses of the province may hereafter require; and to this purpose, the making of such grants in those places, as may resemble the cantonments of an army, with such distinction of favor to the Officers, as will enable them to preserve their authority, and collect the whole, if need should require, into all the arrangements requisite for defence. A communication with Canada should also be attended to, as of great importance.

The Officers of the Provincial Corps have among them, men of the first families, and therefore entitled to be distinguished beyond the ordinary portions which are to be given to mere Settlers, considered as such. Besides the regiment which is now embarked, I reckon that not less than three thousand, provincial military, will soon pass into your province. Such a body, interested to preserve their own property, will, I trust, make a very respectable Frontier; but whether for defence, cultivation or trade, it is in vain to look for prosperity or security on any other foundation, than that of a common Interest, zealously engaging the whole in one mind. These are considerations which I beg leave to recommend to your Excellency's most serious attention, nor can any one article be more effectually employed to excite industry and to obtain defence, than a wise and judicious distribution of land, wherein the Occupier shall be freed from all burthens, except what the defence of his own property, and that of the province may render necessary.[15]

This sounds very much like one of Benjamin Thompson's schemes, advocating a "strong frontier on the river St. Croix", where his regiment, the first to arrive, would get the best place, and its commanding officer, "entitled to be distinguished beyond the ordinary portions", would obtain a large grant. It was unfortunate that this communication was allowed to go forward to Governor Parr. He seized upon its suggestions as an important recommendation and was correspondingly aggrieved when the regimental scouts refused to consider the St. Croix and insisted upon remaining on the St. John.

By the end of May, any hopes which might once
have been entertained of the possibility of shipping to
Nova Scotia or Britain or Canada all the British
sympathizers and of completing the evacuation of New
York early in the summer were dissipated. With the
declaration of peace, and the opening of the season for
travelling by the country roads, many who had taken
refuge within the British lines attempted to return to
their former homes. They soon found out how little they
could rely on the assurances of the peace treaty that they
would not be molested. Some may have been welcomed
by their relatives and former friends, if they were able
to reach them, but most of the refugees met with an
unpleasant reception. Of the numerous sworn statements concerning such experiences, one typical account
will suffice to show the sort of treatment received.

3 May 1783.

The declaration of John Segee a soldiers son in
the Loyal Am'n Reg't who lost one of his Arms by
Accident when he was a Boy of about twelve
y'rs old.

Says

That on the 23d April, in north Castle, he met
with a Charles Ward & three other men who were
strangers to him.

They asked him where he was from, he answered from Long Island. They asked him where he
was going he told them to see his friends in Bedford;
on hearing of which they drew their Swords, and
declared with an oath, if he did not return, they
would cut his head off. He says that he returned
with them, & declares that they flogged him the
whole way from North Castle to the White plains.
That at the white plains they cut his hair, & asked
him whether he would retire within the British
lines if he was set at Liberty; on his answering,

54

yes, Ward gave him between twenty and thirty strokes with his cane, and told him to go about his Bussiness, and let his friends on Long Island know, that every Rascal of them that attempted to come among them would meet with the like treatment.[16]

Other communities did not wait for chance encounters, but publicly advertised in the papers their intentions of discouraging the return of Loyalists. For instance, at a meeting of a number of the freeholders and inhabitants of Poughkeepsie precinct, in Dutchess County, on the 17th of May, 1783,

Determined, that the Constitution of the state of New-York is just and liberal; obtained at the hazard of our lives, and which with our lives we will defend.

That the danger to which it will be exposed, if *those* who have wrapt our cities in flames, and covered our land with blood; and whose principles are utterly repugnant to our free government; are suffered to return, fills us with the most alarming apprehensions.

In our opinion in vain a long tho' successful war; in vain the best blood of America freely sacrificed in its defence; in vain the Constitution of this state, our pride, and the admiration of our neighbours; if persons of the above description are ever enrolled among our citizens, and again partake of those privileges, they so justly forfeited by their treasons. If they had removed from our coasts forever, we would have forgot their crimes; but the idea of again beholding them pollute a land with their presence (now sacred to liberty) fills us with indignation.

Nothing do they deserve from this country but detestation and chastizement.

The spirit of 75 still beats high, and *must* beat high, or American freedom is no more.

The "good people of Rombouts precinct", at a meeting on the 27th day of May, 1783, with Major Andrew Hill in the chair:

Being justly alarmed at the critical situation of public affairs, have deemed it necessary to assemble for the purpose of declaring to their friends in the other precincts, as well as the states at large, their resolutions respecting the conduct proper to be observed by the Whigs, in regard to those abandoned miscreants who deserted their country in its glorious struggle for Independence, and exerted themselves to enslave it, and destroy its peace and happiness: After mature deliberation, they agreed to the following resolutions:

1st. *Resolved*, That the ambition, avarice, and perfidy of the tories have been the chief cause of all the blood that has been shed in the contest between this Country and Great Britain: and though the issue has blasted their malignant hopes, disappointed their sanguinary expectations, and given independence and honor to America, yet the guilt of the tories has not been extenuated; because, from the beginning of the war to this day, they have been guilty of the most horrid and inhuman murders that ever disgraced the records of any country.

2d. *Resolved*, That for the foregoing reasons, those who formerly resided in this precinct, and voluntarily joined the arms of the British King, and aided and assisted in the base attempt of subjugating this country to arbitrary and despotic power, shall never have our consent to live in this precinct: and in case they are so hardy as to return, they shall not be permitted to continue longer than SEVEN DAYS, *after being duly warned to retire*, on pain of

56

experiencing the just punishment due to such infamous parricides.

3d. *Resolved,* That we will exert ourselves to discover the tory fugitives that may now be in this precinct, and those who may hereafter return, and expel them without delay, agreeable to the spirit of the foregoing resolve.

4th. *Resolved,* That we will not associate with any person who may harbour or entertain tory fugitives; but on the contrary we will deem them enemies to the independence and peace of the States, and treat them accordingly.

By order of the Meeting,

ANDREW HILL, Chairman. [17]

Some communities did not allow even seven days to the Tories who came to collect their wives and children and family effects. Benjamin Ingraham, a sergeant in the King's American Regiment, who had lived at New Concord, twenty miles from Albany, on a "comfortable farm, plenty of cows and sheep," which had been seized, the "ploughs and all" sold, and the wife forced to pay rent, came home on September 13, a Friday. The family, who had not heard for four years, "whether he was alive or dead; anyone would be hanged right up if they were caught bringing letters", made all haste to get ready, killing the cow, having candles made of the tallow, with "plenty of beeswax in them to make them hard and good", threshing twenty bushels of wheat and putting it in bags made by the grandmother, packing up tubs of butter and pickles, and a good store of potatoes. "Then on Tuesday," the daughter recalled, "suddenly the house was surrounded by rebels, and father was taken prisoner and carried away." The uncle interceded, and the sergeant was released in the morning, but others were not so fortunate as Benjamin Ingraham.[18]

This attitude on the part of the Americans resulted not only in a very great increase in the number of Refugees in the New York, Long Island, and Bergen communities who asked to be sent to Nova Scotia, but also in an influx into New York of British sympathizers who had hitherto found refuge, as the Rombouts declaration suggests, elsewhere than within the British lines. It became impossible to limit the evacuees, as the first embarkation orders had decreed, to those who had been within the lines for at least a year. It also became impossible to limit the evacuees to those who were destitute. The army transports and victuallers and navy victuallers available were insufficient for the removal of the Refugees whose numbers kept increasing. As the summer wore on, the officials, both in New York and in Nova Scotia, became more and more harried. The thousands with which they had expected to cope became tens of thousands.

Embarkation for the second fleet, usually referred to as the June fleet, commenced as early as May 25, but the vessels did not leave New York harbour until June 15. On June 7, notice had been given to the Refugees that the transports *Two Sisters*, *Hopewell*, *Symmetry*, *Generous Friends*, *Bridgewater*, *Thames*, *Amity's Production*, *Tartar*, *Duchess of Gordon*, *Littledale*, *William and Mary*, and *Free Briton*, which were to carry companies commanded by Sylvanus Whitney, Joseph Goreham, Henry Thomas, John Forrester, Thomas Elms, John Cock, Joseph Clarke, James Hoyt, Christopher Benson, Joseph Forrester, Thomas Welch, Oliver Bourdet, Asher Dunham, Abiathar Camp, Peter Berton, Richard Hill and Moses Pitcher, would "certainly fall down on Monday morning: it will therefore be absolutely necessary for the people who are appointed to go in these companies to be all on board tomorrow evening." The vessels mentioned were lying in the North River and at Brooklyn. Six other vessels, *Commerce*, *Elizabeth*, *Keppel*, *Lord Townsend*, *Nicholas and Jane*, and *Thetis*, and the twelve advertised were reported as sailing on June 10 for St. John and Bay of Fundy ports. A return of June 17 listed 1,654 persons embarked for St. John's River, 205 for Annapolis, 122 for Port Roseway, and 491 for Cumberland, presumably on the above eighteen vessels.[19]

From the Adjutant-General's office, on June 17, a report was issued that, since May 26, 7,656 persons had applied to be removed from New York. The destinations they sought were as follows:

England	615
Ireland	160
Halifax	681
Scotland	19
Jamaica	93
Port Roseway	714
Annapolis	342
River St. John	3,656
Canada	1,218
Island of St. Johns	115
Fort Cumberland	19
Germany	5
West Florida	19

It will be noted that nearly half the applicants expressed a preference for the St. John River, and that of the 3,656 (made up of 987 men, 664 women, 1,439 children, 566 servants) applying, less than half had been sent forward in the June fleet. The ships from the Spring fleet were now making their way back to New York and being revictualled, six on June 18, seven the following day, two on June 21, eleven on the 22d, one on June 23d. Most of the vessels were reported as sailing in July, eight for the St. John River on July 7, eight or nine for the same port on July 8, along with three for Port Roseway and six for Quebec. A return of July 8 showed 1,335 persons "actually Embarked for Nova Scotia", and 516 for Canada. Slowly, the numbers were being reduced.[20]

During July, the Commander-in-Chief received a request from fifty-five gentlemen who wished large grants of land in Nova Scotia, and a counter petition from over six hundred refugees who resented the request of the fifty-five, and pointed out that the persons concerned, several of whom were said to be going to Britain, were most of them in easy circumstances, "and with some Exceptions more distinguished by the repeated favors of Government than by either the greatness of their sufferings or the importance of their Services." The request of the fifty-five (of which more will be heard in Chapter IX) and the counter petition are further evidence of the interest which had been aroused in settlement in Nova Scotia and of the number of refugees who were still in New York in July waiting for evacuation.

An embarkation return of August 5 showed 669 Loyalists and 295 negroes going to St. John River and Annapolis Royal, 173 Loyalists and 420 negroes to Port Roseway, 54 Loyalists and four negroes to Halifax. At some time during the month of August, the memorial of John Smith of New York City, merchant, and agent of upwards of five hundred persons, "Consisting of Men Women and Children, who are now bound with him for their Loyalty to Nova Scotia", was delivered to the Commander-in-Chief, together with a copy of the return which had been deposited with the Adjutant-General's office. Many of his group, Captain Smith pointed out, now residents in this city and on Nassau Island, were obliged to give up their possessions," or in other Words to leave them in the Power of this new fangled Government that is shortly to take place." Captain Smith's friends had heard that there were disputes—some of them

60

indeed had signed the petition against the fifty-five—and that grants were not obtained, but they hoped that they might be able to settle by themselves at or near the St. John River. John Smith's list named 142 men, most of whom can be traced in New Brunswick. The total number of persons was 554 and they were divided among Companies 40, 41 and 42, and perhaps other companies in the group which sailed on August 26.[21]

On August 19, Brook Watson, to whose forethought and practical sense the Loyalists owed so much, had sent a note to Major Mackenzie, the deputy Adjutant-General, to beg him to represent to the Commander-in-Chief that great numbers of "Respectable Loyal Families, driven from their homes for the part they have taken during the late War, and now Claiming the assistance of Government to move them to their intended Asylum in Nova Scotia," were in want of vessels to carry them thither. If His Excellency would authorize the Commissary-General to hire them, on the usual terms and conditions, except that they would be discharged in America, instead of in England as was the custom of the Navy, vessels could be obtained, and at less expense.[22] This suggestion was apparently approved, and from that time on refugees were embarked on the numerous schooners and sloops, the occasional brigs and ships, which were cleared from the port of New York for Nova Scotia, with family effects. A few of these vessels were owned, or perhaps hired, by Loyalists, many of whom were experienced masters of sailing vessels. Other vessels belonged to "patriots" who were not averse to taking a charter under the British at 13 shillings per ton per month. As a result of this change in the method of transport, there is no mention of the sailing of a fleet, from the latter part of August until the completion of the evacuation, with the notable exception of the one which carried the officers and men of the provincial regiments and their dependents.

During the first half of August, the June packet arrived from England with the final orders for the evacuation of New York. On August 17, Sir Guy Carleton addressed a letter to Elias Boudinot, president of Congress, to inform him that the orders had been recently received and that he was doing everything in his power to accelerate the total evacuation. "The violence of the Americans, which broke out soon after the cessation of hostilities," had increased the number of their countrymen who looked to him for "escape from threatened destruction," Sir Guy pointed out, and "these terrors have of late been so considerably augmented that almost all within these lines conceive the safety, both of their property and of their lives, depend upon their being removed by me." It was therefore impossible for him to say when the evacuation could be completed. The daily gazettes and publications were furnishing repeated proofs, Sir Guy continued, "not only of a disregard of the articles of peace, but of barbarous menaces from Committees formed in various towns, cities and districts, and even at Philadelphia, the very place which the Congress had chosen for their residence." He would show an indifference to the feelings of humanity, as well as to the honour and interest of the nation he served, if he were to leave any of the Loyalists that wished to quit the country a prey to the violence they conceived they had so much cause to apprehend. Congress and the subordinate legislatures could, by abating the fears of the Loyalists, diminish the number of emigrants, and speed the evacuation. [23]

In pursuance of the instructions he had received from London, the Commander-in-Chief issued, on August 17 and 18, orders regarding the disbanding of the British American or provincial regiments. Immediately, Gabriel G. Ludlow, on behalf of the officers, sent a protest to the Commander-in-Chief that they should be disbanded, after six years' service, without any positive subsistence for the officers or a provision for the men equal to that of the American Loyalists in general. The season was so far advanced that it would be impossible to have their allotments of land pointed out in time to erect a sufficient covering for the winter, and half their provisions would be expended before they could attempt the improvement of their lands. They had neither tools to build with, implements of husbandry, nor the ability to purchase what they needed. His Excellency was requested to continue the pay of the different corps until a decisive answer was received to the application made for half pay and for permanent rank in America, to grant that the year's provision would commence from the first of May next, and to furnish such tools and implements as their immediate necessities would require.[24]

It was not within the powers of the Commander-in-Chief in New York to delay the disbanding of the regiments, nor to provide half pay, but he could order that implements and tools of any sort available be furnished to the provincials. On embarkation, the regiments received four hand saws each, two cross cut saws, one whipsaw, one broad axe, one hammer, two chisels, two augurs, one jack "plain", one compass, twelve gimblets, three whipsaw files, six handsaw files, three cross cut saw files, one drawing knife, six scythes, several sneads and stones, and each man received one canteen, five pounds of iron, and one hoe.[25] All very helpful, but who had the custody of the regimental hammer?

"We shall all soon be with you—everybody, all the World moves on to Nova Scotia", Joshua Upham, formerly of Brookfield, Massachusetts, Harvard graduate of 1763, formerly deputy inspector of refugees at Lloyd's Neck, Major in the King's American Dragoons, and aide de camp to Sir Guy Carleton, wrote to Edward Winslow from New York, on August 21, 1783.[26] The Commander-in-Chief wrote, with less exuberance, to the commanding officer at Halifax, General Fox, for whom Winslow was acting as secretary at the time, that the several corps should be discharged as contiguous as possible to the lands on which they were to settle and requested Fox to press the governor, not only to determine the spots for each corps, but also to expedite as much as possible the location of lands for the Refugees on the St. John River. Since, despite the exertions they had made, it seemed likely that some of the Refugees would not arrive until late in the year, General Fox was requested to have the barracks and public stores at Annapolis put into repair for their reception. "The British American Troops from this place", Sir Guy continued, with unusual abruptness, "will be sent to the River St. John, as soon as possible."[27] There was a reason for the brusqueness of the statement. Sir Guy's instructions from England had been to send the provincials to Halifax, the military headquarters of Nova Scotia, for disbanding, and he was risking censure by sending them instead to the mouth of the St. John River where they would be near their lands. A less humanitarian and less courageous official would have carried out the instructions without regard to the inconveniences the provincials would thereby suffer.

At the same time, August 22, Carleton wrote to Governor Parr to let him know of the decision he had taken, and again to recommend the provincial troops to his Excellency's protection and favour. The persons employed in the civil departments would also be sent to Nova Scotia, and some of their number would go in advance to choose a suitable location for building a town. For them, and for a "large embarkation of Inhabitants, consisting of Merchants, Farmers, and Mechanics, and many persons of large property," who would bring additional strength and wealth to Nova Scotia, Sir Guy asked Governor Parr's encouragement and assistance.[28]

64

Throughout September and October, and into November, the evacuation of the provincials, the civil departments, and the merchants, farmers, and mechanics continued. Companies 47, 48, 49, and 50, comprising 384 persons, embarked for the St. John River on September 9, and several companies for Annapolis and Port Roseway on the same day. The British and British American Regiments, supposed to sail the 3rd of September, did not get away until the 15th. They had had to be picked up at the various stations where they were encamped and redistributed according to the capacity of the vessels in which they were to sail for Nova Scotia. The married men, in some cases, had to go up country to get their families and household effects, and many of them were delayed, as Benjamin Ingraham nearly was, by the hostility of the people in their home communities. The embarkation return shows the magnitude of the undertaking:

		Total Effectives			
British	Cos.	S	D	R&F	Officers
3rd Battalion 60th..	10	30	22	209	15
4th Battalion 60th..	10	30	22	152	15
British Legion					
(Cavalry)	6	12	6	128	23
Queen's Rangers ..	16	32	11	241	41
King's American					
Regiment......	10	20	10	208	22
Detachment Garrison					
Battalion		1		8	
British American					
New York Volunteers	9	15	2	55	25
British Legion					
(Infantry)	4	5		26	8
Loyal American	10	24	4	89	30
1 Skinners (New Jer-					
sey Volunteers)	10	18	5	152	26

2 Skinners	9	21	6	100	27
3 Skinners	9	27	9	175	29
1 DeLancey's	10	18	1	94	25
2 DeLancey's	9	25	2	105	26
Prince of Wales' American Volunteers..........	10	25	7	113	29
Maryland Loyalists	6	11	2	57	13
Pennsylvania Loyalists	4	2		33	13
American Legion ..	3	7	4	44	12
Guides and Pioneers	7	14	2	118	18
Totals	337	115	2107	400	2959 [29]

Since the 60th and the British Legion, which accounted for 703 of the total 2,959, were sent to Halifax, these returns indicate that 2,256 sailed for the St. John River. The Storekeeper's returns for the issue of spades, axes, and so forth, show a total of 2,306 for the St. John River, but his returns include the detachments of the North Carolina Volunteers and seven South Carolina Royalists. The final report from the Commissary General's office shows 1,826 officers and men of the British American troops gone to the St. John River. With them were 1,770 women, 355 children over ten, 341 children under ten, and 311 servants, a total of 3,396 for the British American regiments and their dependents. Among the missing would seem to be 480 soldiers, with 480 spades, 480 axes, and 480 canteens ....

On the 6th of October, 1783, the Commander-in-Chief was able to report that the British American Regiments had sailed for Nova Scotia; that all the artificers and stores, excepting small stores, were embarked, and the greater part had already sailed for Nova Scotia and England; that transports were allotted

66

for and would soon sail with the British Regiments destined for Nova Scotia and with such discharged British soldiers as wished to settle in that province; that "almost all those Loyalists who expected assistance from Govern't in removing from hence," were provided with shipping and gone to different parts of Nova Scotia, and that ships were preparing for those who still remained.[30]

On November 29, 1783, Ward Chipman, who had been deputy Muster-Master of Provincial Troops, wrote to his former chief and friend, Edward Winslow:

> I have been witness to the mortifying scene of giving up the City of New York to the American Troops. About 12 o'clock on Tuesday the 25th inst. all our Troops were paraded on the wide ground before the Provost, where they remained till the Americans about 1 o'clock marched in thro' Queen-Street and Wall-Street to the Broad-way, when they wheeled to the hay-wharf and embarked immediately and fell down to Staten Island. I walked out and saw the American Troops under General Knox march in, and was one of the last on shore in the City; it really occasioned most painful sensations and I tho't Sir Guy, who was upon parade, looked unusually dejected.[31]

Sir Guy Carleton's task was completed. It says much for his identification of himself with his country that he showed dejection on the occasion of the handing over of New York: he could have been pardoned for showing relief that the sorry business of clearing up the messes made by others was over. He had long since asked, and been refused, permission to return home. Now he could go. With everything against him, the situation, the temper of the times, the administrative awkwardness of the age he had brought to a remarkably successful conclusion the first important evacuation of political refugees in modern times.

CHAPTER FOUR

THE ARRIVAL

To leave New York, under the patronage of the Commander-in-Chief who had the authority to give orders and the assistants to carry out the orders, and under the oversight of a Commissary-General whose efficiency and common sense were backed by long acquaintance with Nova Scotia, was one experience: to arrive at the mouth of the St. John River, where an Irish major in charge of a detachment of soldiers was deputy for a Governor who was waiting for instructions from England, and where the assistant commissary was being replaced by a newcomer from New York, was an entirely different matter. Nor was the disorganization the only feature to make the prospect grim for the arriving Loyalists. Spring comes late along the Bay of Fundy coast, and cold winds and rain are more apt to prevail in May than warm sunshine. In the surrounding wilderness there were few breaks. On both sides of the harbour there were occasional clearings, with a log hut, perhaps occupied, perhaps deserted by its owner who had moved up the river out of reach of the rebel privateers. On the rugged rock at the turn of the river, stood the buildings of Fort Howe, and below the fort was the small settlement where William Hazen, James White, and some of their employees lived. The mast yard, the saw mill, and the scars where limestone had been burned, were further indications of human activity, but elsewhere the rugged hills and the boundless forests were as nature had formed them. The site for the Loyalist town was a rocky peninsula on the eastern side of the harbour, down river from Mr. Hazen's establishment. The ground was uneven and covered with cedars and bushes where swamps and rocks did not preclude their growth. The one advantage of the site was its nearness to the sea.

The fleets despatched from New York consisted of vessels for Port Roseway, Annapolis, Halifax, and other ports in Nova Scotia, as well as the St. John River and Fort Cumberland. From this point on, the concern of this study is with the arrivals at the ports on the north side of the Bay of Fundy, in the part of Nova Scotia which was set off as the province of New Brunswick. With the aid of the Commissary-General's accounts and other sources, it has been possible to discover the names of nearly all the ships which brought Loyalists and Provincials to the ports on the north side of the Bay of Fundy, many details regarding their passenger lists, and the dates of their arrival. It is convenient to consider the arrivals in five groups, the Spring Fleet, the June Fleet, Late Summer Arrivals, the Fall Fleet, Other Autumn Arrivals.[1]

1. *The Spring Fleet.*

New Brunswick historians have generally accepted without question the designation of May 18 as the day on which the Loyalists landed at the mouth of the St. John River, the account by Walter Bates of the arrival of the Spring Fleet, and the list given by Daniel Leavitt of ships he piloted into the harbour as the ships of the Spring Fleet. A further examination of the available records indicates that these three items can be accepted only with reservations. Walter Bates' *Narrative* and Daniel Leavitt's list, of course, were compiled long after the arrival of the Loyalists, and old men's memories sometimes play them tricks.

Why was May 18 chosen as Loyalist Day? If Walter Bates' recollection was correct, the *Union* arrived at Partridge Island on May 10, and next day "was sagely moored by Capt. Dan'l Leavitt, the pilot, in the most convenient situation for landing in the Harbour of

St. John". The passengers, however, did not land, but "remained comfortable on board ship". According to the provision accounts, the passengers remained on the *Union* until June 4. People may have been hustled off other ships, as Bates intimates, but only sixteen passengers were disembarked from the *Aurora* on May 25, and the rest remained on board until June 6. The *Grand Duchess of Russia* discharged all her passengers on May 24, but the *Hope* retained her passengers until June 1. The arrival of the vessels of the Spring Fleet, and the disembarking of the passengers apparently occupied nearly a month. From the leisureliness with which everything was accomplished, it seems likely that May 18 was the first day on which any considerable number of Loyalists landed, rather than a general landing day. A reference by J. W. Lawrence to the 18th of May, 1785, as the second anniversary of the landing of the first Loyalists confirms this supposition. May 18, apparently, was the beginning of the process of landing the Loyalists from the Spring Fleet, a process which occupied three weeks.

Daniel Leavitt or Lovett, who sagely moored the *Union,* and his brother Jonathan Leavitt were New Hampshire-born mariners, who had been brought up to the mouth of the St. John River by James Simonds, who established a trading post there in the 1760's. For many years they· had been masters of vessels employed in connection with the Hazen, Simonds and White enterprises at the mouth of the St. John River. The Leavitt brothers and other masters of sailing vessels, who piloted the ships of the Loyalists, were well acquainted with the twisting channel by which the waters of the St. John River make their way into the Bay of Fundy, through high tide and through low, a place which calls for skilful navigation and understanding of the currents and the state of the tide. This was the first of many instances in which the Pre-Loyalists' familiarity with the region was of great service to the newcomers.

In later years, someone obtained from Daniel Leavitt a list of ships he piloted into the harbour in 1783. As there were twenty ships in the list, *Ann*, *Aurora*, *Bridgwater*, *Britain*, *Camel*, *Commerce*, *Cyrus*, *Emmett*, *Favorite*, *Hope*, *King George*, *Lord Townsend*, *Otter*, *Sally*, *Sovereign*, *Spencer*, *Spring*, *Thames*, *Union*, *William*, and as Walter Bates mentioned that "upwards of twenty sail of ships under convoy left Sandy Hook for Nova Scotia", it seems to have been taken for granted that the twenty ships named were the Spring Fleet. Actually, only seven of the vessels named by Leavitt, *Aurora*, *Camel*, *Hope*, *Sovereign*, *Spencer*, *Spring*, and *Union*, came to St. John in the Spring Fleet, and there is no positive identification of two, *Spencer* and *Spring*. The *Ann* went to Port Roseway in April, but reached St. John in July. The *Bridgwater*, *Commerce*, *Lord Townsend*, and *Thames* arrived in June, the *Sally* and *William* in July, the *Cyrus* in August, the *King George* in September. Of the other four vessels, little information has been found. The *Britain*, which sailed from New York for Portsmouth, England, on November 25, 1783, may have been one of the convoy vessels. The *Emmett* is not mentioned in any of the documents. The *Favorite* was a mast ship which brought provisions from Halifax to Fort Howe in the spring of 1783. The *Otter* is otherwise mentioned only in the Balmain family tradition as the vessel on which their ancestor, William, came to the St. John River.

From comparison of Daniel Leavitt's list, Captain Chads' list, and the victualling returns, the Spring Fleet to the St. John River consisted of these vessels:

Aurora, 369 tons, Thomas Jackson, master, 212 passengers.

Camel, 293 tons, William Tinker, master, 135 passengers.

Grand Duchess of Russia, 308 tons, Stephen Holman, master, 113 passengers.

71

Hope, 286 tons, Robert Peacock, master, 172 passengers.

Lady's Adventure, 750 tons, Robert Gibson, master, 359 officers and dragoons, ?

Mars, 412 tons, James Grayson, master, 210 passengers.

Sovereign, 383 tons, William Stewart, master, 154 passengers.

Spencer, 333 tons, Robert Balantine, master, ?

Spring, 341 tons, Richard Cavers (Cadish on Leavitt's list), master, ?

Union, 287 tons, Consett Wilson, master, 164 passengers.

Since the vessels were supposed to carry one passenger to every one and a half tons, it will be observed that, if the figures for passengers are correct, no ship carried a full load. The *Union* and the *Hope* had carried more than their share of passengers from Huntington Bay and Lloyd's Neck to New York, but had discharged families before setting out on the longer voyage. The item of 359 officers and dragoons for the King's American Dragoons on the *Lady's Adventure* is puzzling, since it bears no discernible relation to the rations from April 17 to May 24, 12,990 days, to the amount of rum consumed, 425 gallons, or to the October returns of the Commissary-General's office which attributed to the regiment a total of 404, made up of 267 men, 45 women, 52 children, 40 servants. The seven passenger lists given make up nearly half of the approximately 2,400 Loyalists sent to the St. John River in April. The *Spencer* and *Spring*, which are put in the Spring Fleet because Daniel Leavitt named them, probably carried less than the 222 and 227 passengers for which they were victualled. There must therefore have been four or five more of Captain Chads' list which sailed for the St. John River:

Ariel, 335 tons, Richard Grigson, master.
Blacket, 400 tons, John Roxby, master.
Brothers, 365 tons, William Walker, master.
Esther, 384 tons, Robert Gill, master.
Grace, 278 tons, William Oxley, master.
Hercules, 250 tons.
Peggy, 360 tons, Jacob Wilson, master.
Providence, 264 tons, John Ritchie, master.
Three Sisters, 240 tons, John Wardell, master.
Venus, 310 tons, John Martin, master.

The only clue to any disposition of these vessels is a letter from Jacob Wilson of Whitby, Yorkshire, master of the *Peggy*, making Henry Nase his attorney to sell the lots and house at Brookland near the "new city of Shelburne, otherwise St. John," because Mrs. Wilson would not hear of his being away any more. Thus was the new city of St. John deprived of a man whom Edward Winslow called "the most extraordinary character in the world".

What preparations had been made for the arrival of the Spring Fleet? The Commissary-General, Brook Watson, and his assistant in Nova Scotia, Roger Johnson, had been making arrangements about provisions and had been endeavouring to find and transport lumber. Although Moses Perley, in a lecture given before the Mechanics Institute of Saint John, in 1841, stated that town lots were laid out by Paul Bedell before the arrival of the first fleet, there is no evidence to confirm this statement. It seems more likely that Paul Bedell arrived in the Spring Fleet, as George Leonard suggests, and that the surveying for lots did not begin until the end of May or the first days of June. Peter Huggeford, a physician from New York, in a petition written on February 8, 1785, said that he arrived in July, 1783, "whilst the town plot was surveying and before any

73

buildings were erected." The accounts for the distribution of boards and shingles commenced on July 5. For the eight ships for which records could be found, there is no mention of disembarkation of passengers before May 23, which suggests that preparations on shore had not been made and that there was not even any available clearing where the two tents provided for each family could be erected.

It is not surprising that the *Union* passengers showed no enthusiasm for landing at the mouth of the river, but waited until three of their number went up the river and picked out a site for settlement. They then left the *Union*, with "Captain Wilson's blessing", Walter Bates characteristically remarks, and embarked on board a small sloop with all their baggage. Walter Bates wrote as if this undertaking were wholly one of the *Union* passengers, but an examination of the names on the passenger list of the *Hope*, one of the few passenger lists available, shows that most of them were Kingston settlers, as were the *Union* passengers, and it would seem reasonable to suppose that they, too, went up the Belleisle as soon as they could arrange for transportation. Christopher Jenkins, who signed the victualling return of the *Aurora*, was also a Kingston grantee, but whether his fellow passengers as a whole took part in the undertaking can only be conjectured. It was unfortunate for the new town at the mouth of the river that the passengers of the *Union* and the *Hope*, and perhaps the *Aurora* and other ships, went up the river at once. They were predominantly a Connecticut group who had been living together on Long Island; they had a strong sense of community; they had ability and initiative, and they might have been able to inject a spirit of fairness and of good sense into the conduct of affairs in the new town.

Another conjecture, for which there is very little actual evidence, is that a large number of passengers in the Spring Fleet went at once up the river to Gagetown.

Anthony Terril, who signed for the *Camel*, and James Peters, who signed for the *Sovereign*, were certainly Gagetown grantees, but there are no passenger lists to confirm the surmise. In any case, since there were many Pre-Loyalists living in the Gagetown area, and since there was difficulty over title to the land, the Gagetown Loyalist settlement was never able to attain the solidarity of the Kingston group. Many of the first arrivals at Gagetown became disheartened by the uncertainity about ownership of the land and withdrew to other parts of the province.

The majority of the Loyalists arriving in the Spring Fleet probably remained at the mouth of the river. Possibly a town meeting was held: anyway directors were chosen, Reverend John Sayre, formerly Rector of Trinity Church, Fairfield, Connecticut, who had been one of the agents chosen by the Lloyd's Neck refugees, George Leonard of Massachusetts, who had been a member of the Board of Directors of the Associated Loyalists, William Tyng of Falmouth, Massachusetts, who had been connected with the Commissary-General's Department in New York and had been picked to replace William Hazen as Assistant Commissary at Fort Howe, and Major Gilfred Studholme of the Royal Fencible Americans, who had been in charge of the detachment of that regiment stationed at Fort Howe at the mouth of the St. John River. Oliver Arnold, a native of Mansfield, Connecticut, graduate of Yale in 1776, was named as secretary of the Board of Directors. Edward Winslow, who reached the St. John River from Annapolis during the first week of July or the last week of June, wrote that an inattention, or want of exertion in the Agents of the Refugees had been the cause of extreme distress to those who had already landed there. "They are at present crowded into one spot without covering," Winslow stated, "and totally ignorant where they are eventually to settle, altho' two townships containing near 300,000 acres of the best land on the River St. John's has been long ago escheated at their application." Winslow thought the "Reverend Gentleman" who was ostensibly in charge unequal to the task, and those were who doing the duty there not the right kind of men. In a later letter, Winslow was even more scathing in his denunciation of the individual who had the direction of all matters civil and military as one "accustomed to dissipation, and who (tho' possessing many pleasing qualities) is as incompetent to the performance of the task assigned, as a Spider wou'd be to regulate the grand manufactories at Manchester."

Events were to make it clear that there was some truth in Winslow's extravagant statements about the mismanagement of affairs in the new town. Complaints became so serious that Governor Parr sent the Chief Justice of Nova Scotia, Bryan Finucane, to investigate the situation in connection particularly with the assigning of lots. Apparently, the passengers in the Spring Fleet thought themselves the only Loyalists coming to the site and laid out a town with large lots. As more and more shiploads arrived, the lots were divided and subdivided, until "the Lotts of those who came first (who had gone to the task and expence in forming the Town) had been reduced to one sixteenth part of their former number of feet—which they had obtained by a fair and legal draft." George Leonard did not add to his explanation what expense there had been in forming the new town. The carpenters employed in building Reverend Mr. John Sayre's house, enclosing the lumber yard, and other public services, from July 20th, were paid by Studholme out of public moneys, and so was "one days Truckage with the Frame of Mr. John Sayre's House with a double Team", charged on August 31. In any case, it is clear that the new town was not ready for the arrival of a considerable contingent of Loyalists by the June Fleet.

2. *The June Fleet.*

On Saturday, June 28, Sarah Frost, a passenger on the *Two Sisters*, recorded that they awoke to find themselves nigh to land on both sides of the ship. At 9.30, the Captain fired a gun for a pilot; soon after 10, the pilot came on board; at 1.15, the ship "was anchored off against Fort Howe in Saint John's River", and some of the passengers were going on shore. Her husband went with them and returned with a fine salmon. The next morning was very pleasant, and Sarah and her children were going on shore. Later she wrote: "It is now afternoon and I have been on shore. It is, I think, the roughest land I ever saw. We are all ordered to land tomorrow and not a shelter to go under." John Clark, a Rhode Island Loyalist, who arrived in the same fleet, stated that only two log huts had been erected by the passengers who had arrived in the first fleet. It was a disheartening prospect, especially after a difficult voyage, with heavy seas for the first few days, and then fog. On the *Two Sisters*, an outbreak of measles had increased the miseries of the long journey, and there was little to cheer the passengers at the journey's end.

For the June Fleet there is more definite information regarding the vessels and their passengers than for the Spring Fleet. Moreover, the advertisement regarding future sailing, Captain Chads' list, another list elicited by the Admiralty in its search into the costs of removing the Loyalists, the victualling lists, and the issuing of lumber at the St. John River, show a correspondence which is remarkable in documents concerning the Loyalists. (One of the ships advertised to sail for the St. John, the *Free Briton*, took a company to Port Roseway.)

Amity's Production, 313 tons, Thomas Reed,
Co. 11, Thomas Welch, 157 passengers.

Bridgwater, 757 tons, Daniel Adnet,
    Co. 9, Joseph Clark, 41
    Co. 10, Jas. Hayt, 43
    Co. 20, Christopher Benson, 42
    Co. 23, James Forester, 122.

Duchess of Gordon, 300 tons, James Holmes,
    Co. 13, Ashur Dunham, 111
    Co. 18, Abiathar Camp, 39.

Generous Friends, 203 tons, Thomas Huntley,
    Co. 6, Thos. Elms, 111.

Hopewell, 208 tons, Mark Richards,
    Co. 3, Henry Thomas, (122?).

Littledale, 253 tons, Richard Kelsick,
    Co. 21, Peter Berton, 145.

Symmetry, 333 tons, Francis Maxwell,
    Co. 4, John Forrester, 111.

Tartar, 261 tons, Andrew Yates (Yetts),
    Co. 12, Oliver Bourdet, 134.

Thames, 202 tons, Abram Ingram,
    Co. 8, John Cock, 104.

Two Sisters, 383 tons, John Brown,
    Co. 1, Silvanus Whitney, (168)
    Co. 2, Joseph Goram, (136).

William and Mary, 320 tons, carried Richard Hill's
    Co. 64 persons, for Annapolis, and probably
    part of Cos. 1 and 2 for St. John River.

In addition to the above:

Thetis, 376 tons, Robert Gordon, Westchester
Loyalists for Cumberland.

From this table it appears that between 1,500 and 1,600 passengers for the St. John River arrived in the June Fleet, in Companies 1, 2, 3, 4, 6, 8, 9, 10, 11, 12, 13, 18, 20, 21, 23. The Commander-in-Chief, it will be remembered, had mentioned to Governor Parr in his letter of April 26, at the time of the dispatch of the Spring

Fleet, that he had given temporary commissions for sixteen companies of militia. Such an arrangement had been continued, and had been systematized by numbering the companies for each destination. By the end of September, the companies sent forward to the St. John River numbered 52 or 54 (there is a discrepancy in the documents as to the numbering of the later companies), 42 for Port Roseway, 17 for Annapolis, and two for Halifax.

Anyone who checks this list with the final *Return* from the Commissary-General's office will notice that the numbers in the companies do not always tally. Abiathar Camp's Company, No. 18, had only 39 persons on the *Duchess of Gordon*, but 203 on the other list. It is possible that Abiathar Camp came up to the St. John River in June with part of his family and part of his company, and then returned to New York. On September 4, 1783, when he was expecting to sail in three days to join his two sons at St. John, he requested help from the Commander-in-Chief. This in part confirms a family tradition that Abiathar Camp made two or three trips in his own vessel, and that on the last trip he carried 203 Loyalists. It also helps to strengthen a hypothesis that there was a great deal of unofficial and unreported transportation of Loyalists from New York, the full extent of which will never be known.

3. *Late Summer Arrivals.*

Although in petitions of Loyalists, there is occasional mention of a third fleet, the records suggest that there was not a regularly convoyed fleet setting off as in April and in June. Since two fleets had arrived without any molestation, it may have been deemed unnecessary to continue making up a convoy. In any case, sailing ships found it difficult to keep together in stress of wind and weather, and tended to straggle into port at intervals. In the June Fleet, for instance, the *Bridgwater* had had difficulty in keeping up with the other vessels and had

79

eventually fallen behind and arrived two weeks or more behind the others.

As far as can be ascertained, these are the vessels which arrived at the end of July and in August.

Ann, 385 tons, John Clark,
    Co. 28, Robert Chillas, 82.
Aurora, 369 tons, Thos. Jackson, 153.
Commerce, 355 tons, Richard Strong, 128.
Elizabeth, 341 tons, John Watson,
    Co. 22, Nathaniel Horton, 70 + 17.
Grace, 278 tons, Wm. Oxley, 62.
Grand Duchess of Russia, 308 tons, Stephen Holman,
    Co. 29, John O'Blenus, 52.
Hercules, 250 tons,   ?   ?
Hesperus, 245 tons, Samuel Clark, sailed July 8,
    remained at St. John.
Joseph, 175 tons, ——— Stokes, 43.
Keppel, 336 tons, ——— Bailey, ?
Kingston, 338 tons, John Atkinson, ?
Lord Townsend, 440 tons, James Hogg,
    Co. 27, Jacob Cook, 50,   (117 passengers)
    Co. 16, John Mersereau, 47.
Mary, 326 tons, ——— Bell, ?
Montagu, 340 tons, Robt. Wilson,
    Co. 7, Peter Huggeford, 105.
Nicholas and Jane, 340 tons, John Ellison, ?
Sovereign, 383 tons, Wm. Stewart,
    Co. 24, John Menzies, 41.
Spencer, 333 tons, Robert Balantine, ?
Three Sisters, 240 tons, John Wardell,
    Co. 30, Wm. Olive, 68.
    Co. 14, Thos. Huggeford, 72.
William, 282 tons, Edward Major,
    Co. 15, Wm. Wright, 85.

The companies mentioned are Nos. 7, 14, 15, 16, 22, 24, 27, 28, 29, 30. The accounts of lumber issues indicate that Companies 17, 19, 26, 32, 36, 37, 38, 39, were also among the arrivals in the late summer. With the exception of Company No. 5, an Annapolis Company which strayed into the St. John River list, and No. 25, whose Captain went to Halifax and whose other officers cannot be traced, all the numbered companies for the St. John River, from 1 to 39, had arrived by the end of the summer.

There are indications of solidarity among the companies who arrived late in the summer, a solidarity which was perhaps enhanced by the inhospitable attitude of the first comers. With one exception, the officers of Companies 7, 17, and 30, became owners of lots on the west side of the harbour. The King's American Dragoons had started a township on the west side, in July, but the authorities at Halifax had decided to move the regiments up the river, and a town site for refugees was laid out on the west side, to the great relief of the Board of Directors of the east side town who were at their wits' end with the problem of providing lots for these new arrivals.

W. O. Raymond has preserved the courteous note of thanks addressed by John Menzies, Captain of Company 24 to Wm. Stewart, Captain of the *Sovereign*, for his generosity, kindness and attention to them while on board his ship, and for the assistance lent them on landing their property from on board. The letter, written on August 12, was by request of the Company, its writer said. Had Company 24 had a meeting? Company 22, which had been disembarked from the *Elizabeth* on August 2, had a meeting, a very momentous meeting as it turned out. A copy of their proceedings on October 28, with Captain Horton in the chair, sent to Governor Parr, aroused that gentleman's apprehensions that a new revolution was being fomented. To modern ears the proceedings sound harmless enough.

81

Proposed that no resolve be passed by this Company, but what we may warrantably publish to the world. Resolved in the Affirmative. Resolved unanimously, that as a considerable number of Inhabitants in this place are educated in the Principles of the National Church of Scotland, Application be made for ourselves and others for Public Grounds to be laid out for a burying ground and erecting a Church for those of that persuasion, with every other encouragement to the National Church of that Ancient *loyal* Kingdom equal to the Church of England.—And if this most reasonable request is refused we *are* determined to petition the Reverend General Assembly so that our case may be laid before his Majesty by the Lord High Commissioner to Kirk of Scotland.

Resolved unanimously, That the chairman of this company be Authorized in *their* name and in their behalf to enquire of Major Studholme and Doctor Sears concerning the Tenor of their Commissions respecting said Loyalists and that a true copy of their Instructions in all respects whatever affecting them may be Communicated to him for their Information so as every Individual may be Satisfied.

Resolved unanimously, That if every necessary Satisfaction is not given that we will employ men in whom we can confide to go to Halifax or Great Britain to represent our case as to our present Situation concerning our Lots in Town and Lands in the Country with an Account of every denomination in Quantity and Quality received by us since our arrival in St. John's River.—

Resolved unanimously that the following are greivances:

1st.   Our proportion of Cloathing has not been adequate to the proposals Shewn us, nor have any of us received equal to those who arrived here before us and a number of the Company have received none.

2d. Blankets Nails Window Glass and Many other Articles which were expected by us have not been received. And the necessaries for erecting of Grist and Saw Mills are not Accounted for.

3d. No Account whatever has been rendered of a Collection of Money to a considerable Amount raised at New York for the Support of the poorer sort of Emigrants.

4th. That a grant of Money to the Amount of £60,000 has been voted by parliament for our present Support of which together with £20,000 by private Subscription we have no Account of and justly fear that it will be appropriated to the use of Averitious men.

5th. That the principal Town Lotts as well as the best of the lands in this part of Nova Scotia have been and are reserved for particular Persons contrary to the Spirit of His Majesty's Gracious intentions.

6th. That we learn five men have applied to the Governor of this Province for a grant of this Township which being done must preclude Our Heirs and Successors of that Valuable priviledge the chusing a Representative or Representatives for us to make Laws to raise Taxes, &c. And Vest that precious Right freely gratiously given us by the Crown in five men only which may in the Sequal prove dangerous to the community and in its nature is unjust.

Signed by order of the Company,

CLAUDIUS CHARLES
Clk. Cy.

Governor Parr had not visited the new settlement at the mouth of the St. John River as he should have done. He had visited Port Roseway in July, 1783, and been acclaimed by the Loyalists there. He had changed the name of the town to Shelburne, and, in his own estimation, smoothed out all difficulties so that now everything would go well and peaceably in that part of his domain. His reason for not continuing to the St. John River, he explained to Whitehall, was the necessity of returning to Halifax to see if instructions from home had arrived. Perhaps with an idea of placating the settlers at the St. John River, the governor had suggested that the town be named **Parr**, but he still knew that he had done less than his duty by the new settlement. That may have had something to do with his seizing upon the communication from Company 22 as a reason for vilifying the place. On December 31, 1783, he sent a copy of the resolutions to Sir Guy Carleton, who had landed all these tiresome problems on him and had suggested that he and the other officials of Nova Scotia forego their fees for land grants, and he wrote the authorities at home that some of the Refugees settled on the banks of the River St. John, "having excited discontents amongst many of those people & managed their proceedings by forming Committees for obtaining Redress of Greivances," in order to check "a disposition so pernicious and banefull", he would withhold grants of land from the principal leaders until His Majesty's pleasure was known. Nowhere was there any indication that the Governor would investigate the complaints or take any steps to redress grievances. "All our disturbances and disagreements in the Province", he wrote to Evan Nepean, "originate at the River St. John, where there are many turbulent Spirits, who are full of groundless complaints, lies and false representations, and their Agents replete with gross partialitys, they give me much trouble and uneasiness, and often make my time uncomfortable". That, of course, was unforgivable.

4.   *The Fall Fleet.*

On the 29th of September, 1783, Colonel Richard Hewlett, commanding officer of the 2nd Battalion of DeLancey's Brigade, who had been placed in charge of the British American corps sent to the St. John River, was able to report to the Commander-in-Chief that the troops under his command had arrived. at their destination on the 27th of the month, with the exception of the *Martha*, on which the Maryland Loyalists and part of his own battalion, the 2nd DeLancey's, had been embarked, and the *Esther*, with part of the New Jersey Volunteers on board. A small part of the Guides and Pioneers had landed, and were going up the river, from the falls, the next day, if the weather permitted. The necessary orders had been given for the troops to disembark on the following day, and to encamp just above the falls, whence they would be forwarded with all possible expedition to their destinations. The want of small craft, however, seemed likely to delay sending the men up river.

On October 13, Hewlett reported that the *Esther* had arrived, but the *Martha* had been wrecked on a ledge of rocks off the Seal Islands between Cape Sable and the Bay of Fundy. The *Bridgwater*, late again, had arrived on October 12, and all the troops had been disbanded. Again, he mentioned the want of small craft and the delays caused. Further information would be given the Commander-in-Chief by Major Prevost, the disbanding officer, who would carry back this letter, but one difficulty was stated, a great confusion among the troops, because small hatchets had been issued them in lieu of axes.

The three vessels mentioned by Colonel Hewlett and those in the victualling accounts make up this catalogue for the Fall Fleet:

Ann, 385 tons, Joseph Clark; Loyal American ✓
Regiment, 74; Guides and Pioneers, 204.

Apollo, 361 tons, John Adamson; Loyal American Regiment, 187; King's American Dragoons, 7.

Bridgwater, 757 tons, Daniel Adnet; Pennsylvania Loyalists, ?

Duke of Richmond, 865 tons, Richard Davis; 1 New Jersey Volunteers, 342; 2 New Jersey Volunteers, 281.

Elizabeth, 341 tons, John Watson; American Legion, 140; Prince of Wales' American Regiment, 77.

Esther, 384 tons, Robert Gill; 3 New Jersey Volunteers, ?

King George, 275 tons; King's American Regiment, 140; Garrison Battalion, 16.

Montagu, 340 tons, Robert Wilson; Prince of Wales' American Regiment, 176 ?

Palliser, 345 tons, James Smith; 2 DeLancey's, 162.

Ranger, 361 tons, John Bell; New York Volunteers, 199.

Sovereign, 383 tons, Wm. Stewart; 1 DeLancey's, 199 or more.

William, 282 tons, Edward Major; King's American Regiment, 161.

The loss of the *Martha* was a sorry business. Captain Kennedy of the Maryland Loyalists, at the official inquiry, gave his opinion that the captain had shown poor judgment in sailing during the night after land had been sighted. He also accused the *Martha's* captain of criminal negligence in jumping into a boat when passengers were stranded aboard the vessel, in refusing assistance offered by the regiments, and in discouraging the inhabitants from putting out to effect a rescue. The captain of the *Martha* tried to excuse himself from this last charge by maintaining that he was convinced that there were no survivors to be rescued, and made other attempts to explain his actions. At the time when the inquiry was held, it was supposed that one captain, one lieutenant, one ensign, four sergeants, five corporals, twenty-two privates, eight women and sixteen children of the 2nd DeLancey's had perished, and one lieutenant, one ensign, six sergeants, two corporals, twenty-seven privates, seven women, nine children, and four servants belonging to the Maryland Loyalists.

The *Esther*, according to the account given by one of the passengers, Mrs. Lewis Fisher, wife of a private in the 3rd New Jersey Volunteers, to her granddaughter, was nearly lost through going on the wrong "track". When they reached St. John, they found the place all in confusion, "some living in log houses, some building huts, and many of the soldiers living in their tents at the Lower Cove." The Fishers joined a party bound up the river in a schooner to St. Ann's. It took eight days to get to Oromocto, and there the captain of the schooner put them ashore, and charged them each four dollars for the passage. The women and children and some of the men went on to St. Ann's the next day by Indian canoes; the rest walked.[2]

John Ward, a lieutenant in the Loyal American Regiment, who commanded the last detachment of Loyalist troops to leave New York, came in a transport ship which was laden with provisions and clothing. Owing to the lateness of their arrival, they were obliged to shelter themselves under canvas tents on the Barrack Square at Lower Cove. The tents Mrs. Fisher saw were probably those of the troops stationed there and of soldiers who could not get up the river, because of the want of small craft mentioned by Colonel Hewlett, or who preferred to remain at the mouth of the river near the provision stores. John Ward mentioned the coldness of the tents, even when thatched with spruce boughs, and the deaths of many women and children during the winter because of exposure and lack of nourishing food.

His son, John Ward, junior, was born in a tent on December 18, 1783. Hannah Ingraham, who arrived the last of September, in the *King George*, presumably, since her father was with the King's American Regiment, said that it was a sad sick time after they landed in Saint John. They had to live in tents, given by the government, and the melting snow and rain soaked up into their beds. Her mother developed rheumatism and was never well afterwards. They too went up the river in a schooner, as far as either Maugerville or Oromocto, and thence in a rowboat hired by Captain Clements of the King's American Regiment.

From Colonel Hewlett's reports to the eleven-year-old Hannah's recollections, all the accounts of the arrival of the Fall Fleet agree that satisfactory arrangements had not been made for the much belated arrival of the provincial corps. Edward Winslow had been very critical of the authorities at the mouth of the river and of the lack of arangements for the refugees, but had he done any better for the provincials? Chosen in April as one of the agents "for the purpose of soliciting & securing grants of land for the Provincial Corps", he had sailed for Annapolis in the *Peggy*, with the captain who was "the most extraordinary character in the world". After a month or more spent in settling his wife and family in Granville, across the river from Annapolis, Winslow had, late in May, gone to Halifax. The first week in July, he was at the mouth of the St. John River, with his friend Major Daniel Murray, who was in charge of the King's American Dragoons, and the two of them were picking the site for a township for the provincials, on the west side of the river, on high ground overlooking the Bay of Fundy on one side and the river on the other, "positively the most magnificent and romantic scene" Winslow had ever beheld. A few days later, he and two brother agents, Major Thomas Barclay of the Provincial Light Infantry, and Lieutenant-Colonel Isaac Allen of the 2nd New Jersey Volunteers, set off to survey the river and choose land for the regiments. Winslow returned to the mouth of the river full of enthusiasm for the country he had seen, but he was met there by news that he had been recommended to the new military commander in Nova Scotia, Brigadier Henry Fox (brother of Charles James Fox), as secretary. Impetuous and impecunious always, Winslow welcomed this appointment, and hastened off to Halifax at once, determined to exploit to the full this opportunity. There, it is to be feared, he forgot his responsibilities as an agent for the provincials and acquiesced in the bestowing of the lower part of the river on the refugees. No wonder, then, that the respectable Serjeants, once hospitable yeomen of the country, addressed Winslow in a language which almost murdered him as he heard it:

"Sir, we have served all the War. Your Honor is witness how faithfully. We were promised land, We expected you had obtained it for us,—We like the country—only let us have a spot of our own, and give us such kind of regulations as will hinder bad men from injuring us."

Winslow and Stephen DeLancey, Lieutenant-Colonel of the 2nd DeLancey's, had been 130 miles up the river just before the regiments arrived, and proposed to the commanding officers that the land should be divided into townships twelve miles square, and that the regiments should draw for their sites. When they took possession of their townships, the regiments would divide them into lots and the settlers actually present would draw for the lots, and any surplus lots would remain at the disposal of the government. After five months, the agents had only this hastily improvised proposal, to which the consent of the governor had still to be obtained. What were the men to do meantime? The land of which they might ultimately receive possession lay ninety, one hundred, one hundred and fifty, two hundred miles up the river. How were they to reach it? How were they to live through the winter? John Ward thatched his tent with spruce boughs. Henry Nase, formerly of Dutchess County, New York, a lieutenant in the King's American Regiment, "hutted" himself and was comfortable in eight days. Lewis Fisher took his family up the river and pitched his tent near the shore, but could not build a log hut because of the lateness of the season. Benjamin Ingraham, however, was not deterred by the lateness of the season. According to Hannah's story, he went up through their lot until he found a nice fresh spring of water.

It was very good so there he built his house. We all had rations given by the government, flour, butter and pork. Tools were given to the men also.

One morning when we awoke we found the snow lying deep on the ground all around us and then father came wading through it and told us the house was ready, and not to stop to light a fire and not to mind the weather, but follow his tracks through the trees, for the trees were so many we soon lost sight of him going up the hill. It was snowing fast, and oh, so cold. Father carried a chest and we all took something and followed him up the hill through the trees to see our gable end. There was a floor laid, no windows, no chimney, no door, but we had a roof at least. A good fire was blazing and Mother had a big loaf of bread and she boiled a kettle of water and put a good piece of butter in a pewter bowl. We toasted the bread and all sat around the bowl and ate our breakfast that morning, and mother said:

"Thank God we are no longer in dread of having shots fired through our house, this is the sweetest meal I have tasted for many a day."

It was not long before father got a good floor down of split cedar logs, a floor overhead to make a bedroom and a chimney built. Who built the chimney. There were no mills then, no bricks nothing but wood. Our chimney was made of stones for the back and a kind of mud mortar. The front and sides were just sticks and mud. They took care to plaster mud all upside the inside of the chimney. Captain Clements came in one day to see father and he said:

"Why, Ingraham, you've got a chimney up before me."

Thus, in one way and another, according to their abilities, the officers and men of the regiments coped with the unsatisfactory conditions they found upon arrival in their new territory. The repercussions were many and far reaching. Some of them will be traced in later chapters.

5. *Other Autumn Arrivals*

Besides the men, women, and children of the provincial regiments, there were refugees arriving during September and October. Indeed, final mopping up operations in New York resulted in the appearance of additional Loyalists in November and even in December.

On September 14, the *Cyrus*, John Wardill, master, arrived at the St. John River with 194 passengers belonging to Companies 41 and 42. The *Eagle*, with part or perhaps all of Company 40, the major part of John Smith's group, was another September arrival. The *Camel*, 293 tons, William Tinker, master, which had sailed also with the Spring Fleet, arrived at St. John on September 18 with "A List of Loyalists and Refugees, consisting of James Reed (Pilot) wife and two children and thirty children over ten years bound as Supernumeraries for Victuals only and victualled at Two Third allowance of all species of Provisions Spirits excepted by Order of Rear Admiral Digby", and "Loyalists and Refugees consisting of 104 men, 50 women, 20 servants", as well as 47 children under the age of ten, who received half allowance. Nearly all the passengers on the *Camel* belonged to the two special companies of Quakers and Anabaptists, and they were sent immediately down the Bay to Beaver Harbour.

In October, these vessels probably brought Loyalists:

Alexander, 420 tons, Roger Alderson,   ?
Hopewell, 248 tons, Mark Richards,   ?
John and Jane, 378 tons, Wm. Dawson,
      Co. 44, Joseph Thorne, 134.
Mary, 315 tons, Francis Rowbotham,   ?
Mercury, 396 tons, Thomas Dawson, 152 passengers.
Nancy, 305 tons, Gilbert Wilson, or to Port Roseway?
Neptune, 400 tons, Thos. Belson, 163 passengers.
Sally, 317 tons, Wm. Bell.

The last voyage of the *Camel* was one that people with experience of the Bay of Fundy in winter will not envy. On November 9, 1783, the *Camel* embarked 167 men, 63 women, and five servants, at New York. On December 14, thirteen passengers were disembarked at St. John, and the ship went on to Digby, where the Loyalists for that area were discharged. On January 7, 1784, more passengers were discharged at Windsor, and the *Camel* may have remained at Windsor for the next two months. On the 8th of March, a few more passengers were deposited at St. John, and two days later, more than forty were disembarked at Passamaquoddy. It is the latest arrival of which any records can be found. In 1784, Thomas Knox reported the "late arrival of a number of families from the American States who profess an interest in settling in this part of the Province and most of whom produce Certificates of Loyalty to the King". There were a few later arrivals who had been detained by illness or imprisonment, and there were others, who had been to England to press claims for compensation or preferment, who sailed across the Atlantic when passage was available. The main body of the New Brunswick Loyalists, however, arrived between the middle of May and the middle of November, in the year 1783.

CHAPTER FIVE

THE ROYAL BOUNTY OF PROVISIONS

Sir

You will issue to the Refugees on board your Ship, One pound of Bread, and twelve ounces of Pork, or, in lieu of Pork, Twenty one ounces of Beef per Man per day. The Women and Children of ten years old and upwards, are to be victualled as the Men, and all under that age, are to receive only half Allowance, but no rum to any.

Such were the instructions issued to Robert Watson, master of the transport *Stafford*, by order of the Commissary-General, on June 24, 1783. The issues varied somewhat from time to time. A printed form of rules to be observed by masters and commanders of transports in victualling land forces was issued to Mr. Samuel Gallilee, master of the *Dorothy and Catherine*, for his guidance in supplying Refugees and Negroes. The 8 Jills of Rum per day were crossed off the list, but the provisions were to be issued according to the table, to parties of six:

	Bread or Flour Pounds	Beef Pounds	Pork Pounds	Butter Pounds	Pease Pints	Oatmeal Pints
Sunday	4		4		2	
Monday	4			1		4
Tuesday	4	8				
Wednesday	4			1	2	4
Thursday	4		4		2	
Friday	4			1	2	
Saturday	4	8				4
Total	28	16	8	3	8	12

Underneath this table was an explanation which will be of interest to modern students of dietetics. One pint of oatmeal, it was explained, was equal to one pint of pease; half a pound of rice to a pint of oatmeal; eight pounds of beef to four pounds of pork; half a pint of wine to one jill of spirits. When the commanding officer ordered vinegar to be issued, a quart per week to six men was the allowance. For Mr. Gallilee's guidance in transporting refugees, the Deputy Commissary added a note that the women and children of ten years of age were to be victualled as the men, but no allowance was to be made for children under ten. He emphasized that neither men, women, nor children were to receive rum. In other cases, instructions allowed two-thirds or one-half rations to children under ten.

The Loyalists, it will be remembered, had requested provisions for the voyage to Nova Scotia and one year's provision thereafter. As the victualling was done from Halifax, the military headquarters for Nova Scotia, it was necessary for Brook Watson, the Commissary-General, to send instructions to his deputy in Nova Scotia, Roger Johnson, regarding the sending of supplies to the outposts where Loyalists would be arriving. In April, 1783, Johnson reported that, by order of the general, he had shipped on board the *Favourite* and *Lyon*, two mast ships, provisions and rum to complete the outposts in the Bay of Fundy to May 31, 1784. More supplies for the ever increasing numbers of incoming Loyalists were received from the surplus stores of the vessels which carried the Loyalists. The *Hope*, one of the Spring Fleet, had in her log a receipt, dated Fort Howe, St. John's River, May 25, 1783, from William Tyng, Deputy Commissary, for 50 sacks containing 5331 pounds of bread, one barrel of beef, ten barrels of pork, six firkins of butter, twelve barrels of pease, seven casks of oatmeal, four puncheons and one hogshead containing 472 gallons of rum. Roger Johnson feared that the stores at Fort Howe would not be able to contain the goods and advised his deputy to pile the wet provisions near the store and to cover them in the best manner possible. Later, Mr. Tyng complained that for want of proper stores, the beef and pork were stolen almost every night, although he had taken the precaution of providing sentinels and counting the barrels every morning and evening. One suspects that some of the dwellers in tents at Barrack Square, near Lower Cove, were able to outwit Mr. Tyng's sentinels.

William Hazen, who had removed from Newburyport to the mouth of the St. John River in 1775, and who was one of the principal partners in the various enterprises carried on there, had been in charge of the commissariat at Fort Howe. On May 31, 1783, Roger Johnson reported to Brook Watson that Mr. Hazen, in consequence of the Commissary-General's letter directing him either to give up his post as commissary or desist from trading, had preferred the former alternative, and Mr. Tyng was taking charge from May 25. William Tyng, who had been employed in connection with the forage department of the Commissary-General's office in New York, did not prove a satisfactory deputy, either to the Loyalists or to Roger Johnson. Johnson complained that Tyng's accounts were late in arriving and when they did come were so "irregular and the form of the receipts so loose" that Johnson, realizing they would not be admitted by the Commissary of Accounts, was obliged to return them. On November 21, 1783, Johnson reported to his superior that he was loading a vessel with flour for St. John. As he had had no returns from Mr. Tyng until that morning, he had not known that flour was needed there. No wonder that Mrs. Fisher recollected that "Supplies expected before the close of navigation did not come, and at one time starvation stared us in the face." Some of the men went down the river with handsleds or toboggans to get food for their famishing families.

William Tyng was relieved of his post at some time during the winter and went up the river to Gagetown for a few years before returning to his former home near Portland, Maine. His place was taken by F. W. Hecht, who was appointed as Assistant Commissary, by orders of Sir Guy Carleton on November 22, 1783, to go to the "River St. John's in the Province of Nova Scotia where there are near 10,000 souls victualed, and there to take charge of the Provisions, Fuel, &c. and be accountable for the same." In 1785, Mr. Hecht's accounts had to be investigated, and his "unaccommodating temper and ill humor" made the task a difficult one. Whether it was Hecht or his deputies who were at fault, Mrs. Fisher said that a full supply of provisions was looked for in the spring, "but the people were betrayed by those they depended upon to supply them." Her husband went up the river to Captain McKay's for provisions, "and found no one at home but an old colored slave woman, who said her master and his man had gone out to see if they could obtain some potatoes or meal, having in the house only half a box of biscuits." Some of the people at St. Ann's, who had planted a few potatoes, were obliged to dig them up and eat them. During the summer, apparently, they discovered large patches of pure white beans, marked with a black cross. Probably these had originally been planted by the French but were then growing wild. "In our joy at the discovery," says Mrs. Fisher, "we called them at first the 'Royal Provincials' bread', but afterwards 'the staff of life and hope of the starving'."

Mrs. Fisher's testimony as to the difficulties of getting supplies up the river to St. Ann's is confirmed by a petition from the officers residing there to Major-General Campbell, who had succeeded Brigadier Fox as commanding officer in Nova Scotia. More than two thousand of His Majesty's faithful subjects would be relieved and aided, the officers pointed out, if his Excellency would be pleased to establish a magazine of provisions at St. Ann's Point. The settlements they were now forming were situated from one hundred to one hundred and fifty miles from the provisions magazine at Fort Howe, and an "infinite variety of inconveniences" resulted from the necessity of sending that distance for their proportion of the Royal Bounty. Major Armstrong of the Queen's Rangers, Captains Andrew Maxwell, Daniel Lyman, Haws Hatch, Lieutenant J. O'Neill and Ensign Oliver Peck of the Prince of Wales' American Regiment, Lieutenant Dugald Campbell of the 42d, Captain Joseph Lee of the 2d New Jersey Volunteers, Captains Samuel Ryerse and Edward Earle, and Lieutenant Josiah Parker of the 3d New Jersey Volunteers, Adjutant Andrew Phair of the American Legion, Ensign Nicholas Humphreys and Lieutenant Garret Clopper of the New York Volunteers, Captains Lemuel Wilmot and William Bailey, Lieutenant Anthony Allaire and Ensign William Edwards of the Loyal American Regiment, Captain James French of the 1st DeLancey's, Lieutenants Isaac Hedden and Henry Barton, and Ensign Reuben Hankinson of 1st New Jersey Volunteers, Lieutenants A. Blundell, Samuel Wilson and William Chew of the Royal Garrison Battalion, Captain Peter Clements, Lieutenants Leonard Reed and Thomas Barker, and Surgeon's Mate Elias Quereau of the King's American Regiment, Cornet Arthur Nicholson of the King's American Dragoons, Captain Ebenezer Brown and Ensign Jonathan Brown of the Guides and Pioneers, signed this memorial on behalf of the officers, non-commissioned officers and privates of the regiments to which they belonged.

Major-General Campbell reported to Lord Sydney that he himself had seen in the course of his tour to the St. John River, in the summer of 1784, the great difficulties which the new settlers had to encounter in procuring their provisions from Fort Howe, and how the hire of the necessary craft, the immense labour and the loss of time discouraged the people and greatly checked the progress of the settlement. He had therefore ordered a storehouse built there. Hannah Ingraham remembered that there was always a sentry on guard, walking up and down with his bayonet fixed, in front of the King's provision warehouse, and that Parson Cooke held services in the warehouse, close by the church green, till the church was ready.

Campbell found the situation of St. Ann's Point "so delightful, the country about it so extraordinarily fertile—and its natural advantages so numerous and considerable, that it cannot fail to become a valuable and important place." To promote these advantages and secure the welfare of the settlement, he ordered a detachment of the 57th. Regiment, under the command of Captain Ovens, to take post at St. Ann's. The exertions of the Loyalists, he thought, did them much credit, and their settlements wore an appearance of great industry and forwardness. This was a more favourable report than usually emanated from Halifax concerning the St. John River and its inhabitants. Joseph Aplin, a Loyalist from Rhode Island, afterwards attorney general of Prince Edward Island, likewise reported favourably after a ten day visit to the town at the mouth of the St. John River. He wrote Chief Justice Smith that, in spite of the uneasiness of the people due to disappointment in getting their lands, about fifteen hundred framed houses and over four hundred temporary ones, constructed of hewn logs, were so far finished as to afford them a comfortable shelter. "Such an Instance of Sudden Exertion cannot be found in the Annals of any People on the Globe," Aplin declared. "During my Stay there, which was about ten days, I frequently amused myself with surveying this mighty Scene of Industry and Labour; and I do assure you, that I have sometimes been almost tempted to discredit my own Eyes."

The delay in getting their lands was making the Loyalists very uneasy indeed. When they had asked for one year's provisions, they had anticipated that they would be sent to Nova Scotia early in the spring of 1783 and that their agents would have had the grants obtained and townships laid out ready for them. On March 31, 1784, Major-General Campbell issued a Proclamation intended to reassure their minds, that the royal bounty of provisions would not cease on the first of May. There was reason to fear that a great number of the Loyalists would be in the most imminent danger of perishing, if rations of provisions were not continued, and he therefore was giving orders that the issue of provisions was to be continued "to such of the Loyalists, at the different settlements, whose necessities may require it, until His Majesty's Pleasure shall be known."

In spite of his concern for the welfare of the Loyalists, as shown in his reports from St. Ann's and in his continuing the issue of provisions, Campbell was not satisfied to allow the abuses which were daily gaining ground to continue. On April 20, 1784, he wrote Lord Sydney that, since he felt that the several Boards in charge were too independent of each other, and from various other reasons had not perfectly answered the purposes he had hoped, he had decided to appoint Colonel Yorke of the 33d Regiment of Foot, Sampson Salter Blowers, Edward Winslow, and Hugh Mackay Gordon Esquires, a Board "for the receiving and considering all claims to Provisions and such other gratuities as are or may be issued by Government under his direction to Reduced and disbanded officers, soldiers and Loyalists setling in the province of Nova Scotia." According to their instructions, the Board were to examine the nature of the application, the quantity of provisions already received, the numbers of the families, the age and description of the persons. They were to inquire if the applicants had lands assigned them and whether they were settled on the land or making preparations to settle. Since the Royal Bounty was intended as "a Relief to Indigence and a spur to Industry", they were to be careful that it was not given to those in a position to support themselves by trade or profession, nor to the dissolute and indolent. Reduced officers and soldiers who did not comply with the evident intention of Government by actually becoming settlers on the lands assigned them were not to be considered as entitled to the Bounty. The Board were to keep an exact record of names and descriptions of the persons applying and of the decision on their claims.

The Board found their task very difficult. "Every man who arrived in this country called himself a Loyalist," Edward Winslow wrote to Brook Watson, on November 12, 1784, "and presumed that he was entitled to the Rations of provisions for himself & his family, and they applied for orders without an idea that any scrutiny could possibly be made either into their circumstances or character, or supposing any conditions required on their part." General Fox decided against issuing provisions to the wealthy or the vicious and indolent, and General Campbell likewise felt that there could be no intention of extending His Majesty's favours to such people. Winslow felt that the Board had corrected many abuses and that all the idle vagrants who had been loitering about the streets of Halifax and committing irregularities, by being deprived of rations, were forced to take possession of their lands and produce certificates of being actual settlers before being restored to the enjoyment of the Royal Bounty. After some experience on the Board, Winslow conceived the idea of parcelling out the province into districts and appointing "persons of activity & judgment to muster all the men, women & children who had actually become settlers." Winslow considered that the expense of these appointments would be compensated by the information they would obtain regarding the precise number and disposition of the settlers and their present situations. By the returns of the muster-masters, he had tried as far as possible "to make the Bounty of Government subservient to the purposes of assisting the civil magistrates—encouraging industry, and contributing to the settlement of the country."

Thomas Knox, who was appointed deputy muster-master for the St. John River and Passamaquoddy settlements, certainly worked at his task with great zeal and earnestness, and sent forward considerable information about the state of the settlements. On his arrival, in June, 1784, he was met with a demand from some recent arrivals, 69 men, 18 women, 21 children about ten, and 16 children under ten. Uncertain of Campbell's orders for a case of this kind, Knox, "upon a Representation of their extreme indigence and a strict inquiry into the merits of their claims", gave them certificates which would enable them to obtain fourteen days' provisions from the Commissary. He had taken the liberty to interfere in behalf of the children who had been born since the arrival of the Loyalists in the province, as there were not many of them, and the necessities of the new settlers required every aid. This suggested "baby bonus" was approved by General Campbell, Knox informed F. W. Hecht on September 1, 1784, and half rations were to be issued for the new babies, as from July 1, 1784. Knox also informed Hecht that a comparison of the figures from the musters he had held, with the numbers formerly drawn for on the St. John River side of the Bay, showed that some 1,000 rations must have been issued on account of persons not existing in the Province, "whereby," added Knox, "the intention of Government in holding out a Reward to Settlers, is not only defeated but grossly abused." Mr. Hecht was requested to observe at the next issue certain rules which Knox thought would make for a more equitable distribution, comparing musters, deducting from persons who drew for others who were not in the province or for servants who could not be accounted for, not deducting from the regiment at large to the injury of the innocent, not deducting for deaths occurring after the issue of provisions, not deducting on presumption of fraud but waiting for an investigation.

When he first arrived at the St. John River, Knox had hoped that if he advertised the musters and consulted with the commanding officers of the regiments and the captains of the refugee companies, he might be able to effect his business. He soon found that it was not possible to arrange for musters at two or three centres: it was too difficult and expensive for men to leave their work and their homes and find accommodation for the two or three days, or perhaps longer, that attendance at the muster would require. To assemble the families was impossible. In the end, Knox yielded to the importunities of the settlers and, as far as possible, saw them at their own homes. It is evident that the people were pathetically glad to see him and to be assured that they were not forgotten by government. They were very anxious to show him the houses they had built, the improvements they had made, the clearing and fencing and planting accomplished. They were likewise anxious to pass on to him complaints regarding the issue of provisions, delays in getting their land grants, any unfair distribution of lots. Although Knox was satisfied that he saw all the new arrivals, there were complaints from both Loyalists and disbanded soldiers, especially from the Miramichi, that they had not been mustered.

As a result of his journeyings among the settlements, Knox was able to discover how unsatisfactory the arrangements for the musters had become. In 1783 and 1784, the newcomers were mustered by regiments and by refugee companies, but the settlers were scattering and not remaining with the regiments or the companies with which they had arrived. Mustering by districts would henceforth be more practicable, and would put a stop to such abuses as one or two persons drawing for a company and then consuming the rations without troubling to distribute them among the distant members of the group. Some such irregularity was probably at the bottom of Mrs. Fisher's complaint about being betrayed by those they trusted to obtain their supplies. Another abuse which Knox hoped to guard against was drawing for absent families. There were genuine cases where families who had been on the point of embarkation had been delayed by illness—there had been a great deal of smallpox in New York, in 1783—or where they were expected to join husband or father when a home was ready for them. Many of these did not arrive: if they were able to survive the hostility of their neighbours in the States for the first months of the peace, they generally remained in their old homes, and the husband or father returned after so short a period that he did not get into the roster of New Brunswick Loyalists. For all Knox's fussing on the matter, it is doubtful if there were more than a dozen or two cases of the kind.

Knox was concerned to find that the captains and crews of many of the transports had drawn provisions as refugees on their first arrival at the St. John River. If the Commander-in-Chief (Campbell) wished to transmit a list of these to the Treasury in order that the amount might be recovered from the owners in England, Knox would collect the amounts and take them to Halifax. "A Mr. Hollinsbury, an Officer in the Navy and Agent of Transports drew at the same time as a Refugee," Knox added sternly. There is no indication that Major-General Campbell undertook to assist the Treasury in recovering from the owners of transports. He may not have been as fond of stirring up hornets' nests as Knox was. "The Officers of Disbanded Corps make great Complaints against me," Knox wrote, "for Striking off nominal servants." The officers asserted that Sir Guy

Carleton had allowed them servants, and that Major Prevost, who had disbanded the provincial regiments, had made the same allowance. That made no difference to Thomas Knox. He persisted in his refusal to allow nominal servants, and thereby perhaps did the new province of New Brunswick some service in discouraging idleness and inattention to their land on the part of officers and servants.

And yet, in spite of his strict adherence to the rules and regulations, Knox granted two months' provisions, "as a donation from Government", to thirty-four families, who mustered 166 children among them, "old Inhabitants who from involuntary causes have been reduced to circumstances of great distress." The involuntary causes which had reduced them to distress were their having been obliged to relinquish their possessions and improvements in favour of Refugees to whom the lands had been allotted. Concerning this blot on the Loyalist escutcheon more will be said in Chapter X in connection with the Loyalist settlement of Queens County.

When Thomas Knox had completed his musters in the area north of the Bay of Fundy, he sent a summary of his findings to Major-General Campbell, along with a table of the previous provisions muster for comparison. A table, listing the regiments in alphabetical order, and including the available victualling lists of September, 1783, the Fort Howe muster of 1783-4, and Knox's 1784 muster, will be found in the Notes. On the whole, the three provision musters show a steady decline in the numbers present. The loss of the *Martha* is reflected in the sharp drop in the numbers of the Maryland Loyalists and the 2d DeLancey's. Except in the case of these two regiments, there is little decline in the number of women from one muster to the next. The men who disappeared were the single and unattached men: the married men remained, and, like Benjamin Ingraham, set about making homes for their families. What became of the men who disappeared? Some of them are accounted for in the increased numbers of servants. Officers would hire privates to clear their land for them. Captain Atwood of the King's American Regiment, for instance, was reported to have forty acres cleared by August, 1784. A few who had been fighting in the Loyalist regiments returned to their former homes. Jacob Smith of the Queen's Rangers, for example, returned to his parents' home in Delaware, where he apparently settled in without any difficulty. Others went to sea, joining in fishing ventures perhaps, or shipping on the schooners and sloops which were bringing lumber for the infant colony, or taking the place of men who deserted from the transports. Some went exploring around the shores of the Bay of Fundy and its numerous inlets. Others crossed the Bay to settlements on the other side, where they had friends or kinfolk or former officers. A few, like the soldier whose body was found in the snow at St. Ann's, drank themselves to death. Smallpox and privations took their toll, a surprisingly small one, in view of the circumstances. There were also the poisonous weeds which Mrs. Fisher mentioned as accounting for a few deaths at St. Ann's.

On March 30, 1785, Knox returned to the St. John River to make a second provision muster. On the journey, he had lost part of his baggage. He had also lost his appointment in Halifax, and he was not in the best of humours. The inability of "your Stores in Halifax" to furnish a regular supply of provisions had been attended not only with great inconvenience to all but very serious distress to many. Had the new governor of the new province not taken it upon himself to secure the settlers up the river by purchasing flour for them before the season of the spring break-up when they could get nothing sent, many people would have perished. The inadequate supplies forwarded by order of the General

had been dealt out "with a sparing hand by a parsi-
monious Commissary, and the old business of striking
off the idle, the dissolute and the wealthy" was now in
full practice. A great part of Knox's time was devoted
to this business of discrimination and to drawing the
line between those who were on their land and those
who were not. Every man who sold his land was being
traced by the records of land transactions and was
being struck off the list.

The 1785 muster, taken by districts, showed that
Knox had found 10,824 hard-working, sober, poor,
disbanded troops and other Loyalists, who had not sold
their land in New Brunswick and were settled on it.
Unfortunately, Knox's list was confined, as will be seen
by an examination of the detailed table in the Notes,
to the Passamaquoddy and St. John River districts.
There was no mention of the Miramichi, the Petitcodiac,
the Memramcook, nor the Tantramar districts, which
all had Loyalist settlers. The distribution shown contains
many surprises. The population of the Passamaquoddy
Bay area was nearly as great as that of the City of Saint
John, and almost one fifth of the total. There were more
Loyalists on the Kennebecasis, the Belleisle, and the
part of the St. John River between, than in the City of
Saint John, and twice as many as in Queens County.
Maugerville had nearly as many Loyalists as St. Ann's
and its adjacent lots (Mill to Phyllis's Creek). Knox's
muster shows one trend which is not surprising, that
settlement was very slow in pushing up the St. John
River beyond St. Ann's. On the difficulties in connection
with the blocks, Chapter IX will have more to say.

With all the discussions, proclamations, regulations,
and complaints about the Royal Bounty of Provisions,
there is no explicit statement as to what the ration was
in Nova Scotia, whether it was the amounts given in
instructions to the master of the *Stafford* or in those to
the *Dorothy and Catherine*. Calculations on the basis of

the return of provisions in the storehouses at Halifax
and in the outposts in Nova Scotia, sent by Major-
General Campbell to Lord North, in a communication
dated December 15, 1783, suggest that the daily ration
was one pound of flour per person, half a pound of
meat, either beef or pork, an infinitesimal quantity of
butter, about half a pound of oatmeal a week, an equal
quantity of pease, and occasionally a little rice. The
store at Halifax had molasses, and most outposts had
vinegar, but these were extras. It was fortunate that the
newcomers to the province could supplement the Royal
Bounty of Provisions with fish, fowl, and flesh from the
abundant supplies to be found in sea, river, brook,
marsh and forest. Flour, as Mrs. Fisher related, remained
scarce for many years, but settlers learned to supplement
their scanty supplies of flour with Indian corn, buckwheat, rye, and oats. Corncake, buckwheat pancakes,
and oatmeal porridge, with the steamed brown bread
that accompanied the Saturday night baked beans and
used any three or four types of meal, were staple articles
in the fare of the settlers for several generations. Sugar
maples, butternut, hazel and beech trees, fiddleheads,
dandelion greens, such saltwater greens as samphire and
gooseneck, wild cherries, strawberry, raspberry, black-
berry, blueberry and cranberry vines yielded variety and
vitamins. But for the first year or two, while Loyalist
and Provincial waited anxiously for their allotted lands,
the Royal Bounty of Provisions was indispensable. If,
in spite of the diligence of Thomas Knox, it nourished a
few unworthies, the discontinuance of the Royal Bounty
forced their withdrawal to easier climates.

CHAPTER SIX

THE OLD PROVINCE

The royal province of Nova Scotia, to which the Loyalists were sent from New York in 1783, included a much larger territory than the present province of Nova Scotia. The area over which the governor of Nova Scotia had jurisdiction comprised the peninsula and the island of Cape Breton which together make up the present province of Nova Scotia, the island of St. John, which is now the Province of Prince Edward Island, and a vaguely defined area of the mainland, which had been included in the French province of Acadie, and which, shortly after the arrival of the Loyalists, was to be set up as the province of New Brunswick. The old documents available made it clear that the western boundary of Acadie and of Nova Scotia was Champlain's St. Croix, but Champlain's stay on that river had been too brief to fix the name to any stream, and arguments could be advanced for claiming as the St. Croix any one of three rivers flowing into Passamaquoddy Bay, the Magaguadavic, the Schoodic, or the Cobscook. The northern boundary of Nova Scotia was equally uncertain, and was variously said to be the great river of Canada, the watershed south of that river, or the Baie de Chaleur, which Jacques Cartier, in the summer of 1535, had discovered on one of its rare hot days.

The territory known as Nova Scotia had had a chequered history. Its coastline had been familiar to explorers and fishermen long before DeMonts and Champlain, in 1604, had spent the winter on Dochet's Island in the St. Croix, and, in the years following, had begun a settlement at Lower Granville on Annapolis Basin. In the seventeenth century, Acadie had been parcelled out to three seigneurs, the North Shore, from Cape Breton to Gaspé, to Nicholas Denys, the South Shore, from Annapolis around the peninsula, to d'Aulnay Charnisay, the mainland, north of the Bay of Fundy, to Charles La Tour. When Charnisay, not content with his extensive territory, claimed rights over the lands of the other two, the endless bickering resulted in the tearing down of whatever was built. Afterwards, Acadie became a pawn in the struggle for control of the continent: it was captured and handed back, conquered and then ceded by treaty to its former owner. Its use as a base for sending out expeditions against the New England settlements to the south roused such bitter resentment there that the capture of Acadie, and the wreaking of vengeance upon its inhabitants, guilty and innocent alike, was inevitable.

One move in the struggle for mastery had been the founding of Halifax by the English, in 1749. The situation of the plantation was determined by the insistent factors of the period, military and naval necessity, and future considerations of political and economic strategy carried no weight. After the capture of the French centres of resistance, Beauséjour and Louisbourg, and the breaking up of the Acadian settlements, English settlers were invited to take over the lands left vacant. Townships were laid out to include the best of the lands the Acadians had improved, and planters from Connecticut, Rhode Island, Massachusetts, Northern Ireland, Scotland, and the north of England arrived to take up land. By the time revolt flared in the colonies to the south, Nova Scotia consisted of Halifax and a number of townships and fishing settlements, with more Acadians on the fringes than any census taker suspected.

In the area north of the Bay of Fundy, the New Brunswick of the future, there were three townships in a relatively flourishing condition, Cumberland and Sackville at the head of the Bay of Fundy, on the former seigneury of Beaubassin, and Maugerville on the St. John River. Cumberland, on the Isthmus of Chignecto, had grown up around Fort Beauséjour, the post erected by La Corne in 1750, as part of the attempt to retain French possession of the area of Acadie north of the Bay of Fundy. The first grant of the township, an area of 100,000 acres including the ridges on which had been built Fort Beauséjour and its English counterpart, Fort Lawrence, and extending from the Aulac River on the west to the La Planche on the east, was made in 1759. The grantees comprised three groups, one of persons connected with the fort and the commissariat, one representing settlers who intended to come from Connecticut, and a third group from Halifax, members of Council and their friends, whose names appeared on the lists of most of the townships. In 1763, and again in 1764, regrants of the township were necessary, and only about twenty of the original hundred names appeared on the later grants. Additions to the grantees were members of the garrison and its hangers-on, further arrivals from Connecticut, new settlers from Massachusetts, and a few arrivals from the British Isles.

Since the 100,000 acres in Cumberland township did not cover all the lands dyked by the industrious Acadians of Beaubassin, two additional townships were laid out, Amherst to the east of the La Planche River, and Sackville to the west of the Aulac, where the extensive Tantramar marshes offered rich promise for future development of agriculture. Amherst, and the eastern strip of Cumberland, between the Missiguash and the La Planche, did not become New Brunswick territory when the new province was set up, but Sackville and the greater portion of Cumberland township lay within the bounds of the new province.

The first settlers in the township of Sackville were a group from Rhode Island and adjacent communities of

Massachusetts. Most of them were members of Baptist churches and they organized a new church for the move to Nova Scotia. The 1761 list of subscribers contained 167 names, but many of the subscribers did not come to the colony at all and of those who did venture to Nova Scotia, several returned after a few years. By 1771, when a census was taken, less than half the 167 subscribers were present. In the meantime, other families had moved into Sackville, some from Cumberland and some from Massachusetts. In the decade of the 1770s, both Sackville and Cumberland received new stimulus and important addition to their population by the arrival of over thirty families from Yorkshire and the north of England. These people, who had emigrated either because their rents had been raised or because they hoped to better themselves, were experienced farmers, with capital and with determination. They proved a most valuable addition, not only to the two townships, but to the two provinces, and ultimately to the North American continent. Several of the families had had close connections with John Wesley and the Wesleyan movement, and they were largely responsible for the establishment of Methodism in the Maritime Provinces and for the founding of Mount Allison University at Sackville as a centre of Methodist education.

On their way up the Bay of Fundy to Beaubassin and Cumberland, both French and English had been slow in exploring the possibilities of the opening on the left, where Shepody Bay receives the waters of the Shepody, the Memramcook, and the Petitcodiac rivers. At the end of the seventeenth century, several enterprising inhabitants of the French colony at Port Royal on Annapolis Basin had established colonies at Chipody, Memramcook, and Petitcoudiak, and, with some difficulty, attained seigneurial rights. After the fall of Fort Beauséjour, these settlements were attacked by the invading forces, and many of the inhabitants fled to the refuge of the surrounding forests, where some of them remained near their old homes, while others travelled west to join their compatriots on the St. John River, and still others found their way eastward to the Gulf of St. Lawrence shore. It is difficult to estimate how many of the 165 families attributed to the region by the census of 1751 may have been able to remain. The 1775 returns for Hillsborough, on the west bank of the Petitcodiac, listed ten Acadians, with 49 in the families named. Up the Memramcook, which was less accessible and did not attract English settlers until after the close of the Revolutionary War, there were probably larger numbers of Acadians.

Hopewell, centred on the Shepody River, Hillsborough, south and west of the bend of the Petitcodiac, and Monckton, north of the Petitcodiac and extending from the bend to the head of tide, were granted as townships in 1765, the year when large grants were made by the governor and council of Nova Scotia. Hillsborough, which had the longest frontage on the river, went to members of the Nova Scotia council, and to one other grantee, the nephew of a Hopewell grantee. The Hopewell proprietors were a Pennsylvania group, whose interest in the region had been excited by a Swiss officer, George Frederic Wallet Desbarres, surveyor of the coast of Nova Scotia. Desbarres had suggested to other Swiss officers serving with the British forces in Pennsylvania that land in this region might be valuable, and they and their Pennsylvania friends had sought grants. Monckton township went to four groups of Philadelphia traders and that egregious colonizer, Alexander McNutt, who had ambitious schemes for filling up Nova Scotia with protestant settlers.

To Hopewell and Monckton, German, Welsh, and Irish settlers were sent from Philadelphia, with the expectation that their efforts would shortly make the property profitable for the proprietors and would yield a livelihood for the settlers themselves. When the expectations of the proprietors were not immediately realized, and when their interest in the colonies they had set up was diverted by pre-revolutionary activities in Pennsylvania, an energetic agent in Hillsborough profited by the unhappy state of affairs in the other two townships to gather in some of their tenants for Hillsborough, in the hope of thus making his principals secure against forfeiture and escheat. One of the proprietors, Joseph Gray, who took over his father-in-law's share of Hillsborough, claimed that, in 1775, the township had had a population of 200. Between that year and 1783, largely because of the raids of American privateers, 87 of the people had removed; in 1783, 27 new families, with 119 "souls" therein, were added, some of the families newcomers to the township, others sons of old residents, notably the sons of Heinrich Stieff (Steeves), who by that time were heads of rapidly increasing family units. The families who had left Hillsborough, it might be remarked, can be traced elsewhere in the New Brunswick area.

After examination of the records of the townships, of the census figures for 1767, 1770, and 1783, of the memorials of the settlers, and of family records, it is possible to suggest that the population of the five townships, Cumberland (which became Westmorland), Sackville, Hopewell, Hillsborough, and Monckton, plus the Memramcook district, was certainly not less than 1200 when the Loyalists came, and may have numbered 1,500 or more. The number of Acadians on the Memramcook and the natural increase of population throughout the area, may have been greater than estimated.

It has been mentioned that, after the capture of Fort Beauséjour and the attacks on the settlements around the Bay of Fundy and its inlets, many of the Acadians fled through the woods to the St. John River. There they joined Boishébert and with him went to the Miramichi, where 3,500 refugees were reported assembled. In addition, many Acadians found asylum along the coast between the Isthmus of Chignecto and the Miramichi. When Colonel James Murray was sent, in 1758, after the capture of Louisbourg, to destroy the French settlements on the Miramichi, he was told that there were numerous habitations dispersed around the bay, and many Indians living in the region, but he reported that, "having two Days hunted all around Us for the Indians and Acadians to no purpose, we however destroyed their Provisions, Wigwams and Houses, the Church . . . and I am persuaded there is not now a French Man in the River Miramichi. . . ." Since no Acadian enumerator followed to show the absurdity of Murray's wishful thinking, future generations can only conjecture that there were probably several hundred Acadians maintaining what existence they could along the North Shore when the Loyalists came.

At the Miramichi, the Nepisiguit, and the Restigouche, when the Revolutionary War began, a few Scottish fishermen and their families were settled. On the Miramichi, the group comprised more than a hundred persons; on the Nepisiguit, half a dozen; on the Restigouche, a dozen or more. William Davidson, who had received a grant of 100,000 acres at the forks of the Miramichi, in 1765, and two or three other Miramichi inhabitants, were forced by the incursions of rebel privateers to take refuge on the St. John River. At least two others are known to have joined the British forces in Canada, and they, like William Davidson, returned to the Miramichi when the war was over.

It seems likely that the St. John River area contained about as many inhabitants as all the rest of the part of Nova Scotia north of the Bay of Fundy. The fishing and trading post which, in 1760, James Simonds had determined to establish at the mouth of the river, had resulted in attracting thither many employees of the

Newburyport firm with which Simonds was connected. An incomplete census of 1775 listed 40 families, totalling 141 persons, at the mouth of the river. More than 60 men had been brought in to work for Simonds and White, and 50 of these, some with large families, were living in the area in 1783.

From the beginning, the settlement at the mouth of the river had maintained a very close connection with the Essex County plantation seventy miles up the river. The Newburyport vessels brought up the Essex County settlers and their supplies, furnished employment for them and a market for their produce. By 1783, the upriver settlement, known first as Peabody's and later as Maugerville, had a population between 350 and 400. The other townships on the river, granted to the Canada Company or St. John's River Society, whose proprietors were interested in shares for speculation rather than for actual settlement, were in a less flourishing condition. Burton, opposite Maugerville, had a population of nearly 300; Gagetown, about 230; Newtown and Sunbury together less than 100. (Conway, the fifth township, is included with the Newburyport settlement at the mouth of the river.) Altogether, the English speaking population of the St. John River area, at the time the Loyalists arrived, was not less than 1,300. The 1783 survey of the area, made by Ebenezer Foster, Fyler Dibble, James White, and Gervice Say, in June and July, at the direction of Major Studholme, officer commanding at Fort Howe, overlooked a number of families in each township and therefore produced a smaller total than this. The survey accounted for between 320 and 330 Acadians, but almost certainly there were others, up the small rivers and creeks, who were not included in the official enumeration.

At Passamaquoddy, which James Simonds had found crowded with traders in 1760, the permanent population, both on the islands and on the mainland, was very small. From what evidence has come to light, it appears that at the time of the coming of the Loyalists there were only about 100 persons settled in the region. There is no indication that any of the few French fishermen or seigneurs who had been connected with Passamaquoddy at one time or another had remained, nor does it appear that any of the refugees from the Acadian settlements up the Bay of Fundy had established themselves at Passamaquoddy.

To sum up, in the part of Nova Scotia north of the Bay of Fundy, two principal groups of settlements had developed, one at the head of the Bay of Fundy, the other on the St. John River, with a fringe of settlement on the North Shore and another in the southwest corner. The English, and German, speaking part of the population numbered probably about 3,000. The majority were American born, although there was a scattering of Irish, Scottish and German-born settlers, and the large group of Yorkshire settlers in Cumberland and Sackville. Most of the St. John River settlers were from Massachusetts; the Sackville and Cumberland inhabitants had come from Rhode Island and Connecticut as well as from Massachusetts and Yorkshire; the Petit-codiac and Shepody settlers included Connecticut and Massachusetts natives as well as several who had been, for longer or shorter periods, in Pennsylvania. The Acadian population may be estimated at 1,500 to 2,000, but the Acadians had been for so many years anxious to keep out of sight that there is little evidence on which to hazard a conjecture as to their numbers.

These settlements in the area which was to become New Brunswick had barely had time to get established before the smouldering resentments in the thirteen colonies blazed into open revolt. By 1775, trade with the other colonies, which had been the lifeline of the infant settlements, had ceased; by 1776, rebel forces were invading Nova Scotia and gathering recruits for the attack on Fort Cumberland; by 1777, the rebel invaders had withdrawn, but rebel privateers were harrying the coasts and raiding the scattered settlements. These events resulted in a few accessions to the population, a few losses, and much shifting about of the inhabitants. The cessation of trade brought William Hazen and George deBlois to the mouth of the St. John, in 1775, but otherwise it checked the inflow of settlers. The evacuation of Boston, which had brought to Halifax a large influx of refugees, some of whom remained as permanent settlers in Halifax and the nearer townships, produced no discernible result in the settlements north of the Bay of Fundy. A few families, the Spragues, the Bonneys, and the Hansons, who apparently had visited Passamaquoddy from time to time for fishing and fur trading, seem to have established themselves in the New Brunswick area during the war. Others from the exposed settlements along the South Shore of the peninsular part of Nova Scotia took refuge on the St. John River. Except for these few, and the Baxters from Alstead, New Hampshire, who arrived in the autumn of 1782, the area north of the Bay of Fundy waited until May, 1783, to receive its first considerable accession of population. The losses of population were the result of the attack on Fort Cumberland. A few inhabitants, notably John Allan and Jonathan Eddy of Cumberland, Reverend Seth Noble and Dr. Phineas Nevers of Maugerville, who had espoused with too much ardour the cause of the revolting colonies, were proscribed and fled.

The harrying of the coasts by rebel privateers resulted in a demand for protection for the settlements. In 1768, General Gage, Commander-in-Chief of the British Forces in North America, had ordered the troops withdrawn from all the forts and military posts in Nova Scotia to Halifax. The attempts to induce Nova Scotia to ally itself with the revolting colonies to the south, and the frequent raids, made it necessary to take steps to

118

retain the allegiance of the inhabitants and to give them protection from the incursions of the enemy. When it was decided, in 1775, to repair, strengthen, and regarrison the forts, Colonel Joseph Goreham and his corps, the Royal Fencible Americans, were sent to Fort Cumberland at the head of the Bay of Fundy. This place they managed to hold against the attacks of Jonathan Eddy and his associates, in November, 1776, until reinforcements arrived from Halifax. Fort Cumberland then became a centre for the area at the head of the Bay of Fundy, with recruits drawn from the neighbouring townships as well as from the more distant Lunenburg and Newfoundland. Many families from outlying settlements, from Hillsborough and perhaps from Hopewell, moved in to the protection of the fort. The business of providing supplies for the garrison and the chances of employment in connection with the rebuilding of the fort attracted additional families to its neighbourhood.

Events showed that Fort Cumberland was unable to provide protection for the St. John River, at which rebel invaders arrived, both by sea and by land, from Machias. The British authorities were spurred to action by the burning of Fort Frederick, and by Allan's attempts to rouse the Indians of the region to attack the settlers. A new fort was built at the mouth of the river, not on the west side site of the old Fort Frederick, but on the east side, on a more commanding site, whose rocky ramparts conveniently towered above the centre of the Hazen, Simonds and White enterprises. Captain Studholme and a detachment of the Royal Fencible Americans were sent to take charge of this new post, which was named Fort Howe. To guard against overland attack, a blockhouse was built at the mouth of the Oromocto, across the river from Maugerville, most of whose inhabitants had shown a disposition to wander from their allegiance to the king, until a visit from the *Vulture*, under command of Colonel Arthur Goold, had recalled them to their duty. A small detachment of the Fencible Americans, under command of Lieutenant Constant Connor, manned the post at the Oromocto. Both Fort Howe and the Oromocto blockhouse attracted a number of "large, poor" families, whose breadwinner found employment either in the garrison itself or in performing various services for the officers and men of the garrison. Officers and men regularly enrolled in the Royal Fencible Americans were treated as Provincials and given grants of land, of which more will be heard in ensuing chapters. The hangers on may be considered as part of the Pre-Loyalist population of New Brunswick, and have been included in the estimated 3,000 inhabitants of the English settlements north of the Bay of Fundy.

Primitive though the economy of these frontier settlements north of the Bay of Fundy was, it nevertheless showed variations from place to place. On the North Shore, the emphasis was on fishing, although there was some trading with the Indians for furs, a little lumbering and less farming. William Davidson of Inverness, who had, in association with John Cort of Aberdeen, received a township grant at the forks of the Miramichi at the time of the lavish granting of land in Nova Scotia, in 1765, protested in later years that he had wanted only fishing privileges and had been embarrassed by the 100,000 acre grant thrust upon him. At the head of the Bay of Fundy, and on the Petitcodiac, the settlements were based on the dyked lands of the Acadians, so that fishing, fur trading, hunting, lumbering, and perhaps even ministering to Fort Cumberland, were overshadowed by agriculture. At Hillsborough, for instance, according to the returns made in 1775, every settler had at least one cow; several of the herds numbered fifteen head or more; and one herd boasted forty-eight head of cattle. All but two of the thirty-four households possessed oxen, and eleven of them reported owning five yoke or more. All but two establishments reported crops of potatoes and turnips, in amounts ranging from 22 bushels to 150; most of them had raised wheat and oats; a smaller number reported crops of peas, barley, and rye; seventeen had raised flax.

Passamaquoddy, again, was a fishing and trading area, with one saw mill, which had been erected during the war years. There is a legend that one settler on the St. Croix protested against the trampling of his beans by the Loyalists' surveyors, but on the whole there was little farming in the area. At the mouth of the St. John River, the Hazen, Simonds and White business had added to fishing and fur trading such industries as lumbering, burning of lime, and shipbuilding. Also, they had dug and shipped a few chaldrons of coal from Grand Lake. Maugerville was essentially a farming and lumbering community, but its inhabitants were not unmindful of other gifts of the river, such as fish and fur-bearing animals. When William Davidson of the Miramichi took refuge on the St. John during the war, he saw the possibilities of "masting", that is, of finding masts for His Majesty's ships of war, and, with some difficulty, persuaded the authorities at Halifax to let him have a contract. The success of Davidson's masting operations attracted the notice of Hazen and White—James Simonds had moved his family up to Maugerville because of the dangers to which they were exposed at the mouth of the river—and they took up masting. Since James White had been deputy on the St. John River for Michael Francklin, the Superintendent of Indian Affairs and former Lieutenant-Governor, who was made partner in the enterprise, it was possible to get official backing at Halifax, and masting proved, for a few years, the most profitable part of the firm's operations. The clashes between the crews cutting for the rival contractors were a foreshadowing of things to come when rival lumbermen on the St. John and its tributaries nearly involved New Brunswick and the neighbouring state of Maine in war.

The political development of the part of Nova Scotia north of the Bay of Fundy was as rudimentary as the economic. As a colonial outpost, Nova Scotia had at first been ruled by a governor and lieutenant-governor appointed by the Lords Commissioners of Trade and Plantations, with a council to assist. When a demand for a representative Assembly arose, Governor Lawrence for some time resisted it, until his desire to attract settlers to the cleared and dyked lands from which the Acadians had been removed, overcame his dislike of such a democratic innovation. In 1765, the territory north of the Bay of Fundy was divided into two counties, Cumberland, which included the townships at the head of the Bay of Fundy, both on the Isthmus of Chignecto and on the Petitcodiac and adjoining rivers, and Sunbury County, which included the St. John River and the Passamaquoddy area. The line between the two counties was defined as running from a point on the Bay of Fundy coast, twenty miles east of the middle of the harbour of St. John's River, and extending due north to the southern boundary of Canada. Since nobody had any certain knowledge of the course of that boundary line, the settlements on the North Shore, at Miramichi, Nepisiguit, and Baie de Chaleur, were considered as part of Halifax County.

Cumberland and Sunbury Counties elected two members éach to the Assembly at Halifax, but as the settlers were much engrossed with their pioneer activities, as the communications with Halifax were slow and uncertain, and as the travelling was difficult, the members seldom attended on their legislative duties. Sunbury County, in particular, was backward politically. Francis Peabody, the nestor of the Maugerville settlement, writing to Captain Hall of Philadelphia, in 1767, mentioned that they had not yet appointed a magistrate nor built their court house. The court house had still not been built, in 1783, when the Loyalists came to the St. John River, and disputes over its location accentuated the bad feelings between the old settlers and the new in the new and smaller Sunbury County. Cumberland was more adequately provided with Land Registry, County Sheriff, and Court of Common Pleas than Sunbury, and had succeeded in maintaining a closer, if not always harmonious, connection with the capital of the province.

For more than two centuries, Nova Scotia has consisted of Halifax and the rest of the province. In 1783, when the province covered a larger area and when means of communication were less developed, the distinction was even more pronounced than it has been in later times. The remoteness, the difference in origin, the undeveloped state, the difficulties in communication, both by land and by sea, of the settlements north of the Bay of Fundy, made their link with Halifax uncertain and tenuous. It was not surprising that the arrival of large numbers of Loyalists at the St. John River and at Passamaquoddy would prove too great a strain on the link, that the link would be broken, and that a new province would be formed.

CHAPTER SEVEN

THE NEW PROVINCE

The link between Halifax and the area north of the Bay of Fundy might have resisted the strain imposed upon it by distance and difficulties of communication; it might even have survived the tension set up by the coming of the large numbers of Loyalists until such time as the settling down of the newcomers to the task of carving farms out of the wilderness eased the tension; the province of Nova Scotia might have remained whole and undivided until the present day had there been wise leadership at Halifax and had there been less skilful handling of situations by the advocates of a new province. The personalities involved, by their pulling and hauling, added the last bit of tension which snapped the link. It is an interesting story, which has hitherto been only partly told.[1]

John Parr, the Irish officer who had been appointed to the governorship of Nova Scotia in 1782, had expected to enjoy his first proconsulship. At first, the emoluments, the luxurious quarters, the consequence the appointment entailed, had seemed most attractive. Then came the Loyalists, and all the advice and instructions from the Commander-in-Chief at New York, instructions which differed from those given him in England. He entertained the important people who came to Halifax, and he bustled about prodigiously, performing, according to his biographer, incredible feats of activity. He lacked, however, such qualities of statesmanship as farsightedness, good judgment, ability to seize upon the salient points in a policy or a suggestion, and let the non-essentials go. Perhaps because it was his first appointment of the kind, he was timid about acting without instructions from home. Moreover, he was badly advised by the officials about him. The members of the Council were even less statesmanlike than Parr, and the question of fees loomed even larger in their eyes than in the governor's. Some, whose past records would not always yield evidence of unswerving allegiance to the Crown, looked with fear rather than with favour upon the arrival of the Loyalists in Nova Scotia. They counselled delay, and they were anxious to make sure that the British government would compensate them for the loss of fees in the grants to the Loyalists. They also wished to have their own considerable grants of land and those of their friends secured, and they were obstructive rather than helpful in the business of escheats and of new grants. The querulous tone of Governor Parr's letters was often due to pressure from members of the Council, particularly from the secretary, Richard Bulkley, and the Surveyor-General, Charles Morris.

These men did the pulling on the Halifax end. On the St. John River end, Edward Winslow, with powerful support, did the hauling. Even before the difficulties about the regimental lands forced him to put every ounce of energy into the advocacy of the new province, Winslow was toying with the idea. On July 7, 1783, when he was waiting passage up the river to look out lands for the regiments, he wrote Ward Chipman that he was determined to distinguish himself by proposing a plan which afforded "the grandest field for speculation that ever offered." It needed only a glance at the general map of Nova Scotia to see how detached the part north of the Bay of Fundy was from the rest, how extensive it was, how many rivers and harbours it contained. Undoubtedly there would be many inconveniences from its remoteness from Halifax, "the metropolis", and from difficulties of communication. "Think what multitudes have and will come here," wrote Winslow, "and then judge whether it must not from the nature of things

125

immediately become a separate government, and if it does it shall be the most Gentlemanlike one on earth." Chipman and one of the party with him at St. John's, he suggested, might go to England and solicit a new government. "You know how Industrious I can be if I please and you may rest assured I will pursue this project with unremitted attention. The people on the other side are already jealous, even the Gov'r fears it evidently, we have therefore been perfectly snug yet."[2] Winslow was to find out in later months how correctly he had estimated the reaction in Halifax.

On the day previous, Winslow and his friend Daniel Murray, who was in charge of the King's American Dragoons, had picked out a site on the west side of the river, where a township for the Provincials could be laid out, with farm lands on the Bay of Fundy and up the river, and Winslow talked airily of a town hut and a country hut and a road between. Doubtless there was much planning and dreaming of future building during the next few days when Winslow and a very congenial group sailed up the St. John River on the most agreeable tour he had ever had. He returned to the mouth of the river, delighted beyond expression with the one hundred and twenty miles of the river which he had explored. Meanwhile, Stephen DeLancey, who had remained at Annapolis while his brother agents were exploring the St. John River, had been told by Amos Botsford, one of the agents for the Loyalists, that the lands on the lower part of the St. John were to be given to the Refugees and that the Provincials' lands were to "commence at Sunbury and go northwest to Canada or elsewhere." Although he could hardly credit so notorious a forfeiture of the faith of Government, DeLancey feared that the report was true. "Could we have known this a little earlier," he wrote, "it would have saved you the trouble of exploring the Country for the benefit of a People you are not connected with."[3]

This was a rude awakening from all the dreams of a town in the most magnificent and romantic situation at the mouth of the river, of regimental lands nearby, of town huts and country huts and roads between, with the most gentlemanlike government on earth dominating a new province. The only hope was that this fortunate appointment of Winslow as secretary to Brigadier-General Fox, the new military commander at Halifax, would give him an opportunity to bring pressure to bear on the authorities in Halifax. Winslow hastened to Halifax, but on the way was delayed at Granville by the death of a son, and reached the metropolis only on August 1, a day after the arrival of his new chief. In Halifax he found that DeLancey's information was only too true. Parr's attitude may be gleaned from a letter written to Sir Guy Carleton, on July 25, 1783, when the governor was in Port Roseway, which he had rechristened Shelburne. This place, he predicted, would "in a short time become the most flourishing Town for trade of any in this part of the World, and the country will for agriculture", but he greatly feared that the soil and fertility of the St. John River had been greatly over-rated by those who had partially explored it, and was certain there would not be enough good land for those already sent there, especially if the Provincial Corps went also. For that reason he had recommended the eastern side of the St. Croix.[4] The jealousy of the St. John River, which Winslow had remarked after his stay in Halifax in June, the fear of having too many people congregated there, and the pressure brought to bear by the Refugees, had combined to fix the governor's decision. Fox, expressing a desire to attend to every wish and opinion of the governor, declined to take up the cudgels on behalf of the Provincials. Winslow, anxious to make the most of this opportunity to get in the good graces of his chief and of the Halifax authorities, acquiesced. On August 7, Isaac Allen wrote from Wilmot, Annapolis County, that Stephen DeLancey had told him that Winslow had relinquished all the Province to the Refugees except the Lands above Sunbury. On August 8, Winslow, in his capacity as secretary to General Fox, was under the disagreeable necessity of writing to Daniel Murray that, since it had been represented to Fox that the King's American Dragoons could not be enhutted at the place where they were at present encamped without great inconvenience to the great number of Loyalists who were forming settlements at the mouth of the River St. John, and since he had been informed that the governor had assigned a certain tract of land for the Provincials, beginning at the eastern boundaries of the Townships of Sunbury and Newtown, Murray had his permission to remove his regiment to that part of the district allotted to the regiment by the agents for locating lands for His Majesty's Provincial Forces. There was the further unwelcome bit of information that it was the General's idea that, since procuring the timber and other necessities for their huts would facilitate the clearing of the land, the huts for the regiment might be built without any public expense.[5]

Fortunately, when Major Murray went up the river to visit the location chosen for his regiment, he returned "in raptures with it." Parr wrote to Carleton, on August 15, 1783, how happy it made him to find that the provincial corps could be accommodated upon the River St. John, near the source of that River, leaving the lower part to the Refuges now settled there; yet, at the same time, he expressed his concern that some of the corps could not be set down on the eastern side of the St. Croix, the frontier of the province, "to resemble the cantonments of an army, agreeable to your Excellency's letter dated the 26th April", a reminder of the suggestion which had probably emanated from Benjamin Thompson. Matters appeared to have been settled to everyone's satisfaction, and Winslow wrote Chipman about getting

128

farms for half a dozen of his friends near Murray's regiment, where there would be a fine prospect, rocks, hills, etc., and no fear of having water near his house. The only reference to the project to which he was to give his unremitted attention was a remark that he would be monstrously pleased when it came his turn to be of some use in the joint concern.[6]

In September, General Fox and his secretary proceeded to the St. John River, where they journeyed one hundred and thirty miles up the river to visit the King's American Dragoons. Winslow mustered the regiment and the general ordered them to be disbanded on October 10. The two then returned to the mouth of the river in time to meet the Fall Fleet arriving with the rest of the British American troops. In reporting to the Commander-in-Chief, and referring him to Major Prevost for details, Fox said nothing of the disturbances reported by Lieutenant-Colonel Richard Hewlett, but it is significant that, although he had previously opposed sending troops to Fort Howe or the St. Croix, he now gave it as his opinion that it was absolutely necessary that troops should be stationed at Annapolis and at Fort Howe, where the operations of civil authority were very feeble and where, on account of the multitudes of people of various orders recently arrived, it was desirable to keep some "appearance of Check on the Licentious and disorderly".[7]

Winslow wrote Chipman that the general was "enamoured with St. John's", that he had taken town lots for himself, Generals Musgrave and Clark, in their neighbourhood at the mouth of the river, and had chosen a spot one hundred and thirty miles from the mouth, at the head of the township located for Murray's regiment, where the three generals, Winslow, and Chipman would have 1,000 acres each. It was characteristic of the times that, although lands had not been located for the

129

"respectable Sergeants of Robinson's, Ludlow's, Cruger's, Fanning's," about whose disappointment Winslow was so eloquent in a letter written seven months later, a reserve for the generals and their friends could be arranged at once. In the letter written on October 10, there is nothing about the disappointment of the regiments, nor is there any mention of a separate government. On December 19, 1783, Winslow wrote Chipman, who by then was on his way to England, and desired him to wait upon General Fox when the latter arrived in England. The General meant to solicit a Government, and "if a separation takes place & a new government is formed at St. John's he will prefer it to any other. In effecting this he will have occasion for the exertion of all your talents—he is perfectly competent to give the necessary information on the subject, and is in possession of maps, papers, &c., but it will be necessary for you to digest the business."[8]

Events were soon to change Winslow's pleasant dalliance with the idea of a new province into vigorous campaigning for the project. Early in January, 1784, Lieutenant John Davidson of the King's American Dragoons, who had been acting as one of the surveyors in connection with the laying out of the tracts for the regiments, arrived with a letter from "Capt. Studholme Late of the Fencible Americans and now acting as a kind of Chief Magistrate acquainting me that *He* cannot (consistent with His Instructions) permit any more of those regiments to proceed up the river and He thinks a township to each regiment is too great an allowance." Colonel DeVeber of the Prince of Wales' American Regiment and other officers arrived at Halifax with a confirmation of what Winslow called "this impolitic prohibition". The Governor had reconsidered the matter, "and these unfortunate men are now preparing to return and intend making another effort to take possession of their Lands when the river is frozen."[9]

"Had the Counsellors of this good man attended in any material instance to the true interests of the Country in those matters which relate to the Settlement of the provincials," Winslow wrote to Brook Watson, on January 10, 1784, "infinite mischief might have been prevented, and instead of an irregular body of men irritated and disgusted to an extreme degree, these people would have form'd a band of obedient and grateful Subjects." Their first proposal had been that the tract located for the provincials should be formed into a county and at once organized, with magistrates appointed from among the officers, so that before the men "Loos'd their ideas of Military Subordination they shou'd feel the more delicate restraint of civil authority." Studholme's incompetence, he intimated, was partly to blame for letting the situation get out of hand. "The common people" were beginning to indulge themselves in all manner of excesses and becoming insolent and rude. "We have yet a gleam of hope that Sir Guy Carleton and yourself may visit this province," Winslow continued, "or that our territory may be separated from it and a General Fox or some other gentleman of distinction may be sent to command it. No other Events can save us."[10]

On January 20, 1784, Winslow wrote to Chipman urging him to be industrious about the business of Nova Scotia, effecting a removal of the present governor and procuring other alterations. The letter was going forward with Reverend Charles Mongan, Chaplain of the 3rd battalion of the 60th Regiment, who would give him "much information on the subject of Nova Scotia." Mongan would also show Chipman a "production of Mr. Aplin's", a memorandum on the partition of Nova Scotia, drawn up by the Rhode Island Loyalist who had visited the St. John River and been impressed with the industry of the inhabitants. Aplin's not very convincing memorandum pointed out the natural division of the two parts of the province, the inconvenience, delay, and expense the settlers in the northern half would suffer, the impossibility of due attention by the governor to the important settlements anticipated: it outlined rearrangements of the governments to overcome these difficulties and suggested that the expense would be little greater than for the present establishments in Nova Scotia and the Island of St. John.[12] Fortunately for the project Winslow was advocating, a much better memorandum was drawn up, probably by Rev. Jonathan Odell, formerly rector at Burlington, New Jersey, Chaplain to the Pennsylvania Loyalists and then to the King's American Dragoons, later secretary to Sir Guy Carleton.

"The British Dominions on the Continent of North America being now reduced to Nova Scotia and a Slip of Canada," this second memorandum[13] pointed out, "it is matter of the most serious consideration how the Country we now possess may be rendered most advantageous to this Nation, and retained as an appendage of it." The first object of every measure respecting the Colonies, therefore, should be the permanence of their connections with Britain, and the second object the advantages to be derived from them. The division of Nova Scotia into two provinces was proposed because of the distance of a great part of the settlers from Halifax, and the name of New Ireland was suggested for the northern half. That name recalled a proposal for a new province, in the region from the St. Croix to the Penobscot, first put forward in 1778. This area was considered to offer an opportunity for the reception of meritorious but distressed people who had been deprived of land in the "revolted provinces", and who would be given grants up to 1,000 acres, free of quit rents for ten years. William Knox, from 1770 to 1782 under-secretary in the Secretaryship of State for America, was the chief proponent of the plan, and on August 7, 1780, Lord George Germaine informed Knox that the King approved the plan.[14] The failure of the British to maintain jurisdiction over the entire area, and the continued existence of a rebel centre at Machias, made it possible for the American Commissioners to insist on the St. Croix rather than the Penobscot as the boundary between British North America and the United States, and precluded any attempt by the British authorities to carry out the original plan for New Ireland. Whether, in the frequent changes of government in Britain, there remained any consistent policy with regard to setting up a new province is a moot point. It was good strategy to suggest for the proposed province north of the Bay of Fundy the name that had been put forward for a project which had received the King's sanction.

The writer of the memorandum referred to the disadvantages under which the Church of England, "the most likely to strengthen the Attachment of the Inhabitants to the British Government and confirm their Loyalty," stood in comparison with any other denomination of Christians, which had its constitution complete and could appoint its own ministers, because orders for Church of England clergy could be obtained only in England. A Bishop should be appointed for Nova Scotia, the country divided into parishes, and glebe lands set aside in each parish. After discussing further details concerning the episcopate, the paragraph ends with two sentences which are noteworthy: "We should give a full toleration to the Roman Catholics and every other Religious persuasion. This would be the most effective Means of diminishing the Republicans, who are principally composed of Presbyterians, and drawing Episcopalians out of the Revolted Colonies." It is to be suspected that the writer meant that the establishment of a Nova Scotia episcopate, rather than religious toleration, would attract Episcopalians to the new province.

The memorandum disposed briefly of the Assembly, the members of which were to be elected annually from

133

the townships, the Council, "to be composed of Persons of the first consequence in the province and of the most approved Loyalty," to be appointed by the King for life, and the Judges; recommended the abolition of Quit Rent; and finished with the request that there should be given to the Colonies "a clear and explicit exemption from all Taxation except by their own Legislatures."

The letters written from London, in March and April, 1784,[15] by Ward Chipman, Reverend Charles Mongan, and General Fox, give support to the cynical view that the partition of Nova Scotia was not a matter of general policy, but a gesture similar to that of a man who finds mosquitoes or hornets annoying him. Winslow's representations sent by Mongan, General Fox's suggestions, Winslow's letter to Chipman requested by Lord Sackville, a memorial from Colonel Willard, Dr. Seabury, and Major Upham, as Agents for the Loyalists, Sir Guy Carleton's views, Odell, who was with Sir Guy and hoping for a post, Judge Ludlow, who was wanting a Chief Justice-ship, great exertions to secure one of the new governments for William Franklin—all these were buzzing around and something had to be done to brush them off. Although Chipman had written from London, on March 13, 1784, that he was authorized to say in confidence that there was no doubt a separate government at St. John's would be established, the dissolution of Parliament in April, 1784, the election, and the change of ministry, delayed action. When Fox wrote to Winslow, on April 14, he said that an express had been sent to him a few days previously, offering the Government of the new province, which was to be called New Ireland, but it was not until May 10, 1784, that the first official intimation of the change was given in a minute of a Council meeting at St. James's, with the Lord Chancellor the Lord President, Mr. Pitt, Marquess of Carmarthen, Lord Howe, the Duke of Richmond, and Lord Sydney

(Thomas Townshend) present: "It is humbly represented to His Majesty that it may be proper to Separate the Province of Nova Scotia into two Governments, by drawing a Line from the mouth of the Musquash River to its Source, and from thence across the Isthmus into the nearest part of the Bay Verte". The minute also provided for the annexation of the Island of St. Laurence (Prince Edward Island) and the Island of Cape Breton to the "Eastern government", and appointment of Lieutenant-Governors at each of these islands, subsidiary to the said Eastern government.[16]

On May 29, 1784, a letter was drafted to inform Governor Parr that on account of representations made of the great inconvenience that would arise to the loyal subjects who had, since the American contest, settled upon the banks of the St. Croix and the St. John and the country adjacent, from the distance of the seat of government at Halifax, particularly when they must needs have recourse to the courts of justice, His Majesty, in consideration of these representations, "and for other Salutary purposes," (to get rid of these bothersome applicants?), had determined to divide the province of Nova Scotia into two governments. The line of separation was intended to be drawn from the mouth of the Musquat or Mesaquash River to its source, and thence across the Isthmus into the nearest part of the Bay Verte. The tract of country westward was to be called New Brunswick, not New Ireland as had been expected. The country to the east was to retain its present name and remain under Parr's government. Cape Breton, under a Lieutenant-Governor, and the Island of St. John (Prince Edward Island), "after reducing the civil Establishment to a parallel with Cape Breton," were both to be annexed to Nova Scotia and to be subject to Parr. The King trusted that this measure might not be considered as the effect of any other cause, "than that of His Gracious disposition to contribute, by every possible means, towards the general convenience and comfort of His faithful and loyal Subjects who had taken refuge in those parts of His Majesty's Dominions". As a further proof of the King's approbation of Parr's conduct during his government of Nova Scotia, Parr was to retain the same appointments after the division of the province as he had heretofore enjoyed.

What was back of this attempt to propitiate Governor Parr? Was there any connection between this and the defeat of Charles James Fox, the offer of the government to Henry Fox and his declining to consider it unless Parr and Haldimand were recalled? Or was it just that Parr had sufficiently powerful friends at home? Certainly he was on good terms with Evan Nepean, who had been under-secretary of state in the Shelburne Ministry and was appointed Commissioner of the Privy Seal in 1784. It seems probable that Nepean wrote Parr privately, suggesting that since a change was going to be made, it would be well if Parr wrote to Sydney recommending the division of the province. In a private letter to Nepean, under date of July 26, 1784, Parr, after complaining that "all our disturbances and disagreements in the Province, originate at the River St. John, where there are many turbulent Spirits, who are full of groundless complaints," (groundless, indeed, was the burden of their complaints, but it is doubtful if the governor intended a pun), added that he was the more desirous matters should soon be settled as he was so ill assisted, "the mode of business in the several Offices in the Province being totally chang'd from what it had hitherto been, by such a great and sudden increase of inhabitants." On the same day, Parr wrote to Lord Sydney that the Loyalists were all happy and contented except upon the River St. John, where party and faction had prevented several families from getting upon their lands as early as they might otherwise have done. He hoped soon to surmount all difficulties, and put forward an interesting theory, that a great part of the animosity was due to the four northern colonies having never looked upon those to the southward as one and the same people. Having thus absolved the Nova Scotia government from all blame for any difficulties, Parr took the liberty of offering his opinion to his Lordship, that it would contribute greatly to the welfare and prosperity of "those unfortunate People" to have the part of the province on the other side of the Bay of Fundy made into a separate government. It might make the people more contented and business could be carried on with more expedition and accuracy, "but this I submit entirely to your Lordships superior judgment." So far, Evan Nepean's pupil followed his instructions; but he could not resist adding another sentence: "I have hitherto found them to be of a turbulent disposition, abounding with groundless complaints and false representations, and their Agents replete with gross partialitys."[17]

With this somewhat doubtful blessing from the governor of Nova Scotia, the new province was launched. After receiving the official notification of the division of the province, Parr wrote, on August 13, that he wished to have "some mark of His Majestys approbation of my Conduct, in order to show some of those designing Rascals, that he thinks I have done my Duty."[18] He did not take advantage of the suggestion made in the final paragraph of the official notification, that "it had been for some time past in contemplation, to make arrangements of some Magnitude, for the better Government of the whole" of British North America, and that if he could not reconcile it with his own feelings to continue to conduct the affairs of Nova Scotia, the writer would be very glad to do anything in his power to make a provision for Parr in any other way that might be more agreeable to him. An earlier attempt to find some equally important post for Parr had been unsuccessful and there was apparently an unwillingness on the part of the ministry to recall him. The division of Nova Scotia was intended to get rid of hornets, not to stir up more.

As soon as he received the first intimation from Ward Chipman that the new province was likely to be established, Edward Winslow passed on the good news to his brother officers on the St. John River, and suggested that an address should be drawn up and signed by the settlers north of the Bay of Fundy. The Address, "dictated agreeable to the general Sense of the Inhabitants of Parr-town on the River St. John and at Passamaquoddy," with officers present to represent the corps they formerly commanded, was signed by upwards of 1,000 "respectable persons who were fully acquainted with its Nature and Contents." It called forth a protest in the "Public News Papers of the 8th June, 1784, at Halifax", and the protest elicited letters from St. John River and Passamaquoddy to confirm that a separate government was indeed requested and that the inhabitants were solidly behind the request. John Coffin, captain in the King's Orange Rangers and later in the New York Volunteers, wrote to Winslow that his town, Carleton, on the west side of the harbour, were "in raptures with the plan and bore me to death for news. You must know my good fellow that I am of some little consequence among the vagabonds. No people in the world could have behaved better than they have during the late disturbance"—one of the few references available to a flare-up as a result of the dissatisfaction on the St. John River.[19]

In April, 1784, Governor Parr had sent Chief Justice Bryan Finucane to the St. John River to investigate the complaints which had been made regarding the distribution of town lots, but his investigation and decisions had done little to quiet the discontent—George Leonard, indeed, charged that they had only stirred up further trouble. The renewal of complaints, and the disturbance mentioned by John Coffin, led to the agents "voluntarily" repairing to Halifax and submitting themselves to trial before Governor Parr, Lieutenant-Governor Fanning, and the Council of Nova Scotia. After a two day public hearing, they were given a certificate that the council were of opinion that Gilfred Studholme, William Tyng, George Leonard, John Coffin, and James Peters, magistrates and agents on the River St. John, had "acquitted themselves in their conduct with fairness, impartiality and propriety." Richard Bulkeley, secretary of the council, signed this testimony to their uprightness at Halifax, on August 3, 1784, but by that time the new province had been decided upon, the new governor sworn in, and it mattered little what the Nova Scotia council thought of the conduct of affairs on the St. John River.[20]

On August 5, 1784, General Fox wrote Winslow that he had declined the government of New Brunswick, partly because his own affairs and his nephew's needed attention, partly because Sir Guy Carleton was not going out as governor-general, Parr was not being recalled from Nova Scotia, nor Haldimand from Quebec. General Musgrave had also been offered and had declined the governorship of New Brunswick, and Sir Guy's brother, Colonel Thomas Carleton, had accepted it. Fox understood that his acceptance was upon a promise of his going to Canada next year, but Fox remarked that next year was a long while. It certainly was in this case, for Thomas Carleton remained governor of New Brunswick until his death in 1817, although he resided in England for the last fourteen years of his life. The position as secretary of the province, which Fox had promised Winslow, had gone to Jonathan Odell, and "there was nothing your friends could think of for you that was not already filled up", his patron added. In an earlier letter, Fox had warned Winslow that some of his letters had been too vehement and had displeased Sir Guy Carleton. Although everything had been set to rights "by your Friends", that incident may have prevented Winslow's getting any appointment other than membership of the Council. Winslow sent his cordial congratulations" to Odell, frankly admitting that he had anticipated the same appointment for himself and had made arrangements for the comfortable enjoyment of it. "Tired of the province of Nova Scotia—its Governor— its inhabitants—", he had determined to move his family to St. John's and had hired a house from Mr. Hazen. As a result of having explored the country, he had much information concerning the inhabitants, soils, productions of the new province. His former appointments with the Provincials meant that he knew most of the principal settlers, and he thought he would be useful to the new government. Certainly, his advocacy of the partitioning of Nova Scotia had made any appointment in that province impossible, and it was necessary to swallow his chagrin and get on good terms with the officials of the new government.[21]

Jonathan Odell, the secretary of the new province, was a native of New Jersey and grandson of the first president of the College of New Jersey. When the revolution began, he was rector at Burlington, New Jersey, and became, successively, chaplain of the Pennsylvania Loyalists, of the King's American Dragoons, and secretary to Sir Guy Carleton. Sir Guy recommended him to Thomas Carleton, and Fox thought he would be going to Canada with Carleton. There was, as it turned out, nothing temporary about the appointment, for Jonathan Odell remained secretary of the province until he handed the position to his son, William Franklin Odell, who relinquished it only on his death, in 1844.

The position of attorney general had been offered to S. S. Blowers, who had been secretary of the Board of Directors of the Associated Loyalists and also of the

Board of Agents, but he preferred to remain in Halifax, where he soon received appointment as attorney general of Nova Scotia. The New Brunswick appointment went to Blowers' friend and fellow student, Jonathan Bliss, a native of Springfield, Massachusetts, and graduate of Harvard in 1763. James Putnam, formerly of Worcester, Massachusetts, graduate of Harvard in 1746, was likewise appointed to the council, and was made a *puisne* judge in the new province. Daniel Bliss, native of Concord, Massachusetts, graduate of Harvard in 1760, Joshua Upham, formerly of Brookfield, Massachusetts, graduate of Harvard in 1763, who had been prominent in Refugee activities and had been appointed major in the King's American Dragoons, Abijah Willard, of Lancaster, Massachusetts, whose name headed the list of the fifty-five petitioners for large grants of land, Ward Chipman, of Boston, Massachusetts, graduate of Harvard in 1770, and Edward Winslow, of Plymouth, Massachusetts, graduate of Harvard in 1765, were also members of the first Council of New Brunswick. William Hazen, native of Haverhill, Massachusetts, who had remained loyal at a time when most of the inhabitants of the St. John River had wavered in their allegiance, and had remained, with great profit to his business, in the good graces of the governing powers, was named to the Council to represent the old inhabitants. Gilfred Studholme, who had been in charge of the detachment of Royal Fencible Americans at Fort Howe, and had acted as deputy for the governor of Nova Scotia, was also appointed to the Council. The only other New Jersey representative, besides Jonathan Odell, the secretary, was Isaac Allen, lieutenant-colonel of the 2nd New Jersey Volunteers, who was also a *puisne* judge. The New York representatives were George Duncan Ludlow, the Chief Justice, and his brother, Gabriel G. Ludlow, who had been colonel of the 2nd Battalion of DeLancey's Brigade, and Beverley Robinson, of a Virginia family, who had married a New York heiress, Susannah Philipse, and settled in Dutchess County, New York, and had been officer commanding the Loyal American Regiment.

Modern ideas of representation of different groups of the inhabitants had no place in the selection of this Council. How little representative it was will be understood when, in the course of the next chapter, analysis of the newcomers is made by colony and by occupation. The Council was heavily overweighted in favour of Massachusetts and of the legal profession. William Hazen was the only member who could be said to represent commerce and industry. Abijah Willard and Beverley Robinson represented the large landowners, but there were no representatives of the yeomen or small holders. The Council was an aristocracy; it was intended by the government at home that it should be such; the governor informed the secretary of state that whereas in Nova Scotia, "everything originated according to the custom of New England with the Assembly," in New Brunswick, "where a great proportion of the people have emigrated from New York and the provinces to the Southward, it was thought most prudent to take an early advantage of their better habits and, by strengthening the executive powers of government, to discountenance its leaning so much on the popular part of the constitution." There is no indication that the Council registered any objection to being considered an aristocracy or to having its power increased.

The Royal Commission, dated August 16, 1784, empowered the governor of New Brunswick to appoint a Council of not less than nine and not more than twelve members from among the "Principal Freeholders" of the inhabitants, and to arrange for general Assemblies of the "Freeholders and Settlers, elected by the Major part." The governor, with the advice and consent of the Council and Assembly, was to constitute and ordain laws, statutes and ordinances for the public welfare and good government of the province and of the inhabitants and of all who should come there, and for the benefit of the king and his heirs and successors. All laws passed were, within three months, to be transmitted to the home government. The governor was empowered to erect, constitute and establish such and so many courts of judicature and public justice as were necessary; to appoint judges, commissioners of oyer and terminer, justices of the peace, and other necessary officers and ministers; to exercise the right of pardon, except in cases of treason and wilful murder; to arrange for the custody of idiots and the management of their estates. He was to levy, arm, muster, command and employ all persons for defence and execute martial law; to raise and build such forts and platforms, castles (the governors of New Brunswick neglected their opportunities in this respect), cities, boroughs, towns, and fortifications as were necessary; he was to appoint captains, lieutenants, masters of ships and other commanders and officers commissioned to execute the law martial during time of war. All public money was to be issued out by warrant from the governor, "by and with the advice and consent of our said Council"—significantly, no mention of the Assembly in connection with the issuing of warrants for expenditure. The governor was to grant lands, tenements, hereditaments, to order and appoint fairs, marts and markets, and so many ports, harbours, bays, havens as were thought necessary. In addition to the Royal Commission, a lengthy document containing ninety-six Instructions was drawn up for the governor.[22]

The distrust of popular assemblies, which the American Revolution had engendered and which the French Revolution was to intensify, was apparent in the Commissions and Instructions to the governor, and was shown even more clearly in Thomas Carleton's words and actions. Although he had reached Halifax on the 30th of October, 1784, and Saint John on the 21st of November, it was the 15th of October, 1785, before writs were issued for the first election of an Assembly. Carleton explained that he felt it desirable to make all possible arrangements, in accordance with the Royal Commission and Instructions, before he called the Assembly. Accordingly, the capital of the province was chosen, the province was divided into counties, the number of representatives for the assembly allocated and election regulations decided by the governor and council, before the ordinary inhabitants had any opportunity to make their voices heard.

It had generally been taken for granted that the town at the mouth of the St. John River would be made the capital of the new province. Another suggestion was made, however, by Edward Winslow. When the idea occurred to him is not known, but in a letter to Ward Chipman, on April 26, 1784, Winslow put forward the suggestion very strongly and marshalled a number of arguments in its favour. The seat of government, he presumed, would be on the St. John River, because of its central location. Establishing the metropolis as far up the river as St. Ann's would have a tendency to extend the settlements and to enhance the value of the land above St. Ann's. It would also facilitate communication with Canada, an important consideration. St. Ann's was delightfully situated, above all freshets and directly opposite the beautiful River Nashwaak. The country around St. Ann's was "inconceivably fertile", and navigation for small vessels was practicable and convenient. "The great town of Maugerville" was in the neighbourhood, and it was so perfectly cultivated as to afford an immediate supply for the market of the town. A communication with Passamaquoddy overland could be easily effected, and the distance was not very great. If the towns at the mouth of the river became great, the governor could take up residence there occasionally, Winslow suggested. The only reason Winslow did not mention was that St. Ann's, by reason of his acquiescence in the handing over of the lower part of the river to the refugees, had become the town of the regiments, and to have it chosen as the capital of the new province would restore Winslow to favour with the regiments.[23]

Winslow doubtless communicated this suggestion to Odell (only the beginning of the draft of the letter appears in the *Winslow Papers*), and to other members of the Council. Although the official reason given for the choice of St. Ann's as the capital was the encouragement it would give to settlements up the river, the decisive factor for Governor Carleton was probably the distance of St. Ann's from the turbulent groups at the mouth of the river, of whose complaints and meetings and tumults he would have received exaggerated reports from Governor Parr. Carleton, like Parr, had served with the 20th regiment, in which a mutiny had occurred, and the experience had left in both officers a fear of what the common people might be plotting and a fondness for repressive measures.

The inhabitants of the towns at the mouth of the river were highly incensed at the choice of St.Ann's as the capital of the new province, and were only partly mollified by a grant of incorporation as a city. A city charter was hastily improvised, based on the colonial charter of New York, with aldermen, assistants, and constables elected by the people, and mayor, recorder, sheriff, and clerk appointed by the government of the province. The city included the towns which had been laid out on both sides of the harbour, Partridge Island, and the establishment of Hazen, Simonds and White at Portland Point. May 18, 1785, the second anniversary of the landing of the first Loyalists, was set as the birthday of the new city. Although the Royal Commission had given the governor power to constitute cities, it had not been anticipated that such hasty action in the matter would be taken, and His Majesty's Government in London expressed disapproval of the incorporation. The charter was not revoked, however, and the new city was permitted to retain its status. Fortunately, Ward Chipman suggested, and the suggestion was adopted, that the city should be called St. John, rather than St. John's. (Recent practice has been to write the name as Saint John, which serves to distinguish the name from other St. Johns.) Governor Parr's unpopularity on the north side of the Bay of Fundy brought about a complete disappearance of the name he had tried to foist upon the east side town, but Sir Guy Carleton's services to the Loyalists caused his name to cling to the west side town.[34] St. Ann's lost its old name. To propitiate authorities at home, the new capital was called after Frederick, third son of George III, at first Fredericks Town, but eventually Fredericton.

Although the people at the mouth of the river could see no justification for the choice of St. Ann's as the capital—the official explanation of encouragement for settlement up the river they scoffed at—there was a nice geographical sense about it. There was also an excellent understanding of geographical factors in the laying out of the counties in the new province. The city of Saint John was given a strip of land along the coast, in each direction, for its county. The Kennebecasis and the Belleisle and the land opposite, on the west side of the River St. John, were made into Kings County. For its shiretown, Kingston served, until changes in the means of communication required shifting of the capital to Hampton. Washademoak and Grand Lake and the Gagetown side of the St. John River became Queens County, with Gagetown as the shiretown. The old township of Maugerville, and its opposite number, Burton, were partitioned off as Sunbury County, the old name for the whole St. John River country. Maugerville hoped to be the shiretown, but a high freshet in 1785 gave that distinction to Burton. The regiments' town, henceforward Fredericton, and the regiments' blocks, and whatever lay in the uncharted wilderness beyond and might be part of New Brunswick, became York County. The Passamaquoddy area and the St. Croix obviously belonged together, and became Charlotte County, with St. Andrews as shiretown. The North Shore including the Miramichi valley, as far as any boundary lines could contain the far reaching figures of the Miramichi's arms, was made into Northumberland County. It was intended that the court house for Northumberland County should be erected at the junction between the Southwest and Northwest Mirami-chi, but an enterprising lot owner further down the river, on the north bank, contrived to have the court-house erected in that less convenient location, where the town of Newcastle eventually developed. The eastern district, including Sackville, the reluctant Cumberland, which was asking to remain with Halifax, and the Petitcodiac River settlements, became Westmorland County. Dorchester, on the Memramcook, was made the shiretown.

It was decreed by the Governor and Council, that St. John city and county were to elect six members, York, Westmorland and Charlotte, four members each, Kings, Queens, Northumberland, and Sunbury, two each. For their first election to the Assembly, the franchise was unusual for the times, since all males of full age, inhabitants for three months, were entitled to vote. The delays in the granting of land were responsible for this democratic innovation: as events showed, any democratic intentions were no part of the policy of the province's rulers.

The inhabitants at the mouth of the river expressed their displeasure at the government's choice of St. Ann's for capital by turning down the government candidates, the Attorney General, Jonathan Bliss, the Solicitor General, Ward Chipman, Christopher Billopp, William Pagan, Stanton Hazard, and John McGeorge, and giving a majority of votes to Tertullus Dickinson, who had been one of the most outspoken denunciators of favouritism in the distribution of Parr Town lots, Richard Lightfoot, Richard Bonsall, Peter Grim, John Boggs, and Alexander Reid. At the final hustings, when it was seen that the "friends of the government" had been defeated, the Sheriff disqualified a sufficient number of electors to change the vote and to enable him to declare the attorney-general, the solicitor-general, and their running mates elected. Little, if any, opportunity was afforded the electors to protest against their disqualification. When a crowd gathered and attempted to push into the coffee house where proceedings were being held, the governor had the military called out to quell the disorder which naturally resulted from the high-handed interference with the election.

At the meeting of the Assembly, in January, 1786, a petition was presented from the indignant citizens in which they stated that they had seen British subjects confined in irons, carried into a garrison, and there examined under the authority of a military guard. Prosecutions were still hanging over the heads of people for supposed offences. One of their legal representatives in the Assembly had been confined in a sentry box at the discretion of a private soldier. They had seen the military introduced during an election, and unnecessarily and unlawfully patrolling the streets during an election, to the terror and alarm of the peaceable, unoffending inhabitants. They had seen officers of the Crown neglecting and refusing to discharge their duty; the freedom of election violated by corrupt and undue influence in the most public manner. They had seen the returning officer behaving with the most unconstitutional and unprecedented conduct; the irreligious and immoral, instead of being punished, encouraged both by precept and example; the Assembly declaring the election for St. John city and county to have fallen upon Jonathan

Bliss, Ward Chipman, Christopher Billopp, William Pagan, Stanton Hazard, and John McGeorge, admitting them and swearing them in, "notwithstanding Tertullus Dickinson, Richard Lightfoot, Richard Bonsall, Peter Grim, John Boggs, and Alexander Reid were chosen by a decided majority according to your Excellency's own regulations."[25]

The answer of the Governor and Council to this petition was the preparation of a bill, drawn up by the Chief Justice, entitled "An act against tumults and disorders, upon pretence of preparing or presenting public petitions or other addresses to the Governor or House of Assembly." No person would be allowed to obtain signatures of more than twenty persons to any petition or complaint, unless such petition were ordered by three or more justices or by the majority of the grand jury of the county in which the complaint originated. When this bill was presented to the Assembly, only four members voted against this outrageous measure, Elias Hardy, member for Northumberland, Peter Clinch, member for Charlotte, Samuel Dickinson, member for Queens, and Stanton Hazard, member for St. John.

Is it any wonder that Winslow complained a few years later of the apathy into which everybody had sunk? What other attitude was possible? Had Winslow himself protested against the actions of the Governor and Council with any of that fine fervour and desire for fairness which had marked his protests against the dealings of the Governor and Council of Nova Scotia? Had he stood forth as the champion of the "hospitable yeomen", on whose behalf he had implored Ward Chipman to carry on the campaign for the establishment of the new province? The inevitable conclusion is that in only one respect was the new province an improvement on the old, in the apportioning of land and in the regulations and arrangements for that purpose. Otherwise, the people had exchanged whips for scorpions. The apathy, the stolid endurance, the preoccupation with getting a living, which enabled the inhabitants to continue for nearly half a century under the unrepentant oligarchy which held sway in New Brunswick from the beginning of the province until the development of responsible government, would have enabled them to survive had the link with Halifax not been broken and had the province of Nova Scotia remained undivided.

CHAPTER EIGHT

ITS NEW INHABITANTS

"Like most of the Loyalists," wrote E. Stone Wiggins of one of the Queens County Loyalists, "he was an upright and exemplary man." The comment is typical of the complacent and uncritical attitude generally adopted by New Brunswickers towards the Loyalists. The schools, rightly, teach that the Loyalists were admirable persons who had suffered for their loyalty to Great Britain and who laid the foundations of the province. Most New Brunswickers, if pressed to add to their general statement regarding the loyalty, sufferings, and pioneering of the Loyalists, will say that the New Brunswick Loyalists came mostly from Massachusetts, that they belonged to the first families of that colony, and that many of them were Harvard graduates. For this impression, the writings of W. O. Raymond are largely responsible. In the articles on Portland Point, published in the *New Brunswick Magazine*, and in the book on the St. John River, the Massachusetts origins of the earliest settlers at the mouth of the river and at Maugerville are emphasized; in the *Winslow Papers*, which Raymond edited, attention was focussed on two scions of important Massachusetts families, both Harvard graduates, Edward Winslow and Ward Chipman. How accurate are these popular impressions?

During the preparations for the evacuation of New York, it became apparent that there were two groups, the Refugees, many of whom belonged to the Associated Loyalists, and the Provincials. The distinction was made sharper by the circumstances of the evacuation and by the division of land on the St. John River. It is possible even today to hear a New Brunswicker state that his ancestor was not a Loyalist but a soldier in the Prince of Wales' American Regiment, or some other provincial corps. Actually, the lines were not so sharply drawn between the two groups. Although most of the Loyalists were Refugees who had been turned out of their homes or forced to flee because they refused to sign "Associations" or to abjure their ancient allegiance, it very often happened that the family had been compelled to seek protection within the British lines because one or more of the family had "run away to join the king's army", and also it very often happened that after the family arrived within the British lines father and sons served in one of the regiments. Moreover, many of the Loyalists had served for a time in the regiments and had then withdrawn from the regiments, perhaps because of wounds or sickness, perhaps because of family responsibilities, perhaps to take employment in one of the civil departments of the army. Also, there were many seconded officers who had been dropped when the regiments were reorganized. These were often eminent citizens who were more successful in recruiting companies for service in the king's cause than they were in leading them into active warfare.

In the eighteenth century, it must be understood, the border line between the recognized battalions of provincials and the companies who served part time, on guard or garrison, on special forays, as guides, or as intelligence officers, was indeterminate. The Westchester Loyalists actually took part in more fighting than the King's American Dragoons, but they lacked a Lieutenant-Colonel Benjamin Thompson and other influential backing to get them recognized by the Commander-in-Chief as a provincial regiment. Beverley Robinson's Loyal American Regiment grew out of a group who had been doing occasional duty as guides and intelligence scouts. An older group, the Guides and Pioneers, who had been serving for six years in similar capacity, barely obtained recognition in time to be included in the evacuation of the British American Regiments. This part time, whole time uncertainty was not peculiar to the British, but existed on the American side as well. Washington's difficulties in keeping his army together are well known. In later years, the United States was most punctilious in recognizing even very occasional services. In tracing an ancestor who fought on the American side, I found that his widow, a second wife, was one of the last recipients of Revolutionary War pensions, although her husband's services had consisted merely of marching to Bunker Hill, where he lost a "pare of suses", and of serving in the militia of Vermont in the "alarm when the Indians came to Royalton".

New Brunswick's new inhabitants, then, were Refugees and Provincials, who were in reality not such different groups and who may both be classed as Loyalists after they have reached New Brunswick and recovered from the initial difficulties of obtaining land. If the authorities at Halifax had been able to view the problem of land granting from an unbiassed and rational standpoint, instead of being prejudiced, fearful, and swayed by personal approaches, the distinction between Refugees and Provincials would barely have existed.

What were the origins of these newcomers to the new province? Were they European born or American born? Were they largely from Massachusetts, as popular belief avers? The European born may be considered first.

The British authorities seem to have deemed it advisable to include in each of the provincial regiments one or more officers and a sergeant or corporal with regular army training. In several cases the Major had been a Captain in a regiment of the line and had been sent to assist the zealous landowners and lawyers, farmers and merchants, who had recruited companies but had little idea how to weld their motley crew of followers into an efficient fighting unit. True, some of the older men, officers, non-commissioned officers, and privates alike, had had experience in the French and Indian wars of the previous decades and others had the alertness and toughness which frontier conditions had bred in them, but regular army methods and discipline were foreign to them and required inculcation. Among the lieutenants and ensigns in the provincial regiments, also, there were several who had been either volunteers or sergeants with regiments of the line. In addition to these officers and men who were planted, more or less deliberately, among the provincials, many officers and men who had taken their discharge in 1763, and settled in the American colonies on grants made available to them at the time, enlisted in the provincial corps. Others rejoined their former regiments, and at the end of the war took advantage of the permission granted to British and German troops to take their discharge on this side of the Atlantic and to receive land and provisions on the same terms as the provincials and the refugees. Those who had had experience of life on the American continent settled down more readily than the regulars who had everything to learn about living in the new country and much to unlearn after several years' experience of eighteenth century army life. Since the British and German troops were sent to Halifax to be discharged, only a few of them found their way to New Brunswick. An appreciable number of old soldiers, who found either the learning or the unlearning too difficult, re-enlisted.

Besides the European born who came with the provincial regiments or with the regulars, there were others, such as Martin Hemen and Thomas Grimmer, who came with the Civil Departments of the Army. One naval officer, Tristram Hillman, and two or three naval ratings would have as much claim to be considered with the Loyalists as would regular army officers and men, but they do not greatly increase the numbers of European born. Of other New Brunswick Loyalists who had been born in Europe, there were some, like Guilford Flewelling and Gabriel Fowler, who had been many years settled in America and arrived at the head of large family groups. Others, such as William Balmain and John Paul, (these chance both to be from Scotland and the former examples from Wales), had arrived only a short time before the commencement of the Revolutionary War, in the wave of emigration from the British Isles which had brought the Yorkshire settlers to Nova Scotia. The total from all these sources is not very impressive. Sampling showed that about one in twenty on the list of New Brunswick Loyalists was European born: even if most of the MacDonalds, Mackays, and so forth, were presumed to be old country born, the percentage is less than ten.

Ninety per cent of the New Brunswick Loyalists, then, were American born. From which of the colonies did they come? It has been possible to ascertain, with some degree of certainty, the former residence of about half the Loyalists on the New Brunswick roster in the Appendix. The lists show that approximately

40 %	came from	New York,
22 %	„ „	New Jersey,
12.9%	„ „	Connecticut,
7.7%	„ „	Pennsylvania,
6.1%	„ „	Massachusetts,
2.3%	„ „	Maryland,
1.9%	„ „	Rhode Island,
1.6%	„ „	North Carolina,
1.5%	„ „	South Carolina,
1.2%	„ „	New Hampshire,
1 %	„ „	Virginia,
.3%	„ „	Delaware,
.3%	„ „	Georgia.

If the former homes of a larger number of the New Brunswick Loyalists could be definitely attributed, there is a strong presumption that the New York, New Jersey, and Connecticut proportions would be increased, rather than diminished. Special care was taken not to attribute individuals to those colonies without checking, and names were not placed in the New York list because one or two persons of the same family name were known to be from New York. For the Loyalist regiments, officers and men in the New York Volunteers and DeLancey's Brigade were attributed to New York, in the Jersey Volunteers to New Jersey, in the Pennsylvania Loyalists to Pennsylvania, in the Maryland Loyalists to Maryland, and in the North Carolina Volunteers to North Carolina, except in the few cases where there was evidence of other origins. Although it had become evident, as this study progressed, that the Massachusetts proportion among the New Brunswick Loyalists was smaller than was generally realized, the relative insignificance of the figure, 6.1%, was unexpected. The well known names, Edward Winslow, Ward Chipman, the Gilberts, Uphams and Coffins, who were almost wholly of Massachusetts stock, had put Massachusetts forward in the minds of all.

If detailed studies were available for the Loyalists in the other provinces of British North America, Nova Scotia, Prince Edward Island, Upper and Lower Canada, it would be interesting to make comparisons. In the absence of such studies, it can only be suggested that the peninsular part of Nova Scotia probably received a larger proportion of Massachusetts Loyalists, partly because enough of the Boston evacuees had remained to attract other refugees from Massachusetts. Nova Scotia would undoubtedly show a smaller proportion of New Jersey Loyalists than New Brunswick, because the New Jersey Volunteers were disembarked at the mouth of the St. John River and most of them settled on that river or on the Kennebecasis or at Beaver Harbour. Nova Scotia would show a higher proportion of North and South Carolina Loyalists, because the King's Carolina Rangers, and the South Carolina Regiment, the North Carolina Highlanders, and the South Carolina Royalists were directed to Halifax, and were given grants at Sheet Harbour, Country Harbour, and others of the long inlets on that deeply serrated coast. For Upper and Lower Canada, the proportion of New York Loyalists would undoubtedly be greater than for New Brunswick, since the regiments settled at Niagara and along the St. Lawrence, Jessup's, Butler's, Colonel Peter's, Governor Henry Hamilton's, Johnston's Royal Yorkers, were almost wholly New Yorkers, and since the majority of the refugees for those areas arrived through the woods or over the lakes from New York's western settlements. From New York City there went to Quebec, according to the final figures for the evacuation, only 1,328 persons, 417 men, 257 women, 244 children over 10, 263 children under 10, 147 servants.

The New Brunswick Loyalists from New York came chiefly from Long Island, Staten Island, Westchester and Dutchess counties. This would be expected, since the New Brunswick Loyalists were made up of officers and men of the provincial regiments based on New York and the refugees from nearby areas who fled for protection to the British lines during the long period when New York was the British Headquarters. The presence of the British army in New York had not only strengthened the loyalism of the Tories, but it had also enhanced the violence of the Whig denunciations of the British sympathizers. The effects were felt not only in New York province but in New Jersey and Connecticut as well. Had the British held Philadelphia for a longer time, the number of Pennsylvania and Delaware Loyalists would have been considerably increased. It is interesting to note that more than half the Massachusetts group

157

among the New Brunswick Loyalists are directly attributable to the British possession of the fort on the Penobscot during the final years of the war.

An examination of the list of New Brunswick Loyalists shows that most of them belonged to families that had been for several generations settled in the American colonies. If one takes, for instance, from the hundreds of names of New Brunswick Loyalists, these which will be readily recognized as typical Loyalist family names, Alward, Baxter, Belyea, Bliss, Brittain, Brundage, Burt(t), Butler, Camp, Carle, Carman, Carpenter, Colwell, Coombs, Corey, Crawford, Cronkhite, Crowell, Curr(e)y, Cyphers or Syphers, Day, Debow, DeLong, DeVeber, DeWitt, Dibblee, Dingee, Drake, Dunham, Dykeman, Earle, Ebbett, Erb, Everett, Fairchild, Fairweather, Fanjoy, Farris, Fisher, Flewelling, Folkins, Fowler, Frink, Ganong, Gerow, Giberson, Gidney, Gilbert, Golding, Gorham, Greenlaw, Guiou, Hagerman, Haines, Hallett, Hamm, Harding, Harrison, Hatfield, Hawley or Holly, Heustis, Holder, Horsefield, Hoyt or Hait, Ingraham, Jenkins, Justason, Keirstead, Ketchum, Knapp, Lamoreaux, Lee, Leeman, Leonard, Lingley, Lockwood, Lounsbury, Mabee, Manzer, Marsten, Melick, Merritt, Mersereau, Miles, Morehouse, Morrell, Mott, Ness, O'Blenus, Odell, Ogden, Olmstead, Parent, Partelow, Perkins, Peters, Pickel, Powell, Pugsley, Purdy, Putnam, Roberts, Ryder, Ryerson, Schofield, Schurman, Scovil, Scribner, Secord, Seeley, Segee, Sherwood, Snyder, Squires, Stackhouse, Starkey, Sterling, Stillwell, Stockton, Strang (L'Estrange), Stymest, Tabor, Teed, Thatcher, Theall, Thorne, Tilley, Tilton, Titus, Underhill, Upham, Vail, Vanbuskirk, Vandine, Vanwart, Wanamaker, Ward, Waterbury, Wetmore, Wheeler, Whelpley, Wiggins, Williston, Wilmot, Winslow, Yeomans, Yerxa, and Younghusband, any one familiar with early American family names will easily see that practically all these names belong to families which had been long established in the American colonies. From the family names which are less readily identifiable because of their more widespread use, Adams, Cameron, Campbell, Clark, Davidson, Ellis, Foster, Gardiner, Gillies, Grant, Gray, Green, Harris, Henderson, Hicks, Hunt, Hutchinson, Jackson, Johnson, Jones, Kelly, Kennedy, King, Lewis, Long, Martin, Matthews, Miller, Mills, Murray, MacDonald, MacKay, Maclean, Macleod, McPherson, Palmer, Parker, Parks, Patterson, Reed, Robinson, Rogers, Ross, Ryan, Scott, Sharp, Smith, Stephens, Stevenson, Stewart, Sutherland, Thomas, Thompson, Turner, Walker, Wallace, Williams, Wilson, Wood, Wright, and Young, there can be added other instances of Loyalists whose ancestors had been settled in the American colonies since the 17th century.

Since the New Brunswick Loyalists represented a cross section of the older communities from which they came and not merely the upper levels or the recent arrivals, and since more than half of them came from New York and New Jersey, it is not surprising to find a considerable proportion of descendants of New York State and New Jersey Dutch among them. There are at least two hundred Dutch family names, and other families had Dutch ancestors. Alexander Clark, for instance, is not a Dutch name, but my Loyalist ancestor of the name had a Dutch wife, a Dutch mother, and a Dutch grandmother. There are about eighty Huguenot names, many from the New Rochelle and Staten Island Huguenot settlements. The German names, about forty, are mostly from the Pennsylvania "Dutch" families, although a few members of the so-called Hessian mercenaries drifted into New Brunswick. Hemen or Hayman, Justason, and Springer seem to represent the Swedish families. The number of Camerons, Campbells, Stewarts, and Macs among the New Brunswick Loyalists show how important was the Scottish element among the Loyalists. The large influx of Irish into the province came in the nineteenth century, but there were a few Irish born and Irish descended Loyalists, especially among the disbanded soldiers. Welsh family names such as Edwards, Fluellin (Flewelling), Jones, Perry, and Williams were well represented.

In analyzing the origins of the New Brunswick Loyalists, one can easily see how erroneous is the impression that they were mostly from Massachusetts. Examination of the occupations of the newcomers dispels the illusion that New Brunswick Loyalists belonged to the first families and were predominantly Harvard graduates. The number of graduates of all colleges, Harvard, Yale, King's (Columbia), or any other college, was insignificant in comparison with any one of such trades as carpenters, smiths, cordwainers, tailors, masons, or weavers, and the number of farmers among the New Brunswick Loyalists belies the legend that "the embattled farmers" were all fighting on the American side.

Three lists, two of incoming refugees and one of more or less established Loyalists, give the occupations of the persons named. The *Union*, one of the vessels in the Spring Fleet, numbered among its passengers thirty-six farmers, eight shoemakers, five carpenters, two blacksmiths, two seamen, and one of each of these occupations, attorney, refiner of iron, joiner, mason, wheelwright, weaver, cooper. Of the 142 men in the company reported by John Smith, New York merchant, there were 69 farmers, 21 shoemakers, 16 carpenters, six weavers, four blacksmiths, two for each of these categories, mariners, millers, clothiers, masons, gunsmiths, and one ship-carpenter, tallow-chandler, merchant, "clark", shopkeeper, baker, fisher, currier, saddler, painter, potter, schoolteacher, "taylor". When the city of Saint John was incorporated, in 1785, over five hundred freemen were admitted, under these classifications:

Yeomen	82	Blockmakers	2
Carpenters	74	Carmen	2
Cordwainers	43	Curriers	2
Merchants	34	House-carpenters	2
Esquires	24	Silk Dyers	2
Tailors	23	Silversmiths	2
Labourers	19	Surveyors	2
Gentlemen	19	Tavernkeepers	2
Masons	18	Tobacconists	2
Blacksmiths	15	Vintners	2
Mariners	14	Auctioneer	1
Bakers	14	Brewer	1
Shipwrights	13	Chairmaker	1
Coopers	7	Clockmaker	1
Joiners	7	Clothier	1
Fishermen	6	Coppersmith	1
Physicians	6	Cutler	1
Barbers	6	Farrier	1
Painters	5	Gunsmith	1
Innkeepers	5	Habitmaker	1
Schoolmasters	5	Hairdresser	1
Tanners	5	Mayor	1
Cartmen	5	Pilot	1
Butchers	4	Sailmaker	1
Brickmakers	4	Sawyer	1
Hatters	4	Smith	1
Printers	4	Stonemason	1
Saddlers	4	Tallow-chandler	1
Cabinetmakers	3	Tidewaiter	1
Gardeners	3	Trader	1
Weavers	3	Turner	1
Grocers	3	Upholsterer	1
Goldsmiths	3	Victualler	1
Shopkeepers	3		

There were so few admissions after 1785 to the roll of freemen, that the figures given above may be taken as fairly representative of the distribution of occupations in Saint John for the first twenty years of the city's history. In 1786, a few merchants and labourers were admitted; in 1790, there were admissions to a few other categories; in 1795, several groups were increased, notably that of the mariners, whose numbers were more than doubled. From 1795 on, the new freemen, for the most part, were sons of the older freemen of the city. The farmers, it is to be noted, had not sought admission to the city's privileges in 1785, nor considered it necessary to obtain permission to use their "art, trade, mystery or occupation within the said City, liberties and precincts thereof". Many of them had already departed to their lands; others were waiting for the long-delayed grants to come before they left their temporary homes in Parr and Carleton; others were among the eighty-two yeomen. After 1785, only three yeomen were admitted, and most of the earlier ones had dispersed to their lands, where they and their neighbours were too much preoccupied with clearing and cultivating to bother with civic affairs. Nor was it only the yeomen who had forsaken the city; many carpenters, cordwainers, masons, and blacksmiths of 1785 had located grants up the St. John and its tributaries, and were rearing their large families on the buckwheat and turnips, the potatoes and corn hoed in around the stumps of their clearings, and perhaps getting occasional opportunities of practising their own particular craft.

Since the other centres of Loyalist population, Fredericton, St. Andrews and St. Stephen, were not incorporated, there are no lists of freemen available, but it seems probable that they were even better supplied with skilled craftsmen than Saint John. St. Stephen, certainly, with its influx of carpenters, smiths, and artificers from the Civil Departments of the Army, was well supplied. St. Andrews' bag was more mixed, but artificers from the fort at Penobscot, along with fishermen, mariners, traders and shipbuilders from the Massachusetts outposts along the Maine coast, were included.

In 1783 and 1784, Fredericton had been the gathering place for the officers and non-commissioned officers of the provincial regiments, and more especially for the married men who hoped to get quickly to their lands. Many of these had been bred to trades, and most of them had possessed their own farms, large or small. The choice of the regimental town as the capital of the province, besides bringing from the mouth of the river several esquires and gentlemen to assume duties in connection with the government, attracted also carpenters, painters, and smiths, who were beginning to find that their services were not in as great demand at the mouth of the river as they had been in the first boom days.

In addition to disproving the first families of Massachusetts-Harvard graduates myth, the analysis of the origins and occupations of the New Brunswick Loyalists shows that they do not fit into the categories usually accepted by American historians, that the Loyalists belonged to the governing, the wealthy, the professional classes, the Church of England clergy, and the recent immigrants. There were a few representatives of all these groups among the New Brunswick Loyalists, but very few. Although there were nineteen Gentlemen admitted as freemen of Saint John in 1785, most of the individuals named were hustling for their daily bread, and were engaged in trade or in agriculture. Only a few of the twenty-four Esquires had received any professional training in the law. The ten clergymen who braved the wilds of New Brunswick could hardly be said to constitute an important section of the New Brunswick Loyalists. Here again, the articulate few have been taken as representatives of the whole group. The Hutchinsons, Wentworths, DeLanceys, Robinsons, Winslows, Odells, were a conspicuous group among the Loyalists, but they were a very small proportion of them. The Loyalists who went to England may have been largely of the governing, wealthy, professional, clerical classes, or recently arrived

Americans. Halifax may have attracted rather more of the governing, wealthy and professional groups than did the area north of the Bay of Fundy, though it is not easy to demonstrate that it had a larger share. The older settlements in the Annapolis Valley were also a drawing card for many, who, like Edward Winslow, found quarters there in 1783, and who, unlike that gentleman, remained where they first found shelter.

These general conclusions regarding New Brunswick Loyalists are confirmed by investigation of the claims presented to the Commission for enquiring into the Losses, Services, and Claims, of the American Loyalists. Of the 5,072 claims presented to the Commission, less than 500 came from New Brunswick Loyalists, and of these only a small proportion were allowed. The first act had required that claims be presented by March 25, 1784, in London, which was almost an impossibility for New Brunswick Loyalists. Although the time for presenting claims was later extended, the Commissioners were very loath to admit claims that had not reached them before the earlier date, and required a detailed explanation as to where the claimant had been between the middle of July, 1783, and March 25, 1784, why he had not heard about the act, and why he had not presented a claim. The majority of the New Brunswick Loyalists had been newly set down in the wilderness, or were on their way thither, or were getting ready to leave New York. Many had not heard of the act before the time had expired, or had heard of it too late to send claims. The Commissioners seemed to have no conception of the difficulties faced by the Loyalists in getting word of the act, in travelling to the mouth of the river (two or three New Brunswick claimants stated that they had nearly lost their lives in the attempt), in finding someone who had paper, pen, ink, and the ability to set down the claim, in producing proofs of losses, in finding the necessary fees. Elias Hardy, the "London Lawyer",

whom Studholme and Parr blamed for every mani-
festation of dissatisfaction on the St. John River, went
to London with claims, but declined to handle any
small claims without a fee of one guinea and larger
claims without a fee of two guineas. Richard Vander-
burgh, formerly of Dutchess County, New York, who
had been a Captain in Emerick's Chasseurs, went from
Burton and took with him many claims from the up river
settlements. There is no mention of his asking a fee, but
in any case he was late in reaching London. Claims that
were on his list were later allowed a hearing. The claims
from the Cumberland area were gathered up by former
officers of the Westchester Loyalists and sent on to Halifax, but did not get overseas in time.

Between 480 and 500 claims were presented by
New Brunswick Loyalists, which means that only some
8% of those listed presented claims. Most of the officers,
like Edward Winslow, contented themselves with their
half pay. Many refugees found the time and expense
involved in getting the claim properly drawn up and
authenticated, and in attending the hearings in Saint
John or Halifax, too great to undertake. Those who
persisted in presenting claims had little reward for their
efforts, for more than half of the New Brunswick claims
were not even granted a hearing, and only a few of the
claims heard were allowed.

Although, according to John Eardley-Wilmot's
statement on the claims, the average claim before the
Commission worked out at over £1,580, only 67 New
Brunswickers, approximately 13% of the claimants,
asked for more than £1,000 sterling. Another 16%
claimed losses between £500 and £1,000; 47% between
£100 and £500; 13% for less than £100. Several claims
were for services or for unspecified amounts. Typical
claims were for a house and furniture, and either a farm
and stock, or a shop and tools. Items such as "6 sheep
well Fatted", a sloop, 86 boxes of soap, carpenter's tools,

a manufactory of starch and hair powder, were enumerated, and one claimant hinted darkly of "Numbers of Other articles I shall thereafter Make Known". Claimants explained the circumstances of their escape to British protection, in a boat during "a very dark night"; of imprisonment when they "suffered every species of barbarity which could be invented"; they told of wives and children turned out of homes with only "the clothes they wore"; of being hoisted on tiptoe, let go "and one of them asked me to eat a Little and then said he Would Rather run a knife through my heart"; of services for eighteen months with rations only, "nor did he choose to live or enrich himself by Plunder". They told of their arrival in Nova Scotia, sometimes naming the transport which brought them; they reported how, within a few days or a month, they had gone up the river; they told of living in the "Deserts of Nova Scotia", of "Low Sercumstances", of wife and five children "in Great Poverty and Distress"; of a family where "one is not being lost in the wilderness and never heard of in attempting to go from one settlement to another." These were the articulate 8% of the New Brunswick Loyalists; the remaining 92%, except for the officers on half pay, were presumably so sunk in "Low Sercumstances" as to be completely inarticulate.

How many Loyalists came to New Brunswick? There are 6,000 names on the list in the Appendix. The list has been carefully screened to delete Pre-Loyalists, Captains of Transports, Nova Scotia Loyalists who had a grant on the St. John River but remained on the south side of the Bay of Fundy, officers who had grants with their regiments but were not present in the province. Disbanded soldiers are not included unless there is some trace of their having actually been present in the province. Eighteenth century spelling of proper names was an endless problem, and the original files were swollen with hundreds of names, which, on closer study, were shown to be variants of other names. The pruning may have been too vigorous, but it seemed better to err on the side of strictness than on the side of laxity.

How many persons do the 6,000 names represent? Since the number of single men was rather large in proportion to the number of married men with families, it would be exaggerating the population to multiply by five. Checks made of various lists which showed numbers of men, women, and children in groups applying to go to Nova Scotia, showed that the totals were three times the number of men and heads of families. The Fort Howe and the Knox musters for the provincials showed rather less than two persons to each man, but the Loyal Refugees total was nearly three times the number of men. The whole muster worked out at about $2\frac{1}{4}$ persons to each man. On this basis, the 6,000 names would represent at least 13,500 persons. A comparison of the number of officers and men who sailed with each regiment and of the number on the New Brunswick list indicated that 1,020 officers and men who sailed for the St. John River either did not remain long enough or did not establish themselves sufficiently to get on the New Brunswick list. This item would bring up the total to 14,520, and there were refugees as well as provincials whose stay was too brief or too unnoticed to have them included in the list. The Commissary-General's return of October 12 gave the total number who had sailed for the St. John River as 14,162. In addition, a few of the Westchester Loyalists, part of the Port Mouton passengers from the Civil Departments of the Army, and the Royal Fencible Americans, the Penobscot Association, part of the King's Orange Rangers, were included in the list of New Brunswick Loyalists. Whichever way it is figured, therefore, the conclusion reached would be that the arrival of the Loyalists meant an addition of 14,000 to 15,000 to the area north of the Bay of Fundy, of whom more than 1,000 made only a brief stay in the area.

CHAPTER NINE

THE PROCESS OF POSSESSION

The apportioning of land is never a simple matter, and there were several circumstances connected with the coming of the Loyalists to New Brunswick which made for additional complications. To begin with, much of the best, the best known, and the most accessible land had already been granted. On the St. John River, the rich interval lands of Maugerville had been granted for the most part to settlers from Massachusetts who were occupying their lands. A few of the proprietors of Conway, Gage, Burton, Sunbury, and Newtown, the St. John's River Society's townships, had sent a few tenants to take possession of their rights in the townships, and in addition members of Maugerville families and families from other Nova Scotia townships had taken possession, with or without the formality of a lease, of other land in these townships. At the head of tide, across the river from Fredericton, the township of Francfort had been granted to Alexander McNutt and four groups from Philadelphia, but had not, so far as can be ascertained, received any settlers from the proprietors. The township of Amesbury, on the Kennebecasis and the St. John, granted to a Halifax group, boasted three or four settlers. James Simonds and his partners had grants on the great marsh near the mouth of the river, and other tracts on the St. John had been granted to Isaac and John Caton of Philadelphia, to William Spry of Halifax, and to Stephen Kemble, Colonel of the 60th regiment. Lieutenant-Governor Andrew Snape Hammond had received a valuable tract at the mouth of the little Kennebecasis or Hammond River.[1]

On the Miramichi, William Davidson's grant at the junction of the Northwest and Southwest was the only township, but several of the Scottish fishermen on the lower part of the river had acknowledged possession, if not formal grants. In the eastern part of the province, the townships of Sackville and Cumberland, of Monckton, Hopewell and Hillsborough, two or three smaller tracts along the Petitcodiac, and one at Baie Verte, were under grant and were partly settled. On Passamaquoddy Bay, several 10,000 acre grants and one 2,000 acre grant, which had not been settled, were easily escheated in 1783. On the St. Croix River, a few settlers were in possession without grants. Other squatters were Acadian refugees, several colonies of whom were living on the Miramichi and along the Gulf shore, on the Memramcook, on the Hammond River, and at several places on the St. John and its tributaries.

Since these grants had been based either on hasty surveys or on cursory observation of the areas, there was the greatest uncertainty about the boundaries. Indeed, in some cases, since the documents were gathering dust in some office in Halifax and neither the proprietors nor their agents nor their tenants had appeared to take possession of the land, the very existence of the grants was uncertain. When it was suggested that the Loyalists at New York might be sent to Nova Scotia, proprietors who had hitherto paid scant attention to their grants in the colony suddenly became active in appointing agents, giving leases to actual and intending occupiers of the land, and bringing pressure to bear on the government of Nova Scotia to prevent escheat.

Although escheat had been long overdue because of non-fulfilment of the terms of the grants, most of the township and tract grants had remained in force, and were still in force when the advance agents of the Loyalists came to Nova Scotia in the autumn of 1782. By the end of 1783, only Amesbury (or Almeston),

Gagetown, Conway, and the Passamaquoddy grants had been escheated. Burton, Sunbury, Newtown, and 20,000 acres in Maugerville were escheated in 1784. The action did not go unprotested. In June, 1784, William Hazen and James Simonds went to Halifax to point out that they had settlers enough in Conway and Gagetown to give them 16,000 acres, but they were asking only 5,000 acres in Conway. Since the land they were asking in Conway would deprive the inhabitants of Carleton, the town on the west side of the harbour, of "a single acre contiguous", Governor Parr refused the request, and Hazen and Simonds had to be content with a tract back of Burton. A few other proprietors were able to show that they had sent settlers and had land cleared, that they had remained loyal to Great Britain, and were therefore entitled to retain ownership of at least part of their land, but most of them were unable to produce any evidence of effort or of loyalty. The necessity of advertising the escheats and examining the claims slowed up the business of clearing titles for regranting the land to the Loyalists and resulted in much confusion and bitterness.

Another difficulty was the ignorance of the terrain. During the 1760's, and particularly in 1765 when there was a rush to obtain grants before the Stamp Act came into effect, a number of agents had traversed the southern half of the part of Nova Scotia north of the Bay of Fundy and had reported their findings to their principals in Halifax, Massachusetts, or Pennsylvania. The reports were then pigeon-holed and forgotten. The Nova Scotia authorities should have checked to see if the land was being settled at the rate of twenty-five families a year for 100,000 acres, but, since members of the Nova Scotia Council and Assembly were among the proprietors of townships where the terms of the grant were not being fulfilled, the authorities in Halifax quietly ignored the distant parts of their domain. Although, during the war, the attacks of the rebels forced them to take notice, from the standpoint of defence, of districts north of the Bay of Fundy, it was probably true that, in 1782, when the Loyalists' agents arrived, Halifax knew less concerning the territory than they had in 1764, when Beamsley Glasier found that "many places was talked of, but none so universally approved as the River St. Johns." Inspection of the townships in the Petitcodiac area was forestalled, but the agents were determined to have the St. John River lands, and a survey, like every provision of the Nova Scotia authorities for the Loyalists, too little and too late, was ordered of the St. John River townships. During June and the first half of July, 1783, two Loyalists, Ebenezer Foster and Fyler Dibble, and two old settlers, James White and Gervice Say, at the direction of Major Studholme, ascertained the number of "settlers" and "souls" in each township. Their report and the establishment of the boundaries of the townships paved the way for the escheats, but even before the survey was made the thousands of Loyalists already arrived at the mouth of the river were clamouring for lands.

An "estimate of the Quantity of Land in Nova Scotia", contained in one of Governor Parr's letters to the authorities at home, hazarded the guess that the province contained 26 million acres, 20 million ungranted, three fifths of which, more than 12 million acres, was supposed to be "Ungranted Lands cultivable". To this uncertainty regarding the terrain, must be added uncertainty concerning the instructions for granting lands. Instructions to successive governors of Nova Scotia had varied. The Lords Commissioners of Trade and Plantations had at one time encouraged grants of townships, and at another time objected to them; they had approved and then disapproved the plans of Alexander McNutt for transporting settlers from the north of Ireland, from Germany, and from other American colonies. The events of the Revolutionary War had changed the whole system of handling colonial affairs, and no one in London, let alone officials in a colony, knew what policies were to emerge in the near or in the distant future. The frequent changes in the ministries had increased the uncertainties regarding what was, or what might in future be, official policy. There was the added complication that Sir Guy Carleton, the Commander-in-Chief in America, under whose jurisdiction and with whose encouragement the whole business of the evacuation of the Loyalists to Nova Scotia had begun, was advocating plans and policies which were at variance with previous orders to colonial governors and, most decidedly, at variance with the selfish interests of Nova Scotia officials. After much searching, an "Abstract of the Instructions to the governor of Nova Scotia with respect to granting Lands" was prepared, and a copy annexed to one of the early proposals for separation of Nova Scotia into two provinces. Briefly, the Instructions permitted granting of 100 acres to the master or mistress of a family, and 50 acres additional for each member of the family, with a further power of granting up to 1,000 acres to a person "of Ability to Improve that Quantity", upon payment of ten shillings to the Receiver General for every hundred acres. Two years after the date of the grant, a quit rent of 2d per 100 acres was to be paid annually.[2]

In London, on the 12th of May, 1783, (when the vessels of the Spring Fleet were beginning to arrive in Nova Scotia), a letter to the Lord President was drafted. Since a considerable number of Loyalists from the United States of America had arrived with their families in the Province of Nova Scotia and others were expected, they would have their different allotments made free of any expense whatever, it was suggested, and they would be indulged with a limited remission of quit rents "to the Utmost extent of their wishes." On June 10, 1783,

172

.instructions were sent to the Governor of Nova Scotia. The first one directed the Surveyor General of the Woods to lay out reserves, particularly upon the rivers of St. Croix, St. Johns and Chibbenaudie (Shubenacadie?), where masting or other timber fit for the use of the Navy was to be found, and directed the Governor to regrant lands which had not been improved or the quit rent paid. The second instruction directed the Governor to grant lands in the proportions set down by the general instructions, but remitted the purchase money of ten shillings per 100 acres for 1,000 acre grants, and further directed the grants to be delivered to the Loyalists without fee, and the expense of running the land to be paid by the Crown. In addition, for the encouragement of the troops who might be disbanded in the province, the Governor was directed to grant 200 acres to every non-commissioned officer and 100 acres to every private, exclusive of the quantity to which they were entitled in right of their families. Every person to whom land was granted was to "subscribe a declaration, acknowledging the King in his Parliament, as the Supreme Legislature of that Province," and the grants were to be void when in tenure of any person who would not subscribe to the declaration. On August 7, an additional instruction was sent, directing the Governor to grant 1,000 acres to each field officer, 700 acres to each captain, 500 acres to each subaltern, exclusive of their family rights, provided they were upon the spot and really meant to improve the land. Where practicable the different corps should be settled together. The Associated Loyalists emigrating from the United States, their commissioned and non-commissioned officers and privates, were to be entitled to the same indulgence as the provincial troops.[3]

These instructions were a reflection of the agreements between Sir Guy Carleton and the Loyalists and the provincial regiments, and of the several memoranda which Sir Guy had submitted to the home authorities and to the Nova Scotia authorities. The unfortunate factor was the time lag. Instructions, drawn up in England in June and in August, and sent forward in the leisurely manner of the eighteenth century, could not reach Halifax until after the great body of the Loyalists had arrived in Nova Scotia. Although Sir Guy Carleton, in his letters to Nova Scotia, had been insistent that the Loyalists should not have to pay fees for their grants, the officials at Halifax had been reluctant to accept his dictum until confirmation was received from London and until arrangements had been made for compensation in lieu of their usual fees. When it was agreed that they should receive half the usual fees from the Crown, it was very much to their interest to increase the fees payable. Joseph Aplin, writing to Chief Justice William Smith, on March 6, 1784, mentioned that the Secretary wanted to make out individual grants, but he took the "freedom of reprobating the Selfish Idea".⁴ Some such instruction had evidently crept into the regulations sent to Studholme for his guidance in dealing with matters on the St. John River. In January, 1784, when Davidson, the surveyor, came to Halifax to report on the difficulties he was encountering, he said that Studholme was requiring every individual to be present on the spot when his land was to be taken up, to be mustered separately by that officer, and to apply separately for a grant, and was not going to admit any "Associations, or Joint Applications". The well-intentioned clause for preventing officers from engrossing large tracts which they had no intention of settling would seem to have been given a wide interpretation. Winslow could understand why jealousy of a separate government on the St. John River might induce the officials at Halifax to oppose the progress of settlement there, but why they should check the exertions of the poor devils who were to remain on their side was a mystery he could not unravel. ". . . one would suppose that from principles of policy the public officers here", he continued, in his letter to John Campbell, "would have exerted all their talents and have endeavour'd to gratify every honest fellow, who had sought an Asylum here, with grants Seals, & Signatures as fast as they applied." The delays and obstructions caused by the shortsightedness of the officials of Nova Scotia were resulting in the departure from the province of many Loyalists, "determined, (although they have persevered all the War) to submit to the grossest Indignities from their Enemy rather than be the sport of the Rebels of this Country: their patience was altogether exhausted."[5]

The obstacles to settlement were enhanced by a similar spirit of self-seeking among the Loyalists. Mention has been made of the fifty-five persons, who, on July 22, 1783, put in an application to Sir Guy Carleton for a tract in Nova Scotia, with field officers' allowances of 5,000 acres each, not, they explained, as a compensation for the losses sustained during the war, but because they were humbly of opinion, "that the Settling such a Number of Loyalists, of the most respectable Characters, who have Constantly had great Influence in His Majesty's Dominions—will be highly Advantageous in diffusing and supporting a Spirit of Attachment to the British Constitution, as well as To His Majesty's Royal Person and Family." The letter book of the Commander-in-Chief shows that much thought was given to composing the note which was to accompany this memorial when it was forwarded to Governor Parr, and the final draft was as neutral as possible: "Names and former places of Residence of those Gentlemen, who by the unhappy Termination of the War, are obliged to leave their Homes and seek an Asylum in His Majesty's Province of Nova Scotia". To obtain this asylum, they had addressed a letter to Sir Guy Carleton requesting a recommendation to the Governor of Nova Scotia for a grant of lands in that province. Parr, who had not read between the lines of Sir Guy's covering note, referred several times to the petition and finally forwarded it to London in April, 1784, with comments opposite each name. Several of the petitioners were noted as "shopkeepers", others as persons with little or no property in America, or as men who had sold their possessions in America and done very well thereby, and it was mentioned that two or three had made their peace with the Americans.[6]

On August 3, 1783, Ward Chipman was repenting of having signed the petition, as he had found several names upon the list which did not comport with his ideas of the business. He was going to decline having any further concern in the business and would rely upon Winslow's having it in his power to provide much better for him than could be done in any other way. The six hundred and more refugees who signed a petition to the Commander-in-Chief against the fifty-five expressed themselves as much alarmed at the application and at hearing that agents had been dispatched to survey the unlocated lands and select the most fertile spots and desirable situations; they had hoped to find an asylum under British protection, "little suspecting there could be found amongst their Fellow sufferers Person ungenerous enough to attempt ingrossing to themselves so disproportionate a Share of what Government had allotted for their common benefit—and so different from the original proposals." The six hundred, more than one fifth of whom can be identified as New Brunswick Loyalists, feared that the large grants asked by the fifty-five would amount nearly to a "total exclusion of themselves and Familys who if they become Settlers must either content themselves with barren or remote Lands Or—submit to be Tenants to those most of whom they consider as their superiors in nothing but deeper Art and keener Policy."[8] It seems probable that the request of the fifty-five and the counter petition of the six hundred influenced the authorities in the new province to take, from the beginning, a very decided stand on the question of large grants to individuals. Although about half of the "respectable Characters" were in New Brunswick for shorter or longer periods, and several of them were members of the Council, they were not able to obtain the large grants for which they had petitioned in July, 1783.

The regulations to be observed "for the orderly and expeditious settlement of the Province of New Brunswick" were inserted between the minutes of the meeting of the Council of New Brunswick for January 12, 1785, and those of January 14, and were printed for distribution. It was ordered first that every petition was to be reduced to writing and delivered to the Secretary of the Province, that it might be considered in its order by the Governor in Council. This was intended to stop any scheming to get the ear of some official and obtain priority influence. The second regulation set forth that any petitioner who asked for vacant land, without specifying a particular spot, was to have his name and place of abode entered on a register, so that he might have his allotment in his turn. This was aimed at casual visitors, seamen on ships, and other persons, who would ask for land, obtain a lot, and then disappear, leaving an unoccupied lot which *bona fide* settlers would have occupied and improved. The third regulation gave detailed instructions for the drawing of lots, whenever a sufficient number of farms had been surveyed. Public notice was to be given to an equal number of persons whose names were first on the register. They were, either in person or by deputy, to attend the drawing, which would be made under the inspection of a deputy surveyor and two or more trustees appointed by the governor. The deputy surveyor, as soon as possible after the drawing, was to show each man his lot and give him possession. There had been numerous complaints about the earlier drafts, where some individuals were fortunate time after time, while others drew blanks in lotteries, even when there was supposed to be land for everyone taking part in the drawing. There had also been complaints that tickets drawn in lotteries did not correspond with the numbers of lots when the district was reached.

A petitioner who asked for a particular lot of land and received conditional approbation of the Governor in Council, was to publish the substance of his petition, for three successive weeks, both in the newspapers and publicly in the settlement nearest to the land asked for. Any person who had a claim to the lot would be given an opportunity to be heard before the Governor in Council, before a warrant of survey for the land was issued. The printers had agreed to take five shillings and no more for the whole of this publication. This precautionary measure was designed to prevent repetition of the many cases where two people had claimed the same piece of land. The entire regulation, and especially the announcement of the price agreed upon with the printers, showed admirable foresight and careful planning.

The fifth and sixth regulations required that all persons who had obtained warrants of survey under the government of Nova Scotia were to transmit copies to the Secretary without delay, and all deputy surveyors were to make returns to the Secretary of their several surveys, and to specify the lots drawn for, that the proprietors might be known and the unappropriated lots assigned to others. The seventh regulation was also intended to furnish necessary information to the Secretary of the Province. The agents of the disbanded corps, or the senior officers of each regiment in the province were to transmit without delay a roll containing the present state of the battalion, troop, or company, enumerating the officers, non-commissioned officers and privates, their wives and children, by name, together with the place of their residence, that all at present in the province and unprovided for, might have their lands assigned them.

By January, 1785, the regiments were so widely scattered that these rolls were not complete. Several fragmentary attempts at enumeration have survived.

The eighth regulation stated that all battalions or companies who were not satisfied with their allotments and were willing to take their lands in any parts unoccupied and ungranted in the tracts assigned for the disbanded corps, on application before April 1, might have farms granted. After April 1, the tracts would be granted to such of His Majesty's Loyal Subjects as first applied for them. For the encouragement of those who would settle above Blocks 6 and 7, the lots would be laid out with forty-two rods frontage on the river for non-commissioned officers and privates and eighty-two rods frontage for commissioned officers. The drafts for such farms were to be conducted under the supervision of the deputy surveyor, the agent, and one or more officers of each battalion, troop or company, and as soon as possible after the draft, the deputy surveyor would show each proprietor or his deputy or agent the boundaries and marks of the lot drawn, which would be considered as a delivery of possession.

It will be remembered that Winslow had proposed to the commanding officers of the regiments, at the time of their arrival in the Fall Fleet, that townships twelve miles square should be assigned to them and that Lieutenant John Davidson and other officers reported, in January, 1784, that Studholme was refusing to allow any more regiments to go up the river to their tracts. The tracts had been assigned as follows:

Block 1, opposite St. Ann's (Fredericton), Maryland Loyalists, grant of 13,750 acres to Daniel Fukes and others, July 14, 1784.

Block 2, Kingsclear, 2nd New Jersey Volunteers, grant of 38,450 acres to Colonel Isaac Allen and others, July 14, 1784.

Block 3, Lower Queensbury, Guides and Pioneers, grant to John Parker and 63 others, November 9, 1787.

Block 4, Prince William, King's American Dragoons, grant to Francis Horseman and 15 others, May 19, 1786.

Block 5, Queensbury, Queen's Rangers, grant to James Brown and 66 others, February 2, 1787.

Block 6, Canterbury, King's American Regiment, grant to Tristman Hillman and 62 others, August 17, 1787.

Block 7, Southampton, Pennsylvania Loyalists, grant to William Burns and others, August 17, 1787.

Block 8, Woodstock, 1st DeLancey's, grant to Robert Brown and 119 others, October 15, 1784.

Block 9, Northampton, 2nd DeLancey's, grant to ?

Block 10, drawn by Loyal American Legion, refused.

Block 11, drawn by Prince of Wales' American Legion, refused.

Block 12, drawn by Loyal American Regiment, refused.

Block 13, drawn by 1st New Jersey Volunteers, refused.

Block 14, drawn by 3rd New Jersey Volunteers, refused.

The blocks with odd numbers were on the east side of the river, the blocks with even numbers on the west side. Block 4, assigned to the King's American Dragoons by Winslow and the other agents, was named Prince William (after the second son of George III), and was possibly not numbered in the draft after the arrival of the Fall Fleet. The King's American Regiment's Block was sometimes referred to as Block 4, and the 1st DeLancey's Block as Block 6. To add to the confusion, the three battalions of DeLancey's Brigade had been reorganized into two before leaving New York, and the men themselves did not always set down correctly their new battalion number, so that it is not strange that the deputy surveyor marked 2nd DeLancey's on the west side of the river instead of on the east.

The Regulations intimate that, even as early as January, 1785, it was becoming apparent that the attempt to settle the regiments by blocks was not succeeding. To begin with, five of the regiments had refused their blocks outright, and the Regulations offered special inducements to anyone who would settle on the upper part of the river, above the DeLancey battalions, on the areas where the regiments had refused even to attempt to take up their land. Of the way in which the officers and men of those regiments scattered, more will be said in the next chapter.

Comparisons of the muster rolls of the regiments with the provision muster and the grants have shown that less than ten per cent of the regiment settled on their block, even when the allotment was near St. Ann's. On Block 1, across the river from the town, the Maryland Loyalists obtained one of the earliest grants. Of the 52 names on the grant, only 48 are Maryland Loyalists, and 23 of those sold their lots in 1784 and the year following. Only ten of the regiment remained on or near Block 1; ten others are traceable, with more or less certainty, in New Brunswick, and one is known to have gone to Upper Canada. Captain Patrick Kennedy and William Owens returned to Ireland and three or four others are known to have gone back to Maryland. Because the regiment was a small one anyway, mustering only about 115 officers and men in 1783, and had suffered heavily by the wreck of the *Martha*, part of the block was given to the New York Volunteers. Although the 1785 muster found only 33 New York Volunteers on Block 1, another document listed 72 as settled on the

St. John River and the Keswick. Nine or ten of the 72, however, cannot be identified as belonging to the New York Volunteers. More than 20 of the regiment remained in the area; three or four others lived in Fredericton; eight can be found in Queens County and about as many more in Kings County; two or three went to Upper Canada; six or seven returned to the States, and another six or seven cannot be traced.

For Block 2, drawn by the 2nd New Jersey Volunteers, the 1784 grant included 143 names (seven of whom seem to have belonged to other regiments), out of a muster roll of 237 in 1783 and an embarkation roll of 154. When a regrant of Kingsclear was obtained in 1799, only 24 of the original names were on the regrant, although three other names may indicate sons of the original grantees. It had been very easy for grantees of Block 2 to sell their lots to officials of the province who wished to have a landed estate within reach of the capital. When Lieutenant Colonel Isaac Allen came up to look for regimental lands in the early summer of 1783, he took up land on the Kennebecasis and placed ten of his "lads" there. Others of the regiment joined them; a few went across the Bay of Fundy to Nova Scotia and a few to Upper Canada; two or three returned to the States.

The Guides and Pioneers, who had drawn Block 3, had not been included in the petition to Sir Guy Carleton from the thirteen provincial regiments, but their commanding officer, Major John Aldington, had asked that they be included for lands in Nova Scotia, since the regiment, or detachments from it, had been constantly on service from the year 1776 to the capitulation of York Town, since all the officers, with one exception, had been more than six years in the service and were mostly refugees whose properties had been confiscated and whose loyalty had rendered them too obnoxious ever to return to their former districts. Of the

153 on the 1783 muster roll, only 93 were present when Thomas Knox supervised the enumeration in 1784, and only 53 families were reported on Block 3 in 1785. When their grant was obtained in 1788, 29 of the 64 grantees were not Guides and Pioneers. Of the 35 Guides and Pioneers named in the 1788 grant, nearly all remained in the neighbourhood, though not necessarily on Block 3. In addition, 75 or 80 of the Guides and Pioneers can be traced within the province. Their long service and their not being one of the regularly constituted British American regiments had resulted in the Guides and Pioneers having greater cohesion than any other group.

When the results were so meagre for the blocks nearest to the town which was chosen as the capital of the province, it is not surprising to find that they were even less noticeable in the blocks further up the river. Blocks 7 and 9 soon lost their identity. Block 8, fortunate in the possession of interval land along the river, and, as the settlers soon discovered, of rich back lands, was more successful in retaining the few officers and men of 1st DeLancey's who ventured up the river than the adjoining blocks.

The final clause in the Regulations for the orderly and expeditious settlement of New Brunswick stated very clearly a policy very different from that suggested by the fifty-five. Except for such commissioned and non-commissioned officers of the disbanded corps as would be willing to take their allowances in one of the twelve-mile tracts assigned to the regiments, no person petitioning for land was to have more than two hundred acres granted him, until the numerous and indigent claimants now in the province should have been heard and provided for. Were there any protests at the Council table against this remarkably democratic innovation? Was Winslow's fine frenzy of indignation against the Nova Scotia authorities responsible for the formulation of this policy? The final Regulation required that all persons be as expeditious as possible in their applications, in order that their lands might be assigned in time for cultivation in the spring, and stated that the Governor would sit in Council on Tuesday and Friday of every week. The response was immediate. A flood of applications poured into the Secretary's office during 1785; the flow diminished in 1786, but kept up through 1787 and 1788, slackening again in 1789, and gradually diminishing to a mere trickle. There were difficulties still over rights of Pre-Loyalist grantees and squatters, over imperfect surveys, over lots left idle while the owners worked at their trades or hired out, generally to officers, but the fairness of the Regulations and their arrangements for written applications and orderly handling of the applications improved relations and speeded up the settling of the newcomers.

An important part of the process of taking possession of the country was the provision of towns. Edward Winslow envisaged a town house and a country house, not to mention a road between. The first act of those arriving in the Spring Fleet, apparently, was to lay out a town at the mouth of the river, and the first demand of those arriving in later fleets was to demand lots in the town. The twelve-mile tracts assigned to the regiments were townships, and there may have been an expectation that a town site would be reserved in the centre of each tract. Blocks 2 and 4 may have achieved a very rudimentary town plot, but in general the desire for river frontage resulted in the tracts being divided up into narrow lots at right angles to the river, with houses strung along as near as possible to the main thoroughfare, the river. Anyway, before the disbanded corps had reached their blocks, another plan had been conceived. After their arrival, at the end of September, 1783, and their disbanding, they had been urged to go up the river to St. Ann's, the site of a French settlement, ninety miles up the river, the starting place of the regimental lands. Lieutenant-Colonel Hewlett, the officers averred in a petition to Governor Parr, sent forward in March, 1784, had promised that they should have a town at St. Ann's. More than four hundred, many of them with large families, unable because of the lateness of the season to wait for the government vessels, had hired passage up the river, and had been at the expense of building shelter and clearing land at St. Ann's. It would have been easier and less expensive to have remained at Parrtown. The expense had been particularly hard on the privates, most of whom had lost good livings in the country and had served faithfully all the war. A market town was needed near the regimental blocks; a town was more wanted at the head of navigation than anywhere else on the river; the situation was excellent and would facilitate settlement up the river—so the fifty-nine officers of the New Jersey Volunteers, the King's American Regiment, the American Legion, the Loyal American Regiment, the DeLancey's, the New York Volunteers, the Pennsylvania Loyalists and the Garrison Battalion argued. Governor Parr approved the laying out of a town at St. Ann's, with small lots not exceeding five acres for gardens, and Charles Morris, the Surveyor General, on April 21, 1784, wrote to Captain Daniel Lyman of the Prince of Wales' American Regiment to lay out the town with streets not less than 60 feet wide and at right angles, "with Proper Public Squares or Cites for Public Building nearly Central as may be". He would explain matters more fully to Lieutenant Dugald Campbell of the 42nd Regiment, who was to assist in the business.[8]

The town was laid out on the lower end of the interval on which the city of Fredericton now stands, with two streets along the river bank, intersected at intervals, and a common behind. On July 25, 1784, Thomas Knox commented that the town was laid out but no house as yet made its appearance. It was just as well that the houses were slow in making their appearance, because changes were to come. Either in January, or early in February, 1785, Governor Carleton, William Hazen, Jonathan Odell, and Thomas Knox went up the river, looked over the site, and decided to make St. Ann's the capital. On February 22, 1785, the Regulations made and ordained by His Excellency the Governor in Council for the speedy building and orderly settlement of a town at St. Ann's point on the River St. Johns, to be called Fredericks Town after the third son of George III, Frederick, Bishop of Osnaburg, were read and approved. Mr. Campbell was to make the survey and division of the town without delay, the streets to be laid down in right lines, a chain wide, intersecting each other at right angles. The lots were to consist of a quarter acre each, 66 feet by 165. This town overlapped the previous town laid out, but was situated further up the river. The officers who had drawn lots in the previous town would get corresponding lots in the new town plat, or, if a house had been built, the lot on which the house stood, if they complied with the conditions. They were to accept in writing, and must, before the 1st of August, commence to build a house at least 16 by 20 feet, and cover it from the weather before a grant could pass. After those who had drawn lots were supplied, the residue of the lots would be drawn for, "regard being had to first applicants in the allotment of the several Blocks, & care being taken that the vacant lots next to the settled ones be occupied in their order." Since there were sufficient lots in the plan for all applicants, licences to occupy would be granted immediately after the survey.

Since it was the governor's intention to remove the seat of government to the new town, "in order to expedite the settlement of the lands in the centre of the Province," the two blocks on which the Barracks and storehouses were situated, and two lots in each block of the two ranges next the river (on Queen and King Streets, that is) were to be reserved for public uses and for the officers of government. For greater regularity in the situation of the buildings and to avoid danger from fire, each person was to erect his house even with the line of the street, and equidistant from the sides of his lot. All outhouses were to be in the rear of the dwelling houses and no thatched roofs would be allowed. No cross lanes or alleys would be allowed to divide the lots and increase the number of highways. Each lot had sufficient breadth to permit a passage from the front to the back buildings or gardens. This placing of the houses on the front line of the lots resulted in giving to Fredericton an old world air on a continent where nineteenth century ideas of town planning called for houses set back from the street. Quaint though the regulations may seem, there was good sense about them, and any departures from them in the nineteenth century have placed the twentieth century at a disadvantage, with streets that are too narrow for modern traffic demands, cross alleys that require paving, lack of space for public uses, districts that are fire hazards, narrow lots with no place for garages or shallow lots with no chance for gardens.

The reaction of the officers to the choice of St. Ann's as the capital and to the regulations promulgated was expressed in a communication of March 21, 1784, from Captains Daniel Lyman, Isaac Attwood, and Frederick DePeyster, on behalf of the officers of the disbanded corps, "Proprietors of Frederickstown". They begged leave to return "their unfeign'd thanks" to His Excellency for "the judicious choice of so centrical a situation, added to the pleasing Sensation of the Honor of your Excellency's residence amongst us"; but they could not help observing that the time limit for building and the restrictions in placing the buildings would be attended with a number of inconveniences to them, and they anxiously solicited "indulgence of a longer period to

187

commence a Building, and that they not may be restricted to the mode prescribed, excepting the size and placing it upon the front line of the lott". Had they planned to subdivide their lots and reap a profit thereby? The fact that they also begged that their concessions might, with all convenient speed, be confirmed by a grant, "upon their making an Improvement", suggests that they had some such intention. It is still possible to see evidences on the older streets in Fredericton that the Governor in Council refused to change the requirement that the houses should be placed in the centre of the lot.[9]

The original plan of Frederickstown provided for a large square in the centre of the town plat, with land for the church, the school, the town hall, and other public purposes included. The Old Burying Ground of Fredericton occupies part of this area. The parish church was built on another site, nearer the river, perhaps because the parson and many of his parishioners had land across the river. The river also attracted the business establishments, and the town centre was never developed as planned. The commons for pasture and garden lots, left back of the two town sites, were gradually built upon and eventually covered with houses, railroads, factories and warehouses. The eighteenth century practices of reserving a green belt close to the town, and of building on the hill, as Benjamin Ingraham and others of the Loyalists did, were more in accord with twentieth century principles of land use.

The inhabitants of the town sites at the mouth of the river, as has been mentioned, were not pleased at the choice of St. Ann's as the capital of the province. Besides granting them a city charter, the Council tried to propitiate them by arranging that the governor should reside in Saint John for part of the year. Although the shifting of the capital meant a serious blow to pride and the transfer of a few officials of the government, it was the end of the Royal Bounty of Provisions which was the real cause of the sudden collapse of the boom in the new city. There was no longer any advantage in remaining near the provision store at Fort Howe, and there was every reason for moving to the farm where materials for building houses, fuel, food, and clothing could be obtained, with much expenditure of labour, but with very little expenditure of cash. The carpenters and blacksmiths, who had found employment in the first two or three years when the new towns were building, the labourers and cordwainers, even the merchants and gentlemen were beginning to find that the only means of providing the necessities for their growing families was to get on their land. Very few could sell their lots, except the fortunate ones who had drawn near the Upper Cove, the Prince William Street, King Street area, which was becoming the commercial centre; renting was possible for even fewer; for the most part, the lot owners had to abandon their lots and the rude shelters they had built thereon. The accounts of occasional visitors to the city tell of the desolation of much of the Loyalist town plat, and their testimony is corroborated by the records of land transactions. It was not until the second decade of the nineteenth century that purchasers were interested enough to get in touch with Queens County farmers, New York citizens, settlers in Upper Canada, and arrange for transfer of ownership. From that boom during the Napoleonic wars until the tragic destruction by fire in 1877, the Loyalist city enjoyed great prosperity, and became the fourth ship-owning port in the world.

In the St. John River area, two other towns were attempted, Gagetown, on Grimross Creek, part way between St. John and Fredericton, and Kingston, on Kingston Creek. Gagetown was promoted by James Peters, a native of Long Island, New York, who had been living in Orange County in that province, and had been sent, with his family, within the British lines in 1778.

James Peters had been in charge of the passengers on the *Sovereign,* one of the vessels in the Spring Fleet, and objections were made to the size of the lot assigned to him in Parrtown. He was also one of the magistrates and agents whose conduct was complained of by the settlers, but was found satisfactory by the Council of Nova Scotia, on August 3, 1784. Possibly because of this unpopularity, he withdrew to Gagetown, where he thought a town of importance must develop because of the situation, halfway between Saint John and Fredericton, and the point of transhipment for Grand Lake and the Washademoak. When the grant of the town was obtained, March 31, 1792, there were only seventeen proprietors for its 112 lots, and the town has never fulfilled the expectations of its promoter. Kingston, at the head of the creek or inlet near the foot of the Belleisle, was founded by the Connecticut Loyalists of the Spring Fleet, who were joined by others of their friends from later fleets. Walter Bates says that they picked out the situation for their church and school house, and the surveyor, Frederick Hauser, laid out a road six rods wide, and numbered twenty-two lots on each side. "Before the lots were exposed for draft," Bates records, "it was agreed that one acre off each adjoining corner of the four first numbers should be allotted the place for the Church and that lot number one on the west side should be reserved for the parsonage." The water privilege was to be reserved for those who would engage to build a grist mill and saw boards enough for the church and school house. The charm that Kingston still retains attests to the good sense and harmony of this plan for a centre in a rural township.

At least three other town sites were laid out by the Loyalists, two on the St. Croix, St. Andrews and St. Stephen, and one on Passamaquoddy Bay, Bellevue at Beaver Harbour. St. Andrews, like Parrtown, was intended to be the centre for persons with farm lots along the Bay of Fundy and up the river. Provision was made also for defence, and a considerable area was reserved for barracks and fortifications. The names of Parr, Bulkley, and Morris, used for the divisions of the town plat, indicate clearly under whose patronage St. Andrews was laid out. The site further up the river, at the fishing falls, was laid out rather later, possibly in July, 1784, by a group headed by Nehemiah Marks, as the centre of their settlement. Bellevue, on Beaver Harbour, where the Quakers and Anabaptists who arrived in the *Camel* in September, 1783, were sent, was the third town, and had a very elaborate layout, with town lots, five acre lots and ten acre lots behind the town, and farm lots ringed around those. On paper, and in the eloquence of the agent, it was very impressive, and many people applied for lots. Of the subsequent development of those towns more will be said as the distribution of the New Brunswick Loyalists is considered.

CHAPTER TEN

THE DISTRIBUTION

In 1785, when the final provision muster was made, the Loyalists were largely concentrated near the mouth of the St. John River, where they had been disembarked at the time of their arrival two years earlier. There were lesser concentrations in the Maugerville area, where the Pre-Loyalist settlement afforded shelter and a welcome break in the surrounding wilderness, and at St. Ann's, where the four hundred and more officers and men of the disbanded regiments had made their way in order to take possession of the blocks on the upper part of the river. At Passamaquoddy Bay and up the St. Croix River there were other considerable groups. Of the eastern and northern half of the province, the muster said nothing. It was not long before the picture began to change.

In the first place, the establishment of the new province, with facilities for granting land and for conveying ownership, and the publication of the regulations respecting granting of land, gave new hope of obtaining title to land, and of obtaining it conveniently, speedily, and fairly. Loyalists who had remained in their huts at the mouth of the river awaiting the outcome of lotteries, now renewed their search for desirable locations. There was the added spur of necessity, with the end of the Royal Bounty of Provisions in sight, and the increasing numbers of mouths to be fed. The carpenters, masons, and blacksmiths, who had found plenty of work in the building of houses for the few moneyed Loyalists and for the officers on half pay, found the prospects of employment decreasing, the prices of food rising, and all circumstances conspiring to induce them to join in the rush for land. As a consequence, immediately after its birth, the infant city of Saint John lost weight alarmingly. The condition was aggravated by the choice of St. Ann's as the capital, for office holders and office seekers moved up the river to the new town of Fredericton, and disbanded officers and men, who had not looked with much favour on their opportunities for getting land up the river, thought it might be worth while to assure a place near the capital.

It was not only the city itself that lost population. The high tides, the cold winds, the fogs, the rocky hinterland, had belied the first promise of easy food from sea and marshland along the shores of the Bay of Fundy. A few hardy folk remained along the coast, gathering by the creeks which afforded landing places for fishing boats and a patch of interval land where crops could be raised, but many who had at first sought land along the Bay moved up the river. The rugged shores of Grand Bay and of Kennebecasis Bay, and the islands at the entrance to Kennebecasis Bay, likewise proved less attractive than they had seemed at first, and grantees from those areas explored further, up both the Kennebecasis and the St. John. One noteworthy migration was that from Kingston. The Connecticut Loyalists, who had flocked to Kingston in such numbers upon their arrival, found themselves in a hilly country of great beauty, with a wealth of forest surrounded by burnt over areas, but with little good agricultural land. In five years' time, many of the families were moving up the St. John River to Woodstock, where one of their number, John Bedell, had been engaged in surveying, and where another, Samuel Raymond, was entitled to land with the De-Lancey's. Bedells, Dibblees, Raymonds, Ketchums, Hoyts, Lanes, Bryants, and Marvins were among the families who left the Kingston settlement. Others of the Kingston settlers, finding that the Kennebecasis River lay at the back of their farms, followed that river to the fertile valleys which lay further up the river, beyond the rugged shores of Kennebecasis Bay.

Other settlers moved, not because their land was too hilly and rocky, but because it was too low. Many of the newcomers of 1783 had seized upon the fertile islands and intervals built up by successive deposits of silt throughout the centuries. The 1785 muster, for instance, reported 170 people on Long and Musquash Islands, in the lower part of Queens County. In the late spring of that year, a very high freshet covered the islands and forced the unfortunate residents to flee to higher ground. Loyalists who had intended to build on the islands looked around for higher ground. One man wrote bitterly to the Council that he had been promised 200 acres of land, he had received seven acres and it was under twelve feet of water. Maugerville, a strip of interval between the St. John River and the chain of lakes known as French, Maquapit, and Grand Lakes, likewise suffered from the inundation of 1785. Its popularity declined and it lost its position as shiretown of Sunbury County to the settlement across the river, Burton, which was able to keep its head above the floods.

Although Governor Parr had suggested that the soil and fertility of the St. John River area had been greatly overrated by those who had partially explored the region, it turned out that fuller and more complete exploration discovered fertile areas previously unknown. There had been previous knowledge of the interval land near the mouth of the important tributary of the Kennebecasis, the Nauwigewauk, and Sir Andrew Snape Hamond had secured a large grant there before he resigned as Lieutenant-Governor of Nova Scotia, a grant which caused much annoyance to the Loyalists who found themselves on desirable territory thus pre-empted. Simon Baxter, a New Hampshire Loyalist, who had had the astuteness to seek out land in Nova Scotia in the autumn of 1782, and Gilfred Studholme, the officer commanding at Fort Howe, had obtained grants further up the Kennebecasis, where other tributaries afforded good meadows. Seekers after land, forced to follow the diminishing stream still further, found the wide valley at the confluence of the Salmon, the Trout, Smith Creek and Ward Creek. To this region, known as Sussex Vale, came a large number of Loyalists, headed by George Leonard of the Board of Associated Loyalists and of the Board of Agents of Parrtown, and Oliver Arnold, who had been secretary to the Parrtown agents. Gradually, settlement pushed up the valleys of all four streams. Similarly, above the lakelike expansion of the Washademoak, interval land was discovered, and was settled, in the 1790s, by the Alwards, Coreys, Humphreys, Keiths, Thorns, and the Pre-Loyalist Prices. Before long, this group, and other settlers who had joined them, pushed beyond the watershed of the upper Washademoak, which they had named the Canaan River, to the brooks running into the Kennebecasis and into the Petitcodiac.

Much of the land adjoining both the Washademoak and Grand Lake had been swept by forest fires some years before the Loyalists came. Daniel Micheau, a Loyalist from Staten Island, who surveyed along the Washademoak in July, 1785, reported that the lands on the northwest side of the river had been burnt but had grown up with young timber, chiefly white birch and poplar, "with almost every Species of timber Interspers'd Among it." Lots without merchantable timber were unwelcome, for the settler had to depend for cash, in his first years on his land, on the wood he could sell for fuel or for lumber. One man, petitioning for more land, explained that he and his sons had cut all the trees on the land formerly granted him and it was no use to him. Because of the importance of the forest cover, newcomers who drew lots on the Washademoak and Grand Lake in the first drafts and came up to look at the location were discouraged and declined the lots. This led to much confusion and to slower settlement in those areas. The streams entering Grand Lake had nothing like the Canaan River's meadows to attract settlement. In later years, Grand Lake itself, with its resources of coal and trees grown to profitable size, attracted Loyalists and nineteenth century immigrants, who were able to supplement their farm incomes by building wood scows for transporting coal, wood, and hay to the Saint John market.

In 1785, there were 17 Loyalists on the Oromocto River and several Pre-Loyalists as well. Others joined them and followed the far reaching branches of the Oromocto, the Rusagonis, and the Waasis. The Nashwaak, which enters the St. John River opposite Fredericton, had been a thoroughfare to the Miramichi and the North Shore from time immemorial, and that function continued. At first, there was a great scramble for lots on the Nashwaak and its tributaries, but nearness to Fredericton could not compensate for the hilliness of much of the terrain. The area above the Tay, laid out in very narrow lots for the 42nd Highlanders and others, under the leadership of Lieutenant Dugald Campbell, was for many only a stopping place on the way to the Miramichi, where wider river frontage and the presence of other Scots were a double attraction. The mill sites on the Nashwaak and the proximity to the capital tempted promoters to pile up large holdings of land; these speculative holdings prevented settlement. A few Loyalists followed the Nashwaaksis and the Keswick to upper meadows on those streams, above the lots taken up by the regimental blocks.

Ironically enough, the blocks rejected by the regiments turned out to have the best land above Fredericton. During the summer of 1784, a group of men from 1st DeLancey's, under the leadership of

Benjamin Griffith, who had served in the battalion as Lieutenant before he was taken prisoner, made their way up to Medoctec, fifty miles above St. Ann's, the site of a former Indian village. For the journey, they made use of Durham boats, the flat scows, thirty or forty feet long, eight feet wide, equipped with oars and mast, the invention of Robert Durham for use in connection with the coal mines on the Delaware. The centre of the DeLancey settlement, which they called Woodstock, was on the interval, down river from the present town of Woodstock, where the varying levels worn by the river's erosion afforded good farming land. From Kingston, and from less fortunate blocks down the river, where rocky hills discouraged settlement, other Loyalists, Refugees and Provincials alike, and Pre-Loyalists as well, came exploring, tempted by the promise of wider frontages on the river. They liked what they saw and sought for grants. It was not long before the settlers found that the land back of the river farms was also excellent. Grants to officers and men, most of them disbanded provincials, who served during the Napoleonic Wars and the War of 1812, in the King's New Brunswick Regiment and in the 104th, encouraged further settlement. Before the first generation of Loyalists had passed away, York County had become so top-heavy, that the upper half was made into the County of Carleton.

The movement of Loyalists from the St. John River to the Miramichi was started by William Davidson, the salmon fisherman from Inverness in Scotland, who had received a grant of 100,000 acres at the junction of the Southwest and Northwest Miramichi in 1765. During the war, he had taken refuge on the St. John River to escape the frequent visits of privateers in his own area. After the war, when the Nova Scotia townships were liable to escheat where sufficient settlers had not been established on the land, Davidson offered inducements to Loyalists and Pre-Loyalists who would settle on his grant. Many newcomers and old-timers went to the Miramichi, "having a fairer prospect of doing better for themselves there than by remaining on St. Johns River, which place they left last May 1784", as James McComb of the Queen's Rangers expressed it. Daniel Micheau, formerly of Staten Island, who had been engaged in surveying on the Miramichi, asked a grant there in place of his lot on the "French Canebecacious" (Hammond River), which was so "high above all Navigation as not even to admit a Bark Canoe (the Greater Part of the Summer) within some miles", but afterwards Micheau thought better of the Kennebecasis area and made it his permanent home. The 42nd Highlanders from the Nashwaak, as has been mentioned, and other Scots from the North Carolina Volunteers' detachment on the Keswick, and from the Queen's Rangers on Block 5, moved over to the Miramichi. Between eighty and a hundred Loyalists moved to the Miramichi, but not all of them remained permanently. There were enough to cause bitterness between the new and the old settlers in the area, although not enough to make the Miramichi an important part of the Loyalist community. Further north, on the Restigouche River, a few Loyalists, some from the St. John River, others from the Loyalist settlements on the north side of the Baie de Chaleur, in Lower Canada or Quebec, joined the Acadian and Scottish fishermen who had remained throughout the Revolutionary War.

In the settlement of the Loyalists, the eastern part of the area north of the Bay of Fundy had been overlooked, except for the sending of the Westchester Loyalists to Fort Cumberland. Nowhere has any clue been found as to the reasons for sending the Westchester Loyalists to the head of the Bay of Fundy. Had their agents come up and chosen the location? Had the Commander-in-Chief thought it advisable to send them to a different part of the country from the Associated

Loyalists and the Provincials? Was it deemed desirable to send a group of Loyalists to Cumberland where republican sentiments had flourished in the past and might be expected to exist in 1783? Whatever the reasons for sending them to Fort Cumberland, the Westchester Loyalists were a not unimportant factor in the Loyalist settlement of New Brunswick. Although the grants allotted to them, Ramsheg or Wallace on Northumberland Strait and Cobequid on Cobequid Bay, were both in the peninsular part of Nova Scotia, many of the Westchester Loyalists remained in the part of Cumberland township which became part of Westmorland County, New Brunswick, and others drifted, as Cumberland settlers had done in previous years, to the adjoining township of Sackville and to the Petitcodiac River settlements. Others found their way to the Memramcook River, where many Acadians were still living, and especially to Dorchester on that river, when Dorchester, because of accessibility by boat from the Petitcodiac River settlements, was made the shiretown of Westmorland County.

In the course of a few years, other Loyalists reached the Petitcodiac River from the St. John. The desire of the new province to open up communications between its centre and its periphery had led to the offer of bounties to inhabitants who would settle on the wilderness parts of the new roads projected, and especially to those who would provide accommodation for travellers. The Westmorland Road, designed to connect the St. John River with the eastern part of the province and to provide a through way to Halifax, was one of the most important roads, and a special effort was made to induce settlers to build inns on the portage between the Kennebecasis and the Petitcodiac. Eventually, these settlers pushed on to the upper part of the Petitcodiac where they encountered the pioneers from the Canaan settlements on the upper Washademoak, the Pre-Loyalists and the few Loyalists who had come up the Petitcodiac River beyond the reach of its overwhelming tides.

Another expansionist movement, in which both Loyalists and Pre-Loyalists shared, was along the Northumberland Strait shore, in the district later formed into Kent County. A fishing and lumbering area, with little agricultural potential, it offered commercial and, in later decades, shipbuilding opportunities which made it an important part of the province. But with account taken of all the Loyalists in the eastern and northern sections of New Brunswick, it can still be said that the Loyalist element there was relatively insignificant in comparison with the Pre-Loyalist and the Post-Loyalist elements in the population.

In the southwestern corner of the province the situation was quite different. Passamaquoddy Bay and the east bank of the St. Croix were predominantly Loyalist territory. There were a few fishermen and traders with rights, and in a few cases with grants, on various islands or in coves along the mainland. The Loyalists found also a handful of squatters on the east bank of the St. Croix. These men may have moved up of their own accord, or they may have been encouraged by John Allan, one of the leaders in the attack on Fort Cumberland, who had been banished and who was endeavouring to have all the territory as far as the Magaguadavic River taken over by the United States. The main body of Passamaquoddy or Charlotte County Loyalists was made up of five groups. The first and largest group was the Penobscot Association, composed chiefly of loyal refugees who had been living under the protection of Fort George on the Penobscot, and many of whom had been employed in the various services connected with the military establishment. They were given town lots in St. Andrews, at the mouth of the St. Croix, and farm lots along the river and the shore. Associated with the Penobscot Association in the town of St. Andrews was the 74th Association, officers and men of the Argyll Highlanders, who had been stationed at Fort George and who had taken their discharge in Nova Scotia in preference to returning to Scotland. There were 125 men in the 74th Association, but only 32 wives and 48 children, a contrast to the Penobscot Association, whose 178 men headed a total company of 649. In addition to the men discharged from the 74th, there were other discharged soldiers among the Charlotte County Loyalists, small groups from the 84th, the 70th, the 64th, the North Carolina Highlanders, the Royal Garrison Battalion, the King's Orange Rangers, one man from the 42nd, two from the Nova Scotia Volunteers, and three "Brunswick Soldiers late of the Regiment of Specht". Most of these received town lots in St. Andrews and farm lots along the shore of Passamaquoddy Bay.

Some eighteen miles up the St. Croix, at the fishing falls, the Port Matoon Association laid out another townsite. This group, composed largely of men employed in the Civil Departments of the army and of Armed Boatmen, had been sent from New York, late in November, to Port Mouton, on the south shore of Nova Scotia. On February 3, 1784, Governor Parr had reported to Sir Guy Carleton that the only people not pleased were the Commissary-General's Department, and he was afraid that they had great reason to be discontented with the lands above Port Mouton. The governor had empowered Major Mollinson to look out for a better situation in any part of the province so that they might remove there early in the spring. Nehemiah Marks, formerly of Derby, Connecticut, who had served with the Armed Boatmen, surveyed possibilities in many places and had put his name on the lists for grants in several areas, with the Maryland Loyalists opposite St. Ann's, and at Digby, for instance. Eventually he selected the Schoodic or St. Croix as a desirable site, and several boatmen, employees of the Ordnance and the Barrack-Master-General's, as well as of the Commissary-General's Department, joined with him. The census takers of 1784 noted that there were 201 Loyalists with Nehemiah Marks at the fishing falls. When they were laying out the townsite, St. Stephen, they were supposed to have interfered with the garden of one of the squatters, who protested that his beans would be ruined. Nehemiah Marks is said to have answered that the King was a gentleman and would pay him for his beans.

A fourth group of Charlotte County Loyalists was located east of the St. Croix, at Beaver Harbour. This was a group of Quakers and Baptists (called Anabaptists in contemporary documents), who arrived on the *Camel* in September and had been sent from the St. John River down the coast. Their agent, Samuel Fairlamb, who had been striving to attract as many Loyalists as possible to the town of Bellevue, was able to report in the summer of 1784 that 192 settlers, with 60 women and 112 children, were present, and hundreds more had applied for lots. Although the harbour was excellent and the fishing good, the rocks and swamps of the environs discouraged agriculture, and the settlement dwindled. A forest fire completed the ruin of the once hopeful town of Bellevue, and the few surviving families moved to the plateau behind, which they called Pennfield Ridge. On two occasions the Yearly Meeting of the Society of Friends in Philadelphia sent gifts and members to minister to these and other Quaker settlers in New Brunswick and Nova Scotia, but the missioners reported sadly that the meetings were not kept up and the children were not trained in the thought and discipline of Friends.

East of the Quaker settlement, on L'Etang peninsula, the Fencible Americans had been assigned land, where 108 of them, with 40 womenfolk and 54 children, were reported present in 1784. Since many of the men had been resident at Fort Howe for several years and had acquired connections and interests at the mouth of the St. John River, they preferred to return thither. The forest fire which swept through the Quaker settlement destroyed also the Fencible Americans' first attempt at settlement, and the few who remained in the area moved to the falls on the Magaguadavic, where a group from the Queen's Rangers, under the leadership of Lieutenant Hugh MacKay, and a few other disbanded provincials and Loyalists had taken advantage of the good harbour, the falls, and the meadows, to start a settlement, which became the town of St. George.

The Passamaquoddy-St. Croix groups, although they were later in arriving than the St. John River Loyalists, showed much more energy and direction than the groups at the mouth of the St. John. While the Parr Town Loyalists were still nursing grievances, the St. Andrews Loyalists were building their town, setting up saw mills, making plans to "supply the whole British West India Islands with Boards, Plank, Scantling, Ranging Timber, Shingles, Clap Boards and every species of Lumber that can be shipped from any part of New England, oak staves excepted", and, before the end of May, 1784, were sending cargoes of lumber to the West Indies and to several ports in Nova Scotia. The West India trade, the fishing, the lumbering, the ship-building, not to mention the opportunities for smuggling, were all turned to good advantage by the energetic and skilful settlers on the St. Croix. For several decades, theirs proved to be one of the most flourishing of the Loyalist settlements.

The twentieth century, with its many and easy methods of travel, is wont to assume that people in the eighteenth century did not move around a great deal. Actually, they moved around very freely, and with surprising ease, in canoe, small boat, schooner or sloop, with little trouble in packing up their few and simple movable possessions. Consequently, it is very difficult to determine the numbers settling in any district, for some families were moving out and others moving in every few years. A few generalizations are possible. There were apparently about twice as many Loyalists in Kings County as in Queens, but it is to be remembered that Kings County tended then, as it does now, to be the country residence of Saint John citizens. There was, however, far more of an economic and less of a recreational aspect about the eighteenth century ownership of country estates. A large family could be more economically fed and also more usefully employed in the country than in the city—but of this more will be said in the next chapter. In spite of all the migrations from Kings County, into the city, up the St. John, across the low watershed to the Petitcodiac, there remained a large and influential Kings County Loyalist group. With the predominance of New York families among the Loyalists, there tended to be a large proportion of former residents of New York province in every county, but in Kings County the New York proportion was smaller than elsewhere. Connecticut Refugees were important in Kings County. From Kingston, where most of the Connecticut Loyalists had gone when they arrived, they spread up and down the Belleisle and the Kennebecasis. On the Kennebecasis, there was also a nucleus of New Jersey Volunteers, placed there in the summer of 1783 by Lieutenant-Colonel Isaac Allen of the 2nd Battalion, on a tract of 3,000 acres for possession of which he had made arrangements with a Halifax merchant. This nucleus attracted other New Jersey men, especially from the 1st and 3rd Battalions, whose blocks had been located so far up the river that the battalions refused them.

Yet another group in Kings County came from South Carolina. These were part of a shipload of refugees who had arrived at Halifax in November, 1782, under the care of Colonel John Hamilton, commander of a unit variously referred to as the Royal North

Carolina Regiment or the Ninety Six Regiment. From Halifax, Colonel Hamilton had gone to New York to solicit clothing and supplies for the destitute group from South Carolina, and from New York he had sailed to England to press his claims for compensation. On his return, finding that several of the families had moved to the St. John River and thus had missed receiving their share of the clothing sent to Halifax, he petitioned the local authorities on their behalf. Colonel Hamilton and his protégés received grants on the Belleisle, where most of them remained, although Hamilton himself, in 1790, received appointment as British Consular Agent in Norfolk, Virginia, and departed to a warmer climate, giving up his appointment as registrar of deeds for Kings County. (His clear and legible handwriting has never been equalled by any registrar of deeds in New Brunswick.)

In addition to its Connecticut, New Jersey, and South Carolina groups, Kings County had a small band of German-born settlers among its Loyalists. For no apparent reason, there were remarkably few Scottish settlers in Kings County.

Queens County was the most solidly New-York Refugee-settled of any part of the province. By the same token, it had many Dutch and Huguenot families among its inhabitants, and a larger proportion of Scottish families than Kings County. In spite of the fact that Lieutenant-Colonel Richard Hewlett of 2nd DeLancey's, who had been in charge of the Fall Fleet, settled in Queens County, very few of the officers and men of the provincial regiments followed his example. On their first arrival, the Queens County Refugees had taken possession of land without any consideration for the rights of the old inhabitants, and the persons to whom two months' provisions were ordered, "as a Donation from Government, on acct of their Indigent Circunstances", were mostly Queens County Pre-Loyalists. Eventually, the Loyalists were required to pay compensation for the lands, "on the ground of the King's having been deceived in the same, for that otherwise as he can do no wrong, it cannot be supposed if the real estate of this settlement had been known a grant would have passed to a Stranger over the head of the first Occupier and Cultivator." A King, it might be noted, has his uses when it comes to making explanations. In spite of belated justice, the hasty and unjust eviction of the old inhabitants gave Queens County a bad start, with a nasty fracas (for their part in which several newcomers were sent to gaol), and a feeling of bitterness which has never wholly disappeared.

In Sunbury County, the old inhabitants, more firmly established than in Queens County, were better able to hold their own against any unjust encroachments by the newcomers. Maugerville, in particular, rented them shelter, leased and sold small lots, large lots, whole farms, sold them food, sold them lumber. Officers of the disbanded corps, with the money from final settlement for their services, and the prospect of half pay, were only too glad to buy land already under cultivation, and houses into which they could stow their families at once. The Maugerville families, used to the country, used to clearing land and building houses, bought lots from soldiers who had no liking for carving a farm out of the forest, or accepted William Davidson's offer of tenant farms on the Miramichi. Sunbury County's nearness to Fredericton made it popular with both officers and men of the disbanded corps, who came upon it and were sometimes disembarked there on their way to St. Ann's in the autumn of 1783 and later, and they left little room for refugees within its narrow confines.

Although, as has been observed, it had been the intention that the disbanded officers and men should settle on the upper part of the St. John River, in point of fact they scattered widely throughout the province. Mention has been made of the tendency of Scottish soldiers to join their fellow-countrymen on the Miramichi, of various groups who settled in the Passamaquoddy area, of New Jersey Volunteers on the Kennebecasis, of officers at Maugerville and elsewhere. Partly because of the lack of small boats when the regiments arrived, partly because of the delay in assigning blocks, partly because of the provision stores and other attractions of the mouth of the river, many of the officers and men remained in Parr Town. Members of the King's American Dragoons, who had started to build on the west side of the harbour before the regiment was ordered up the river to Prince William, refused to move one hundred and forty miles up the river. One group of the Prince of Wales' Volunteers, under the leadership of Lieutenant-Colonel Gabriel deVeber, went west, to Musquash; a smaller group, associated with Lieutenant Michael Ambrose, sought lands eastward on the Bay of Fundy; others settled on the Nashwaak. 3rd New Jersey Volunteers were to be found up the Kennebecasis, up the Nashwaak, up Little River, behind Maugerville. The King's American Regiment sought land on the Nash-waaksis, opposite Fredericton, or in other regimental blocks. Men from the Loyal American Regiment ✓ claimed discovery of the Penniac, a tributary of the Nashwaak, and took up grants there.

Even where the regimental block was taken up, the men did not remain on it, but moved to another block or to another part of the province. John and William Cliff, sergeants in the King's American Dragoons, sold their grant in Prince William and moved across the river to the Guides and Pioneers' block. The Closes, who had land with the Guides and Pioneers preferred Prince William. Lot Mills Patterson, a sergeant in the Queen's Rangers, who had land in Block 5, on the east side of the river, moved to the west side, where his descendants still reside. Sometimes the reason for a move may have been that distant fields looked greener; more commonly, absorption into the wife's family group may have been the reason. Jesse Gillies, who had been a sergeant in the New York Volunteers, was to be found on the Belleisle instead of on the Keswick, because he had married a daughter of Captain Thomas Spragg, who had sailed from New York as head of Company 46. Daniel Parent, a refugee from Westchester County, bought land in the Guides and Pioneers' block in 1789.

The provincials had protested because the lower part of the river was assigned to the refugees, but refugees in great numbers moved to the upper part of the river to the land the provincials refused. When the regimental blocks came up for regrant, at the turn of the century, only five or six per cent of the regiment were on their own block. New Brunswick's experience with group settlement was similar to that in many places and at many periods: group settlement is successful only if there are strong religious bonds, or social customs and tabus comparable to religious ties, to cement the group. Otherwise, economic considerations, out marriage, or passing fancies, disrupt the group and upset the planned settlement.

In the end, York County had more disbanded provincials than it otherwise would have had, but only a very small number in comparison with what it was expected to have. From the first, there was a continual infiltration of Refugee Loyalists and of Pre-Loyalists, and there was a continual progress of settlement, both up the river and back from the river, wherever suitable land was found, by all three classes of inhabitants. In the lower part of the county there was some preponderance of New Jersey settlers; in the upper part, the New York and Connecticut Loyalists were in the majority. The 42ders on the Nashwaak made that part of the county a Scottish stronghold, and Fredericton, from its very early days, contained a large group of Scots.

It could not be expected that a group who showed such propensity to shift from place to place would confine their migrations within the limits of the province of New Brunswick. There were a few, half a dozen or so, who risked yellow fever for the sake of the warmth of the West Indies. There were officers, and a small number of private soldiers, who, after brief experience in New Brunswick, found that their roots were in the old world, and returned to England, Scotland, or Ireland. To Europe went a few others, some, like Edward Winslow's cousin, Benjamin Marston, in the hope of government preferment, some, like Alexander Reid, to extend a trading venture. There were at least forty who, in most cases within a few years of their arrival in New Brunswick, betook themselves to the British Isles.

The Bay of Fundy was less of a barrier to the movement of people in the time of the Loyalists than it is at the present time, and the other side of the Bay was the easiest place to which a restless Loyalist could migrate. In addition to its nearness, the other side of the Bay was attractive because of the close ties of blood and of former association between the peoples settled there and on the St. John River side. Fowler, Gidney, Hatfield, and Thorne are only a few of the names common to both Annapolis and St. John River Loyalist settlements. Hudson River Dutch and disbanded Hessians crossed the Bay to join compatriots, and New Jersey Volunteers went over to settle near officers who had bought farms in the older settlements of the Annapolis valley. Some sixty or more whose names appear on the list of New Brunswick Loyalists are known to have crossed the Bay and settled in Nova Scotia. In addition, many other disbanded officers and men, paid off at the mouth of the St. John River and drawing their rations there for a time, but not sufficiently settled to be included in the list of New Brunswick Loyalists, eventually made their homes in Nova Scotia. Among the Refugees, it was common practice to solicit grants on both sides of the Bay and to take up whichever lot circumstances or fancy dictated, a practice which makes it difficult to determine whether some individuals are to be considered as New Brunswick or Nova Scotia Loyalists. Consider, for instance, the case of the family of Elisha Jones of Weston, Massachusetts. Elisha died at the St. John River in 1783, and the family moved back and forth between Sissiboo (Weymouth, Nova Scotia) and Prince William. Stephen, as a cornet in the King's American Dragoons, received grants in Prince William, but settled in Sissiboo, and relinquished his rights to Nahum, who later became a merchant in Saint John. Simeon, a brother of Elisha, who lived in Prince William for a time, later moved to Sissiboo. Although the oldest son of Elisha, Elisha, was in Saint John for the hearing of claims by the Commissioners, the escheat of his and his mother's grants, in 1800, suggests that he returned to the States and took his mother with him.

The movement to Nova Scotia, then, while larger than the migrations to the West Indies and to the British Isles, did not account for any very large proportion of New Brunswick Loyalists. In any case, it was part of a two-way movement, and of a back and forth migration which has continued to the present.

The largest outward movement of New Brunswick Loyalists, naturally, was back to the country from which they had come. Undoubtedly, there were among the newcomers of 1783 those who came because transportation and provisions were being handed out, and who returned when the Royal Bounty of Provisions was no longer distributed to them. Unless these persons came on the few ships whose passenger lists have been found, or were in John Smith's group, or were named on the early grants, their names are not known and do not appear on the appended roster of New Brunswick

Loyalists. It is impossible to ascertain the number of these "rice Christians". The New Brunswick list contains 6,000 names, but includes the Fencible Americans, who had been stationed at Fort Cumberland and at the St. John River. The Commissary-General's returns show 5,280 men sailed for St. John River, 184 (most of whom settled in Nova Scotia) for Cumberland, and the Passamaquoddy muster lists show 567 from Penobscot and Port Mouton, a total of 6,031. These figures, therefore, provide no basis for supposing that many returned to the States.

A check of the four ship musters yields a wide divergence. Of the passengers who came on the *Union*, in the Spring Fleet, a closely knit group, most of whom went to Kingston, 97% remained in New Brunswick, and only 3% returned to the States. In the case of the *Hope*, another vessel of the Spring Fleet, most of whose passengers went to Kingston, 76% can be followed in New Brunswick; of the remaining 24%, some are known to have returned to the States, and some cannot be traced. The passenger list of the *Cyrus*, which arrived in September, shows a 72% survival in New Brunswick or other Loyalist communities, and 28% either untraceable or known to have gone back to the States. The *Camel*, in spite of the fact that its Quaker and Anabaptist passengers were hustled down the Bay of Fundy coast to Beaver Harbour, provided between 63 and 75% permanent Loyalist settlers, for New Brunswick and Nova Scotia. (The fantastic mis-spelling of the names on the ship's muster and the late discovery of the muster account for the uncertainty.) The only other check possible is John Smith's group, who were apparently late comers to the Loyalist ranks, who were certainly late in gathering for transportation, and who were distributed amongst several vessels and several companies. About 60% of this group can be assigned to the permanent Loyalist community. Of the 40%, others may possibly have remained, for many of them were carpenters, masons, and shoemakers, who may have lived in rented quarters, married, had children born to them, died, and been buried, without notice of any of these proceedings appearing in any available records. After a few years, John Smith and probably his lieutenants went back to New York, and others of the 40% doubtless followed their example.

From the New Brunswick list of Loyalists, some 200 are known to have returned to the United States, and probably as many more joined in the trek. Even if twice as many more returned, the proportion is only 10%. Some observers, not realizing that the majority of the Loyalists belonged to families long settled in America, have jumped to the conclusion that any Loyalist family name encountered in the United States indicated a returned Loyalist. Actually, the New Brunswick Loyalists were very often one or two members of a large connection, the majority of whom remained in their old homes. Sometimes genealogies record the names of the Loyalist members, occasionally they list their descendants, but frequently family records omit all mention of what were considered, if known to have existed, as erring members of a family which numbered many "patriots". Of the exodus to the United States in subsequent generations, more will be said in Chapter XI: for the Loyalists themselves, the conclusion is that less than 25% of all arrivals returned, and less than 10% of those who were in the province long enough to be identified as New Brunswick Loyalists.

Somewhat smaller in numbers, but more important for the future of British North America, was the migration of New Brunswick Loyalists to Canada, and particularly to Upper Canada. At the time of the evacuation of New York, more than 1,300 men, women and children had been sent by ship to Canada, and hundreds more had toiled through the woods and along the rivers and lakes to the same destination. As happens in all such forced migrations, family groups were broken up and some members went to Nova Scotia and some to Canada. There were Secords on the St. John and on the Niagara. There may have been other instances similar to that of Robert Land and his wife and family. Land, imprisoned by the Committee of Safety, escaped to find his home burned and his wife and family missing. Supposing that they had perished, he made his way through the woods to Niagara, and then to the end of the lake, where the city of Hamilton now stands. His wife and children, however, warned by an Indian whom they had be-friended, had escaped with their lives, and, with the aid of the Indians, had succeeded in reaching the protection of the British lines at New York. From there they sailed with the first fleet to the St. John River, where they remained for some time, until a friend who had been to Niagara told them of seeing the name of Robert Land carved on a beech tree near the falls. Mrs. Land and her two sons left Saint John, and by way of New York and their former home in Delaware (where the eldest son had been able to buy back the former estate), journeyed to Niagara. For several years they could find no trace of Robert Land at Niagara, until a trader told them of a hermit by the name of Land who lived at the head of the lake. Once again they set out along the forest trails, and this time they found the lonely cabin and the long lost husband and father.

One, or even a dozen such dramatic reunions would not explain the movement of two hundred New Brunswick Loyalists to Upper Canada. The impetus came from the appointment of John Graves Simcoe as Lieutenant-Governor of Upper Canada and his desire to have officers who had served under him in the Queen's Rangers as members of his Council. Land was promised in lavish quantities, especially to disbanded officers, and there followed during the ensuing decade a migration from New Brunswick of such proportions as to call forth the term, "Niagara Fever". Although checking with the Ontario Land Papers and local histories produced only 200 names, it seems probable that the migration was much larger than this and that many of the untraceables disappeared in the direction of Upper Canada. Especially does it seem probable that many disbanded private soldiers who had been living in New Brunswick as hired men on farms, in saw mills or grist mills, or on vessels, joined in the trek to the new province. So many sergeants and corporals, not only of the Queen's Rangers but also of all three battalions of the New Jersey Volunteers, the Loyal American Regiment, and others, can be identified, that the supposition of a large migration of privates is strengthened. In applying for land in Upper Canada, particularly in the later stages of the movement thither, the petitioner often omitted to mention that he had lived in New Brunswick and had had possession of or been entitled to a grant there—an omission which does not help identification of applicants for land in Upper Canada.

The migration to Upper Canada was largely recruited, so far as can be ascertained, from three areas in New Brunswick, from the Miramichi, from Grand Lake, and from the Penniac. All three areas were marginal, and all are still relatively undeveloped in comparison with other parts of the province. The Miramichi had latent possibilities in other resources than agricultural, but the fishing was in the hands of the old inhabitants, and the shipbuilding and lumbering potentialities were to be realized only at a later period. It was not difficult for John Willson, the New Jersey Loyalist who had gone to the Miramichi as one of William Davidson's tenants, to gather up a party of sixty and set sail for the St. Lawrence. Similarly, the nineteenth century prosperity of Grand Lake could not be foreseen, nor the possibilities of the coal resources appreciated, and a considerable group of Refugees who had drawn lands along Grand Lake looked for broader acres with less swamp and greater fertility. The Loyal Americans who had exulted over finding the Penniac had been soon undeceived as to the value of their discovery, and they, along with neighbours who had served in the Prince of Wales' American Regiment, sought the new El Dorado. Chance brought to notice the removal to Upper Canada of two or three Fencible Americans from their unpromising peninsula on the Bay of Fundy coast, and it seems probable that they were not the only ones from that area to become infected with "Niagara Fever".

One of the interesting features of the movement to Upper Canada was the participation of New Brunswick Pre-Loyalists, not only in the actual migration, but in the sharing of the rewards of land grants, and in bequeathing to their descendants the opportunity of considering themselves as United Empire Loyalists. The first wave of migration from New Brunswick to Upper Canada reached its peak around the turn of the century, but the migration continued throughout the nineteenth century, at first to take up land in "Canada West", and later to take part in the industrial expansion of central Canada.

CHAPTER ELEVEN

LOYALIST INTO NEW BRUNSWICKER

*In fro what partie of the earth that men dwell, either
aboven or benethen, it seemeth always to hem that
dwellin there that they gow more right than any other
folk.* SIR JOHN MANDEVILLE.

As they moved up and down the rivers, over the
watersheds, along the coast, Refugees and Provincials,
farmers and merchants, carpenters and lawyers, victims
of mobs and volunteers to the king's army, men who had
been known for their loyalty to the king in 1775 and men
who had gone along with their neighbours for a time but
had later rebelled against the tyranny of committee and
mob, New Yorkers and South Carolina Irishmen, New
Jersey Quakers and Connecticut Churchmen, Massachusetts traders and disbanded Highlanders, developed
gradually some consciousness of being New Brunswickers.
It was unfortunate that His Majesty's Council had not
foreseen what an awkward and uneuphonious term
would have to be used to describe the inhabitants of the
new province. Acadian, Nova Scotian, Loyalist, the
older, pleasanter sounding names had to be laid aside
for the new to explain the new product, fused from the
many and diverse elements. If the melting pot analogy
were valid, it would be simple to explain the process,
instead of having to consider the interplay of the
complicated relationships between groups of families in
a community, of the beliefs, backgrounds, physical
environment, circumstances, all of them continually
changing with the passing of the years.

For most of the newcomers, the process of develop-
ing from Loyalist into New Brunswicker meant betaking

216

themselves and their families to the two hundred and more acres along one of the many rivers or lakes in the new province, felling trees, putting up a cabin, putting in crops around the stumps of the trees, cutting down more trees, sawing and splitting wood for use at home and for sale in the towns, hauling out the stumps, getting land cleared and ready for the plough. The process of building was explained in detail for immigrants expected in New Brunswick in later years:

The Habitations which new settlers first erect are all nearly in the same style, and constructed in the most simple manner. They consist merely of round logs, from five to twenty feet in length, laid horizontally over each other, the logs being first notched near the ends, to permit their sinking into and resting on each other at the corners of the walls. One log is first laid on the ground or foundation on each side, to begin the walls; then one at each end, and the building is raised in this manner by a succession of logs, crossing and binding each other at the corners, until seven or eight feet high. The seams are closed with moss or clay; three or four rafters are then raised to support the roof, which is covered with boards, or with the rinds of birch or spruce trees; bound close with poles tied down with withes. A wooden frame-work, placed on a foundation stone roughly dressed, is raised a few feet from the ground and leading through the roof with its sides closed up with clay and straw kneaded together, forms the chimney. A space large enough for a door, and another for a window, is then cut through the walls, and in the centre of the cabin a square pit or cellar is dug for the purpose of preserving potatoes or other vegetables during winter. Over this pit a floor of boards, or of logs hewn flat on the upper side, is laid, and another over head to form a sort of garret. When a door is hung, a window-sash, with six, nine, or sometimes twelve panes of glass, is fixed, and a cupboard and two or three bed-stacks put up, the habitation is then considered ready to receive the new settler and his family.

Peter Lugrin, formerly storekeeper of His Majesty's Hospitals, when he petitioned for a grant of land, stated that he had built a house 27 feet by 21, "of Squared Logs," and two other houses, but most of the settlers built of the round logs. The first houses in Saint John, Peter Fisher remarked, "were constructed of wood, many of them were low and ill shaped. These when removed by fires or other causes, are generally replaced with handsome brick buildings, which is making a great improvement in the appearance of the city." In the city, the first log cabins might be replaced by brick houses, but elsewhere frame houses were constructed, sometimes a few years after the arrival of the Loyalists, and the log cabins were then used for stables or for workshops. The series of disastrous fires in Saint John have removed every eighteenth century building, but Kingston, Fredericton, and occasional farms afford examples of houses constructed by the first generation Loyalists. Unfortunately, very few of these fine old colonial houses have survived the frequent fires of the wooded, wood-burning region, and nineteenth century replacements were often of undistinguished or frankly regrettable architecture.

The labour of clearing the land and getting it ready for the plough was hard and time consuming. Felling the trees was only the beginning of the task; the branches had to be lopped off and disposed of; the logs had to be cut in lengths and hauled away; the stumps had to be burned or dug out, or hauled out by oxen. The burning of the stumps and of the brush frequently resulted in an uncontrollable conflagration, such as that of June 18, 1784, which burned over a large part of the Loyalist

218

town at the mouth of the river. There were other dangers which menaced, the slipping of the axe, the unexpected falling of a tree, the attack of a bear. William Perry was treed by a bear one night, and, unable to get one foot out of the bear's reach, and afraid to call for help lest his wife rush out of the cabin into the bear's clutches, had to submit through the long hours of darkness to the bear's clawing of his foot.

It was a hard life, and it was for many of the Loyalists a step backward from the ease and comfort they had inherited, to the toil and hardship of past generations. It was not surprising that a later observer wrote of the sons of the Loyalists "forgetting their fathers' loyalty and inheriting only their regrets." The same observer, however, pointed out that, "in every part of the province, those who for a series of years had confined their attention to farming alone, had all, without exception, done well." The means by which a settler could make his way in the country was explained by Lord Edward Fitzgerald, a major in the 54th Regiment, who arrived at Halifax in June, 1788, and made his way around the head of the Bay of Fundy to Saint John.

The country is almost all in a state of nature as well as its inhabitants. There are four sorts of these; the Indians, the French, the old English settlers, and now the Refugees, from the other parts of America; the last seem the most civilized.

The old settlers are almost as wild as Indians and lead a very comfortable life; they are all farmers, and live entirely within themselves. They supply all their own wants by their contrivance, so that they seldom buy anything. They imagine themselves poor because they have no money, without considering they do not want it; everything is done by barter, and you will often find a farmer well supplied with everything, and yet not have a shilling in money. Any man that will work is sure in a few years to have a comfortable farm; the first eighteen months is the only hard time, and that in most places is avoided, particularly near the rivers, for in every one of them a man will catch enough in a day to feed him for a year. In the winter, with very little trouble, he supplies himself with meat by killing moosedeer; and in summer with pigeons, of which the woods are full. These he must subsist on till he has cleared enough to raise a little grain, which a hard working man will do in the course of a few months. By selling his moose skins, making sugar out of the maple trees and by a few days work for other people, for which he gets good wages, he soon acquires enough to purchase a cow. This, then, sets him up, and he is sure in a few years to have a comfortable supply of every necessity of life. I came through a whole tract of country peopled by Irish, who came out not worth a shilling, and have all now farms, worth (according to the value of money in this country), from £1,000 to £3,000.

The equality of everybody and of their manner of life I like very much. There are no gentlemen; everybody is on a footing (provided he works) and wants nothing; every man is exactly what he can make himself, or is made by industry. The more children a man has the better; the father has no uneasiness about providing for them, as this is done by the profit of their work. By the time they are fit to settle, he can always afford them two oxen, a cow, a gun and an axe, and in a few years, if they work, they will thrive.

In a few years, if they worked, they would thrive, but meantime, there were a few amenities which the most civilized group, the Refugees, missed. "I received a Letter from your Sister Sally, dated from Gagetown, St. Johns River, Novascotia, 20th September last, which came to hand the 20th of December," wrote Edward

Chandler from Chelsea, February 10, 1785. "It was wrote upon a sheet, of the bark of a Tree, a thing I never saw before in all my Excursions through America." A Benedict Arnold, on leaving the province, might advertise for sale such possessions as "exceptional feather beds, mahogany 4-post bedsteads, a suit of elegant cabriole chairs covered with blue damask, sofas and curtains to match", and such other luxuries as "card, tea and other tables, looking-glasses, a secretary desk and bookcase, fire screens, and girandoles, lustres, an easy and sedan chair, an elegant set of wedgewood gilt ware, two tea-table sets of Nankeen china, a variety of glassware," such useful appurtenances as "a terrestial globe, a double wheeljack, and a great quantity of kitchen furniture", but most Loyalists were fortunate if they had the one chest, one square table, four chairs, one "tramel", one pot and pair of tongs, one porridge pot, one pewter platter, four pewter plates, one "pewter cason", that Martha Lyon had been allowed to carry with her from her old home in Fairfield, Connecticut.

The move to New Brunswick was not without its compensations. Daniel Lyman, reporting in 1793 to Lord Hawkesbury, President of the Board for management of affairs relating to Foreign Plantations etc, said that "the salubrity of the air, and the healthfulness of the inhabitants surpasses almost belief." Amelia Harris, daughter of Captain Samuel Ryerson of the 3rd, formerly the 4th, New Jersey Volunteers, told how her mother "brought from the healthy climate of New Brunswick four fine children, all of whom she buried in eight weeks at New York. She gave birth to four more; three of those died also and she felt sure if she remained there she would lose her only remaining one." In 1794, the family set out for Upper Canada, where the only child survived and another was born.[1] The healthful climate of New Brunswick was no figment of the imagination. The abundant sunshine, the precipitation, partly in the form of snow, the deep cold of winter which killed germs, the quick growth of summer provided excellent growing climate not only for children, but, as forestry experts have discovered, for trees as well.

The healthfulness of the climate and the vigorous outdoor work increased the virility of the males and made possible a reproduction rate which modern sedentary occupations forbid. Families which had been accustomed to three to eight children in their former homes had six to eighteen children after the move to New Brunswick. For the first two generations, thirteen was a usual number of children in New Brunswick families, and it was not unusual for every child born to reach maturity. Living was simple, for the great majority of the people, reduced to the primary requirements of food and shelter and warm clothing. The family all worked on the task of meeting these requirements, the women and children helping with the building of the log cabins and plastering the chinks with clay and moss, with the constant providing of fuel, with the planting, hoeing, and harvesting of the crops, and with tending the stock. As Lord Edward Fitzgerald said, the more children the better. They were economically an asset, not a liability. The boys were off to the woods at an early age, and doing a man's job by the time they were in their middle teens.

At eighteen and nineteen, the sons were cutting down trees on their own land and stacking logs for a cabin. Girls of sixteen and seventeen were weaving blankets and dress lengths, and assiduously watching over a new-born calf and a lamb which would be part of their dowry. The early marriages, as well as the climate and the economic advantages, promoted large families. There was also a psychological factor which encouraged large families. Among a group set down in a new country, whether in the wilderness or among strangers, there is always the urge to increase the size of the group. The loneliness, the sense of being overwhelmed by the forest, the desert, or the strange races around, act as a powerful stimulant to family increase. Plural marriages are, of course, the quickest means of achieving this increase of the group, and if supernatural sanction for such a method can be proclaimed, the pioneering community can be very rapidly increased in numbers. It is not surprising that New Brunswickers, both Loyalist and Pre-Loyalist, were won over to that quintessence of pioneering, Mormonism, and were to be found in the ranks of the Mormons in Utah. Mormon churches and schools, though not, as far as is known, the practice of plural marriage, were to be found in more than one backwoods community in New Brunswick during the nineteenth century.

Along with the remarkably high birth rate, there existed, for the first fifty years at least, until the coming of the cholera, a phenomenally low death rate. In the first two or three years, the number of deaths may have been fairly large, because of the disorganization, of the diseases, especially measles and smallpox, brought from New York, of the dependence on the royal bounty of provisions, which was at times in short supply, often of doubtful quality, and never very sound dietetically. After that, except for deaths from drowning, which were all too frequent in a country where the rivers and lakes and bays were the principal means of communication, there were very few deaths in the Loyalist communities. The Society for the Propagation of the Gospel would receive reports from a missionary, in 1800, that he had, in five years, baptized 295 infants, married 48 couples, and buried 17 persons; for 1811 and 1812 that he had baptized 115 infants, married 40 couples, buried 8 persons.

That was the story among the sober, industrious, rural part of the population, but it was not the whole story. Sobriety and steady industry were not characteristic virtues of the entire population. The trade with the West Indies, which every writer on New Brunswick in its early days noted with pride, brought return cargoes of rum and molasses. Gin, it used to be said, was the shortest way out of Manchester: rum, for the discouraged, for the casuals, for the thriftless, was the shortest way out of New Brunswick, and particularly out of the slums of Saint John. The irregularity, the disagreeableness, the dangers, and sometimes the traditions of the types of employment open to labourers, seafaring, fishing, lumbering, shipbuilding, encouraged hard drinking. The resort to rum intensified the discomforts of working conditions and of living conditions and sank whole sections of the province's population into misery and degradation. Temperance societies were formed, and even religious bodies which had developed no particular conscience on the matter were forced to take a stand against the enemy which was threatening to ruin the province.

The wretched living conditions, in the rows of hovels which were built at the edges of the town plots, were both a cause and an effect of the rum drinking. Their inmates were a prey to the diseases which came along, the Asiatic cholera, which was a scourge to Atlantic seaports in the 1830's, the scarlet fever and diphtheria which swept through the province with an intensity and destructive force unrealized by later generations, the typhoid and typhus which were the result of the filth and squalor and lack of sanitation, the ever present smallpox, and the later menace of tuberculosis. Infantile mortality rates in the towns were much higher than in the country, and Saint John, like other cities of the era, had constantly to be renewed and strengthened by influx of the country born and country reared. As the nineteenth century wore on, the conditions which had operated for the first two generations ceased to stimulate the increase of population at as rapid a rate. In addition, changed conditions brought a higher death rate. The building of frame houses, heated by a stove, meant greater comfort, but it also meant greater susceptibility to disease. My grandmother's brothers died in infancy of black diphtheria; my father's brothers died in young manhood of tuberculosis. Again and again, in studying New Brunswick families, I have heard a similar report. Although the towns were beginning to learn something about sanitation, it was still expected, in the 1890's, that an attack of typhoid fever would be part of the course for pupil teachers attending the Provincial Normal School.

The large families of the Loyalists meant that the outward movement, which was noted in the last chapter, continued to exist. Although the land a Loyalist received could support a large family, it could not be expected to support several rapidly increasing families. There was a constant reaching out for more land, for more opportunities, as the children of ten years and upwards on the victualling lists, then those under ten, then the first New Brunswick born, then the children of the men who had married soon after arrival, reached their early maturity. Wherever the land was suitable, the gaps, caused by the disappearance of disbanded provincials and other newcomers who had no desire to settle or of those who preferred other areas, were soon filled in. The back country was then explored and the land along the smaller tributary streams. As often as not, the older sons pushed on to new farms within the province or outside it, and the old home ultimately descended to one of the younger members of the family. By the end of the eighteenth century, when the movement to Upper Canada was in full swing, many second generation Loyalists were looking out for places, and they went along to Upper Canada, sometimes as sons-in-law of families who were making the move. Throughout the first half of the nineteenth century, in spite of the difficulty of the long journey, New Brunswickers went to that "Canada West" which today is that essentially eastern part of Canada, Ontario north of Lake Erie.

Political differences and the violence of the fearful victors could not entirely wipe out ties of blood. Sisters wrote back and forth, whenever opportunity offered by a trading vessel, and a mother, "under a decai of old age", sent word of her longing to see again her first-born. A few old folk, leaving their families established in the new country, went back to end their days among the scenes of their childhood, or with members of their family who had not made the trek to New Brunswick. Others seized at the offers made by brothers and sisters to give their children the opportunities for schooling which were largely missing in the pioneer settlements, and the young people were sometimes absorbed into the older communities their fathers had left. Settlement was pushing west of the thirteen colonies, and in the newer frontier settlements old resentments were forgotten and New Brunswick pioneering experience was valuable. There had been an Indiana, an Illinois, a Michigan, a Wisconsin fever, James Finlay Weir Johnston reported in 1851, and there was then a California fever. A continuing core of the family may have remained in New Brunswick, and did, in most instances, but members of Loyalist families were to be found in every expansionist movement on the continent, from Maine to California. New Brunswick became, what it has ever since remained, a notable nursery of men and women. It is doubtful if any comparable area has so greatly contributed to the population of North America. At the same time, the province's own population has shown steady increase in every decade of its existence.

There arises the question which emerges in every discussion of migration in Canada, how far was this emigration a result of displacement by immigration? Were Loyalists displaced from New Brunswick by post-Loyalist immigration? Which suggestion in turn leads to the question, did the Loyalists displace the Pre-Loyalists. Did the Pre-Loyalists displace the Acadians? Did the Acadians displace the Indians? At this starting place, consideration of the problem can usefully begin. Under the Indian hunting and fishing economy, with a very trifling development of agriculture, the population of the area was about one to the square mile. When the French came, with their better weapons and tools, and their access to European markets, the whole economy of the region entered on a new phase, in which both Indians and French shared, and there was no question of displacement. There was room for both groups in this improved hunting, fishing, and agricultural economy.

The struggle for the mastery of the American continent, which was partly the rivalry of two political entities and partly the clash of two differing economies, resulted in partial displacement of the Acadians in the New Brunswick area by military force. The removal was intended to be total, but the Acadians' knowledge of the country, their skill in adapting themselves to life in the forest or along the more remote parts of the coast, their usefulness as dyke builders and as hewers of wood and drawers of water, enabled them to survive, even at the relative disadvantage in which supposed military necessity had placed them. At the suggestion of one of their number, those who remained in the St. John River area, after the Loyalists came, were given grants of land three hundred miles up the river, near the entrance of the Madawaska River, the principal thoroughfare to Quebec.

Thanks to their greater capital, their wider knowledge of crops and processes, their beginnings of industry, their nearer markets in Massachusetts and Philadelphia, the Pre-Loyalist settlements had been able to make some small progress in the ten years before the outbreak of the Revolutionary War stifled development. The descent of the Loyalists was almost as sudden as the appearance of an army, but except for the few instances which have been mentioned, it was much less arbitrary. Of the thirty-three families for whom Thomas Knox ordered a special donation because their land had been taken by Loyalists (William Graves, Nathan Bragdon, Charles Skinner, Jeremiah Tracy, John Morgan, Peter Connor, Stephen Young, Tamerlane Campbell, Andrew Harrington, James Browne, William and John Spragg or Sprague, Nathan Simons, Mrs. Robishaux, Ezekiel and Benning Foster, Mary Stimson, Robert Lasky, John Messenger, John Casey, Daniel Ralph or Rolf, Jeremiah Frost, Elijah and Ebenezer Estabrooks, Archelaus Hammond, Elias Clarke, George Morley, John Hendrick, Jabez Salisbury, Caleb Finny, Amy Armstrong, Widow Smith, Abner Brooks), two or three were displaced to the Annapolis, but, with one or two exceptions, the rest remained in New Brunswick and made as considerable and as valuable a contribution to the province as any twenty-five families one could name. In spite of the curious remark by Colonel Dundas, one of the Commissioners on Loyalists' Claims, that the old inhabitants were "a despicable race, ready to sell their improvements, as the Loyalists are enabled to purchase from them", the Pre-Loyalists were in fact taking part in a shrewd, sensible, and useful transaction. They could buy land elsewhere in the province for a trifling sum, and, with the additional funds at their disposal from the sale of their former holdings, they could in a short time be more comfortable than before. The prompt attention of the new provincial administration to grievances warded off further trouble between the new settlers and the old, and intermarriage between the two groups wiped out the feeling of separatism. Eugenically, the coming of the Loyalists was the salvation of the Pre-Loyalist communities, for the Burpees and the Stickneys, the Barkers and the Jewetts, on the St. John River, the Steeves and the Lutz families on the Petitcodiac, the Dixons and the Blacks on the Tantramar, were as much intermarried as was desirable, and new strains were needed. Economically, the Pre-Loyalists benefited by the increased local demand for their lumber, their crops, their cleared land, their house room, their skills, as well as for their daughters. In spite of the petition of Benjamin and Nicholas Weymouth of the River Kennebec claiming that they had had to move from lands in Sunbury County for the accommodation of Loyalists, there is no evidence to show that there was any considerable displacement of Pre-Loyalists by Loyalists, and there is every reason for thinking that the displacement was negligible.

As has been shown, the outward movement of Loyalists from New Brunswick began almost immediately after their arrival and continued throughout the eighteenth century. The arrival of a few families from Perthshire, about 1801, after the movement to Upper Canada had reached its peak, could hardly be considered as affecting that migration. Otherwise, New Brunswick had to wait until after the close of the Napoleonic Wars for any considerable immigration. From 1819 to 1826, the fragmentary figures available suggest that upwards of 12,000 immigrants arrived, the majority of them Irish or north Ireland Scots. Then, and in later decades, many arrived at New Brunswick ports but went on at once, or as soon as transportation was available, to the United States. The immigrants who remained in New Brunswick settled on land between the Loyalist communities, for instance, between Grand Lake and the Washademoak, or in the eastern and northern parts of the province, areas which had hardly been affected by the influx of Loyalists, or went to work in the Saint John shipyards. The decade of the 1820's was a transition period, when the process of handing on to the next generation was completed by the Loyalists of 1783. The few old men and old women, who remembered another, more civilized milieu, reminisced unheeded. The sons

229

of the Loyalists knew only the frontier life, two thirds lumbering, one third farming; their formal education had been neglected and they could barely read or write; the land they inherited was sufficiently cleared for the subsistence type of farming which was all they knew; it was no longer a brave new world, and apathy succeeded the determination of the previous generation. Until the setback of 1825, when there was a decline of fifty per cent in the value of New Brunswick ships, shipbuilding and lumbering were an outlet for the more ambitious Pre-Loyalist, Loyalist, and Post-Loyalist, and the two industries, after a brief respite, once more enjoyed a boom. The financial crisis of 1825, and the Miramichi fire of the same year, had more to do with any emigration of Loyalist families from the province than the moderate immigration from the British Isles in the post-Napoleonic period.

The next considerable immigration was in the 1840's, when the Irish famine resulted in the arrival of thousands of half-starved Irish, many of whom did not long survive the horrible conditions under which they had been shipped to the new world. As before, many went on to the United States. Although nearly 59,000 newcomers were reported as arriving from 1841 to 1850, the census of 1851 showed only 40,432 immigrants in the province, comprising 20.8% of the population. Of the immigrants, 71% were Irish. When Professor Johnston visited the province, in 1849, he found that the emigrants from the province could be divided into four groups:

1. Those engaged in lumbering who left because of the failure of trade in the previous two years.

2. Persons in debt.

3. Unskilful farmers who were overwhelmed by the partial failures of the corn and potato crops.

4. Those with friends and relatives in the Western states.

General economic conditions, and a continuation of the migratory movement of the past, were thus the explanation of the emigrations, and the emigrations would have occurred anyway, regardless of the influx of Irish immigrants. The 1850's and the 1860's were the great decades of the wooden ships, when Saint John became the fourth ship-owning port in the world, and her ships, her ship captains, her shipyards, and her fleets of ships became famous. On all the creeks and inlets of the Bay of Fundy, ships were being built, and the farmers grew prosperous in supplying the lumbermen and the shipbuilders with food and fuel.

The passing of the era of the wooden sailing vessel and the opening up of the great wheat lands of the western prairies set in motion a greater emigration from New Brunswick than had previously occurred; the Pacific Coast lumbering, and the industrial development, first of Massachusetts and adjoining states, then of central Canada, became the next lures which increased outward movement from New Brunswick. The wonder is that in spite of all these migratory movements there remained within the province a considerable core of Loyalist families, as well as of their predecessors and their immigrant successors. Although it is the impression of casual observers that the Loyalist families have largely vanished from the scene and that few of them are to be found in the province today, this study of the Loyalists has shown how many descendants of the newcomers of 1783 are still to be found in New Brunswick. In many cases, where the original family names are not to be found, descendants through daughters and grand-daughters are surprisingly numerous. The Loyalists, in fact, neither displaced nor were displaced. All groups in New Brunswick were equally affected by economic

231

conditions and by the general restlessness of the North American inhabitants.

Consideration of the movement of population has entailed mention of the principal means of livelihood, farming, lumbering, shipbuilding, and shipping. The West India trade, into which the Loyalists, particularly at St. Andrews, had entered eagerly, flourished until 1830, when the West India trade was thrown open to American vessels. Shortly afterwards, the enterprising merchants of St. Andrews projected a railroad to Quebec, but the final settlement of the boundary awarded much of the territory through which the railroad was to run to the United States. From the double blow, St. Andrews did not recover. St. Stephen captured the lumber business, and St. Andrews sank into a lethargy from which the tourist business of the twentieth century has hardly roused her.

The Napoleonic embargo, which prevented England's access to Baltic timber, gave the British North American colonies a market for their lumber, and an opportunity to build the large sailing vessels which were more economical for carrying bulky cargoes than the small and expensively built ships of English oak. It was unfortunate for later generations, in Saint John and in the province generally, that much of the wealth accumulated during the heyday of the wooden sailing vessel was swept away by the great fire of Saint John, in 1877. Although the city was rebuilt, the cost of replacement was a serious burden at a time when the end of the era of the wooden sailing vessel was at hand. When no alternative industry or chance of employment offered, a period of stagnation ensued. The half century from 1880 to 1930 was one of the most difficult the province experienced, especially as the depression came at a time when other parts of the continent were prospering; but in the next decade, the descendants of the Loyalists found that New Brunswick homesteads had advantages

232

over the bread lines of the idle cities and the dust-buried farms of the western prairies. In becoming a New Brunswicker, the Loyalist of 1783 had bequeathed to his children a goodly heritage, little chance of great wealth, to be sure, but unspectacular, moderate, and continuing prosperity, if they were willing to work.

And the mention of work brings up the other phase of the development of Loyalist into New Brunswicker which remains for consideration, for it was the work, the long, hard, unceasing toil necessary under pioneer conditions in the new province, which made it possible for the Governor and Council to extend and strengthen their control of affairs in New Brunswick. As the years passed, the "little court" of Fredericton became more and more divorced in outlook and educational background from the rest of the province. The ordinary county members elected to the Legislative Assembly were at a great disadvantage when they came to the sessions, and were easily overawed by the assurance and haughtiness of those who were familiar with the situation and with the procedure of the Assembly. The first reformer, James Glenie, like many of the early mill-owners, met with financial disaster and had to leave the province, and it was difficult to find leaders who would stand forth against the usurpation of power and privilege by the oligarchy. The Assembly took its cue from the Council and was haughty in repressing criticism. When George Handasyde, a New York Loyalist, in McPherson's Coffee House, on the evening of January 24, 1786, ventured to express his indignation at the action of the House of Assembly in voting that the Sheriff of Saint John, in giving seats to the candidates who received a minority of the votes cast, had "conducted himself legally, fairly, and with impartiality", the printer for the House of Assembly, Christopher Sower, reported his remarks to the Assembly. Handasyde was arrested and brought before the Assembly, whose pardon he was compelled to ask, on his knees, for his contempt and breach of privilege. After being reprimanded by the Speaker, and compelled to pay a fine, the prisoner was then discharged. Could there be any hope that such an Assembly would champion the rights of free speech, of fair trial, or the abolition of privilege?

Not content with their right to veto acts of the Assembly, the Council continued the practice, considered so important at the time of the first election, of having a few either of their own members or of the select circle sit in the Assembly. Acts of the Assembly had to receive the approval not only of the New Brunswick Council but also of His Majesty in Council, and this led to further measures of undemocratic purport. The election act passed by the first Assembly, giving the right to vote to freeholders whose land was worth £20, was, after a lapse of four years, disallowed by the authorities in England (who had doubtless received highly coloured reports of the first election), and a £25 qualification was requested. The Council was responsible only to the Governor, and he was responsible only to the King in Council. The salaries of Governor, Chief Justice, Attorney-General, Surveyor-General, Agent of the Province, Naval Officer, and certain contingencies, were voted by Parliament at Westminster for a few years, and the Governor had control of the casual and territorial revenue and of the customs. In addition to their salaries, the officials received fees for their services, and in some cases the fees amounted to more than the salaries. If the remarkably democratic and fair regulations for the distribution of lands, as drawn up in 1785, had quieted the dissatisfaction engendered by the delays of the Nova Scotia government in 1783 and 1784, and had made the people feel that their interests were being well looked after by the New Brunswick government, an awakening was due by 1819. A return of that year showed that the fees on a Crown grant of 300 acres or less amounted to £11. 13s. 4d., of which the Governor received £4. 1s. 8d., the Secretary, £3. 7s. 6d., the Attorney-General, £1. 10s. 10d., the Surveyor-General, £2, and the Auditor-General, 13s. 4d. Those fees, which enriched the officials, were a deterrent to poor settlers, who would have improved the land and become valuable inhabitants of the province, and an encouragement to land speculators.

By every possible means, the Council increased their solidarity and their continued participation in the positions of power and privilege. Intermarriage made the group more closely knit and concentrated the control within a narrow circle which became known as the Family Compact. Education and religion were both made tools of their dominance. Before the Loyalists left New York, a proposal had been made for establishment of a college in the province to which they were going, and in December, 1785, a petition was presented to Governor Carleton for his consideration, regarding "the necessity and expediency of an early attention to the establishment in this Infant Province of an Academy or school of liberal arts and sciences." A tract of about 6,000 acres adjoining Fredericton was accordingly set aside for the use of the school, and in 1800 a charter of incorporation was obtained. The college was hardly more than a collegiate school until 1829, when the college moved up the hill and the school took over the old premises near the church. Both school and college were considered the special preserve of the few families who controlled the Council, and their sons made life miserable for students from outside the circle. The college was criticized by Professor Johnston, in 1849, as sectarian and expensive. It was then providing a formal, classical education for only fifteen students, and its efforts served only to intensify the contrast between these fortunate few and the rest of the inhabitants, who were dependent on an occasional itinerant schoolmaster or on their own efforts for what little book learning they received.

Many Loyalists had found themselves in the position of Henry Nase, who had four fine boys, and "no other means of providing for them but learn them to work and make them farmers." Others, like Hezekiah Wyatt, formerly a sergeant in the King's American Regiment, bound their sons as apprentices and trusted to their getting some education under the terms of the apprenticeship, set forth in a quaintly worded document such as the one which, under date of March 6, 1787, bound William Wyatt to Abraham DePeyster for nine years, and stipulated that:

> he the said apprentice his said Master shall faithfully serve his secrets keep, his lawful commands everywhere gladly obey He shall do no Damage to his said Master; nor see it to be done by others, without letting or giving notice to his said Master, He shall not waste his Master's goods, nor lend them unlawfully to others, He shall not commit fornication nor contract Matrimony within the said term, at Cards Dice or any Unlawful game he shall not play whereby his said Master may be Damaged, with his own goods or the Goods of other during the said term, without Licence of his said Master, He shall not buy or sell; He shall not absent himself Day nor Night from his said Master's Service without his leave, nor haunt Ale House Taverns or Playhouses but in all things behave himself as a faithfull apprenticed Servant ought to do during the said term, and the said Master shall procure and provide for him the said apprentice sufficient meat, Drink, apparel, washing and Lodging, fitting for an apprentice Also to cause him to read Write and Cipher and at the expiration of said term give and provide him with a good suit of Cloaths, one pair of three Years Old Steers, and one Cow or Heffer three Years Old with Calf . . .

Regardless of the Maugerville Congregationalists, the Sackville Baptists, the Cumberland Methodists, the Petitcodiac Lutherans, the Highland Scottish Catholics and the Scottish Presbyterians on the North Shore, the Acadian Catholics, the Quakers and Anabaptists sent down to Beaver Harbour, the Church of Scotland adherents for whom Company No. 22 spoke, the Irish and Scottish Catholics in provincial regiments, the Governor and Council considered the Church of England as by law established, and refused recognition, pecuniary aid, or permission to perform marriages, to other denominations. It mattered not that church practices developed in the compact, long-settled villages and squirearchies of England, the morning and evening prayers, baptism of infants, churching of women, publication of banns, marriage by the ordained priest, burial in consecrated ground, ordination of "gentlemen" of university education, were well nigh impossible in pioneer New Brunswick. Any attempt to adapt the practices of the church to the democratic conditions of the settlements was frowned upon. When the church at Kingston made the pews free, the Bishop of Nova Scotia, in August, 1809, significantly enough after he had reached Fredericton, wrote that it gave him no small concern on his visit to Kingston to learn that the pews in the church of Kingston were all held in common, and that none were appropriated to individuals.

I never knew an instance before this, in Europe or America, where the pews were thus held in common, and where men—perhaps of the worst characters—might come and set themselves down by the most religious and respectable characters in the parish. This must ultimately tend to produce disorder and confusion in the church and check the spirit of true devotion and piety.

When a man has a pew of his own, he can leave his Bible and prayer books in that pew when public worship is ended on Sunday, and he will be sure to find them in his pew on the next Sabbath.

The infirmities of age and bad health require attention to the comfort of warmth, especially in the winter. A man may procure that comfort by lining his pew with some kind of cloth and covering the floor.

It is needless to say that the mode of holding the pews in common must necessarily preclude these with many other benefits and conveniences that might be named.

What could occasion such an innovation—such a departure from the usage of the Church of England I am unable to conceive; the greatest disorder must be the consequence, if this mode be continued, when the country becomes populous; in some places it would at this day be ruinous to the church.

It was no wonder that the Methodist circuit rider, the Baptist missionary, travelling through the woods on snowshoes, with their willingness to hold services at any time and in any place, with their simple, stern, and stirring messages, with their emphasis on the salvation of the individual, on his inner spiritual growth and his daily conduct, with their hope of a better world, gathered up large followings in the scattered settlements. The missionary of the Society for the Propagation of the Gospel might write hopefully of "preventing the people from being misled by the wild enthusiasm of strolling Teachers", but a journey of one hundred and forty miles through a thickly settled country where there was no clergyman of the established church showed how little headway the Church of England as by law established had made among the settlers of the province. It showed also how illusory had been the hope of the writer of the memorandum on the partition of Nova

Scotia that easing the requirements for ordination would result in rapid filling of the ranks of the Church of England clergy.

The continued dominance of a few was bringing about a situation which might have led to a second American Revolution. The similar oligarchic control in Upper Canada called forth the vigorous protests which resulted in the Rebellion of 1837. In New Brunswick there was no uprising, and responsible government was gradually and quietly brought into being. Three factors accounted for this orderly transition. In the first place, the power of the oligarchy was broken by the nemesis of their own situation. Being friends of the government and maintaining a position on the Council involved a standard of living and a type of expenditure for dress, for accommodation, for equipage, for education of the sons of the family, which made it absolutely necessary to have a position with a good salary or sufficient perquisites. Attending to the duties of the position, and keeping up the style of living required for the Government House set, made it impossible for the official to work himself on his "estate", (even if such homely occupation had not been *infra dig*), or to give adequate supervision to farm or mill or woodland or fishing right. Borrowing to develop any of these properties usually turned out to be as disastrous as borrowing for such expenditures on consumption as building a house, educating a son, marrying a daughter. Plagued by debts, tiding over one crisis after another, a man might get by as long as he lived and kept in the circle: his death upset the precarious equilibrium of centripetal forces, and collapse was then inevitable. Creditors swallowed up house and land and furnishings; friends had to intercede for a pension for widow and unmarried daughters and find places for sons not yet established, who must, of course, be placed so as to maintain that station in society to which they had been born. An inheritance of debts, a desire to keep up appearances, a scorn of work and of practical knowledge, were a poor start for the second generation. The Family Compact tended to disintegrate from within and to become a mere hollow semblance of what it had been.

Secondly, there was no uprising because, whatever an observer might say about the sons of the Loyalists forgetting the loyalty of their fathers, there existed in New Brunswick a deep and abiding loyalty to the British crown and the British government, and revolt against the King's representative in the province was unthinkable. In the earlier days of the province this loyalty took forms which no longer exist, virtual establishment of the Church of England, denial to Dissenting clergy of the right to perform marriage or to sit in the legislature, division of the province into parishes as units for local administration, recognition of the anniversaries of King Charles, Martyr, of the Restoration of King Charles II, of the coronation of George IV, of the Gunpowder Plot, and of such events in the church's calendar as St. Patrick's Day, Whit Monday, Whit Tuesday, St. John the Baptist's Day, Michaelmas, and St. Andrew's Day, as public holidays. These manifestations of loyalty, most of them unsuited to the province's development, have vanished (as indeed most of them have gone in Britain), but the sense of loyalty has remained. In spite of the nearness of the American neighbour, in spite of the obvious material advantages of becoming a part of the United States, in spite of the existence of an occasional annexationist, New Brunswickers have maintained their attachment to the crown of Great Britain and their conviction that their place is and will continue to be, with the rest of the Canadian provinces, within the framework of the British Commonwealth.

The third factor was also one of the intangibles which exist and influence the course of a people's development more strongly than such obvious factors as climate, soil, or natural resources. The belief in constitutional procedure for redress of grievances, like the loyalty to the British crown one of the fundamental tenets of the Loyalists, meant patience and a conviction of the ultimate triumph of justice. It meant respect for law and order and for orderly procedure. It meant unwillingness to resort to violence, and willingness to wait for years rather than to jeopardize ultimate victory by depending on summary methods. It has been part of the invisible barrier which separates all of Canada, and particularly New Brunswick, from the neighbour to the south. It is the basis for the respect and the high place which Canada has achieved among the nations of the world. As the Loyalist developed into New Brunswicker, this was the most valuable contribution he made to the new province and to the nation of which it ultimately became a part. This abides.

NOTES

Since a complete *apparatus criticus* would be two or three times the length of each chapter, the notes are confined to brief mention of sources quoted or used.

CHAPTER I.

[1] John C. Miller, *Origins of the American Revolution*, (Boston, 1943), *passim*.
[2] John C. Crane, *Colonel Thomas Gilbert, the Leader of New England Tories*, (Worcester, 1893).
[3] George Atkinson Ward, *The Journal and Letters of Samuel Curwen . . .*, (4th ed., 1864). Dr. D. C. Harvey of the Provincial Archives of Nova Scotia checked the Halifax residents.
[4] Carleton Papers, (hereafter CP), *passim*. *Collections of the New Brunswick Historical Society* (hereafter NBHS), 1904, v, 220-1. Public Records office, London, War Office papers (hereafter WO), 1/13, f. 41.
[5] CP 9941, 8252, 8255.
[6] Lorenzo Sabine, *Biographical Sketches of Loyalists of the American Revolution*, (Boston, 1864), i, 339.
[7] Force's *American Archives*, Series IV, iii, 1247. New York Historical Society, 1883, p. 252.
[8] Clinton Papers.
[9] *Winslow Papers, passim*.
[10] Clinton Papers.
[11] Colonial Office papers (hereafter CO), 5/175, ff. 451, 453.
[12] CP 4443 and *passim*.
[13] Clinton Papers, *passim*. Ontario Land Papers, under Vernon.
[14] Harris, *History of Long Island*.
[15] Beamish Murdoch, *A History of Nova Scotia, or Acadie*, (1867).
[16] CP 5577.
[17] CP 4191, 4741.
[18] CP 10307, 5267.

CHAPTER II.

[1] CP 5328.
[2] CP 4693.
[3] CP 5447.
[4] CP 5649, 5760. W. O. Raymond, *The River St. John*, (Saint John, 1910), p. 507.
[5] CP 6641.
[6] CP 5662.
[7] CP 5828.
[8] J. B. Brebner, *The Neutral Yankees of Nova Scotia*, (New York, 1937), p. 352.
[9] CP 6110, 6176, 6468.
[10] Murdoch, *op. cit.*, iii, 13.
[11] CP 6291.
[12] *Winslow Papers*, 87-9.
[13] CP 7127.
[14] CP 7141.
[15] CP 7139.

CHAPTER III.

[1] WO 60/16.
[2] CP 7192.
[3] CP 6458.
[4] WO 60/25.

5 W. O. Raymond, ed., *Kingston and the Loyalists of* 1783, (Saint John, 1889).
6 WO 60/27, AD 36/various.
7 CP, *passim.*
8 CP 7272.
9 WO 60/27 and 29.
10 CP 7400.
11 CP 7427.
12 WO 60/27, CP 9728.
13 CP 7558.
14 CP 7557.
15 CP 7557.
16 CP 7623.
17 CP 7796.
18 Women's Canadian Historical Society of Toronto, 1912.
19 Raymond, *The St. John River*, p. 502, CO 5/110.
20 CO 5/161.
21 CP 8938.
22 CP 8755.
23 CP 8740.
24 CP 8754.
25 WO 60/29.
26 *Winslow Papers*, 124.
27 CP 8779.
28 CP 8783.
29 CO 5/111, f. 149.
30 CP 9305.
31 *Winslow Papers*, 152.

CHAPTER IV.

1 WO 60/25 to 30, AD 49/9, AD 36/9430, 10381, &c., Carleton Papers, Volume on St. John River in Public Archives of Nova Scotia, Raymond, *op. cit., Winslow Papers*, J. W. Lawrence, *Foot-Prints*, (Saint John, 1883) were the principal sources used for working out the story of the arrival of the Loyalists.

Return of the Number of Loyalists gone to St. John's River in Nova Scotia as per returns left in the Commissary-General's.

	Men	Women	Children over 10	under 10	Servants	Total
Amount of an Alphabetical List	790	433	536	464	211	2434
of a List which begins with Joseph Cooper.	489	341	364	398	311	1903
of Captain Dickenson's Co.	25	10	25	13	2	75
of Captain Barret's Co.	31	12	21	16	2	82
Quaker Company	40	14	9	20	19	102
Anabaptist Company	20	11	10	6	—	47
of Captain Huggeford's Co. (No. 14?)	28	18	17	26	16	105
Numbered Companies.						
1. Sylvanus Whitney Samuel Miles Jonathan Knapp	42	27	39	48	12	168
2. Joseph Goreham Solomon Ferris Joseph Dickson	31	20	40	38	7	136

3.	Henry Thomas James Etridge John Burnet	32	26	19	33	12	122
4.	John Forrester James Oliver Benjamin Stanton	51	30	46	27	31	185
5.	Richard Hill James Hughston Thomas Griggs	68	37	39	38	38	221
6.	Thomas Elms Thomas Smith John Kirk	30	19	14	13	45	121
7.	Peter Huggeford Timothy Whetmore Thomas W. Stanton	34	25	59	16	18	151
8.	John Cock James Reed Anthony Reece	32	21	19	29	10	111
9.	Joseph Clark John Cochrane Frederick Dibble	36	25	22	26	52	161
10.	James Hoyt Nathaniel Dickinson Nathaniel Hubbert	42	31	22	39	85	219
11.	Thomas Welch Henry Straeder Alexander McKee	62	27	55	34	20	198
12.	Oliver Bourdett George Younghusband Charles Cook	55	36	18	29	42	180
13.	(Asher?) Dunham Samuel Haines Smith James Leonard	31	19	39	18	5	112
14.	Thomas Huggeford Thomas Davenport Henry Fowler						
5.	(William) Wright John Flewelling Enoch Supplee	45	21	25	19	11	121
16.	John Mersereau Stephen Bedle Uzall Ward	34	15	28	23	9	109
17.	(Donald) Drummond Edward Batie Thomas Yearly	25	20	16	7	22	90
18.	Abiathar Camp Abiathar Camp Jr. John Camp	52	36	39	28	48	203
19.	(William) Perine Joseph Shotwell Matthew Perrine	41	25	17	19	21	123
20.	Christopher Benson, Sr. Christopher Benson, Jr. William Benson	5	5	4	1	3	18

21. Peter Berton Nathan Underhill Joshua Gidney	31	20	25	26	30	132
22. (Nathaniel) Horton William Loraine James Bell	45	23	18	22	57	165
23. James Forrester David Elmston George Livingstone	35	25	22	25	15	122
24. John Minzies Philip Phoenix John Harrison						
25. Edward Pryor John Houseman Thomas Goudge						
26. Robert Chillas (No. 28?) John Burgess John Jenkins						
27. Jacob Cooke Peter Paterson Wm. Beers						
28. Joseph Cooper James Berry Joseph Beck						
29. John O'Blenus William Secord John Crab						
30. William Olive William Young Robert Peel						
31. Peter Grimm Frederick Wiser Jacob Ieroleman						
32. Richard Squires Joseph Cavely (?) Latting Carpenter						
33. Daniel Fowler Zachariah Sickles Robert Cunard						
34. William Gray Isaac Hatfield Daniel Ward						
35. Richard Walker Robert Hicks Thomas Mallard						
36. James Spence James Thorne John Lumsden						
37. Abel Hardenbrook William L. Roome Henry Roome	58	29	22	25	13	147
38. Robert Camble Alexander Milne Alexander Gardiner	69	35	46	25	15	190

39.	John Cluett Richard McMichael Jonathan Burnham	59	41	43	41	37	221
40.	John Smith Thomas T. Smith Albert Van Nostrandt	73	41	63	63		240
41.	(James?) Dickinson Samuel Peers Samuel Searles	46	25	38	33	5	147
42.	(Thomas?) Merrit Willet Carpenter Henry Fowler	23	13	11	16	2	65
43.	John Ford Oliver Taylor Stephen Hunt	44	22	16	20	4	106
44.	Joseph Thorne Edward McIlroy William Thorne	42	22	28	34	8	134
45.	(Samuel?) Dickinson John Youmans John Wishburne	11	5	1	14	7	38
46.	Thomas Spragg John Underhill Weeden Fowler	32	20	10	10	4	76
47.	Thomas Woolley Daniel Nostrandt Edward Sands	69	43	73	18		203
48.	Thomas Fairchild Seth Fairchild Nathan Whitney	13	5	16	2		36
49.	Joseph Ferris Joshua Curry Abijah Barker	36	18	21	18	1	94
50.	William Lewis Richard Bonsall Francis King	15	7	10	9	10	91
51.	Bartholomew Crannell John Smith Isaiah Smith	84	65	73	54	24	300
52.	John Whitmore John Van Winckle Richard Carman	53	29	40	42	14	178

2 Peter Fisher, *History of New Brunswick*, (Reprint, Saint John, 1921), 126-33.

CHAPTER V.

Based on WO 60/25-30, CO 217/41, 42, CO 5/111, Fisher, *op. cit.*, 129-30.

PROVISION MUSTERS
September, 1783, Fort Howe, 1783-4, Knox, 1784.

	Men	Women	Children over 10	Children under 10	Servants	Total
American Legion	72	20	14	14	20	140
	60	18	9	12	13	112
	57	19	8	13	11	108

247

1 DeLancey's	140	33	27	28	38	266
	127	32	26	21	37	243
	108	32	19	20	15	194
2 DeLancey's	184	42	44	38	26	334
	121	34	29	11	20	215
	107	32	15	29	15	198
Fencible Americans	—					
	116	33	20	51	19	239
	45	14	17	27	0	103
Garrison Battalion	12	3				15
	—					
Guides & Pioneers	100	32	16	40	15	203
	106	29	25	23	21	204
	93	31	21	25	6	176
King's American Dragoons	267	45	52		40	404
(July, 1783)	194	43	24	23	32	316
	143	39	19	24	6	176
King's American Regiment	148	35	50	30	16	279
	153	47	79	22	44	345
	144	35	68	28	18	293
King's Orange Rangers	—					
	93	20	2	17		132
	59	14		12		85
Loyal American Regiment	117	39	42	47	18	263
	108	46	49	40	46	289
	95	39	45	32	8	219
Maryland Loyalists	84	12		12	14	122
	47	6	2	1	16	72
	43	3	1	2	3	52
1 New Jersey Volunteers	153	67	48	50	12	330
	171	61	63	41	35	371
	158	57	57	39	9	320
2 New Jersey Volunteers	134	46	38	29	25	272
	135	49	55	23	36	298
	132	45	44	38	14	273
3 New Jersey Volunteers	229	94	70	64	33	490
	101	32	34	16	6	189
	173	64	47	42	6	332
New York Volunteers	89	30	38	12	17	186
(& South Carolina Roy.)	110	30	34	11	32	217
	73	18	21	10	12	134
North Carolina Volunteers	25					25
	—					
	17	3			5	25
Pennsylvania Loyalists	51	12		11	6	80
	38	13		9	13	73
	36	14		8	5	63

Prince of Wales Amer. Regiment	173	68	37		28	330
	157	65	54	23	56	355
	152	39	22	15	33	261
Queen's Rangers	244	63	17	38	37	399
	222	66	21	41	47	397
	210	64	22	42	23	361
South Carolina Royalists (with N.Y.V.)	6					6
	19	16	9	13	3	60
Loyal New Englanders, (Knox only)	5	4	8	1		18
British Regiments (Knox only)	199	48	17	43		307
Black Companies (Knox only)	89	58	9	26		182
Loyal Refugees (Knox only)	1966	1028	1159	949	248	5350
	4131	1719	1630	1438	441	9359
Provincials, Ft. Howe	2059	624	526	385	473	4067
Provincials, Knox	1847	575	436	418	187	3463

General Return of all the disbanded Troops and Loyalists setling in New Brunswick, who are now receiving the Royal Bounty of Provisions. November 25, 1785.

	Men	Women	Children	Total
Passamaquoddy	819	363	395	363	1940
Musquash Cove	31	11	11	8	61
Manawagonish	25	16	13	7	61
From Red Head to Quaco	61	32	29	32	154
Hazen's Marsh	11	6	10	7	34
City of Saint John	867	484	302	357	2010
From the Falls to the Boars Head	89	42	41	33	205
Back Lotts on the Grand Bay	7	3	3	4	17
Kennebeckasis	365	193	265	197	1020
From Boar's Head to Mckeans at Head of Long Reach	308	178	197	166	849
Belleisle Bay	58	27	35	27	147
From McKeans to Maugerville	101	64	80	67	312
Spry's Grant	51	21	37	16	125
Township of Gage	97	70	86	84	337
Washademoack	47	30	30	24	131
Grand Lake	53	31	32	35	151
Long Island	24	18	21	15	78
Musquash Islands	29	21	23	20	93
Maugerville	243	117	103	120	583
Burton	122	69	100	79	370
Oromocto and its Brook	17	11	15	11	54
From the upper Boundary of Maugerville to the Nashawack	24	14	11	11	60
From the Oromocto to Mill Creek	44	21	31	19	115
Nashawack	157	47	31	40	275
From Nashawack to Madamkeswick	58	29	13	14	114
From Mill to Phillis's Creek	315	127	122	105	659

New York Volunteers &s on Maryland

Block No. 1	33	17	17	11	78
Prince William	60	20	7	17	104
Block No. 2 (NJV)	122	50	55	34	261
Block No. 3 (GP)	53	26	16	25	120
Block No. 4 (KAR)	31	13	11	9	64
Block No. 5 (QR)	33	11	4	8	56
Block No. 6 (DeL)	25	11	9	10	55
Additions	46	28	29	28	131

10,824

CHAPTER VI.

Based on a study of grants, township records, wills, family histories, official correspondence, records of deeds, memorials. In E. C. Wright, *The Miramichi*, (Sackville, 1944), *The Petitcodiac*, (Sackville, 1945), *The Saint John River*, (Toronto, 1949), and "Cumberland Township: a focal point of early settlement on the Bay of Fundy", *The Canadian Historical Review*, March, 1946, xvii, 27-32, further details of Pre-Loyalist settlements are given.

CHAPTER VII.

[1] Marion Gilroy, "The Partition of Nova Scotia," *The Canadian Historical Review*, December, 1933, xiv, 375-91.
[2] *Winslow Papers*, 99-100.
[3] *ibid.*, 105-6.
[4] CO 217/56.
[5] *WP*, 118-9.
[6] CO 217/56, *WP*, 121, 127, 128.
[7] CP 9283.
[8] *WP*, 139, 158.
[9] CO, 217/59, f. 9.
[10] CO 217/56, f. 449.
[11] *WP*, 163.
[12] CO 217/56, f. 393.
[13] CO 217/56, f. 408.
[14] *Dictionary of National Biography*, Knox, William.
[15] *Winslow Papers*, 163-178.
[16] CO 217/56, f. 502.
[17] CO 5/111. CO 217/56, *passim*.
[18] CO 217/59, Aug. 13, 1784.
[19] *Winslow Papers*, 205-7.
[20] *ibid.*, 217.
[21] *ibid.*, 176-8, 219-220.
[22] NBHS, 1905, vi, 391-408.
[23] *Winslow Papers*, 194.
[24] Lawrence, *op. cit.*
[25] James Hannay, *History of New Brunswick*.

CHAPTER VIII.

The analysis of the Loyalists is based on the list of New Brunswick Loyalists and on researches into their origins, on the Register of Freemen of Saint John, on Loyalist Claims in the Public Records Office, AO 13.

CHAPTER IX.

1 This chapter is based on a study of the grants of Nova Scotia and New Brunswick, memorials, &c.

2 CO 217/56, f. 404.

3 CO 217.

Names, and former places of Residence of those Gentlemen, who by the unhappy termination of the War, are obliged to leave their Homes and seek an Assylum in His Majesty's Province of Nova Scotia, to obtain which, they by Letter of the 22d July 1783 Address'd His Excellency Sir Guy Carleton KB General and Commander-in-Chief &c. &c. Requesting a Recommendation to His Excellency the Governor of Nova Scotia, for a Grant of Lands in that Province.

Names	*City, Town or County*	*Colony or Province*
Abijah Willard	Worcester	Massachusetts Bay
The Revd. John Sayre	Fairfield	Connecticut
Anthony Stewart	Annapolis	Maryland
Nathaniel Chandler	Worcester	Massachusetts Bay
John Potts	Potts-Grove	Pensylvenia
Rufus Chandler	Worcester	Massachusetts Bay
Christopher Billopp	Richmond	New York
Abel Willard	Worcester	Massachusetts Bay
William Wanton	New Port	Rhode Island
Benjamin Seaman	Richmond	New York
Richard Seaman	Ditto	New York
The Revd. Charles Inglis, D.D.	New York	New York
Nathaniel Coffin	Boston	Massachusetts Bay
James Anderson	Ditto	Massachusetts Bay
Walter Chaloner	New Port	Rhode Island
Abiathar Camp	New Haven	Connecticut
Bartholomew Crannell	Dutchess	New York
James Clarke	New Port	Rhode Idland
Joseph Taylor	Boston	Massachusetts Bay
Stephen Skinner	Middlesex	New Jersey
Thomas Knox	New York	New York
William Taylor	Boston	Massachusetts Bay
James Peters	Orange	New York
Samuel Donaldson	Suffolk Town	Virginia
Thomas Blane	Westmorland	Virginia
The Revd. Henry Addison	Prince George	Maryland
Joseph Taylor	Trenton	New Jersey
John Le Chevalier Roome	New York	New York
The Revd. George Panton	Trenton	New Jersey
Hugh Henderson	Portsmouth	New Hampshire
Samuel Goldsbury	Suffolk	Massachusetts Bay
Aaron Cortelyou	Richmond	New York
John Smyth	Middlesex	New Jersey
William Taylor	Monmouth	New Jersey
Ward Chipman	Boston	Massachusetts Bay
Isaac Wilkins	West Chester	New York
Philip John Livingston	Dutchess	New York
The Revd. John Bowden	New York	New York
The Revd. James Sayre	Dutchess	New York
James Fairlie	Chesterfield	Virginia
Edward Golston Lutwyche	Portsmouth	New Hampshire

Isaac Longworth	Essex	New Jersey
Benjamin Davis	Boston	Massachusetts Bay
William Campbell	Worcester	Massachusetts Bay
Thomas Horsfield	Kings	New York
Colin Campbell	Burlington	New Jersey
Colburn Barrell	Boston	Massachusetts Bay
Harry Peters	New York	New York
John Mawdsley	New Port	Rhode Island
Thomas Bannister	Ditto	Rhode Island
John Moore	New York	New York
John Watson	New Port	Rhode Island
David Seabury	New York	New York
George Taylor	Monmouth	New Jersey
Andrew Bell	Somerset	New Jersey

Of these fifty-five gentlemen, the number from

New York	was	17,	of whom 11 or 12 can be traced in New Brunswick.
Massachusetts		13,	4 or 5
New Jersey		9,	2 or 4
Rhode Island		6,	4 or 5
Virginia		3,	0
Connecticut		2,	2
New Hampshire		2,	0
Maryland		2,	0
Pennsylvania		1,	0
		55	23 or 28

Analysis of the list shows that about half the number were in New Brunswick for longer or shorter periods, and about one quarter were permanently identified with the province (Abijah Willard, Rev. John Sayre, Christopher Billopp, William Wanton, Walter Chaloner, Abiathar Camp, Bartholomew Crannell, James Clarke, James Peters, William Campbell, Thomas Horsfield, Colin Campbell). It is interesting to note that the list is heavily weighted in behalf of Massachusetts and Virginia, and that the New Brunswick contingent included all the Connecticut members, a larger proportion of the New York, New Jersey, Rhode Island members, and a smaller share of the Massachusetts petitioners.

CHAPTER X.

All sources previously mentioned were used in compiling this chapter.

CHAPTER XI.

[1] *Loyalist Narratives from Upper Canada*, Champlain Society, 1946, "Historical Memoranda" by Mrs. Amelia Harris, p. 109.

APPENDIX

KEY TO LIST OF NEW BRUNSWICK LOYALISTS

Although every care has been taken to make this list as accurate and as complete as possible, errors will doubtless be found. The vagaries of eighteenth century spelling (a few of which have been indicated) and the diversity of sources used heightened the difficulties of coping with several thousand names. The Mc, Mac problem was especially serious, and the 80 Smiths. The abbreviations are:

a.b., Armed Boatmen.
absc., absconding debtor.
A.Co., Albert Co., N.B.
A.Co., Albany Co., N.Y.
B.Co., Bergen Co., N.J., Bucks Co., Pennsylvania.
BCV, Bucks Co. Volunteers.
Bel., Belleisle, Kings Co., N.B.
BH, Beaver Harbour, Charlotte Co., N.B.
BL, British Legion (Tarleton's).
BMG, Barrackmaster-General's Department.
Carl., Carleton Co., N.B.
carp., carpenter. carpenter, 85, admitted as freeman of Saint John, 1785.
Chap., Chaplain.
Char., Charlotte Co., N.B.
CMG, Commissary-General's Department.
Cmpb, Campobello Island.
Cn., Carleton (West Saint John).
C17, Lot No. 17 in Carleton.
Cpl., Corporal.
Ct., Connecticut.
Ctld., Courtlandt Manor, N.Y.
Cumb., Cumberland, N.S., part of which became Westmorland Co., N.B.
d., died.
dr., drowned.
D.Co., Dutchess Co., N.Y.
DeL., DeLancey's Brigade.
Dig., Digdeguash, Charlotte Co., N.B.
Dip. Har., Dipper Harbour, Charlotte Co., N.B.
Dorch., Dorchester, Westmorland Co., N.B.
Em. Ch., Emerick's Chasseurs.
Eng., England.
Engr., Engineering Department.
Fr. Lake, French Lake, Sunbury Co., N.B.
F'ton, Fredericton, N.B.
GB, Great Britain.

Ger., Germany.
Gn., Gagetown, N.B.
GP, Guides and Pioneers.
Gr., Grand (Lake, Bay, Manan, &c.)
Ham.R., Hammond River, Kings Co., N.B.
Hfx, Halifax, Nova Scotia.
Ir., Ireland.
KAD, King's American Dragoons.
KAR, King's American Regiment.
K.Co., Kings Co., N.B.
Ken., Kennebecasis, N.B.
Kes., Keswick, York Co., N.B.
Kn., Kingston, Kings Co., N.B.
KOR, King's Orange Regiment.
Kt.Co., Kent Co., N.B.
LAL, Loyal American Legion.
Lanc., Lancaster, N.B.
LAR, Loyal American Regiment.
LC, Lower Canada (Quebec).
L.I., Long Island, N.Y.
LNE, Loyal New Englanders.
LR, Long Reach, Kings Co., N.B.
Lt., Lieutenant.
Maj., Major
Maquapit, Maquapit Lake, Queens-Sunbury Co., N.B.
Mass., Massachusetts.
Maug., Maugerville, Sunbury Co., N.B.
Md., Maryland.
Me., Maine.
Mir., Miramichi, Northumberland Co., N.B.
ML, Maryland Loyalists.
Mspc., Mispec, St. John Co., N.B.
Msx.Co., Middlesex Co., N.J.
Musq., Musquash, St. John Co., N.B.
Musq. Is., Musquash Island, Queens Co., N.B.
Nash., Nashwaak, York Co., N.B.
Ner., Nerepis, Kings Co., N.B.
N.J., New Jersey.
NJV, New Jersey Volunteers.
N.S., Nova Scotia.

N.Y., New York.
O.Co., Orange Co., N.Y.
Or., Oromocto, Sunbury Co., N.B.
Ord., Ordnance Department.
P17, Lot No. 17, Parrtown (Saint John).
Pa., Pennsylvania.
Pass., Passamaquoddy Bay, Charlotte Co., N.B.
PEI, Prince Edward Island.
Pen., Penobscot, Maine.
pens., pension.
Pet., Petitcodiac River, N.B.
Phila., Philadelphia, Pa.
PL, Pennsylvania Loyalists.
Pr.Wm., Prince William, York Co., N.B.
PWAR, Prince of Wales' American Regiment.
Q.Co., Queens Co., N.B.
Qnsby, Queensbury, York Co., N.B.
QR, Queens Rangers.
re-enl., re-enlisted.
RFA, Royal Fencible Americans.
RGA, Royal Garrison Artillery.
SC, South Carolina.
Sch., Schoodic (St. Stephen), Charlotte Co., N.B.

SCL, South Carolina Loyalists (SCR, Royalists).
S.Co., Sunbury Co., N.B.
Scot., Scotland.
Shef., Sheffield, Sunbury Co., N.B.
Shel., Shelburne, N.S.
St.A., St. Andrews, Charlotte Co., N.B.
St.Geo., St. George, Charlotte Co., N.B.
St. Is., Staten Island, New York.
St.J., Saint John, N.B.
svd., served, in some capacity.
Sx., Sussex, Kings Co., N.B.
UC, Upper Canada (Ontario).
USA, United States of America.
Va., Virginia.
Wash., Washademoak, Queens Co., N.B.
W.Co., Westchester Co., N.Y.
Wdstk., Woodstock, Carleton Co., N.B.
Wstm., Westmorland Co., N.B.
WJV, West Jersey Volunteers (afterwards united with NJV).
WV, Westchester Volunteers.
Wls., Wales.
Y.Co., York Co., N.B.

The list shows, where information could be obtained, the names of heads of families or single men of eighteen years of age and upwards, their former homes, their service during the Revolution, their first grants, their subsequent grants and/or place of residence.

Abbott, Joseph, *see* Ebbett.						
Abell, John	N.J.	3 NJV		Kings County		
Abernethy, William		42nd	Nash.	York County		
Abram, James		40th	St. John Co.	re-enl.		
Acheson, James		RFA	Maq. 84			
Achison, *see* Atchison						
Acker, George		NYV				
Jacob	3 NJV		York Co.			
Ackerley, *see* Akerley						
Ackerman, Abraham	N.J.	LAR		Carleton Co.		
Cornelius	N.J.	3 NJV	Fredericton	Carleton Co.		
James	N.J.	3 NJV	Fredericton			
Peter	N.J.	?				
Ackerson, Cornelius			York Co.	Kings Co.		
Garret	N.Y. Or. Co.		Maug.			
Jacob	N.Y. Or. Co.	KOR				
Thomas	?	KOR				
Acle (Ackel), James	N.Y. W. Co.	WL	St. John Co.			
Ac(y)rig, Rachel	N.J.?		P1137		to N.J.	son/rem.
m. Garret Jacobus						
Adair, Robert (carpenter)	Pa.?		P1350	York Co.		
Adams, Cornelius				York Co.		
Isaac		Cpl. PWAR		York Co.		
Jabez	Ct.	PWAR				
James	Ct.	2 NJV	C159,170	Kings Co.		UC?
Jane or Jean			St. A. 84			age 10.
John (1)	N.J.	CMG?	P703	Sunbury Co.		
John (2)	Ct.?	Sgt. KAR	Nash.	Carleton Co.		
John (3)	N.Y. A. Co.	2 NJV	Bl.2	Kn.?		
John (4)		PWAR	Nash.			
Jonathan (1)	?		Sunbury Co.			
son of John (1)						
Jonathan (2)	Ct.?	PWAR	Kings Co.			
Nathaniel, blacksmith	N.Y. W. Co.	WL?	Kings Co.			
Stephen		KAD				
William, mariner	N.Y.	BMG	Ken.	St. John		d. '92
Agnew, John	Scot./Va.	Chap. QR	Nash.			
Stair	Va.	Capt. QR	Nash.			
Aiking, Moses			Maug.			
Akehorn, Jacob			St. A.			
Akerley, Benjamin		LAR	York Co.			
David	N.Y. W. Co.		Albert Co.			
James, carpenter	N.Y.		Wash.			
Moses			Queens Co.			
Obadiah	N.Y. Ctld.	WL	Cumb. Co.	Hampstead		
Oliver	N.Y. Ctld.	WL		Hampstead		
Albright, John	N.J.	2 NJV	P381	Grand Lake		
Alcorn, James	Pa.	PL	Bl.7			
Alder, Robert, cooper, 90			St. George			
Alderade, Wm.			Dig. 84			
Aldington, John	b. Eng./N.J.	Maj. GP		England		
Alexander, Gershom			York Co.			
Hugh		3 NJV				
Sarah			Charlotte Co.			
Algee, Algie, *or* Elgee,						
Alexander	Scot./N.Y.		P914	Queens Co.		
David				Queens Co.		
James			P919	Kings Co.?		
John, weaver, 85		CGP	P901	Queens Co.		
Allaby (Aliby), Isaac	N.J.	2 NJV	Bl. 2	Ken.		
Allaire, Anthony, New Rochelle	N.Y.	Lt. LAR	Fredericton			
Alld, William, millwright			Nash.			
Allan, Adam	Scot.	Lt. QR	Pr. Wm.			
Anthony			P1192			
Allen, Aaron			Gn.	Grand Lake		
Alexander			Mir.			
Benjamin	Scot.		P377	Msp.		Baie Verte
Daniel		1 NJV				
David		GPdr.	Bl. 3			

Name	Origin	Unit	Col. A	Col. B	Col. C
Allen, Isaac, lawyer	N.J.	Lt.Col. 2 NJV	P 56, 57	York Co.	
James	Pa.?	Sgt. LAR	Grand Lake Burton	Kings Co.	
John, Hackensack	N.J.			York Co.	
Jonah		3 NJV	Pr. Wm.		
Jonathan	Pa.?	1 NJV	York Co.		
Lawrence		3 NJV	Maq.		
Peter		3 NJV	Bl. 3		
Samuel		Cpl. KAD	Woodstock		
Thomas, son of John		3 NJV	Y.Co.	St. John Co.?	
William (Van)	Pa.	Lt.Col. PL	P13	England	
William			Campobello		
Allicock, Charles		Lt. SCL	St. John		
Allison, Edward, widow Sarah	N.Y. Q. Co.	Capt. 2 DeL.	Bl.9	d.	
Allison, Wm. *see* Ellison					
Alloway, John		KAD	York Co.		
Allward, *see* Alward					
Alsop, John		BMG	Ken.		
Alstine, Alston David, carp.		3 NJV	P1007	Wash.	St. John
Joseph			P781	Kings Co.	
Alstine, Alston Lewis			P320	Kings Co.	
see also Elston.					
Althouse, John	Ger.	Capt. NYV	York Co.		
John Jr.	Scot.	Lt. NYV	P1288	to U.S.A.	
Alward, *or* Allward, Asher	N.J.		Maug.	Queens Co.	
Benjamin, carpenter	N.J.	St. Is.			
Benjamin, Jr. carp.			Wash.	New Canaan	
Daniel				U.C.	
John	N.J.	St. Is.	Ken.	Wash.	
Alwood, Joseph	N.J. Mx. Co.		P343	St. John	
Alward, Joseph, carpenter	N.J.		P187,1408	Kings Co.	
Oswald	N.J.		P300	New Canaan	
Silas, farmer	N.J.		P573		
Alyea, Peter		KOR	St. J. Co.		
Ambrose, Margaret	S.C.		C355		
Michael	Ir./S.C.	Lt. PWAR	C332	St. John Co.	
Amor, *see* Aymer					
Anderson, Archibald			Shel.	Mir.	
Benjamin	Ct.	2 DeL.	P74		
Cornelius	Scot.	2 NJV	Bl. 2	UC	
David			F'ton		
George (1)	Pa.		B.H.	Dip. Har.	
George (2)	S.C.		Bel.		
Henry	Mass.?	Engr.	P1351	Ken.	
James (1)		CMG?	C245	Cn.	
James (2)		74th.	Char. Co.		
Jeremiah	N.Y. W. Co.		Gn.		
John (1)		Cpl. PWAR	St. John Co.		
John (2)		PL	Bl. 7		
John (3)		NYV	Kes.		
John (4)		83d.	Mir.		
Joseph	N.Y.	LAR	P1027	Sussex	
Peter, baker, 85	N.J.?	5 NJV	P973	St. John	F'ton
Reuben			BH		
Simon				Queens Co.	
William (1)	Pa.?	KAR	York Co.	Carleton Co.	
William (2)	N.Y.	WL	Shel.	St. John Co.	
Andrew(s), Benjamin	N.Y.		BH	Kings Co.	UC
George			P128	Halifax	
Israel	R.I.		C26	Charlotte Co.	Halifax
John, house joiner	R.I.?	KOR?	Char.		
Robert, joiner, 85			C168	St. John	
Samuel, Rev., Yale '59	Ct.		Char.		
Angevine, John	N.Y. D. Co.	WL	Cumb.	St. John?	
Angus, Robert, carpenter, 85		carp.	P1414	Queens Co.	
Annis, *see* Innis.					
Ansley, Daniel	N.J.	2 NJV	Bl. 2		N.Y.
John	N.J.	2 NJV			
Ozias, farmer	Eng./N.J.	Adj. 1 NJV	Kings Co.		N.Y.
Thomas		1 NJV	Kings Co.		
Anstruther, William		Maj. RGA	Char.	Nash.?	
Aplin, Joseph	R.I.		St. John		P.E.I.

Appleby, Benjamin	N.Y.	Sgt. 3 NJV	P688		
David			Wash.		
Elnathan, carp., 85		Sgt. QR	Bl. 5	Ken.	St. John
Henry			Wash.		
James			Wash.	pens. 36	
John		3 NJV	Gr. Lake		
Lucas			Wash.		
Peter				Kn.	
Arbuckle, Samuel			Queens Co.		
Archer, Robert, painter, 96			F'ton		
Ariot, Philip			Gr. L. 84		
Arrhour, Mary			P1323	Bel.	
Armstrong, Richard	Eng.?	Maj. QR	C233	F'ton	
Zwiri, black	Ct.				
Arnold, Amos, yeoman, 85	Mass./S.C.		P66	LR	
Andrew			Char.		
Benedict	Ct./Pa.	Col. LAL	F'ton	St. John	Eng.
John		2 NJV	F'ton		
Oliver, Yale '76	Ct.	Lt. Vol. NE	P95	Sussex	
Rosewell	Ct.			Ken.	
Arnott, David, mariner			St. A.		
Arran, John			Musq.		
Arrowsmith, William			P1326	Queens Co.	
Ash, James ?				Char.	
Ashburn, Patience, widow			Maug.		
Ashford, William			P436	St. John	
Asten, Aston, *or* Austen,					
Benjamin		GP	Bl. 3	Wash.	
Caleb		GP	Bl. 3		
Caleb (Bergen, s.)			C28		
David			BMG	F'ton	
Martin		GP	Bel.		
Samuel (1), tailor	Ct.		P1295	LR	
Samuel (2), carpenter	Va.		Fr. Lake		
Solomon		LNE, QR			UC
William, labourer, 95	N.C.?	RFA	Char.	St. John	
Atchison, John	Eng.	Ens. 1 NJV	Burton	F'ton	
Atkinson, Alexander		Lt. RFA	?		
John	Mass.?		St. John		
William	Md.?		P196	Mir.?	
Atherston, Benjamin ?			Char.		
Peter ?			Char.		
Peter, Jr. ?			Char.		
Atwood, Isaac, pract. of physic	N.J.	Capt. KAR	Bl. 4, P1177	U.S.A./93	
Aymer, Francis	N.Y.		P1125	Queens Co.	Md. St. A.
Babb, James		GP	Bl. 3		
Babbitt, Daniel, blacksmith	Ct./N.Y.		Gn.		
Babcock, William, carpenter	N.Y, O. Co.	2 NJV	Burton	Mir.	
Backhouse, John, carpenter, 85		1 NJV	C318	L.R.	UC?
Backstaler *or* Backstead, Ignatius			Burton	York Co.	
Bailes *or* Bayles, Edward		KAR	P1054		
Bailey, Benjamin	Eng.		Or.	Gr. Lake	
Edmund			St. A.		
Edward		PL	Bl. 7		
Henry		1 NJV	Penniac	Bel.	
Joseph			P648		
Nathaniel	Mass.		St. A.		
Oliver, sailmaker			P593	LR	
Philip, Lt. 72d.	Eng./N.H.?	Capt. RFA	Char. .	d./85	
Samuel			St. A.		
William (1)	Eng.	Capt. LAR	F'ton		
William (2), yeoman, 85			St. John Co.		
Zachariah	Md.	ML	Bl. 1		
Bain, Alexander		42d.	Nash.		
? George, whitesmith			St. John		
John			Kings Co.		
Baird, William, carpenter, 96		carp.	P1210		
Bairnsfair, William			St. A./84		
Baisley, James			Gr. L./84	St. John	
see also Bazeley.					
Bakeman, William, black			Gr. Lake		

257

Name	Origin	Service	Loc1	Loc2	Loc3
Baker, Anna			Char.		
Anthony		a.b.	Kn.	Carleton Co.	
Charles			LR	Sunbury Co.	
John, seaman	Mass.		left		
John	N.Y. W. Co.	Lt. KAD	P464	Ham. R.	
Jonathan			Queens Co.		
Joseph		smith	St. A.		
Josiah		Lt. 3 NJV	Sch.		
Prince and Polly, servants			Sch.		
Baldwin, Daniel			BH		
John	Pa.?		St. A.? 84	St. George	
Balentine, Alexander			P1097	Gr. Lake	
Samuel		2 DeL.	Maug.	Gr. Lake	
Ballou, Edward			Kn.		
Balmaine, William	Scot./N.Y.		P506	Gr. Lake	
Balster, William, merchant, 85			Gr. Lake		
Bampton, Paul		RFA	3 ch.		
Bancroft, Daniel	N.J.	Surg. 2 NJV	Bl. 2		
Bancker, see Bonker					
Banks, David			St. John		
James			Wash.	Maug.	
William		Ens. 2 NJV	Bl. 2	Queens Co.	
Banner, Charles, tailor, 85					
Bannister, Thomas	R.I.	Vol. NB guide			
Barber, John		a.b.	Sch.		
Barbarie, John	N.J.	Capt. 2 NJV	P1191	Bl. 2	Sussex
Oliver	N.J.	Lt. LAR	P1193		Sussex
Barcelon, Sarah			Gr. L./84		
Barclay, or Barkley, Abraham			P963		
James	N.Y.			St. John	
John		Ord.	Sch.		
Thomas	N.Y.	Maj. LAR	P202-4	N.S.	
William			P964	Ken.	York Co.
Bardin, Peleg			Ham. R.		
Barge, William		a.b.	Gr. Lake	Musq.	
Barker, Abijah, 2d. Lt. Co. 49			P1260	Musq.	N.Y.
Ephraim			Char.		
George			Gr. Lake/84		
Thomas (1)	N.Y. D. Co.	Lt. KAR	Penniac	F'ton	
Thomas (2), mariner, 85	N.Y. Ctld.		P2		
William, blacksmith,90	N.Y. W. Co.		Char.	St. John	A. Co.?
Barlow, Edmund			Ken.		
Ezekiel, shipwright			Ken.	St. John	
Jesse, shipcarpenter, 93					
Jonathan			Sackville		
Joseph		carp.	Ken.	Port.	
Thomas	Pa.	SHB	P1015		
Barnard, James			Char.		
John, Harv. '62	Ger.			d./85	
Moses			St. A./84		
Barnes, or Barns, Joshua	N.Y. Ph.	Capt. LAR	LR		
Peter		KAR			
Robert			Char.		
Thomas			P1152	Kings Co.	
Barnet, James		a.b.	Mir.		
Barnhart, John		NYV	Kes.	Bel.	
Barnum, Nathan	Ct.	Ens. 2 DeL.			UC
Barr, John			Mir.	Scot.	
Peter		74th			
Barrett, Caleb		Lt. WJV	BH		
James			BH		
John		1 DeL.	Nash.		
William			Nash.		
Barry, Edmond		Cpl. RFA	Mag.		
James		Cpl. 1 DeL.	Bl. 8		
John		QR	Mir.		
Lewis			P444		
Thomas			P902	LR	
Bartley, James		1 NJV	York Co.	Mir.?	
Barton, Dennis		64th.	Pass.		
Edward, baker, 85			P899		
Henry, farmer	N.J.	Lt. 1 NJV	Maug.		
James, farmer	N.J.	Ens. 1 NJV	Maug.		

Barton, Michael			P1359			
Roger	N.Y. L.I.	Ens. NYV	Kes.	Gr. Lake		
Bartow, John			BH			
Bartrum, David		2 NJV	Bl. 2	N.S.		
Bass, Daniel		2 NJV	F'ton			
Bashford, Sally, m. John Cooke						
Bassa, *probably for* Racey						
Bates, Alexander		Cpl. QR	Bl. 5	Carl.		
Samuel		Sgt. QR	Bl. 5			
Walter, shoemaker	Ct.		Kn.			
William	Ct.	Sgt. QR	Bl. 5	UC		
Batson, Lawrence ?			Char.?			
Bauch, John			Mspc./84			
Baxter, George			P789			
Joseph	N.H.		Norton			
Richard			Gr. Lake/84			
Simon	Ct./N.H.		Norton			
Stebbins, cordwnr, 85	N.Y. W. Co.		P1446			
Stephen	N.Y.		P968	U.S.A.		
Bayer, James ?			Gr. Lake/84			
Baynard, William		ML	Maug.			
Bazeley, Abraham			Queens Co.	N.S.		
William			Kings Co.	N.S.?		
Beach, Lewis			Kn.	U.S.A.		
William			Kn.	U.S.A.		
Beale, Richard	R.I.		P1358	St. John		
Beam, *see* Boehm						
Be(a)man, Ebenezer	Mass.		Lanc.			
Thomas	Mass.	Lt. Assoc. Ref.				
Bean, Enoch			Kings Co.			
John (1), yeoman, 85			C407			
John (2), carpenter			St. A.			
Thomas, carpenter, 84	N.Y.		P90	St. John Co.		
William			Or.			
Bearbright, *see* Bourght.						
Beard, Enoch		Cpl. PWAR	York Co.			
Beardsley, Abel	Ct.		Bel.			
John, Rev.	Ct./N.Y.	Chap. LAR	P151	Maug.		
Nehemiah		2 DeL.	Or.			
Paul			Or.			
Zephaniah	Ct.	2 DeL.	Maug.	Kings Co.		
Beaty (Beatteay), Edward, Sr.			C71	Cn.		
Edward, Jr.			C70			
John	R.I.?		P207	Ken.	St. A.	
Joseph, mariner, 99 ?			C129	Ken.		
Polly			C72			
Thomas,		QR	Bel.			
cabinet maker, 95 ?						
William		KAD?	C130			
Beck, Joseph, 2d. Lt. Co. 29	Eng./Pa.		P903	Gr. Bay		
Beckwith, Ichabod		Sgt. LAL	Mir.			
Bedell, Daniel, farmer	N.Y. L.I.					
John (1), merchant, 85	N.Y. St.I.		P7	Kn.	Wdstk.	
John (2), barber, 85						
Joseph			P8, 33	Burton	Ken.	
Paul, merchant, 85	N.Y. St.I.		P32			
Richard				Ken.		
Stephen, Lt. Co. 17	N.Y. L.I.		P152			
William			P338	Ken.	UC	
Beebe, Edward	N.Y./Ct.?	KAD	BH			
Samuel	Ct.	KAD				
Seth		KAD				
Beers (Godbeer), William		Engr.	Maug.			
2d. Lt. Co. 27						
Beeton, John			Char.			
Begar, *see* Biggar						
Beggs (Bigg?), William			Gr. Lake			
Behn, see Boehm						
Belding, Daniel, merchant, 95			Chance Har.			
Jasper			Ken.	Kent Co.		
Bell, Isaac, Sr., merchant	Ct.		P169			
Isaac, Jr., gentleman, 90	Ct.				N.Y.	
Jacob, farmer	N.J.		P19			
James, 2d. Lt. Co. 22	Ct.		P1349	F'ton		
James		2 NJV?	Gr. Lake			

259

Bell, John, carpenter	N.J.	Ord.?	P1442	Gr. Lake	
Joseph ?			BH		
Robert			Cmpb.	St. John	
Thomas			St. A.		
William	Pa.?	3 NJV	Pr. Wm.	Carl.	
Belmind, Garret ?			BH		
Belyea, Beyea, or Bulyea,					
Abraham	N.Y. Ctld.	WL	Oak Pt.		
Beyea, Benjamin, bro. Jas	N.Y.				N.Y.
Henry	N.Y.		Kings Co.		
James, son of Henry	N.Y.	WL	Wash.		
Beyea, James	N.Y.		Ham. R.		
Beyea, John, labourer, 95 ?	N.Y. Ph.	LAR			
Belyea, Beyea, or Bulyea,					
Joseph, son of Henry	N.Y. Ctld.	WL	Wash.		
Robert, son of Henry	N.Y. Ctld.		Kings Co.	Kent Co.	
Widow, two sons			Musq.		
Benedict, Comfort	Ct.		St. John		
Eli	Ct.	Lt. GP	Bl. 3	Ct.	N.B.
Jabez			Gr. Lake		
Bennet(t), Elijah		Cpl. PWAR	Ham. R.	Sussex	
James		2 NJV	Bl. 2		
John, ship carpenter		Sgt. BL?	St. A.		
and smoker of herrings					
Joshua			Ham. R.		
Lewis		Cpl. NYV	Kes.	U.S.A.?	
Thomas	Pa.?	2 DeL.	St. St.		
Bennison, George, mariner	S.C.		P109	Char.?	
Benson, Isaac		Cpl. PWAR	York Co.		
Seth			Kn.		
William, 2d. Lt. Co. 2C			P478	Gr. Lake	
Bent, Samuel, stationer, 87 ?					
Bentley, John, merchant, 96 ?			P130	St. A.	
John (2)		GP	Bl. 3		
John (3)		PWAR	Bl. 9?		
Berdan, Albert		Sgt. 2 NJV	Bl. 2		UC
Berdun, Isaac			St. John Co.		
Bergan, or Bergin, James,	N.Y.				
tallow chandler, 85					
Peter			St. John		
Bernard, see Barnard					
Berry, George		GP	Bl. 3		
James, Lt. Co. 29,			F'ton?		
merchant, 85					
John			Char.		
Lewis			P524		
Robert			Ken.		
Samuel, blacksmith, 95?					
Berton, George D.			F'ton		
Peter, Capt. Co. 21	N.Y. L.I.		C270	Kings Co.	
Betner, Henry			Ken.	York Co.	
Betson, Joseph		CGP	Sch.		
Thomas			Or.		
Bettle, Everard			Gn.		
John		Lt. WJV?	Bl. 2	Ken.?	
Betts, Azor	N.Y.	Surg. QR	Kn.		
David		2 DeL.		Carl.	
Ephraim		Sgt. 2 DeL.	F'ton	Mir.	
Jared, cordwnr		Sgt. PWAR	F'ton		
Beveridge, David, barber, 85			P1415		
Beyea, see Belyea					
Bickle, see Pickel					
Biddle(stone), John	Pa.	GP	Bl. 3		
Biggar, Bigart, John, tailor, 95?		CGP?	Kn.	N.S.	
Billopp, Christopher	N.Y. St.I.				
Birdsall, or Birdsill, Archibald			Ham. R.		
Benjamin	N.Y. D. Co.		Jemseg		
Caleb, cooper		KAR	Sussex		
Isaac, blacksmith					
Robert			Ham. R.		
Birmingham, James, yeoman, 85		Sgt. PWAR	P834		
upholsterer, 85					
Patrick		1 DeL.	Bl. 8		
Bishop, Silvanus	Ct.	Sgt. PWAR	Nash.	left	
Bispham, Joseph, hatter	N.J.		BH/84	d./85	

Bissett, George, Rev.	R.I.		St. John		
William			Gr. Lake		
Blaau, Waldron	N.Y.	Capt. 3 NJV		d./83	
Black, James			P909	Dip. Har.	
John		Cpl. 1 DeL.?	Char.		
Joseph			St. A./84		
William		NCO 40th.	Mspc.	Gr. Lake	
Blackburn, Francis	N.Y. Q. Co.		Gr. Lake		
Blackie, James			C305		
Blackmar, Andrew	Ct.?	2 DeL.	BH/84		
Blackmore, Joseph			Woodstock		
Blades, Christopher			P1396	Kings Co.	
Blaicker, Jacob David		Sgt. 38th	F'ton		
Blair, David, merchant, 85	Scot.		P122		
			C109		
George		guide	P239	Nash.	
James, mariner			P1363	Halifax	
John		3 DeL.	F'ton	Penniac	
Malcolm		RFA	Mag. R.		
Peter, merchant, 92?					
Blakeney, or Bleakney, David	Ir./S.C.	mil	P776	Ken.	Pet.
William	Ir./S.C.		P777	Westm. Co.	
Blakeslee, Asa, soapboiler, 95	Ct.	KAR			
Blauvelt, Cornelius	N.J.	3 NJV	Gr. Lake		
Blewer, see Brewer					
Bliss, Daniel, Harvard '60	Mass.		Or.		
Jonathan, Harvard '63	Mass.		C341	F'ton	
Esquire, 85					
Samuel	Mass.	Lt. 84th	Pass.		
Blizzard, Samuel	N.Y.		Maug.		
William, shoemaker	N.Y. D. Co.		Wash.		
Bloodworth, Nathaniel		Sgt. QR	Bl. 5	Carl.	
Bloomfield, David		2 NJV	Bl. 2		
Blume, John Nicholas,			C408	Ken.	
freeman, 85					
Boatman, Jeremiah			Char.		
William			Char.		
Bodtner, Johan Scharls	Sax.		Ken.	U.S.A.?	
Boehn (Beam), John	Swed.	Hess.	Ham. R.		
Boerhight, see Bourght.					
Bogart, Gysbert	N.Y. O. Co.	Carp.	Burton		
Isaac			P337		
Leffert			Queens Co.		
Thamar, widow			Gn.		
Boggs, John, tailor, 85		Engr.?	P1304	Kings Co.	Scot.
John ?	N.C.			Queens Co.	
Bogle, William	Va.		P987	Albert Co.?	
Bohle, Frederick			Sussex		
Boice, see Boyce.					
Boland, Nicholas			P833		
Boltenhouse, Bedford		LAR	N.S.	St. St.	Dorch.
Bolton, William		Ord.	Char.		
Bond, Abraham, weaver	N.Y. L.I.		Queens Co.		N.Y.
Jacob, farmer	N.Y. L.I.				
Elizabeth			BH		
Sarah			St. John		
Bonker, Abraham,		3 NJV	P581	Gr. Lake	
carpenter, 85					
Bonnell, or Bunnell, Benjamin			LR		
Daniel			Kn.		
Gershom		2 DeL.	Fredericton		
Isaac	Ct.	PWAR	Kn.		
Bonsall, Richard, Lt. Co. 52,	Wls./N.Y.		P672, 1413		
merchant, 85					
Bookhout, John, labourer, 85		Sgt. LAR	P1028		
Boone, Henry			Or.		
John		LAR	Or.		
Samuel, Sr.					
Samuel, Jr., farmer	R.I.		P1263		
William, farmer	R.I.		Gn.	Kes.	
Booth, John, watchmaker, 95	N.Y.	Engr.			
Joseph, farmer	Ct.				
Joshua	N.Y.	Sgt. QR			UC
Boras, James ?			York Co.		

Bostwick, Daniel	Mass.		P843	Bel.	
Isaac			P1313	Kn.	
Nathan			Wash.		
Bosworth, Thomas, cooper	Eng./N.Y.		P1324		
Botsford, Amos, Yale'63	Ct.		P202, 3, 4	Westm.	
Bottom, William		70th	Pass.		
Bough, John		KAD	C380	Ken.	
Bourght, Philip		Cpl. LAR	F'ton	dr./86	
William			Kes.		
Bourn, (Bowen), Ansell, carpenter			P1109	Sussex	Boston
Ashley	N.J.	Sgt. 1 NJV	Penniac		
Francis		3 NJV	P726		
Henry			Dig.		
James, brickmaker, 96		Sgt. RFA.?	Kn.	St. John	
Peter, tanner, 98					
William	N.Y.		P588	Ken.?	
Bower, Alexander		2 NJV	Ken.		
Bowler, John			St. A.		
Bowman, Andrew, tailor, 85			C41		
Conrad	N.J.	1 NJV	Penniac		
Henry, Sgt. 84th	Ir.	Ens. PWAR			
Bowra, or Boura, Peter, mariner, 96			St. John		
Boyce, Isabella			St. A.		
Joseph		2 NJV	Ken.		
Susannah			St. A.		
Boyd, John, house carpenter		74th	St. A.		
Michael	Pa.	PL	Bl. 7		
William Robert E.			St. John		
Boyer, Charles			Gr. Lake	Carl.	
Samuel, yeoman, 85			Bel.		
William, mariner, 90			St. John		
Boyle, Adam	N.J.		Queens Co.		
Hugh, prob. Doyle					
Patt		GP	Bl. 3		
Richard	Ir.	Ens. 1 DeL.	Bl. 8		
Terence		KAR	Bl. 6	Woodstock	
Bowlby?, Thomas		2 NJV	Ken.		UC
Boyne, Alexander, carpenter			P483	Gr. Lake	St. John
James			P1422	Gr. Lake	
Richard			Wash./84		
Boynton, Caleb	Mass.		Dig.		
Brace, James, merchant	Eng.	Maj. RFA	Ft. Cumb.		
Bradbury, John			St. A.	York Co.	
Bradford, Benjamin	Mass.		St. A.	Char.	
Richard			Ham. R.		
Bradley, James, gardener, 85	Mass.	1 DeL.			
John		CMG	UC	Carl.	
Lewis			F'ton		
Neil			Ken.		
Richard			Musq.		
Thomas		Gar. Bn.?	Gr. L. esch.		
William Brown			York Co.		UC
Bradshaw, James	N.Y.	2 DeL.			UC
William		NYV	Kes.	St. John Co.?	
Brady, Richard			Sch.		
William		2 NJV	Ken.	Gr. Lake	
Bragg, Joab (Joel?), mariner			St. A.		
Brannah, James, merchant			Kings Co.	Fredericton	
Brannen, Charles		2 DeL.	F'ton	Nash.	
Ezekiel, carpenter, 95			P794	Or.	
Peter		64th	Char.		
Thomas, shipwright		Cpl. 1 DeL?	Ken.		
Branscombe, Arthur			P975	Gr. Lake	
Branson, Eli	Va./N.C.	Capt.	P1169	Eng.	
Brawn, see Brown					
Breir, John, yeoman, 85					
Brennah, Michael			Bl. 6	Fredericton	
Bretney, see Britney					
Brett, Anthony		KOR	St. John Co.		
Brewer, or Brower, Adolphus			Queens Co.		
Cornelius			Kes.		
Daniel	Mass.	KAD			
John			York Co.		
Mary	N.Y.		P1256		

262

Brewerton, George L.	N.Y.	Ens. 1 DeL.	P1271		UC
James	N.Y.	Ens. 2 DeL.	P1273		UC
Bricker, *see* Bonker					
Bridal, John Scott	Pa.?	3 NJV	Gn.		Pa.?
Bridgham, Ebenezer	Mass.		P46		
Bridgeman, Henry			Maq.		
John			Kings Co.		
Thomas			Maq.		UC
William			Maq.		UC
Bridges, Joshua			Dig.		
Briggs, Abiel	N.Y.		Queens Co.		
Ebenezer	N.Y.		Shef.		
John, mariner	N.Y.	KAD	P1389		
William	Ct./N.Y.		Gn.		
Brill, David, farmer	N.Y. D. Co.		Gr. Lake		
Jacob	Ger./N.Y.		Gr. Lake		
Joseph, tailor	N.Y. D. Co.		Gr. Lake	U.S.A.	
Brinkerhoff, Abraham	N.Y.	Sgt. 1 DeL.	P1279		
Brinley, Francis	R.I./Mass.	Surg. NYV	Kes.	N.S., R.I.	
Brisley, Thomas Dennis, blacksmith			Or.		
Brit(te)ney, Jacob	Pa.	BCV, QR	Pnfd.		
John	Pa.	BCV, QR	Kn.		
Brittain, James, farmer	N.J.	Lt. 1 NJV	P1051	Kings Co.	
Joseph	N.J.	Ens. 1 NJV	P1052	Kings Co.	
William	N.J.	1 NJV	P1050	Kings Co.	
Britton, John			C135		
Brock, Nicholas		ML	Bl. 1, sold.		
Brockeberry (Brackenby), Robert		Sgt. 40th	St. John Co.		
Bromehead, Jonathan		Lt. 54th		d.'88	
Brooker, Jacob		PWAR	Bl. 5?		
Brooks, Benjamin, mariner, 85, silk dyer, 85		Em. Ch.?	Wash.		
Daniel			/85		
Jesse ?			C317	Cn.	
Stephen			LR		U.S.A.
Brothers, Joseph, shipwright, 95			C8		
William	N.J.	2 NJV	C417	Bl. 2	
Brown, Abraham		QR?	Mir.		
Adam		3 NJV	P727		
Alexander			Nash.		
Alexander, mason, 85			Wash.		
Asher	Pa.		BH/87		
Benjamin Field	Pa.		BH		
Bostwick	Ct.		P1319	Kings Co.	
Charles			P1142		
Christopher	S.C.?		Sch.		
Daniel (1)	Ct.		P1328	Kings Co.	
Daniel (2)	Scot./Me.		St. St.		
David, Dr. of Physic	Scot.	Hosp.	St. John		
George (1), cooper			Mir.		
George (2)		1 NJV ?	Sussex		
Henry Barlow, schoolmaster			Char.		
Hugh	S.C.		P322	Bel.	
James (1)		Cpl. QR	Bl. 5		
James (2)			St. A.		
James (3)	S.C.		Bel.	d./85	
James (4)		1 DeL.	Bl. 8		
John (1)		1 NJV	Ken.		
John (2)	Ga.	QR	Bl. 5		
John (3)	N.J.	3 NJV	P311	Carl.	
John (4)		GP	Bl. 3	d./85	
John (5)			St. A.		
Jonathan (1)	N.Y.	Sgt. 3 NJV	Shef.	Carl.	
Jonathan (2)		Ens. GP	Bl. 3		
Joshua		CGP	St. A.		
Josiah Sawyer	Ct.	KAR		Carl.	
Margaret	N.J.		Gn.	Irld.	
Matthew			Maq.	Pa.	
Nathan		NYV?	Kes.		
Neill		74th			
Noah			Sch.		

Brown, Rachel, wdw. Capt.	Ct.		Wash.		
Hezekiah, PWAR					
Richard (1)	N.H.		St. A.		
Richard (2)			C89	Bel.	
Robert				Pass.	
Samuel	Mass.	Cpl. RFA	Mag. R.		UC?
Silvanus, son of					
Ebenezer					
Thomas		1 DeL.	St. A.		
Titus			LR		
William (1)		2 NJV	Bl. 2	Gr. Lake	
William (2)		3 NJV	Burton	Carl.	
William (3)		1 DeL.	Bl. 8	Carl.?	
William (4)			Ken.		
Zachariah Barnard,	Mass./L.I.	Lt. 2 DeL.	Burton		
farmer					
Brownell, Joshua	N.Y. D. Co.		P1269	Wash.	
Brownrigg, John		BMG	P42, 43		
Richard F.		Capt. LAR?		Irld.	
Bruce, David	S.C.?	42nd	P244	Nash.	Mir.
John		42nd	Nash.	Fredericton	
Brundage, Andrew			P969	Wash.	
Benjamin		QR			
Daniel, d. 9. 11. 83		ex QR	P856		
Jeremiah,	N.Y.		C256, 257		
silversmith, 85					
John, tailor, 85			C171		
Joshua	N.Y. D. Co.	WL	P977		
Josiah		Em. Ch.	P1074	Or.	
Nathaniel, son of			P850		
Daniel, carman, 85					
Brunson, Daniel	Am.	Ens. PWAR	Nash.		LC
Brush, John Rodolph	N.H.?	1 DeL.	Bl. 8		
Samuel	N.Y.		P333	Sussex	
Bruster, John			Burton		
Bryan, Michael		KOR			
Samuel, labourer, 97					
Bryant, John	Va.?	Cpl. PWAR	St. John Co.		
Robert	N.C.?		Kings Co.		
Seth	Mass.		P1335	Kn.	Wdstk.
Buchan, William		42nd	Nash.	Fredericton	
Buchanan, Robert			St. John		
Samuel		3 NJV	F'ton		
William			Mag. R.		
Buckelow, Isaac		1 DeL.	Bl. 8		
Sarah			P388	Bel.	
Bucket, William		NCO 2 NJV	C418	Char.?	
Buckingham, Stephen		Cpl. KAR	Or.?		
Buckley, Daniel		1 DeL.	Bl. 8		
James, shipwright, 85			C36		
Thomas, Sr.	Pa.		P1122	Pnfd.	
Thomas, Jr.	Pa.			Pnfd.	Halifax
Buffington, Jacob, carpenter	Pa.		BH		
Richard	Pa.		BH	St. John Co.	
Bughner, Henry		1 NJV			UC
Bulkman, Samuel		KOR	Pass./84		
Bull, George	N.Y. U. Co.	Lt. LAL	Woodstock		
Jacob	N.Y. D. Co.		Gr. Lake		
Richard	N.Y. O. Co.	NYV	Ham. R.		
William			Ham. R.		
Bullen, Samuel, potter, 97			LR		
Bullock, Thomas		RFA	Mag. R.		
Bulmer, Joseph ?			Sackville		
Bunce, Joseph			P129, C181, 2		
Bunnell, see Bonnell					
Bunting, Roland		Cpl. 1 NJV	Penníac	Loch Lomond	
Burchil, John		KAD	Bl. 4		
Burden, John		1 NJV			
Thomas	Mass.	Lt.?	P816	Burton	
Burditt (Bourdett), Oliver,	N.J.		P1118, 1237		
Capt. Co. 12,					
merchant, 85					
Stephen, mariner, 85			St. John		
Burdick, Freeman		BMG	Kn.		UC

264

Name		Service			
Burgain (Burgoin), Edward		Sgt. PWAR	Nash.		
Burgess, Benjamin, mariner		Sgt.?	St. John	St. St.	
Daniel	Pa.	Gn.			
David			Ken./84		
John, Lt. Co. 27		1 NJV?	P1459	Ken.	
Josiah		Gn.			
Burk(e), Edward	Pa.		BH	L.I.	
Jacob			Burton		
John	Pa.		Burton	BH	
Richard		Sgt. 3 NJV	BH		
William, shipwright					Gr. Man.
Burkestaff, Frederick	N.Y.	3 NJV	F'ton		
John		RFA	Mag. R.		
Burkitt, William,	Pa.				
prob. Bucket					
Burling, Samuel	N.Y.	guide	Shel.	St. John	
Burlock, Hester, wdw.	Ct.		Gr. Lake	Or.	
David			Gr. Lake	Norton	
Samuel					
Burnett, John, Lt. Co. 3					
Samuel		Sgt. QR	Bl. 5	Maug.	
William		Sgt. QR?	P765	Ken.	
Burnham, Jonathan, 2d. Lt. Co. 39		guide	Sackville		
Burns, Charles		1 NJV			
Daniel		GP	Bl. 3		
James	Am.	Capt. RFA	St. John		
John (1)		Sgt. RFA	Mir.	Ken.	
John (2)		Sgt. PWAR	LR	U.S.A.?	
Moses		Sgt. RFA	Mag. R.		
Patrick ?			Mir.		
Philip, labourer			St. A.		
Samuel			P768?	U.S.A.	
			P1438		
William		QR	Mir.		
Burrell, Joseph, baker, 85		LAR?			
Burris, or Burrows, James		GP	Bl. 3		
Burt (Burtt), Benjamin, Sr.	Ct.	ex QR	Burton	d.	
Benjamin, Jr.	Ct.		Maq.	Kes.	
David	Ct.	ex QR	Kes.		
David, shoemaker	N.Y. D. Co.				
Isaac, prob. Butt					
John, carpenter, 85		QR?	Bl. 5	St. John	
Joseph	Ct.		Gr. Lake	Kes.	
Burtis, Benajah, hatter, 85	N.Y. W. Co.				
Mary, wdw.	N.Y. W. Co.				
Thomas, blacksmith	N.Y.		Gr. Lake	U.S.A.?	
William, cartman, 85	N.Y. W. Co.	WL	P578		
William, farmer	N.Y. L.I.		LR	U.S.A.	
Burtless, Thomas		1 NJV	LR		
Burton, James			LR	U.S.A.	
Burwell, James	N.J.	Cpl. 2 NJV	Ken.		UC
Bush, Gilbert, shoemaker	N.Y. L.I.				
Buskirk, Abraham, see Vanbuskirk					
Garret			Kings Co.		
John		BMG	Gn.		
Lawrence	N.J.		Nash.	Queens Co.	
Bustin, Thomas, carpenter, 85	Va.		P1005		
Buswin (Buswell?). Richard, mason, 85					
Butler, Alfred			Pass.		
Benjamin, tailor, 85		ML	Bl. 1, sold.		
David			Deer Is.		
Ephraim		2 DeL.	Kn.		
Gillam, Boston evac.	N.H.		Char.		
James, Boston evac.	Mass.		P326		
John	N.J. ?	PWAR	Ken.		
Josiah, mariner, 85	Ct.	BMG	P1356		
Michael, yeoman, 85	Ir.		P1213	Kings Co.	
Peter		2 DeL.?	P1439	Maug.	
Samuel			BH	Kn.	
Thomas, farmer	Pa.		P323		
Butt, Isaac		40th	Mspc.	enl.	
Butterworth, Moses		Cpl. 2 NJV	C390	Bl. 2	
Bydder, Richard			York Co.	burned'86	

Byles, Mather, Rev.,   Mass.   St. John
  'Harvard, '51
  Mather, Jr.   C137   Fredericton   W.I.

Cable, Ann, wdw. of John Ct.   Kn.
  Anthony, cooper, 85   Ct.
  Jabez   Ct.   P1315
  James, cooper, 95   Ct.
  John, cooper, 95   Ct.   Kn.   St. John
  Peter, cooper, 85   Ct.   Kn.   St. John
Cain, (see also Cane, Kain, Kane).
  Barney, farmer   Pa.
  John (1)   N.Y.   Wash.
  John (2)   dr. PWAR St. John Co.
  Michael, labourer, 90
  William   PWAR   Nash.
Cairnes, or Carne(s), John (1)   Ken.   N.Y.
  John (2), merchant   2 DeL.   Nash.   Fredericton
  Robert, yeoman, 85   Sgt. QR   P697
Calder, John   KAR
  Robert   74th   Campb.
Caldwell, Thomas   2 NJV   Gn.
  William   Eng./Pa. guide   Queens Co.
  William, mariner, 96
Caleff, John   Mass.   Surg.   St. John   St. A.
Calkin, Ezekiel ?   St. George
Call, John   3 NJV   Pr. Wm.
Calla(g)han, Dennis   dr. ML
  James   GP   Bl. 3   Maug.   F'ton
  Nicholas   Ct.   P1327
  Patrick   Mass.   St. A.
  Susannah, wdw.   Ken.
    (Jos. QR?)
  Thomas   1 DeL.   Bl. 8
Callender, William   Sch.
Calley, William   Ken.
Calverley, Craven,   Md.?   St. John   Kings Co.
    victualler, 96
(Caverly), Joseph, Lt. Co. 32
Calvin, John   2 NJV   Ken./83
Camber, John, carpenter   PWAR   Kes.   Carl.
  William   dr. PWAR Kes.
Cameron, Alexander (1)   Lt. Navy St. John Co.
  Alexander (2)   74th   Dig.
  Daniel   Scot.   Lt. 1 DeL. P1272
  Donald   St. A..
  Duncan (1)
  Duncan (2)   3 NJV   P924   Gr. Lake UC
  Hugh (1)   Gr. Lake
  Hugh (2)   74th   Dig.
  James   42nd   P247   Nash.
  John (1)   42nd   Nash.   Mir.?
  John (2)   Scot./N.Y. 54th   Nash.
  John (3)   Lt. KOR Gr. Man.
  Stephen, merchant   Kes.   Fredericton
  William,   carp.   Wash.
    carpenter, 85
Camp, Abiathar, Sr., Capt. Ct.   P26   d.'88
    Co. 18
  Abiathar, Jr., Lt.   Ct.   P25, 69,992 Jemseg
    Co. 18
  Eldad   GP   P641
  Hiel   Ct.   C161   Pr. Wm.
  John, 2nd Lt. Co. 18, Ct.   Ens. 2 NJV P16, 499
    mariner
  John, Jr.   Ct.   Fife. 3 NJV P935
  Neil ?   C303
Campbell, Archibald   Lt. 74th St. A.
  Charles   C173
  Colin, Sr., merchant Va.   Lt. 74th St. A.   St. John
  Colin, Jr.?   St. A.   Dig.
  Colin, Esquire, 87   Mass.
  Colin   Scot.   Lt. 1 DeL. d./85
  Donald, Esquire, 85 Scot.   Capt. 3 NJV C160, 172 Musq.   N.Y.

266

Name	Origin	Regt./Rank	Grant/Loc.	Settlement
Campbell, Donald		Lt. 74th	St. A.	
Donald		KAD?		
Dugald (1)	Scot./N.Y.	Lt. 42nd	C604, 5	Nash.
Dugald (2)		Lt. KAR	P426	Fredericton
Dugald (3)		74th	St. A.	
Duncan		a.b.	St. A.	
Finlay			York Co.	Carl.
Hugh (1)		74th	Sussex	
Hugh (2), yeoman, 85		42nd	C444	Dip. Har.
James		Lt. 40th	Pass.	
John (1)		Sgt. KAD	Carl.	
John (2)		Sgt. 74th	St. A.	
John (3)		74th		
John (4)		74th		
John (5)		74th	Dig.	
Kenneth		Lt. 74th		
Lauchlan		carp.	P991	Queens Co.
Malcolm, labourer			Kings Co.	
Mary, wdw. of Alex of Boston			P707	St. John
Peter (1), farmer	Pa./N.J.	Capt. 2 NJV	Bl. 2	d./22
Peter (2)		Sgt. GP	Bl. 3	W.I.
Richard, sailor			C29	Ken.?
Robert, Sr., Capt. Co. 38 surveyor, 85	N.J. Msx.	enl. GP	P708	
Robert, Jr., ae. 12	N.J.		P709	
Robert		3 NJV?	Carl.	
Robert		1 NJV	Penniac	
Walter, Esquire, 95	Scot.	Capt.PWAR	P177, C124, 606	Scot.
William, Esquire, 95	Scot./Mass.		Halifax	St. John
William (2)			Sch.	
William (3)		PWAR	St. John Co.	
Canby, Joseph, merchant, 85	Pa.	BCV	P1006	
Thomas, blacksmith		KAD	Kn.	
Cane, see also Cain, Kain, Kane.				
Jeremiah		KOR	St. John Co.	
John		GP	York Co.	
Canniff, John				UC
Cannum, Thomas, labourer, 87	Pa.	PL	Bl. 7	Nash.
Canter, James			Carl.	pens.
Cantwell, Richard			P756	Queens Co.
Card, Elijah, shipwright, 85			P1021	
Henry			Deer Is.	
Carew, David			Kings Co.	
John		NSV	Pass.	
Carey, Edward, carpenter, 85				
John Henry, mariner	Md.		F'ton	Cn.
Carhart, Hacaliah		Qm. QR	Bl.5	N.Y.
Carle, Jonas			P827	
Joseph			Ham R.	
Lewis	N.Y.		Gn.	U.S.A.
Phebe, spinster			1st. fl.	
Robert			Queens Co.	
Thomas, farmer	N.Y. D. Co.		Gn.	Gr. Lake
Carlisle, Robert, barber, 85		RFA	P809	Sussex
Carlow, John C.			St. A.	St. John
Martin			St. A.	
Carman, Elkanah, farmer	N.Y. L.I.			
Richard, 2nd Lt. Co. 23			P82	Maug.
Willet, farmer	N.Y. L.I.	QR?		
Carmichael, Donald		74th	Char.	
Dugald		74th	Char.	
Carne, see Cairne				
Carnell, William, victualler, 95 see also Cornwall		Sgt. KOR	Mspc.	
Carney, see Kearney				
Carpenter, Archelaus, cordwnr.	N.Y. W. Co.		Queens Co.	
Coles	N.Y. W. Co.		Queens Co.	
John, trader			Shel.	Mir.
Latting, 2nd Lt. Co. 32	N.Y.			

Name	Origin	Service	Place 1	Place 2	Extra
Carpenter, Thomas, Sgt., Guards	Eng.	Adj. 2 DeL.	P1165	U.S.A.	
Willet, Lt. Co. 42	N.Y. W. Co.	WL	Queens Co.		
William True		Sgt. KAD	C347, 309		
Wilson		KAD	BH		
Carr (or Kerr), Charles mason, 85			Gr. Lake		
James			Mspc.	York Co.	
John		guide	St. John	Queens Co.?	
Lawrence			P896		
Thomas			Char.		
Carre, Henry, arr. Dec. 83			P505	Kings Co.	
Robert Bulfil	N.Y.		St. John	Kings Co.	
William			P711	Or.	
Carrell, James			Ham. R./84		
(or Carnet), Robert		GP	Bl. 3	Maug.	
Carrick, Charles		74th	St. A.		
Carrington, Tamar, wdw. of Abr.	Ct.		P413	Queens Co.	
Carroll, Daniel, clerk	Pa.				
John, labourer, 87	Pa.	PL	Bl. 7		
Joseph, saddler		ML	Bl. 1	Fredericton	UC
Carson or Casson, Jacob		1 DeL.	Bl. 8		
James, weaver			Maug.	Kings Co.	
Carten, see Keirstead					
Carter, Christopher, druggist	Pa.	Hosp.	Halifax	St. John	
Edward		2 NJV	Ken.		
George			Musq.		
James (or Wm.?)		1 DeL.	Bl. 8		
Samuel, black			St. John		
Thomas		3 NJV	P317	LR	
Carton (Carson?), Thomas			P830		
Carty, James		2 NJV	Bl. 2	Ken.	N.S.
Carver, Caleb	Mass.		P1209	Bel.	
? Jacob, yeoman, 85					
Carvel, Jacob		Sgt. 2 NJV	Ken.	Fredericton	
Cary, Daniel, black			Maug.		
Case, Elisha	R.I.		P1250		
John			P1458		
Casey, John		1 DeL.	Nash.?		
Samuel		KAR?	Nash.		
William			Nash.	Mir.?	UC?
Castilla or Costilla, Francis		3 NJV	P884	Ken.	
Caswell, John			Gn.	Queensbury	
Joseph, blacksmith			Gn.	Queensbury	
Cathran, Alexander			C194		
Cayford, Jenny	N.J. Cmb. Co.		Gr. Lake/84		
Cayton, John		ML	Bl. 1		
Chadeayne, John			Kn.		
Chaloner, Benjamin, mariner, 97			Bel.	St. John	
John, gentleman, 95			Bel.	St. John	
Walter, gentleman, 85	R.I.		P58	Bel.	
Chambers, James			St. John Co.	Kings Co.	
Robert		Sgt. 1 DeL.	Bl. 8		
Champ(i)er, or Schomber, Lewis or Ludwig, carpenter, 85			P384	St. John	
Champney, Benjamin } Ebenezer } Francis	?		Char.		
Chancy, Edmund, aet. 10			St. A./84		
Chandler, Thomas		W. Vol.	St. John Co.		
Charles, Claudius, surgeon			P1303		
William	Ct.	Sgt. PWAR	Burton	York Co.	
Charl(e)ton, Henry			York Co.		
Robert			Ken.	U.S.A.?	
William, merchant			St. John		
Chace, or Chase, Ebenetus			Gr. Lake		
Isaac		2 DeL.			
James	Mass.		Maug.	Gr. Lake	
Lydia			P171	Gr. Lake	
Reuben, carpenter	N.Y. D. Co.		Gn.		

Name	Origin	Regiment	Location	Ref	County	Extra
Chace, *or* Chase, Seth			Wash.			
Shadrach, farmer	Mass./R.I.	Ens. 2 DeL.		P568		d. St. J.
Walter			Gn.		Maug.	
William, shoemaker			P386		Ken.	
Chasser, *or* Cheshire, Thomas	N.Y.		P481		Queens Co.	
Chatty, Charles		74th				
Chayton, John			St. A.			
Chestnutwood, Sebastian		1 NJV	Ken.			
Chew, Joseph	N.J.	CMG	C193	UC?		
William	N.J.	Lt. 3 NJV	C447	Maug.		
Chicase, James			Gn.			
Chichester, Rachel	Ct.		P306	Or.		
Chick, *see* Scheck						
Chidister, John		2 NJV	Ken.	York Co.		
Childs, Robert		2 NJV	Ken.			
Chillas, Michael			Ham. R.			
Robert, Capt. Co. 27	Eng./N.Y.	Capt.				
cabinet maker, 85		NYCV	P1424			
Chipman, Ward, Esquire, 85	Mass.		C195			
Chisholm, Hugh	Scot.		Sch.			
Christie, *or* Cristy, George			Char.			
Jesse			Char.			
James		Sgt. 3 NJV	P922	Sussex		
John			Sch.			
Peter			Char.			
Samuel			Char.			
Shadrach, farmer			P771			
Thomas			Char.			
William (1)		RFA?	Char.			
William (2)		KAD	Bl. 4			
Chubb, John, cordwainer, 85	Pa..		P1151			
Church, William	N.Y. A. Co.	KAR	F'ton			
Clapp, James, yeoman, 85		a.b.	Gr. Lake	UC?		
Jesse			Ham. R.			
Thomas, mariner, 85			St. John			
Clapson, William			St. A.			
Clare, William John	Eng. N.E.		F'ton	Kent Co.		
Clark(e), — — widow			Dig.			
Abraham			Queens Co.	Fredericton		
Alexander (1)	N.J.	ex NJV	P1232	Maq.	St. John	
blacksmith and carpenter, 85						
Alexander (2)			Gr. Lake			
Archibald			Gr. Lake			
Benjamin ?			St. John			
Benjamin	N.J.?		Queens Co.			
Charles Leach			Sussex			
Dawson			Musq.			
Dougald		74th	Char.			
Gardner			Queens Co.			
Isaac, fm Me., 77			Queens Co.	Fredericton		
Jacob			Rusagonis			
James (1), baker, 85	R.I.	CGP	P1225, 1340			
James (2), Jr.	R.I.		P1339			
James (3)		Cpl. PWAR	F'ton	Mir.		
Jehiel, mariner, 95						
Jeremiah		RFA	Mag. R.			
John (1), cordwainer, 85						
John (2), merchant, 85						
John (3)			P974	Queens Co.		
John (4), painter			P1140			
John (5)		70th	Char.			
John Hunter			St. A.			
John, Jr.			LR			
John Wright			Queens Co.			
Joseph, Capt. Co. 9	Ct.	Surg.	P313	Maug.		
Joseph, Jr.	Ct.		LR	Char.?		
Latham	R.I.		St. John			
Nehemiah, phys./85	Ct.	Surg.Em.Ch.	P314			
Ninian			Char.			
Peter		1 DeL.	Bl. 8	Carl.		
Richard Samuel, Rev.	Ct.		Gn.	St. St.		
Yale, '62						
Robert			Char.			
Samuel, weaver, 85	Eng./N.Y.	ex QR	P784			

Clark(e), Stephen		Cpl. LAR	York Co.	
Thomas, grocer			P1113	
Thomas, carpenter		KAD	Queens Co.	
William (1)			Char.	
William (2), Esquire, 85	R.I.	Capt. LNE	C120	
William (3)	N.C.		Gn.	
William (4)		4th R. Art.		Mir.
Clawson, William	N.J.		LR	
Clay, Jonathan, blacksmith, 85		KAD	Bl. 4	
Clayton, Samuel (1)		Cpl. KAD	Bl. 4	P124
Samuel (2)		Ct. QR	C210	Bl. 5	Y. Co.
Clearwater (Clowater),		KAR	Penniac	
Frederick				
Cleary, Daniel ?			St. St.	
Cleaves, Ebenezer				
Harrison				
John	?		Char.	
Nathan				
Robert				
Clements, John		dr. ML	Bl. 1	
Peter	N.Y.	Capt. KAR	P1055	York Co.
Cle(a)veland, James		RFA		
Katurah			P805	
William			P1312	
Clews, or Clues, John			P730	Mspc.
Cliff, John		Sgt. KAD	Bl. 4	
William		Sgt. KAD	Bl. 4	
Clinch, John		Adj. RFA		
Peter, merchant	Ir. Pa.	Lt. RFA	Mag. R.	
Clindenen, David				
David, Jr.	?		Char.	
Robert				
Cline, Peter		PL	Bl. 7	
Clinton, William, cordwainer			P719	Bl. 3	Absc.
Clopper, Garret, merchant	N.Y.	Lt. NYV	P114	Fredericton
clerk				
Close, Abraham	N.Y. W. Co.	Lt. GP	Bl. 3	
Benjamin	N.Y. W. Co.		Pr. Wm.	
Tertullus		Vol. GP	Bl. 3	d.
or Cluss, Caesar, black			St. John	
David			P604	Gn.	U.S.A.
Clowes, Gerhardus, farmer	N.Y. L.I.	Capt. 2 DeL.	P120, 407	Or.
John	N.Y. L.I.	Lt. 3 DeL.	P139	Burton
Samuel, farmer	N.Y. L.I.	Lt. 3 DeL.	P85		N.Y.
Timothy Bagley			P53	Ham. R.
Cluett, John James, Capt. Co. 39			P105	Gn.
attorney-at-law, Gn.				
Cobe, John		KOR	St. John Co.	left
Cochrane, John, Lt. Co. 9	N.H		P113	Lanc.
John			Char.	
John Corlet			Gr. Bay	U.S.A.?
Jonas			Dig.	
Jonathan			Gr. Bay	
Peter			Char.	
Robert			Char.	
Samuel			St. John	
Walter		74th		
William, labourer			P916	
Cock, James		2 DeL.		
John, Sr., Capt. Co. 8	Eng.		C206	
yeoman, 85				
John, Jr. m. gardener, 85			C205	·Bel.
Jordan	N.Y.		P511	U.S.A./00
Kelah			C507	
Sarah			C212	
William			C437	
Cockburn(e), John (1)		74th		
John (2)		31st	St. John Co.	
Coddington, Asher			LR	
Jacob		NYV	Kes.	
Codner, James, merchant, 85		Ens.Vol.Irld.	P48	
Coffield, Thomas	N.C.	Lt. NCV	P1167	Md.
Coffin, Guy Carleton			P141	
Isaac			C244	

270

Name	Origin/Unit	Rank	Code	Place	Extra
Coffin, John		Capt. NYV	C223, 4 242, 3, 602	Ner.	
Jonathan			C241		
Nathaniel	Mass.		C246, 283 384-6, 603		
Thomas A.		CMG	C281		
William, Harvard, '72	Mass.		C30, 285	Halifax	Que.
Coffman, or Cufman, John		3 NJV?	Nash.		
Coggeshall, James	N.Y.C.	CMG	St. John	d./86	
Cohee, Samuel (Lemuel?)		Sgt. ML	Bl. 1		
Coker, John James Thomas			Musq.		
Co(u)lborn, Charles, mariner	Am.	Lt. LAR	St. John	N.S.	
Colby, John			Queens Co.	York Co.	
Colden, Cadwallader D.			St. John		
Thomas, Esquire, 85	N.Y.	Capt. PL	C121, 2	Bl. 7	N.Y.
Cole, Alben		KAD .	Bl. 4		
David, carpenter		3 NJV	P1185	Wash.	
Henry		2 NJV	Bl. 2		
John, gentleman, 85	N.Y.				
John (2)		LAL	Gr. Bay		
John (3)		dr. LAL	Ken.		
Jonas			Kn.		
Richard			P918	Sunbury Co.	
Stephen			P292		
William		Ord.	P.767		
Coleman, Abraham			Ken.		
Daniel			St. John Co.		
Nathaniel		KAD	BH		
Robert			Kings Co.		
Thomas			F'ton	Ken.	
William		RFA	N.S.		
Co(o)ley, John, Black			St. John		
Colgin, Patrick			Burton	Mir.	UC?
Collard, Edward, blacksmith		GP	Bl. 3	Carl.	
James, Labourer, 97			St. John		
William, ship carpenter	Pa.				
Colley, Ishmael			P441		
Collins, Alexander		NYV	Kes.		
Benjamin		1 DeL.	Bl. 8		
David			St. A.		
James	Pen./83		St. A.		
John			St. A.		
Michael			Musq.		
Morris			Ken.		
Peter		Pilot	Shel.	Wash.	
Thomas		Cpl. 1 DeL.	P414	Pass.	
Colquhoon, Duncan	Can.	QMG	Or.	Fredericton	
Coltart, Robert, cartman, 85			Or.		
Colton, Isaac	N.E.		Or.		
Colville, John, merchant, 85	Scot.	Ord.	Sch.	P10, 59	
Colwell, John	N.J.	Ens. NJV	Kes.	Queens Co.	
Thomas		2 NJV	Ken.		
Co(o)mbs, Dennis, Coachmaker	N.J. Msx.	Adj. 2 NJV	P410	St. John Co.	
John, farmer	N.J.	Lt. 2 NJV	Bl. 2	Fredericton	
Micajah			P852	Gn.	LR
Nathaniel, carpenter	N.Y. L.I.	CMG	Queens Co.		
Nathaniel, farmer	N.J.	Ens. 2 NJV	F'ton	N.J.	
Noah, weaver	N.Y. L.I.		Ken.		
Robert		CMG	Gn.		
Samuel, carpenter, 85			P650		
Thomas, carpenter	N.Y. L.I.		Or.	Queens Co.	
William, farmer	N.Y. L.I.		Or.		
Com(e)ly, Robert, mason	Pa.		So. Bay	Kn.	
Compton, Ebenezer	N.Y.		Maug.		
John (1), bricklayer	Mass.		St. A.		
John (2), shoemaker. 95	N.Y. D. Co.		Gn.	St. John	
John (3)	N.J. Som.		Maug.		
William, carpenter, 85	N.J.		P1104	St. John Co.	
Conder, Elinor		RFA wdw.	Mag. R.		

271

Condon, Thomas		KAD	Bl. 4		
Coney, *see* Conway					
Conklin, Edmund		KAR	Or.		
Gilbert	N.Y. W. Co.	LAR?	St. John		
Joel			Bel.	U.S.A.?	
Samuel	N.Y.		P1344		
Conley, Connelly *or* Connolly,					
Dennis			P1064	Mspc.	
John	Ir./N.J.	3 NJV	P895	St. John Co.	
Patrick		RFA	Mag. R.		
William		RFA			
Connard, *see* Cunard					
Connell, Charles			Carl.		
Edward		BH		St. John	
Conner, *or* Connor, Constant	Ir./Mass.	Lt. RFA	P64		
Hugh		RFA	Mag. R.	Halifax	
James		disb.	Halifax	Mir.	
John (1)		a.b.	St. A.		
John (2), mason		QR?	P1011	Gr. Lake	
Peter		PWAR	Kings Co.		
Robert		Ord.	Sch.		
Conrad, *or* Conrod, John		2 NJV	Ken.	Sussex	
Conrey, John	Ct.	WL	Queens Co.		
Conway, Arthur		Sgt. PL	Bl. 7		
James, merchant, 85					
Cook(e), Charles, 2nd Lt.	Ir./N.J.		P1014		
Co. 12, mariner					
Daniel		PWAR	York Co.		
Edward			Mspc.		
Jacob, Capt. Co. 28			P1441	Maq.	Ken.
Jedidiah *or*	Ct.	BMG	Or.	U.S.A.?	
Zedediah, Sr.					
Jed. *or* Zed., Jr.			Or.		
John, merchant, 85			P1398		
Peter			Burton	Deer Is.	
Robert	Mass.	CMG	P1318	Ken.	Mass.
Samuel, Rev.	Eng./N.J.		F'ton		
Thomas			BH/87		
William	Ct.	Ord.	BH		
Zoar	N.Y. W. Co.				
Cookson, William	Mass.		St. A.		
Coon, William, blacksmith	N.J.	WL	Cumb.	Mir.	
Cooper, Andrew	S.C.?		F'ton		
Edward			C438		
John		Cpl. 3 NJV	Penniac		
Joseph, Capt. Co. 28,			C202	UC	
yeoman, 85					
Richard, farmer	N.J.	Lt. 3 NJV	Nash.		
Roger			Nash.		
Copeland, John		PWAR	St. John Co.		
Corey, Francis, merchant	R.I.	Lt. LNE	Gr. Lake		
Gideon, cooper	R.I.		C162	Gn.	New. C.
Gilbert	N.Y. L.I.	Br. pte.	Queens Co.		
Griffin	N.Y.		Queens Co.		
Sarah	N.Y.		Gn.		
Silvanus			Jemseg		
Thomas	N.Y.	Cpl. NYV	P1376	Queens Co.	
Cork, John			Wash.		
Corneck, John *or* Joseph		RFA	Mag. R.	Char.	
Cornelius, Daniel			St. A.		
Corneli(u)son, John		dr. 2 NJV	P493	Ken.	
Cornwall, Andrew			P1230	Kings Co.	
William,			P847		
cordwainer. 85					
Corn(w)ell, Charles, farmer	N.Y. L.I.				
Samuel, carpenter	N.Y. L.I.		Cumb.		
Corvin, John			Sch.		
Cosgrove, Thomas		PL	Bl. 7		
Costin, *see* Carton					
Cotterell, Jonas	N.J.?		BH		
William	N.J.?	KAD	BH		
Cott, (*for*) Mott?, Johannas V.	N.Y. L.I.				
Cotter, Michael			P1159		
Patrick		QR	Mir.		
Cottingham, Ephraim	Md.	ML	Bl. 1	Md.	

Cottle, Nathaniel	Mass.?		Queens Co.		
Cougle, John, farmer	N.J. Sx. Co.	Capt. 1 NJV	C249, 610, 1	Sussex	
Coulter, Andrew		Ct. BL			
Courser, John	N.Y.	Engr.	York Co.		
Couzins, Edward		1 DeL.	Bl. 8		
Covernam, Henry			Rus./84		
Covert, Abraham	N.Y. D. Co.	Lt. WL	A. Co.	Queens Co.	
tavernkeeper, 95 ?					
Cowan, John (1)		GP	Bl. 3		
, John (2)		Ord.	St. A.		
Cowie, Joseph			P799		
Robert		74th	Sch.		
Cowper, William	Mass.		?		
Cowperthwaite, David	N.J.		Or.	Gr. Lake	
Hugh	N.J.	WL	Burton	Shef.	
Cox, Charles		QR	St. George		
George	N.Y.?	Lt. KAR	Bl. 6	Fredericton	
Henry			Mace's Bay		
John	N.Y.	KAR	Bl. 9		
Robert, mariner?	Pa.		Gn.	Gr. Lake	
William	N.Y.?		C163	Bel.	
Coxetter, Bartholomew,					
tailor, 93, ar. w. parents.					
Cozens, Daniel, farmer	N.J.	Capt. 2 NJV	St. John		
Samuel	N.J.		C416	UC	
Crabb, James		3 NJV	P465		
John, 2nd Lt. Co. 29	N.Y. D. Co.		P565	LR	
John, Jr.	N.Y. D. Co.		P647	Kings Co.	
Stephen	N.Y. D. Co.		P646	Gn.	
Craddock, John			Ham. R./84		
Thomas			P297		
Craft, John	N.Y. D. Co.	WL	C266	Ham. R.	
Reuben	N.Y. D. Co.	WL	Ham. R.		
Craig, David		74th	St. A.	Dig.	
James		1 DeL.	Bl. 8	P983	Carl.
John (1)		GP	Bl. 3	d./85	
John (2), cooper			LR		
Robert (1), cooper, 85		Engr.	P1094		
Robert (2)		84th	Mag. R./84		
Cram, Robert ?			Mir.		
Crandall, George		KAD	BH		
Lewis, 2nd fleet			Gn.		
Crandlemire, William			Or.		
Crandy, John			P1076		
Crane, Daniel		NYV	Kes.		
Joseph		2 NJV	Ken.		
Crannell, Bartholomew, Capt.	N.Y. D. Co.		P88		
Co. 51, Esquire, 85					
Frances	N.Y. D. Co.		P428		
Isaac Van Hook			Gr. L.	Ct.	
Lemuel	N.Y. D. Co.		P431		
Cranston, Elizabeth			Ham. R.		
Crawford, Francis			St. John	Ken.	
James (1)	N.Y. W. Co.		Kn.		
James (2)			Ken.		
Joel			Kn.		
John (1)	N.Y. W. Co.	WL	P1012	Cumb?	
John (2)	Ct.		Ken.		
John (3)			St. A.		
Samuel		KAR	Bl. 3		
Thomas		Cpl. QR	P848	Queens Co.	
William, Sr.,	Ct.		P1316		
yeoman, 85					
William, Jr.,	Ct.		P1317		
cooper, 85					
William	Ir./Mass.	BMG	Kn.		
Creighton, Thomas, blacksmith			Queens Co.		
Thomas, Jr.,			St. John Co.		
blacksmith, 95					
Crickmore or Creekmore, Jesse			Bl. 5	Or.	
Crillon, Willard			LR/84		
Crispie(n), Matthias		3 NJV	P875		
Cristall, John	Scot.	Surg. PL	P227	Scot.	
Cristy, see Christie					
Crockford, James, baker, 85					

Crocker, Robinson			St. A.	
Cro(w)foot, Elihu	Ct.	Sgt. PWAR	St. John Co.	
Crombs, James ?			Char.	
Cromwell, Gerardus		QR	Jemseg	
James				New Canaan
John			Bel.	
Thomas, carman			Queens Co.	St. John
Crone, Israel		84th	Mag. R.	
Cronk, David, mariner, 97	N.Y.		LR	
Cronk(h)ite, Henry	N.Y. D. Co.	KAR	Bl. 6	Carl.
John	N.Y. D. Co.		Ken.	
Crookshank, George	Scot./N.J.		St. John	UC
Crookshanks, Joseph			St. A.	
Cropley, William		Bergen		
Cross, William		KAD		
Crossing, William	R.I.	Surg. LNE	Kings Co.	
Crossman, Robert		RFA		
Crow, William			Dig.	
Crowell, Joseph, farmer, Esquire, 85	N.J.	Capt. 1 NJV	C378, 395, 6	
Sarah	N.J.		C377	
Thomas	N.J.		C24	N.S.
Crozier, Ezekiel		Cpl. 2 NJV	Ken.	
Cudney, Ezekiel			P543	Shef.
Isaiah			Maug.	Kings Co.
Cullen, Isaac		Cpl. ML	P219	Bl. 1
Walter	Ir.	Surg. Mate RFA	Pass.	
Cull(e)y, John, cordwainer, 85		KAD	C298	
Culvar, Jonas, Sr.		1 NJV	P958	
Jonas, Jr.		1 NJV	P957	UC
Cumberland, John ?			BH	
Cumming, Alexander		Adj. KAR	P427	Scot.
Cummin(g)s, Daniel (1)		KAD	P1278	Maug.
Daniel (2)		1 DeL.	Bl. 8	
James		ML	Bl. 1	
John (1)		74th		
John (2), gentleman			Burton	
Silas, blacksmith			St. A.	
Cunard, Jonathan		Engr.	Ken.	St. John
Robert, 2nd Lt., Co. 33	Pa.		P1008	K. Co. Ptld.
Cunliffe, Joseph, merchant	Eng./N.J.	Capt. 1 NJV		Fredericton Carl.
Cunnabel, Edward G.			St. John	
Cunningham, Charles			P112	
Henry			Queens Co.	
John, Sgt.	Ir.	Adj. LAR	Or.	Qnsb.
Miles		RFA	P811	Mag. R.
Richard		3 NJV		
Thomas	Ir.	Lt. 1 DeL.	Bl. 8	Qnsb.
Curr(e)y, Charles			Gr. Lake	
David			P653?	Or.
John		dr. LAR	P1217	Bl. 8
Joshua, Lt. Co. 49	N.Y.	ex LAR	P655	Gn.
Patrick		KAD	Bl. 4	
Richard	N.Y.		P652	Queens Co.
Currie, Ross	Pa.	Adj. PL	P225	York Co.
Currier, Issachar			Cn.	Bl. 2
Curtis, Andrew, cooper, 85			P721	
Ebenezer			Char.	
Solomon		GP	Bl. 3	d., 1 daughter
Cushannon, Richard ?			Char.	
Custard, Samuel	Pa.		Burton	
Cuthbert, James	Scot.		P1429	Kings Co.
Cutler, Abigail, wdw. John		CMG	Bl. 4	
Elizabeth			Bl. 4	
Hannah			Bl. 4	
Joseph		RFA	Ken.	
Luther			St. John Co.	
Cyphers, George	N.J.	Adj. 2 NJV	Bl. 2	

Dafford, Abraham ? Gr. L./84

274

Da(i)ley, David		QR	St. A.		
John		KOR	St. John Co.		
Dalne, *see* Doiley, James					
Dalley, Cornelius, cooper		Engr.	Gr. Lake	UC	
Dalton, Benjamin			St. A.		
James			Mspc.		
John		QR	Mir.		
Dalwick, Casper			P148		
Dalzell, Edward, mariner, 85			P1243	absc./96	
Dan(n), John, mariner, 85	Ct.		P828	Kn.	
Selleck			P1156	Bel.	U.S.A.
Dane, Daniel			Char.		
Luther			Char.		
Daniel, Joel, carpenter		Cpl. 1 NJV	Penniac	Sussex	
Timothy	N.Y. W. Co.		P1033	Kings Co.	Y. Co
William		42nd	Nash.	Mir.?	
Darby, Charles		a.b.	Sch.		
Darbyshire, Daniel, *Cyrus*			?		
Darington (Derington), John	N.Y. D. Co.		Ken.		
William		3 NJV	Ken.		
Dasher, Benjamin	N.C.	NCV	Kes.		
Davenport, Gabriel	N.Y.	KAR	Bl. 6	Carl.	
Thomas, Lt., Co. 14	N.Y.				
Davi(d)son, Andrew			Ken.		
George			Wash.		
Hamilton, carpenter, 85			P1233	York Co.	
James		1 NJV	P378		
John (1), saddler, 85			P1101		
John (2)	N.H.	Lt. KAD	C239, 424, 5	York Co.	
John (3)	N.J.	Engr.	St. George	?	
Davis, Abel			Rest.	Mir.	
Benjamin		1 NJV	Kes.	Rest.?	
Burrows, gentleman, 95		QMR LAL	C111, 2	Kings Co.	
Caleb			Bel.		
David		GP	Bl. 3	d.	
Edward			Ken.		
Elisha	Pa.	BCV	P782	LR	
Germain		1 NJV	BH	St. George	
Honor			St. A.		
James	Ct.?	KAD? 1 DeL.?	LR		
John (1)		CMG	St. A.		
John (2), cordwainer, 85		GP?	P640	Ken.	
John (3)		LAL? 1 DeL.?	Gr. Lake	St. John	
Joseph	Ct.?		Char.		
Thomas	N.Y.	WMD	Mir.	Bel.?	
William		74th	Char.		
Dawson, George		Capt. BL	P482	Dip. Har.	Pa.
Henry			Gr. Lake		
James		Capt. BL	Eng.	Mace's Bay	
Samuel		1 DeL.	Bl. 8		
Thomas			P421	St. A.	U.S.A.
Day, Abraham			P920	Gr. L. esch.	
Hendrick		CMG	P1123	Queens Co.	
James			Kings Co.		
John (1)	N.J.	2 NJV	Bl. 2		
John (2)	N.Y.C.	CMG	P1135	Queens Co.	
John (3), cordwainer, 90			St. John		
Peter	N.J.		Shel.	Queens Co.	
Thomas		Engr.?	Sch.		
William, carpenter, 95			P1131	Wash.	N.Y.?
Dayton, John		QR	Bl. 5		
Dealy, Michael		RFA	Mag. R.		
Dean(e), Jacob, freeman, 90			Queens Co.		
John, labourer, 90	Ct.		St. John		
William, cordwainer, 85		Sgt. LAL	Gr. Bay		
Debaw, *or* DeBow, James, bricklayer, 95		1 NJV	P952	Ham. R.	
DeBeck, John Ludwig		Lt. NYV	Kes.	d., wdw.	

DeBlois, Lewis	Mass.		St. John		
Gilbert	Mass.		St. John		
Decew, *or* DeCou, Jacob	N.J. Sx. Co.			UC	
Decker, Henry			P699	UC	
Reuben			P335		
Stephen, blacksmith, 95			Kn.		
Dee, David		RFA	Kings Co.		
D'Ehrenstein, Frederick	Ger.	Lt. Lsbg.	Maug.	Fredericton	
DeForest, Ephraim, shoemaker	Ct.		Kn.	Fredericton	
Nathan		Cpl. KAD	Kn.		
Deil (?), John		1 NJV?	Ken.		
Delaney, James		Ens. 1 DeL.	Bl. 8		
John	N.Y.		Queens Co.		
DeLong, Aaron		LAR	Gn.	Kn.	
John		LAR	Queens Co.		
Simon		LAR	N.S.		
DeLue, Jacob, mariner			LR	St. John	
DeMarest, James		KOR	P921		
Simon		3 NJV	P934	Kings Co.	U.S.A.?
DeMerchant, John			Carl.		
Philip		Cpl. 1 DeL.			
DeMill, John, carpenter, 85			P1138	Kings Co.	
Dempsey, Simon		KOR	St. John Co.		
Dennis, Cornelius, millwright	N.Y.		P1221		
Henry	Pa.		Char.		
John	Pa.		Shel.	Pnfd.	UC
Lewis	N.J.	Engr.	York Co.	Mir.	
Nancy			Pass.		
Peter		NYV	Kes.		
Dennison, John, Jonathan			Char.		
Michael		1 DeL.	Nash.		
Denskill, James			BH		
Denton, Robert			Queens Co.	left?	
Samuel	N.Y. L.I.		Or.	Queens Co.	
Solomon	N.Y. L.I.		Or.	N.Y.	
DePeyster, Abraham	N.Y.	Capt. KAR	P21, 103		
Frederick	N.Y.	Capt. NYV	P84	Kes.	N.Y.
Joseph Reed			Gr. Lake/84		
Derickson, Jacob, farmer	Pa.		Jemseg		
Derrick, Christopher		KAR?	Sch.		
Derry, James	N.Y. W. Co.	WL	Westm.		
John	N.Y. W. Co.	WL	Westm.		
Deveau, *see* Devoe					
DeVeber, Francis		Ens. 2 DeL.	Bl. 7	Musq.	
Gabriel, Sr.	Eng.	Lt. Col. PWAR	P99,115	Musq.	
Gabriel, Jr.		Lt. DeL.	Burton		
John		Ens. PWAR	P100	Musq.	
Sarah			P98	d./85	
Devereaux, Margaret			Sch.		
Devire, *see* Dyer					
Devoe, Daniel, cartman, 85	N.Y.	Sgt. LAR	St. John		
Frederick, cordwainer, 85	N.Y.	guide	P1184		
Lewis	N.Y.	NYV	St. John		
Dewar, *or* Duer, John		42nd	Nash.	Mir.	
Dewit(t), Evert or Ewart	N.Y.	a.b. St. Is.	Or.		
Henry			Or.		
Jacob		KAR	Or.		
John		3 NJV	Or.	Pr. Wm.	
Peter			Or.		
Dexter, John		QR	Gn.	Mir.	
Dibbins, Henry		1 NJV	Ken.		
Dibble(s), Frederick, 2nd Lt. Co. 9	Ct.		P117	Kn.	Wdstk.
Fyler, attorney	Ct.		P60	d., wdw. Polly	
Jonathan	Ct.		BH	d.	
Ralph	Ct.		Kn.		
Walter	Ct.		P116	Kn.	Sussex
William	Ct.		Kn.	Woodstock	
Dick, James		74th			
John (1)		74th	Char.		
John (2)	N.Y.		Mag. R.	St. John	

Dickerman, Abraham, shoemaker	Ct.		St. John			
Dickey, *or* Dickie, Adam			Char.			
Hector	S.C.		Jamaica	Ken.		
Jonathan			Ken./84			
Dicki(n)son, Amos	N.Y.		Maug.	Wash.	Carl.	
Darius, tailor	N.Y. L.I.		F'ton			
Gilbert	N.Y. D. Co.		LR	Queens Co.		
Hannah			C548			
Isaac, tailor, 85			P814			
James, merchant	N.Y. D. Co.		P164	Bel.	Gn.	
Nathaniel, Lt., Co. 10	Mass.	CMG	C428, 436	West.		
Samuel	N.Y. D. Co.		P96,398	Queens Co.		
Tertullus	N.Y. D. Co.	BMG	P78	Gn.	Wdstk.	
Dicks, *or* Dix, Joanna, wdw.	N.H.		Gr. Lake			
Dickson, or Dixon, Andrew		GP	Bl. 3			
Charles, labourer		QR	Bl. 5			
Gabriel			Gr. Lake			
Humphrey			Shef.			
John, carpenter		Cpl. ?	Sch.			
Joseph (1), 2nd Lt. Co. 2		Ens. AL	Kn.	Bel.		
Joseph (2)		1 DeL.	Bl. 8	Woodstock		
Richard, black	N.Y.		St. J.			
William			Sch.			
Diemar, Augustus		Ens. LAR	York Co.			
Dier, *or* Dire, *see* Dyer						
Dif(f)endorf, George	Pa.		BH	N.S.		
Jacob	Pa.		BH	N.S.		
Dignam, Christopher			Bel.			
Dignon, Patrick		2 NJV	Ken.			
Dill, Job (gr. as Jacob Dale)			W. St. John			
Dillon, William			P1019	LR		
Dilworth, Jasper ?			Maug.			
Dinbow, Joseph ?			Dig.			
Dingee, Elijah	N.Y.		Gr. Lake	Shef.		
Solomon, carpenter	N.Y. L.I.		Gn.			
Dingwall, Arthur, shopkeeper, 85	Scot.		P1348			
Dinn, William ?			Maq.			
Disbrow (Desbrow), Henry			Ham. R./84			
Noah, mariner, 95			St. John			
Samuel			Ham. R.			
Divis, Robert, ar. Sept.	Va.		BH	son		
Doane, Rachel	Pa.					
Dobbie, John		74th	Char.			
Dobbins, Alexander		CMG	Pt. M.	St. A.		
Dobbs, Elias			Or.			
Hewlett			St. John Co.			
Martin	N.Y. D. Co.		Or. rej.			
Zachariah	N.Y. D. Co.	Cpl. KAR	P717	Queens Co.		
Dobie, Robert			Sch.			
Dodd, Thomas			Sch.			
Dodge, Abraham, mason, 85						
Samuel, Sr., bricklayer, 85			St. St.			
Samuel, Jr.			Char.			
Dodley, William ?			Kes.			
Doggett, John, mariner			St. A.			
Doiley, James		64th	Pass.			
Dolan, Patt		GP	Bl. 3			
Dolph, Stephen			Or.			
Dominick, Francis, carpenter, 85		Engr.	P144, C169			Digby
Donahoe, Thomas, joiner		2 NJV	P1184	Ken.		Sussex
Donald, Alexander			Penniac			
James			Mir.			
William, mariner, 90	Scot.		P1018			
Donaldson, John	N.H.		St. A.			
William, merchant, 85	Scot./Va.		Shel.	St. John		Jam.
Don(n)ally, Barney (Bartholomew?)		Ord.	Mspc.			
Patrick		PWAR	St. John Co.	Nash.		
Donland, Timothy		Vol. NYV	Or.	Carl.		

Name	Origin	Regiment	Ref.	County	Location
Dooley, William		NYV	Kes.		
Dop (Drost?), Peter?			Queens Co.		
Doran, Peter		PWAR	Sch.	Fredericton	
Dougherty (Doherty), John			P1141	Gr. Lake	St. John
Doughty, Doty, Doughts, *or*					
Dotens, James	S.C.?		St. A.		
Nathaniel, farmer	Md.				
Douglas, Daniel, plasterer			St. John		
Dove, John	N.J. Msx.	Engr.	P324	Sussex	
Sarah			Gr. Bay		
William		GP '78	P160		
Dowdney, *see* Downing					
Dowling, Abraham			C216		
John		NSV	St. A.		
Lawrence,	Ir.		C153		
carpenter, 85					
Samuel,			P571		
bricklayer, 85					
Downer, Thomas			P1060		
Downey (Downie), Abraham		KAR	Kings Co.		
Margaret, wdw.	S.C.		Bel.		
Downing, John	N.C.?		Westm.		
Nathaniel			BH	Char.	
Downs, Patrick			Ham. R./84		
Doyle (Doyall), Hugh			Sussex		
James, shipwright?			St. John		
John		1 NJV?	Sussex		
Drake, Benjamin	N.J. Msx.		BH		
Francis, shoemaker	N.Y.	Sgt. 2 DeL.	Maug.	York Co.	
Michael			BH		
Peter, yeoman, 85	N.Y.		Bel.		
Uriah, labourer, 98			P1071		
Drew, Joseph, tailor	Scot./S.C.		P576	Bel.	St. John
Driscoll (Driskell), Daniel		KAD	Kings Co.?		
Jeremiah		RFA	Kings Co.?		
Drost, Peter, mariner, 85			P712	Queens Co.	
Drummond, Alexander,		Surg. KAR	C105	Nash.	
Physician, 85					
Ann, daughter of			C106	York Co.	
Donald, m.					
McGibbon					
Ann, wdw. of			C82		
Donald					
Donald, Capt.,					
Co. 17					
Jacobina, m.			C81	Nash.	
Dugald Campbell					
James			P1418	Rest.	
William,					
prob. Dryden					
Dryden, William		Lt. 1 NJV	Gn.	Kings Co.	
Dubbins, Patrick			Mspc.	N.S.	
Dubois, Culf		fifer 2 NJV	Bl. 2		
Dudgeon, Thomas?		KOR '78		Albert Co.	
Duer, Donald		74th			
Duffell, Edward, yeoman, 85	N.J.	1 NJV	C320	Bel.	
James	N.J.	Sgt. 2 NJV	C127		
Duffer (Dufe), Angus			BH	York Co.	
Duffus, Charles,			St. John		
schoolmaster, 95					
Duffy, Samuel, mariner, 85			P629		
Duftin (Dustin?), Paul			Char.		
Duggin (Dougan), John		1 DeL.	Bl. 8		
William			Ken.		
Dunavan (Donavan), Anna			Char.		
Cornelius		KOR			
Daniel		KOR			
Dunbar, Elizabeth			P1355		
George		Capt. 1 DeL.	P49	Nash.	
John		ML?	Sch.		
Duncan, John, shoemaker			St. John		
Dundrick, Leonard			Mspc.		
Dunfield, Michael		RFA	P812	Mag. R.	Ken.
Dunham, Asher, Capt. Co. 13	N.J.Mor.Co.	Lt. NJV sec.	P1116	N.S.	
Daniel, joiner, 85	N.J.		P687	St. John Co.	

Name	Origin	Rank/Regt.	Grant	Location
Dunham, David	N.J.		P293	Kings Co.
Isaac, tailor	N.Y.		P301	Ken.
John		KAD	P306	Gr. Bay
Jonathan, black-smith, Capt. Co. 13		LNE		
Lewis, house carpenter			F'ton	
Seth			Kn.	
Thomas		Engr.	Kn.	UC
Dunlop, Charles or John?		Ct. QR	Bl. 5	
Dunmore, John			Sch./84	
Dunn, Benjamin			BH	
Daniel	N.Y. W. Co. WL		Gn.	Mir.
Jeremiah, farmer			BH	Campobello
John	N.Y.		St. A.	
Jonathan, farmer			BH	Campobello
Mary, m. Fitzgerald			P564	Gn.
William, mason, 85	Pa.		P911	Maq.
Duphnack, Charles		Brunswick Regt.	St. A.	St. John
Dure (Durl), Patrick		42nd	Cn.	
Durfee, William	Ct.	CMG	P638	
Durlon (Durling?), Joseph, carpenter	N.Y. L.I.			
Durney, John		Sgt. RFA	P405	Campobello
Durose, Charles		Cpl. KAR	Or.	
Dusenberry, Henry, clothier	N.Y. W. Co.		Wash.	U.S.A.
Dustan, see Duftin				
Dutton, Mrs.			Kn.	
Dwyer, Dyer, Dier, Devire, Edmund,	Mass.	CMG	Queens Co.	
Henry, farmer	N.Y. Or. Co.		P475	
James (1)		Cpl. 1 DeL.	Bl. 8	Carl.
James (2), farmer	N.Y. Or. Co.		Kings Co.	
James (3)		QR	Bl. 5	York Co.
(Droyer), John Frederick			Gr. Lake	
Jonas			Dig.	
Dykeman, Garret	N.Y.		P660	Jemseg
Gilbert			Queens Co.	
Joseph or Josiah			P1447	BH
Dymond, or Dumont, William Van		Lt. 1 NJV	Maug.	
Eagan, Edward		RFA	Mag. R.	
Eagles, John	N.Y. W. Co.	Capt, QR sec.	Ptld.	
Earle, Charles	Scot./Va.	Surg. 1 NJV	F'ton	
Edward (1)	N.J.	Capt. 3 NJV	Gr. Lake	N.Y.
Edward (2)		Sgt. 3 NJV		
John		KOR		
Justus, merchant	N.J.	Lt. 3 NJV	P890	Gr. Lake
Michael			Bel.	
Philip			P1103	F'ton
Eastman, David	Pa.		St. A.	
Easton, James	Scot./N.Y.		Queens Co.	
Eaton, Francis		KAD	Bl. 4	
Ebbett, Joseph, shoemaker	N.Y. L.I.		Gr. Lake	Burton
Eccles, James	Ir.	Lt. PWAR	P226, C315	York Co.
Echron, John			St. A.	
Edgett, Joel		WL	Albert Co.	
John		WL	Albert Co.	
Edison, George				
Edwards, Edward, farmer	Eur.	Navy?	P121	Ken.
Richard, labourer, 87		CMG	P1214	
William (1)		Ens. LAR	F'ton	
William (2)		KAD	Bl. 4	
Effa (Effee), John Caspar, gunsmith, 85	Ger.		P1387	
Egan, Nicholas			P316	Dip. Har.
Egbert, Anthony, carpenter, 85	N.Y. St. I.	Engr.	P107	
Eldred, Peter		a.b.	Sch.	
Eldridge, Rebecca, m. Phillips			St. A.	
William	N.J.?	2 DeL.	BH/87	

Fairweather, Benjamin	R.I.		P1400	K ngs Co.	N.S.
Jedediah, mason	Ct.		P1329	Kings Co.	
John		74th			
Samuel			Sussex		
Thomas	Ct.		P802	Kings Co.	
Falcken (Falkenham?), John, yeoman, 85			C441		
Fanjoy, William		Cpl. PL	Bl. 7	Gr. L.	
Fanning, David	Va./NC	var.	Queens Co.	N.S.	
Farington, Margaret			BH/84		
Farmer, Henry		Sgt. 1 DeL.	Bl. 8		
Farnam, Ephraim, mariner			Pass.	St. A.	
Farr, Francis			Char.		
Farrah, Peter, cordwainer, 85			St. John		
Farrand (Ferrand), Stephen, cordwainer, 85	N.J. E. Co.				
Farrell, Elizabeth		RFA	Mag. R.		
William		1 NJV	P1039	Bl. 7	
Farren, James		a.b.	Sch.		
Farris (Ferris), Abraham			Gr. Lake		
Ahasuerus			BH		
Caleb	N.Y. W. Co.				
George	N.Y. W. Co.		P658	Jemseg	
John (1), clother, 85		3 NJV	P938		
John (2)		5 NJV	Gr. Lake		
John (3)		GP	Bl. 3		
Joseph (1), Capt. Co. 49			P554	N.Y.	
Joseph (2), joiner	Ct.		Ken.	Ct.	
Joseph (3)		Lt. But. R.		Char.	
Joshua	N.Y. W. Co. WL?		P553	UC?	
Larkin		PWAR?	York Co.		
Peter	N.Y. W. Co.		P548		
Samuel		Cpl. KAR	Penniac	F'ton	
Solomon, Lt., Co. 2	Ct.	Ens. AL	BH		
Fauvrick, John ?			St. A./84		
Fay, Henry E.			C92-5, 138-9		
Featherby (Feareby, Federby?), Thomas		NJV	Ken.	Sunbury Co.	
Feed (Teed?), Isaac			Gr. Bay/84		
Fenny, Cillap (Phoenix, Philip?)			Ken.		
Ferdinand, Peter		74th	Sch.		
Ferguson, Alexander			St. A.		
Henry	Pa.	Ens. 1 DeL.	P1274	Bl. 8	
John		Lt. LAL	P691	Musq.	
Robert	R.I.		P504	Dip. Har.	
William	Pa.	Sgt. 29th	Tracadie		
Fernald, Noah			P1017	Queens Co.	
Fero, Christian		Sgt. Kar.	Penniac	Carl.	
Ferris, see Farris					
Fick, Peter	N.Y. D. Co.		Maug.	Or.	
Field(s), Ambrose			BH/84		
Cornelius			Mspc.	Gr. Lake	
George	Pa.		BH/87		
Patrick		Sgt. 1 DeL.	Carl.		
Fife (Fisk?), William			Mspc.		
Finch, Charles		KOR			
Edward	N.Y. D. Co.		P1307		
Henry, mariner, 95	N.Y. D. Co.		LR		
Martha, wdw.			Or.		
James			Or.		
Reuben	N.Y. D. Co.		P859		
Titus		PWAR	Nash.	UC	
Finlayson, John		42nd	Nash.?		
Finn, Darby		RFA			
Dominick		GP	Bl. 3		
Patrick, labourer			St. John		
Finnamore, Charles	N.J.	2 NJV	Ken.		
David			Sussex		
Richard	N.J.	Ens. WJV	C55	Jemseg	
Fish, Alexander		a.b.?	Sch.		
Thomas	N.C.	NCV	Kes.		
Fis(c)her, Adam			St. John Co.		
Andrew	Pa.		Gr. Lake		

Fis(c)her, Barbara, wdw. John,		ML	Bl. 1	
m. Joseph Scribner				
Henry		1 DeL.	Bl. 8	
John (1),			P1217	
mariner, 90				
John (2)	N.J.?	PWAR	Bl. 3	
Lewis (Ludwig)		3 NJV	F'ton	
Peter		74th		
Fisk, William, carpenter, 85		Engr.		
Fith (Fitz), Jeremiah			BH/87	
Fithie (Fitch), George ?			Gr. Lake	Master *Nancy*
Fitzgerald, Daniel		LAL	Bl. 5	
John		1 DeL.	Bl. 8	LR
Matthew			Mspc.	
Morris		RFA	Mag. R.	
Thomas			Gr. Lake	
Fitzpatrick, James		Sgt. 1 DeL.	Bl. 8	
Fitzrandolph, David, *et al*	N.J.		BH	N.S.
Fitzsimmons, Peter, vintner, 85			P1416	
William			St. John Co.	
Flaglor, Simon	N.Y. D. Co.		Kings Co.	
Fleetwood, William		Cpl. LAR		
Fleming, Andrew	Ir.		St. John	
Charles		1 NJV	Penniac	
James	Md.?	74th	Kings Co.	UC?
John, black			Bl. 2	
Richard		GP?	St. A.	
Fletcher, Dan			Queens Co.	
Duncan		Capt. Lt. LAR		Scot.
Isaac		KAR	Penniac	Bl. 7
James		3 NJV	Wash.	
Flew(w)elling (Flueling), Abel	N.Y. U. Co.	pilot	P6¹⁷	Kings Co.
Enos		KAR	Kn.	
Francis	N.Y. W. Co.	WL	Wash.	
Guilford	Wls. N.Y.		Bel.	Calif.	K. Co.
John, Lt. Co. 15	N.Y. U. Co.		Kings Co.	
Joseph,	N.Y. W. Co.			St. J.
fisherman, 95				
Morris	N.Y. U. Co.		P838	LR	St. J.
Thomas	N.Y.		Kings Co.	
Flinn, David		1 DeL.	Bl. 8	
Henry			St. A./84	
John		3 NJV	Gr. Bay	
Patrick		RFA	Mag. R.	Deer Is.
Flint, James		QR	York Co.	
Flood, William			Bl. 5	
Florence, Lewis			Mir.	
Flower(s), Gilbert,			Queens Co.	
carpenter, 85				
John			Queens Co.	
William		LAL	Or.	
Floyd, Richard	N.Y. L.I.	QMR 2 DeL.	Maug.	U.S.A.
Fogo, David, Capt., Schooner			St. A.	
Polly				
Folkins, Joseph	Ger.?		Queens Co.	Kings Co.
Forbes, Henry ?				d./1843
James		42nd	C44	
Force, Philip	N.J. Sx. Co.	1 NJV	Ken.	Ptld.	UC
Ford, Elizabeth, wdw.			BH/84	Pocologan
John (1), Capt. Co. 43	N.J.	Lt. NJV sec.	P309	Ken.
John (2), jeweller	LNE	KAD	Bl. 4	
Forman, James		Sgt. KAR	Penniac	York Co.
Forrest, Daniel	Scot.		Jemseg	
Thomas			F'ton	Bl. 9
For(r)ester, James, Capt.				
Co. 23				
John, Capt. Co. 4, R.I.			P1239	Kings Co.
yeoman, 85				
John, Jr.			P1248	
Joseph, shipwright			P1083	Ken.
Joshua			LR	
Mary			C131	
Forsdyke, John,		Sgt. 2 DeL.		
? *same as* Forsythe *following*				

Name	Origin	Military	Location	Location 2
Forsythe, John, carpenter, 85			P502	Dip. Har.
Robert	Pa.		Mir.	
Fosdick, Nathaniel			Bel.	Cn.
Foshay, Isaac	N.Y. Ph.		Maq.	Jemseg
Peter	N.Y. Ph.			Jemseg
Foss, Elias	Ger.	CMG	Or.	
Foster, Caleb	N.J.?	KAR	Sunbury Co.	
Charles			F'ton	Carl.
Ebenezer	N.J.		Kings Co.	
Elias, Sr.	Ct.		LR	
Elias, Jr.	Ct.		LR	
Jacob			Gn.	
Josiah		Cpl. 2 NJV	Ken.	Carl.?
Joshua			LR	
Stephen		CMG	Kn.	
William		WL	Westm.	
Fought, George, cordwainer, 90			P1322	
Foulk, Moses	Pa.?		BH	Pennfield
Founds (Fowns), William, blacksmith, 85			P432	St. John Co.
Fountain, Stephen, blacksmith	Ct.	QR?		N.S.
Thomas, black			St. John	
Fowler, Aaron, carpenter, 85	N.Y.		P356	Bel.
Andrew	N.Y. W. Co.		St. John Co.	
Benjamin, carpenter, 85		Cpl. QR	Norton	
Caleb		Ens. LAR	F'ton	
Cornelius			P419	Bel.
Daniel, Capt. Co. 33, cabinet maker, 85			LR	
Gabriel	Wls./N.Y.	WL	Ham. R.	
Henry, Lt. Co. 42	N.Y.	WL	Ham. R.	
James (1)	Wls./N.Y.		Ham. R.	
James (2)	N.Y.		P1026	Ham. R.
Jeremiah, carpenter, 85	N.Y. W. Co.	Sgt. LAR		
John, farmer	Ct./Mass.		Kn.	UC
Josiah (1)		a.b.	Sch.	
Josiah (2)	N.Y. W. Co.	WL	Maug.	Sussex
Joshua	N.Y. W. Co.		Burton	Queens Co.
Oakley			Ham. R.	
Oliver			Queens Co.	
Robert		Sgt. 1 DeL.	Bl. 8	Gr. Lake
Thomas			P411	Ken.
Thomas, Jr.		1 DeL.	Bl. 8, P1277	Carl.
Walter			P355	Bel.
Weeden, 2nd Lt. Co. 46			P1025	Ham. R.
William	N.Y.	Capt. LAR	F'ton	
Fox, Frederick		KAR	York Co.	
George		KAD?		
John Christian	Pa.?	KAR	Bl. 6	
Koses		GP?	Kn.	
Patrick			Bel.	Maug.
Foy, John		PWAR	Nash.	
Thomas		1 DeL.	Bl. 8	
Frankar, Lewis		GP	Bl. 3	
Franks, Frances		1 NJV	Sussex	
Thomas		Sgt. QR	F'ton	
Fraser, (Frazier, Frazee),				
Abraham			St. John	
Alexander			Mag. R.	
Charles		Sgt. KAR	Bl. 6	
Daniel or Donald			Mir.	
James (1)		Ord.?	St. St.	
James (2)		3 NJV?	C426, 7	
John (1)		42nd	P257	Nash.
John (2)		QMR. KOR?	Sch.	St. A.
Lewis (1)		Cpl. NYV	P955	Kes.
(Frazee) Lewis (2)			C380	Sussex
Michael, baker, 85			P1401	
(Frazee) Oliver		2 NJV	C351	Sussex
Simon			Kemble Manor	

Name	Origin	Rank/Unit	Code	Place	Place
Fraser, Thomas		Cpl. 42nd	Nash.		
William, Sr.,		Sgt.?	Sch.		
William, Jr.			Sch.		
(Frazee) William		CMG	C337	Ken.	
Fredenburgh (Vradenburgh?),	N.Y.		Kings Co.		
Nicholas					
Frederick, Conrod			F'ton		
Peter		KOR	St. John Co.		
Free, William	N.Y. W. Co.	WL	Burton	Kn.	
Freeland, Hartman		2 NJV	Bl. 2	Kings Co.?	
Nicholas		Sgt. 3 NJV	P923	Ken.	
Freely, Charles		2 NJV	Burton		
Freeman, Benjamin		Engr.	BH	U.S.A.?	
Lewis		Ct. KAD	C190	Bl. 4	N.S.
Mark		Cpl. KAR	Bl. 6	Carl.	
Samuel		Cpl. KAR	Bl. 6	Carl.	
Thomas		NYV	P1047	Kes.	Kn.
French, Charity	Ct./N.Y.		P1286	Pet.	Dip Har.
James (1)		Capt. 1 DeL.	P1293	Nash.	
James (2)	Pa.	Cpl. 2 DeL.	BH/86		
Thomas		Capt. 1 DeL.	P1292	Bl. 8	U.S.A.?
William		Ens. 1 DeL.	P1291		
Frink, Nathan	Ct.	Capt. LAL	C110, 123, 250, 1	St. St.	
Fritch, John	Pa.	QMR	Ken.		
Frost, Abraham, tavernkeeper, 85			P9		
John, carpenter, 85		LAR			
Joseph (1)		Cpl. LAR	LR		
Joseph (2)		RGB	Mag. R.		
William	Ct.		P15	Kn.	
Fry, William			BH/84		
Fukes, Daniel		ML	Bl. 1		
Fuller (Fullard), Daniel		KAR	York Co.		
David		PWAR?	York Co.		
Fullerton, John B.		2 DeL.?	P792	Ken.	
Susannah, wdw. Stephen	Mass.	Ord.	Queens Co.	St. John Co.	
Fullington, John			St. John		
Fulson (m?), Nanny			Pass.		
Fulton, James	N.H.	Capt. KAD	Bl. 4	UC	
Norman			P146		
Robert			Char.		
Furlong, William		Lt. LAL	Bl. 4		
Furnell, see Fernald					
Gabel, David, Sr., baker, 95	Ger.		P382, 1342		
David, Jr.			Gr. Lake		
Gage, David		2 NJV		Carl.	
John			Pass.		
Gaines, Josiah			P1030	Kings Co.	
Thomas		RFA	Mag. R.		
Gale, Thomas		KAD	Bl. 4		
Gallant, Matthew		QR	Queens Co.		
Gallop, William	Mass.		St. A.		
Galloway, John		Sgt. QR / Sgt. KAD	P860		
Peter			Gr. Bay		
Gamble, John		Surg mate	P154, 610	UC	
Thomas			Gr. L.	Pass.	
Gammon, William			St. A.		
Gandle, Elijah		Cpl. NYV	Kes.		
Ganong, John	N.Y.	WL	Or.	N.Y.	
Thomas	N.Y.		Kn.		
Ganter, Peter		KAD	Bl. 4	Kn.	
Garden, William	S.C.		F'ton		
Gard(i)ner, Alexander, 2nd Lt. Co. 38		Whf.	P710		
Edward			P1189	Queens Co.	
George, blacksmith, 95		1 NJV	P903		
Henry, baker, 90			P971		
Jacob			P972		
John		42nd			

Gardi(n)er, Joseph			Musq.		
Mary, wdw.			Musq.		
Miles		3 NJV	P893	Ham. R.	Nash.
Thomas			Gn.	Bl. 3	
Garity (Gerratee), Andrew			Gr. Bay		
Garnett, Joseph	Md.		Nash.	St. A.	
Garrison, Abraham		1 DeL.	Bl. 8		
John			BH	St. John	
Garvey, Alexander		1 NJV	Ken.		
John		1 NJV	Ken.	St. John Co.	
Gater (Gutter?), Charles			Ken.		
Gaunce, Jeremiah			P550	Gn.	
Gay, Richard		GP?	Bl. 3, abs.		
Gaynor, James,	R.I.		P579		
blockmaker, 85					
Peter,	R.L.		P418		
blockmaker, 85					
Gearish, Enoch, gentleman			Or.		
Gee, Cornelius		Cpl. KAR	Bl. 6	Carl.	
Gentle, George ?			Gr. Lake		
George, William			Sch.		
Germain, George		2 NJV	Ken.		
Gerow, Andrew	N.Y. W. Co.				
Benjamin			Wash.		
Charity, wdw. Isaac,	N.Y.		P1200		
Capt. QR					
Daniel, farmer	N.Y. W. Co.		Wash.		
Henry	N.Y. W. Co.			UC	
Isaac	N.Y. W. Co.		Wash.		
James	N.Y. W. Co.		Wash.		
Gerrard, William (1)		QR	P761	Fredericton	
William (2),			C69		
cabinet maker, 85					
Gerrish, Moses			St. A.	Gr. Manan	
Gersham, Alexander,		2 NJV	Ken.		
or Alexander, Gersham?					
Gesner, Abraham		KOR		N.S.?	
Henry		KOR		N.S.?	
Geyer, William M.			St.Andrews/84		
Giberson, Gilbert	N.J.		Shel.	BH	Pa.?
John		KAD	BH/84	Carl.	
William			BH	Char.	
William, Jr.			BH		
Gibson, David			Bl. 1/85		
John (1)	Ir.	Engr.	P886		
John (2)	Scot.	Sgt. 3 NJV	F'ton		
Gidney (Gedney), Jacob			Kn.		
John	N.Y. W. Co.		Kn.		
Joseph	N.Y. D. Co.		Gr. Lake		
Joshua	N.Y. D. Co.		Gr. Lake		
Gifford, Gardiner		KAR	Maug.	Ken.	
Matthew	Eng./Mass.	Navy	P21	Kn.	
Gigge (Guiggey), John		LAR	Kings Co.		
Gilbert, Benjamin ?			F'ton		
Bradford,	Mass.		P23		
merchant, 92					
Caleb		2 DeL.	Bl. 3	UC?	
Isaac		Sgt. QR	Bl. 5	Queens Co.	UC
Josiah		Cpl. KAR	Bl. 3		UC
Perez	Mass.		Gn.		
Thomas, Sr.	Mass.		Gn.		
Thomas, Jr.	Mass.		Burton		
Gilbourn, Knight		Sgt. LAL	Kings Co.	Ptld.	
Giles, John			Bl. 2		
Gil(l), John, printer, 85	Pa.		BH	Pocologan	
Thomas	Del.	Ens. ML	Bl. 1		
Gillespie, Sarah			Or.		
Gillies (Gillis), Archibald,			C1, 613		
shipwright, 85					
Daniel		NYV	P898		
Jesse	N.Y. U. Co.	ex Sgt. NYV	Kes.	Bel.	
John			Char.		
Gilman, John	N.H.	2 DeL.	Char.	York Co.	
Gilmore, Joseph	Pa.	Cpl. 2 DeL.	P807	Nash.	
(or Gilner), Edward			Sch.		

Name	Origin	Service	Location	Location 2	Location 3
Gilzean, Alexander, yeoman, 85 ?					
Givin (Gavin), John		a.b.	St. John		
Gleeson, Donald		84th	Pass.		
Glenie, James	Scot.	Lt. Engr.	Nash.	Or.	Eng.
Glover, Andrew, carpenter, 85			C213		
Elias, farmer	Ct.	Capt. vol.			
Goddard, John		BMG	Albert Co.?		
Goff, Charles	Del.	pilot	Albert Co.?		
Golder, John, carpenter	N.Y. L.I.		Kn.		
James		NYV	ar./88	York Co.	
William		Sgt. NYV	Kes.		
Golding, Abraham			Wash.	N.Y.	
Benjamin	N.Y. D. Co.		Queens Co.		
John	N.Y. D. Co.	WL	Queens Co.		
Joseph	N.Y.	guide	Queens Co.		
Nathaniel, tavernkeeper, 95		KAR, WL	Ham. R.	St. John	
Stephen			Wash.		
Thomas			Queens Co.		
Goldsmith, Henry			St. A.	Halifax	
Richard			Char.		
Gondelo, John		Sgt. 1 DeL.	Bl. 8		
Good, Abraham			Gr: Lake		
David		?	Burton	Carl.	
Goodspeed, Thomas ?			Sunbury Co.		
Goodwin, Jacob		1 NJV	Penniac		
(or Wingood), Matthew			Sch.		
Gordon, Alexander			Mag. R.		
Francis			Maq.		
James, merchant 85	Scot./Ga.		Musquash		
John (1), farmer	Ct.		Gr. Lake		
John (2)		Ens. RFA?			
Gor(e)ham (Gorum), John, weaver, 85	Ct.	Sgt. QR?	P30		
Jonathan	Ct.		LR		
Joseph, carpenter, 90	Ct.		Engr.	Kn.	
Nathaniel, Capt. Co. 2	Ct.		P1020	Kn.	
Samuel			Kn.		
Gorman, James			Mir.		
John		1 NJV	Sussex		
Gorts, George		LAL?	Gr. Bay		
Goslee, Matthew		Sgt. PWAR	Ken.	UC	
Gosling, James	N.J.	CMG	St. A.	N.S.?	
Goss (Goff?), Charles			Char.		
Samuel			Char.		
Goucher, Joseph		1 NJV	P815	Penniac	
Goudge, Thomas, 2nd Lt. Co. 26					
Gould, Abraham			P341	Dipper Harbour	
Catherine			P340	Dipper Harbour	
John, Jr., hairdresser, 87	Mass.	Hosp.	P330		
Gove, Jonathan	N.H.		Char.	Gn.	
Grace, Thomas		Ord.	Sch.		
Graham, Henry		Engr.	Mspc.	U.S.A.	
Martha			Sch.		
Granger, Robert			St. John		
Sarah			P286	Ken.	
William			Pass.		
Grant, Daniel, shopkeeper, 90		BMG	St. A.	St. John	
Donald		74th			
Hugh			Char.		
James, cooper		CMG	Mspc.		
John		1 NJV	Ken.		
Penuel, wdw.			Bl. 6		
Major James,		KAR			
Peter		Ens. KAR?	Bl. 6	Navy	
Robert		Ens. NYV	Kes.		
Sarah, wdw.			N.S.		
Major Alex		NYV			
Samuel		Sgt. GP	Kes.		
William (1)		KAR	Bl. 6	Carl.	

Grant, William (2)	Scot.	QMR. 71st	Sch.	St. George
Grass, Jacob, husbandman		1 NJV	Or.	
Grawburgh, John, shoemaker	N.Y. D. Co.			
Gray (Grey), Abraham		1 NJV	Bl. 3	Bel.?
Alexander		1 NJV	Bl. 3	
James, Sr.	Ct.	GP	Bl. 3	Bel.
James, Jr.	Ct.	GP?	Bl. 3	Mir.
John (1), hairdresser			St. A.	
John (2)		42nd	Nash.	Carl.?
Lyman		KAD	Bl. 4	York Co.
William (1), Capt. Co.34	N.Y. W. Co.		Maug.	Bel.
William (2)		Lt. QR, Capt. NYV	P1224	Bl. 5	UC
Greely, Exekiel			Char.	
Joseph			Char.	
Samuel			Char.	
Green, Daniel, chairmaker	Pa.	KAD?	Queens Co.	St. John
Elizabeth, wdw. Thomas, (Emerick's Chasseurs)	N.Y.		F'ton	
Henry		Sgt. GP	Bl. 3	Carl.
Isaac		dr. GP	Bl. 3	drowned
James	Ct.	Sgt. KAR	Wash.	
John	N.J.	BMG	P841	Queens Co.	UC
Joseph (1), tailor, 85			P1229	
Joseph (2)		Maj. 1 DeL.	Bl. 8	
Nancy			St. A.	
Patrick			Nash.	
Rufus	N.Y. D. Co.		Sussex	
Thomas	Pa.	LAL?	Kes.	
William, tobacconist, 90			P1427	N.Y.
Greenlaw, Alexander			St. A.	
Ebenezer			St. A.	
Elijah			St. George	
Jonathan			St. A.	
Greenwood, John, cooper	Del.?	CMG	P305	Halifax?
Gregg (Griggs), Alexander, cooper			Mir.	
David			Char.	Mace's Bay
Thomas, 2nd Lt. Co. 5	N.Y.		Char.	
Gregory, Moses			P1091	U.S.A.	UC
Richard, yeoman, 85			P826	Kn.
Grier, William		Sgt. PL	Bl. 7	
Grierson, James	Scot./Ga.?	74th	St. A.	St. George
Griff, Peter			P485	
Griffin, Joseph		LAR	Pennisc	
Michael		NCV	Kes.	
Obadiah, farmer	N.Y. D. Co.		P1374	UC
Stephen		LAR	York Co.	
Thomas, weaver		NYV	P1452	Gr. Lake
Griffith, Benjamin Peck	N.Y.	Lt. 2 DeL.	Bl. 8	
Evan, husbandman	Pa. Y. Co.		BH	
Robert	Ct.		Kn.	U.S.A.
Grigor (Gregor), James, carpenter, 85			St. John	
Grim, Peter, Capt. Co. 3, grocer, 85	N.Y.		P136	
Grimmer, Thomas	Ger.? Pa.	Ord.	Sch.	
Grindley, John			P1226	Scot.
Grisdall, Thomas, blacksmith, 85	N.Y.		LR	
Griswold, Seth		Cpl. LAR	Or.	York Co.
Groom, Enoch		54th	P.E.I.	Albert Co.
Grothe, John, farrier, 85		84th.?	Char.?	
Grumble, George ?			Kings Co.	
Gua (Guiou), Isaac		KAR	York Co.	Kings Co.
Guerrier, William		Sgt. PL	Bl. 7	Kes.
Guildy (Gelden), Isaac, shipwright			P485	Dipper Harbour
Guess (Guis), John			F'ton	
Gummersall, Thomas			York Co.	
Gunn, Alexander		42nd	Nash.	Mir.
George		BMG	St. A.	Digby
James (1)		42nd	Nash.	Mir.

Name	Origin	Rank/Unit	Code	Place 1	Place 2
Gunn, James (2)		QR	BH	Char.	
Gunter, Abraham	N.Y.		Wash.	UC	
Andrew, carpenter		Engr.	Queens Co.		
Charles	Ger.	Hosp.	Bl. 3		
Conrad, carpenter	N.Y.	Engr.	Wash.	N.Y.	
Guthrie, Joseph, cordwainer, 85			Norton		
Robert			Norton		
Guyer, Peter	Ct.		Kn.		
(or Guyon), John			BH/86		
Hackett, Alexander, mariner, 85	Scot.	BL	Gr. Lake		
Kary Ann	N.J.?		P1257		
Rebecca			Gr. Lake		
Hadden, (Haddon), James, carpenter, 85			P935		
Joseph, Sr.			Mspc.		
Joseph, Jr.			Mspc.	Or.	
(Heden?) Mary			P336	Queens Co.	
Hagerman, Francis			Gr. Lake		
John		NYV	P1449	Gr. Lake	Carl.
Haid (Hade), Jonathan			P1003	Mspc?	
Haight, Benjamin		Ens. QR?	P182	UC?	
Hailey, or Hayley, Nathaniel			St. A.		
Thomas			St. A.		
Thomas, Jr.			St. A.		
Hain(e)s, David, tailor			Wash.	Gr. Bay	U.S.A.
Helena			Sch.		
Joseph	N.Y. W. Co.	Cpl. NYV	Kes.		
Matthew			C298		
Peter		NYV?	Kes.		
Hait (Hayt, Hoyt), Azor			Ken.		
Daniel Keeler	N.Y.	KAR	Bl. 4		
Israel, shoemaker	Ct.		Kn.		
James (1), auctioneer, 85	Ct.	BMG	P7	Ct.	
James (2)	Ct.		Maug.		
Jesse	Ct.	pilot	N.S.		
Jesse, Jr.					
Joseph (1)	Ct.	PWAR	C334	Maug.	
Joseph (2)		capt. a.b.	P24		
Joseph Lamson			Ham. R.	U.S.A.	
Monson		Lt. PWAR	F'ton	St. John	Ct.
Stephen, Esquire, 85	Ct.	Capt. PWAR	C107	N.Y.	
Stephen, Jr.	Ct.		C33	LR	
Sylvanus	Ct.		Kn.		
Hake, Samuel			Shel.	St. John	absc.
Hale, Thomas			Cn.		
Hall, Cornelius			Gn.	dr. '85	
Isaac, fisherman, 85		LAR	Ken.		
John (1)			P1390	Queens Co.	
John (2)			St. A.		
Martin		RFA			
Moses			P228		
Thomas		NYV	Kes.		
Hallett, Daniel		Lt. 1 DeL.	P208	Nash.	
Joseph			P212	St. Croix	
Moses, carpenter	N.Y. U. Co.		P232		
Robert		Cpl. 1 DeL.	Bl. 8	Carl.	
Samuel, Sr., Esquire, 85	N.Y.	Capt. 2 DeL.	P209, 210		
Samuel, Jr.	N.Y.		P101	Sussex	
(H)allibach, Pater, sawyer, 85			C42	Kings Co.	
Halsey, Elisha	N.Y. L.I.		P1258	BH/86	
Halstead, Samuel		WL	Cumb.	St. John	
Haltridge, David			P796	d. '87	
Ham(b)len, William		NCV	P370	Kes.	
Hamerly, Peter		KAD	BH/84		
Hamilton, Asa ?			Ken.		
George		NJV	Ken.		
Gavin			P1391	Ham. R.	
Henry		Sgt. Maj. 40th			

```
Hamilton, James
    John (1)              Scot./S.C.      Lt. Col.      St. A.      Kn.         Consul,
                                          96 Regt.      P613                    Va.
    John (2),             Ir./S.C.                      Pet.
      labourer, 85
    John (3)                              2 NJV         Ken.
    Robert                                Sgt. 70th     St. A.
    William, baker                        RFA
Hámm, Andrew              Pa./NC          NCV           Gr. Bay
    Deel or Thiel         N.Y. A. Co.     KAR           F'ton
    Frederick                                           LR
    Thomas                N.H.            Em. Ch.?
Hammell, John, physician, 85              Surg. 3 NJV   P1150
Hammon(d), Burney                                       P716
    Ezra                                                Gn.
    George                                RFA           Mag. R.
    James                                                St. A.
    Zebedee, mariner                                    St. A.      absc.
Ham(p)ton, Abner, fisherman, Pa.                        P1065
    cooper, 85                                                      C339
    Andrew                Pa.                           C338        Ken.
Hanbury, Coroyden                         svd.          Mir.
Hance (Hants), Peter,     N.Y. O. Co.     Engr.         Gr. Bay
    yeoman, 85
Hancock, Joseph, fisherman, 85            Sgt. 1 NJV
Hand(s), John, carpenter  N.J.                          BH/84
    (Handy), Molly                                      Or.
    Priscilla                                           Or.
    Samuel                                              BH/87
Handasyde, George, clerk  N.Y.                          Burton      Kings Co.
Haney (Heney?), Thomas                    Sgt. KAD      Sussex?     Deer Is.?
Hanford (Hanforth), Joseph Ct.                          LR
    Thomas (1), mariner   Ct.             pilot         C227, 273
    Thomas (2), Jr.       Ct.                           C256
    Thomas (3),           Ct.                           P186
      merchant, 85
    Thomas (4),
      gentleman, 85
Hankins, John                                           BH/84
Hanley, William, labourer, 85             2 DeL.
Hannah, James            Scot.            svd.          St. A.
Hanselpacker, Philip     N.J.             Cpl. 3 NJV                Sunbury Co.
Hanson, Christopher,                      BMG           Kes.
    carpenter
    John                                               Chamcook Island
    Michael                                            Kes.
Happie (Happy), George,  N.Y. D. Co.                   Kn.
    shoemaker
Harbel(l) (Hargill), Christian R.I.                    Gr. Lake
    Christopher           R.I.            Vol. LNE      P1106
    Cornelius, butcher, 95
Harbord, William                          QR            Bl. 5       UC?
Hardenbrook, Abel, N.Y.                                 P1098
    Capt. Co. 37, sailmaker, 85
    Nicholas                                            St. John
    William                                             Musq.
Harding, Christopher                                    Sch.
    Daniel                                BL?           Or.
    George                                guide         Maug.
                                          Lt. PL?
    Israel               Ct.                            Queens Co.  N.S.
    James                                 3 NJV         York Co.
    Valentine                                           Bel.        Maug.
    William              N.Y. U. Co.      (Ann/82)      P5          Bel.      Maug
Hardy, Elias, Esquire, 85 Eng./Va.                     P417
Hare, John                                             Char.
Haren, Joseph, butcher, 85
Harger, Joseph                            Cpl. PWAR
Hargill, see Harbel
Hargrove, William        Eng./Va.                      Shel.       Kes.
Hark(e)y, David          N.C.             CMG           Gr. Bay
Harley, William,                                                   UC
    cordwainer, 85
Harmack, John                                          P102
Harman, John                                           Gr. Bay     Queens Co.
```

Harned, Benjamin		1 NJV	BH	Sussex	
Nathaniel	N.J.		P1128		
Phinehas, shoemaker	N.Y.			N.J.	
Harper, Thomas, yeoman, 85			St. John		
William		KAD	Bl. 4	Pr. Wm.	
Harrington, Andrew			Gr. Lake	Deer Is.	
Benjamin			P877	Ken.	
John, joiner, 85			Sussex		
Joseph			Kn.		
Harris, Abraham	N.Y. R. Co.		Ham R.		
George, yeoman, 85			C118, P131	Kings Co.	
Isaac		ML	Bl. 1		
James (1), cartman		3 NJV?	LR		
James (2)	Pa.		BH	Lepreau	
John, yeoman, 85	N.Y.?	QR?	Kings Co.		
Joseph			P824		
Martin		KOR			
Mercy, seamstress	R.I.		Gn.		
Robert		Sgt. ML	Bl. 1	V2.	
Samuel		Sgt. St. Is.	York Co.		
Thomas	N.Y. W. Co.	WL	P966	Maq.	UC
William (1), labourer, 85		2 DeL.	P823		
William (2)			C125	Kn.	
Harrison, Charles	Ir./N.J.	Capt. 2 NJV	P91	Maug.	
James	Ir./N.J.	Lt. 2 NJV	P14	Maug.	
John, 2nd Lt. Co. 24			P508	Maug.?	
Joseph		Sgt. LAR	Or.		
Thomas	N.C.? N.Y.?		P1140		
William			St. Croix		
Hart, Jacob	R.I.		Ham. R.	Cn.	
Joseph	N.Y.?	Cpl. GP	Kes.		
Nathaniel			Bl. 4		
Samuel	Pa.	guide	BH/87		
Tucker	N.Y. D. Co.	KAR	Kings Co.	N.S.	
Hartley, George Adkin	Eng.	Sgt. KAR	Bl. 6		
Hartshorne, David			P291	Queens Co.	
John			Wash.		
Harvey (Howey?), David		PL	Bl. 7		
George		RFA			
John	Pa.	2 NJV?	P818	Or.	
Hastie (Hasty), John		Ord.	Sch.		
Hatch, Christopher	Mass.	Capt. LAR	P81	York Co.	St. A.
Hawes	Mass.	Capt. PWAR	P157	Nash.	U.S.A.
Hataby (Hately), Richard, carpenter, 85		Cpl. LAL	P690	Gr. Bay	
Hatfield, Abraham, carpenter	N.Y. W. Co.	WL	P1163		
Daniel, blacksmith	N.Y. W. Co.		P1161	Bel.	
David, labourer, 90	N.Y. W. Co.		P1160	Bel.	
Frederick			LR	d.	
Hepzibah			Or.		
Isaac, Lt. Co. 34, yeoman, 85	N.Y. W. Co.		P1164	Bel.	
John Smith, carp., mariner, 85 ?	N.J.				
Hatheway, Ebenezer	Mass		Burton		
Hatt, Henry		RFA			
Hatton, Michael, labourer, 85, see McElhatton					
Hauser, Frederick			P6, 34		
Jacob		BMG	C208	Ken.	
Hautzman, see Kautzman					
Haviland, Anchineas		Lt. WL			
Isaac, yeoman, 85			P1155 . LR		
Hawes, W. B., labourer, 85		LAL	Dipper Harbour		
Hawkins, Michael	N.J.	AL?	Kes.		
William		RFA	Char.		
Hawley (Holly), Abigail	N.Y. W. Co.		wdw., 5 ch.		
Daniel		2 DeL.	Bl. 3		
Ebenezer, freeman, 85	Ct.	Sgt. PWAR	Kn.		
Elnathan	Ct.	Sgt. PWAR			
Henry, farmer	N.Y. W. Co.				
John, farmer	N.Y. W. Co.				
Samuel (1), farmer	N.Y. W. Co.				
Samuel (2)	Ct.	Sgt. 2 DeL.	Bl. 9		

Hawley, Walter   Ken./84
 William   P315   Ken.
Hawn, Peter   1 NJV C74   Kn.
Hawkhurst, Isaac, carpenter   BH   Queens Co.
 Jotham, carpenter N.Y. W. Co.   Gr. Lake
Hay, John   Mass.
 Robert   Mspc.
 Samuel   Bel.
Haycock (Hecock), Daniel N.Y. O. Co. LAL Gr. Bay
 Morris   N.Y. L.I. Sgt. Maj.   Brier Is.
            QR?
 Thomas   N.Y. O. Co. KAR Gr. Bay
Hay(e)s, (Hazsis), George   Or.
 John, baker, 85   1 NJV?
 Thomas   2 NJV Bl. 2   Ken.
 William, farmer N.Y. L.I.   P1382
Hayman, Nehemiah Md.   ML   Bl. 1
Haynes, Charlotte,   (Wm. CMG) Queens Co.
 m. Wm. Peters
Hayt, see Hait
Hayter, John   Eng.   Roy. Art. Gr. Bay
 William, carpenter, 85   Gar. Bn. P970
Hazard, Stanton, merchant, 85 R.I.   West Indies
 Stephen   R.I.   Queens Co.
Hazelton, Charles   QR   Bl. 5
Hazen, Daniel   Sgt. 1 NJV   UC
 Joseph   WL   P569   Wash.
Hazsis, (Hayes?) George   Queens Co. Kings Co.
Hearne, Patrick ?   Gr. Lake
Heater, (Hayter?) John, labourer, 85,
Hecht, Frederick William Ger./N.Y. CMG St. John N.S.   Eng.
Heddon, Isaac   Lt. 1 NJV F'ton
 Zopher   17th   P1388, 1437   Mspc.
Hefferman, John   Va.   St. A.
 Michael   St. A.
Heginer, Widow, of ?   Penniac/89
Heister, Andrew, painter, 85 N.Y.   P1148
Helbert, Bernard   Cpl. NYV Kes.
Heller, Elizabeth   P137   Musq.
Helm(s), Henry   1 DeL. Bl. 8   Carl.
Helnick, Frederick,   Mspc.
 cordwainer, 85
Helsey, John   P849
Hemen (Hayman), John   KOR
 Martin   Sweden CMG St. St.
Henderson, Alexander   .RFA Ken.
 Hugh   N.H.? 74th   St. A.
 James   Pa.   Engr. Ken.
 John   pilot   Ken.
 Thomas   Lt. LAR F'ton   Char.
 William   Engr. BH   LR
Hendricks, Conrad, baker N.J. Mon. Co.   P1134   d. '84
Hendrickson, John, farmer N.Y. D. Co.   Kn.
Hen(d)ry, George   Scot.   Wash.
 James, housewright Scot.   Queens Co.
Henley, James   Lt. ML P217   Bl. 1
 Maurice   St. A./84
 Simon   BH/84
Hennessy, Richard   QR   York Co. Mir.   U.S.A.?
Hennigar, Adam,   Ger./N.Y.
 tobacconist, 85
 Christopher,   Ger./N.Y.   P369?   Ken.
 tanner, 85
 John   N.Y.   Ken.
 Michael, butcher, 85 Ger. N.Y. KAR Bl. 8
 Rudolph   2 NJV
Henricke, Henry,
 chimney sweep
Henriques, Philip, freeman, 85 N.C. NCV Kes.   UC
Henry, James, yeoman, 85   P1491
 John   2 NJV
Hers(h)a, Benjamin   P877   UC
Heslop (Hislop), James   Ken.   Scot.
 John   Lt. 3 NJV P892

Heustis (Hustice,) John Hunt	N.J. Sx. Co.	Cpl. 1 NJV	P1172		
Lewis	N.Y.	GP?	P1262	York Co.	
Philip, yeoman, 85			C262		
Robert			Ken. Is.		
Stephen		Lt. KAR	P75		
Timothy		GP	P1203	Bl. 3	
Hewett (Huit), George, labourer, 85		KOR	St. John Co.	;	
Hewey, John			St. A.		
Hewlett, Charles			Gn.	Woodstock	
Richard	N.Y. L.I.	Lt. Col.	P12, 55	Queens Co.	
		2 DeL.	C234		
Hickey (Hickie), James		KOR	Mag. R.		
William		1 DeL.	Bl. 8		
Hickman, William ?		NYV	Westm. Co.		
		Em. Ch.			
Hicks, Edwards	Pa.?		Mspc.	UC?	
George		KAR	Bl. 6		
Jesse		KAR	F'ton	Carl.	
John		Hosp.	P462	Sussex	
Robert, Lt. Co. 35			P392, 912	BH/84	
Samuel, ship carpenter, 95			Mspc.		
William, shipbuilder	Eng./N.J.	LAR	Kn.		
Hickscox (Hickox), Reuben	Ct.?		Nash.	Carl.?	
Hierlihy, Philip	Ct.	Sgt. PWAR	Mir.		
Higbee (Higby), George		LAR	P1188		
Jacob			Wash.		
Jonas		Cpl. 1 DeL.	Bl. 8		
Uriah		2 NJV	C392		
Higgins, Abraham	Ct.		P791	Ken.	
Barnabas			St. A./84		
James			LR		
John (Francis ?)		QR	Bl. 5	Carl.	
Michael			Bl. 8		
William		3 NJV		Carl.	
Hildebrandt, Ludovick		Specht Regt.	St. A.		
Hilkiner, George			Mag. R./84		
Hill, Barto			Wash./84		
Daniel		Sgt. LAL?	Sunbury Co.	St. John Co.	
John (1), shopkeeper, 85	Mass.		C174	Maug.	St. John
John (2), mason, 85		1 NJV		UC	
John (3)		QR	Bl. 5		
Richard, Capt., Co. 5	Ir./N.Y.				
Samuel	Ir./S.C.	BMG	Ken.		
Solomon		Cpl. LAR			
Hillman, Tristram		Lt. RN	Bl. 6		
Hillsgrove, John		Cpl. LAL	Bl. 6	Carl.	F'ton
Hillyard, Gersham		QMR.		St. John	absc.
		Em. Ch.			
Nathaniel		Kings Co.	Gn.		
Hillyer, Nicholas, tailor			St. John		
Hilt, William, brewer, 85					
Hilton, Jonathan		QR	Bl. 5	Carl.	
Hinchman, John	N.J.Gl. Co.		BH	Eng.	
Hinds (Hines), Banjam'n			Kn.		
Hitchcock, John			P619	UC	
Jotham, rigger, 97			St. John	absc.	
Solomon			York Co.	U.S.A.	
Hitchin(g)s, Amos	N.H.		St.A.	St. David	
David	N.H.		Char.		
Josiah	N.H.	71st	Char.		
Hoag(e), Alexander			Dig.		
Hobby, Jabez	Ct.	WL	St. John		
see also Obbens					
Hoffman, John		KAR	York Co.		
Hogarth, Aaron		RFA	Mag. R.		
Hogg, Joseph			Char.		
Holden, David			Char.		
Thomas		QR	Bl. 5		
Holder, Jacob	Pa.	BCV	P566	Kn.	
John	Pa.	2 DeL.?	P572	Wash.	
Holland, Hannah			C59		
Henry		1 NJV	Penniac		
Jesse			P1059		

Holland, John, Esquire, 85	N.H.	Ens. PWAR	C113, 4		
Joseph W.,	Mass.	Vol. LNE	C134		
Richard		Lt. LNE	P197, C57		
Richard D.,			C68		
Holl(o)day, William		KAR?	Or.		
Hollowood, Charles, freeman, 95		dr. KAR			
Thomas			Bl. 2	Carl.	
Holmes, Absalom, cordwainer, 85	Ct.	guide	P211		
Henry, see Helms					
James	N.Y. W. Co.		Mir.?		
John, shoemaker	N.Y. L.I.		Or.	Queens Co.	
Moses		1 DeL.	Bl. 8	York Co.	
Peter			St. John	N.Y.	
William (1)		GP	Bl. 3, absent		
William (2)		CMG	Sch.		
Holt, Andrew		Cpl.	Bl. 8		
Moses		Lt. PL	P228		
William Johnson	N.J.	Ens. PL		Montreal	
Holton, Peter			BH		
Homer, John		1 NJV	Mir.	UC?	
Hooper, James		RFA			
Richard			St. George		
Hopkins, Jeremiah		QR		Carl.	
Hopp, John			St. A./84	age 10	
Hopwood, Thomas			Rusagonis		
William, sailmaker, 95					
Hore, Henry		Sgt. 3 NJV?	Kings Co.	Carl.	St. A.
Horn, Frederick			St. A.		
Horner, John	N.J.	1 NJV	BH/87		
Horsefield, James	N.Y. L.I.		P110		
Thomas	N.Y. L.I.		P92	St. John	
Horseley, Thomas			P693	Mspc.	
Horseman, Francis, labourer, 85		KAD	St. John		
Horton, David		Sgt. NYV	Kes.	N.Y.	
James	N.Y. W. Co.		Shel.	Mir.	
John	Scot.	Ens. NYV	Kes.	Burton	
Nathaniel, Capt. Co. 22, mariner, 85		guide	P180		
Hortwick, Lawrence, carpenter, 85	N.Y.		St. John		
House, Abraham			Burton	Kes.	
George			Kn.		
Housinger, Philip, yeoman, 85		KAR	York Co.	Ken.	
Houzer (Howzer), Andrew		KOR			
Ruleph		KOR			
Hovey, Ichabod		Sgt. 2 DeL.			
Howard, John	N.Y. D. Co.	Capt. KOR	C413	St. John Co.	
William			Nash.	Sunbury Co.	
How(e), Caleb	N.H.	Lt. QR	P195	Bl. 5	Ken.
John, City bellman			St. John		
Nathaniel		KAR	Or.		
Stephen			Char.		
Howell, Chaney		KOR	St. John Co.		
Howland, Elinor			P563		
Hoxie, Joseph, carpenter, 85					
Samuel			P803	BH/84	
Hoyt, see Hait					
Hubbard, Frederick		1 DeL.	Bl. 8		
Isaac	Ct.	AL	Burton	Carl.	
Nathaniel, 2nd Lt. Co. 10	Ct.	AL	Burton		
William	Ct.	Ens. 2 DeL.	P165	Burton	
Hubbill, Ammon		2 DeL.	Or.		
Nathan		Capt. a.b.		Ct.	
Hubbs, Huber, see Obbens					
Huckings, Samuel			Dig.		
Huddleston, Annanias			Nash	St. John	
Hudgens, James (Hugg?)			York Co.	UC	
William		QR?	Bl. 5	UC	
Huff, Henry		3 NJV	York Co.	Carl.	

Huggeford, Peter, Sr., Capt. Co. 7	Eng./N.Y.	Surg. LAR 2 years	P150	N.Y.	
Peter, Jr.			P149		
Thomas, Capt. Co. 14		WL		N.S.	
William L.		Lt. LAR	P147	N.S.?	
Hughes, John		NYV	P905	Kes.	
Samuel	Mass.		P800	Wash. gr. d./83	
William Evan			BH	St. Croix	
Hughson (Hewson?), James,	N.Y.		Bel.		
Joshua	N.Y.		Bel.		
Nathaniel			Bel.		
Hull, Sylvester			P1022		
Hulshart (Hiart?), David			Ham. R.	N.J.	
Humbert, Stephen, baker, 85	N.J.		St. John		
Hume, Eli		1 NJV guide	P951	Kn.	
James, mariner, 97					
John (1), farmer	Ct.		Kings Co.		
John (2), mason	W.I.		Ptld.		
Humphrey (Humfrey, Humphries),					
Abel			LR	Deer Is.	
James	Pa.		Char.		
John		BL	Char.	Mir.	
Joseph	Pa.		Kn.		
Nicholas	Ir./Pa.?	Ens. NYV	Kes.		
Simon		ML	Bl. 1		
Thomas		GP?	Kings Co.		
William or Walter		CMG	Char.		
William	Pa.		P288	LR	New Canaan
Hunlocke, Thomas, Esquire, 85		Capt. 2 NJV	C609, 610	Bl. 2	
Hunt, Cosby	N.Y.	Lt. NYV	P949	Kes.	K.'Co.
Daniel		3 NJV	Penniac		
James			Pocologan		
John		Lt. GP	P1321	Bl.[3	
Rachel, wdw. Thomas		KAD?	P325		
Samuel	Mass.		LR	U.S.A.	
Stephen, 2nd Lt. Co. 43					
Thomas, blacksmith, 85			Kings Co.	St. A.	
Hunter, James (1), labourer, 85			St. John Co.	UC?	
James (2), carpenter, 87			F'ton		
Joseph		KAD	Bl. 4		
Mary			Ham. R.		
Huntley, William			St. John		
Hurd, Jonathan		Cpl. 2 DeL.	Wash.	St. John	
Hurley, Thomas			Mspc.		
William		RFA	St. George		
Husband, Andrew		Lt. GP	Bl. 3		
Huston (Hewston), Gabriel		Sgt. GP	Bl. 3	Gn.	
Thomas			Sch.		
Husted, Jabez, butcher, 85	N.Y. W. Co.	CMG a.b.			
Philip			Queens Co.		
Hutchin(g)s, William, blacksmith, 85	Mass.		St. John Co.		
Hutchinson, Agnes, wdw.			Sussex		
Alexander, cordwainer		NYV	Kes.	F'ton	
John	N.J.	Capt. Lt. 1 NJV	C44	Ken.	
Marmaduke		Engr.	Gr. Lake		
Robert			York Co.		
Samuel			Maug.		
William		Capt. 1 NJV	C13, 106	Ken.	UC
Huton, Morris		LAL?	Gr. Bay		
Hutton, William		RFA	St. John		
Hutz, (Olts?) Nicholas			Gr. Lake		
Hydecker, George, armourer		KAD	P1075	Gr. Bay	
Hyler (Isler), Henry, yeoman, 85	N.J.		C415	Ken.	
Iliff, Jacob		2 NJV	Ken.		
Stephen		Sgt. GP	Bl. 3		

I(I)sley (Eysley), Jacob	Del.		LR		
Ingham, Isaac			P296	Ken.	dr. '85
Ingleby (Ingolsby), Thomas		ML?	St. John		
Ingles, Alexander	Ga.?		P1222		
James			Mir.		
Ingraham, Abijah	Ct./N.Y.	Cpl. KAR	Bl. 6	Bl. 3	
Benjamin	Ct./N.Y.	Sgt. KAR	F'ton	Bl. 3	
James			Or.		
Inman, Richard		Cpl. 1 DeL.	Bl. 8	Carl.	
Innis (Ennis, Annis), Francis			Gr. Bay/84		
James, Sr., merchant, 85		RFA	P399	Ken.	
James, Jr.		RFA	P237		
John (1)		1 NJV	Ptld.		
John (2)		Sgt. Roy. Art.		Musquash	
Iredell, Abraham	Pa.	Lt. GP	Ken.	UC	
Ireland, Adam	N.Y. W. Co.		St. John		
Ireton, Barnabas			Mspc.		
Irvin (Erwin), Edward, carpenter, 85		Sgt. GB	Queensbury	N.Y.	
Thomas, merchant, 85		74th?			
Isaacs, Micajah			F'ton	Bl. 3	
Ives, David	Ct.		P994	Burton	
John, carpenter	R.I.				
Jack, James		PWAR	St. John Co.		
Robert	.		Mir.	left	
Jackson, Basil		Ens. GP	P206	Bl. 3	N.Y.?
Harry, shipwright		Lt. 2 DeL.	C276, 7	Nash.	Kn.
Joseph, farmer	N.Y. L.I.		Gr. Lake		
Peter	Ct.	2 DeL.			
Robert			P937		
Stephen		Cpl. NYV	Kes.		
William (1)			St. St.		
William (2)	S.C.?	Sgt. 1 DeL.	Bl. 8	Woodstock	
Jacobs, Harbut		dr. PWAR	St. John Co.		
Jemima ?			P852		
Joseph			Gn.		
Richard		CMG	Musquash		
Jacobus, Garret, mason, 85	N.J.		P853	Wash.	
Jaffrie, Alexander		74th			
James, Benjamin, cooper	Ct.	CMG	C284		
Daniel	Pa.	QMR. 2 NJV	Bl. 2		
Joseph		KOR			
Robert, cordwainer, 95	Ct.		St. John		
Jamieson, Benjamin, blacksmith	N.Y. L.I.				
Bulson, gunsmith	N.Y. L.I.				
(Timison?), Casper, carpenter	N.Y. L.I.				
Israel		KAR	BH?	Ham. R./84	
William		DeL.?		UC	
Janns, Mary, wdw. of Jacob	LAR?		Mir.		
Jarvis, Hannah			P729?		
John, blacksmith, 85	Ct.		Ken.		
Munson, Esquire, 85	Ct.	Lt. PWAR	P87		
Nathaniel, boatbuilder			P910	Burton	
Ralph			Ken.		
Samuel	Ct.	CMG	P86	U.S.A.	
Stephen	Ct.	Lt. SCL	F'ton	UC	
William	Ct.	Ct. QR		UC	
Jeffray, Acton, innkeeper, 95			C158, 180		
Jenkins, Christopher			Gn.	Kn.	
Daniel	N.Y. Cmb. Co.	Sgt. 1 NJV	Bel.		
David		KOR			
John (1)	Eng./S.C.	Lt. 2 NJV	Bl. 2	F'ton	
John (2), 2nd Lt., Co. 26, carpenter		Engr.	P1341		
Nathaniel	N.J.	1 NJV	Bel.		
Jennings, John		1 DeL.	Bl. 8	Carl.	
Luke		KAR?	Bl. 5	Carl.	
Samuel		Engr.	Bel.	Ct.?	
Thomas (1), blacksmith		2 DeL.?	Bl. 8	St. John	

Name	Origin	Unit/Rank	Location		Note
Jennings, Thomas (2)	Mass		P977	Gr. Lake	
Jennison, William, schoolmaster, 95			Maug.		
Jenson, Robert		KAD	Bl. 4	Carl.	
Jetter(s), John			Dipper Harbour		
Jewel(l), Abraham	N.Y. D. Co.		P530	Gr. Lake	
Ezekiel	N.Y. D. Co.		P521	Gr. Lake	UC
William		LAR	Queens Co.		
Job(es), Samuel		1 NJV	C323	Ken.	
Johns, John		Navy	Sch.		
Johns(t)on, Archibald		74th	Char.		
Charles		2 DeL.	Penniac	Queensbury	
Cornelius			P1066	Or.	
David		GP	Bl. 3	Gr. Lake	
George		Mate, a.b.	Sch.		
James		CMG	St. John Co.	U.S.A.	
Jeremiah	Ct.	Cpl. QR	Gr. Lake		
John (1)		GP	Bl. 3	Gr. Lake	
John (2)		RFA	Mag. R.		
John (3)		74th	Char.		
Lawrence	Pa.?	LAR	Penniac		UC
Nathaniel			P321	Kings Co.	
Peter		Cpl. LAR	Penniac		UC?
Reuben		Sgt. 1 DeL.?	Bl. 8		
Robert	N.J.	3 NJV	P936		
William		vol.	P1063	Gr. Lake	
Widow, KAD, of Samuel? m. James Niles			Bl. 4		
Joiles, Jacob & John ?			BH/84		
Jones, Caleb	Md.	Capt. ML	P211	Bl. 1	
David		KOR			
Edward	Pa.	BCV	C445	Queens Co.	
Eliphalet			Ken.	York Co.	
Garret			BH/84		
George		KAD	Bl. 4	York Co.	
Henry		Cpl. LAL	York Co.		
Hugh		3 NJV	P942		
John (1), farmer	Pa.		P1457?		
John (2), mason, 85	Eng.		P1380	St. John	
John (3)	R.I.	a.b.	LR		
John (4)		17th	P906?	St. John Co.	
John (5), cordwainer, 85					
John (6)	Me.		St. A.	Me.	
Jonathan, farmer		guide	Kings Co.		
Joseph (or John?)		1 DeL.	Bl. 8		
Mary, wdw., not on provision list					
Nahum, merchant	Mass.		P28, 77		
Richard			Maug.	Ken.	
Samuel		3 NJV	P1168	UC?	
Simeon	Mass./N.H.	Lt. KAD	P76, C238	Bl. 4	N.S.
Stephen	Mass.	Ct. KAD	Bl. 4		UC?
Thomas		Lt. NCV	Kes.	d., wdw. to U.S.A.	
William	N.J.		Bl. 5	Carl.	
Jordan, Francis			P967		
Gilbert, fisherman. 85					
James, fisherman, 85	N.Y.	CMG	Bel.	p 1032	
John, fisherman, 85	N.Y. W. Co.		P1031		
Joslin, Andrew, farmer	R.I.	Sgt. LNE	P372	York Co.	
David		KAD	Bl. 4		
Isaac			York Co.		
John			C99		
Moses		KAD	Bl. 4		
Jouet (Jowett), John	N.J.	Ens. 3 NJV	York Co.		
Xenophon	N.J.	Ens. 1 NJV	York Co.		
Joyce, James			St. A.		
Judd, Reuben			BH/84		
William		PWAR	BH	Nash.	
Judson, Chapman, carpenter, 85	Ct.		P1114	Ken.	
Justason, Isaac	N.J.		Pennfield		
Justus	N.J.		Pennfield		

Kain (Kane, Cain), Dennis		KAD	Bl. 4	
Hugh			P371	Mspc.
⸱ Jeremiah		KOR		
Kaiser (Kaizer, Keyser),				
Frederick		QR		
John	N.Y.?		Queens Co.	
Kaiser, Matthias		BCV	Char.	
Kautzman, Catharine,			P97	N.Y.
m. D. Aymar				
Kavanagh, James, blacksmith				
Kavond, see Kevand				
Kay, George			St. John	
Kean, Michael, labourer, 85		PL	Bl. 7	
William		Adj. PL	P231	Bl. 7	Or.
Kearney (Carney), Alexander		Sgt. 1 NJV	Queensbury ⸱ Carl.	
Francis		Maj. PL		Ir.
William			Bel.	
Keating, Ann, wdw. Robert,			C231, 256	
Ens. PWAR				
Keech, Robert	N.Y. U. Co.	WL	Westm. Co.	
Keef or Keith, Daniel,		17th	P766	New Canaan
cordwainer, 85		Sgt. QR		
James		Engr.	P1013	Ken. Is.
Keen, Benjamin			BH	
Jesse		Sgt. 1 NJV	BH	N.S.
Kehoe (Kaher), Edward			P488	Char.?
Keirstead (Kierstead), Benjamin			P714	Or.	Ken.
Hezekiah	N.Y.		Gn.	Kings Co.
Isaiah	N.Y.		P715	Kings Co.
James	N.Y.		Wash.	Kings Co.
Johns(t)on	N.Y.	2 NJV?	Gn.	N.Y.
(Casted), Luke			Ken.	
Kellam (Kellum), John		Sgt. PWAR	Maug.	
Kelly, James	S.C.		Mag. R.	
John (1), carpenter		CMG	P625	Kn.	St. John
John (2)	N.J.	Sgt. 2 NJV	Bl. 2	
Joseph			Char.	
Luke		3 NJV	Bl. 3	
Michael		Cpl. RFA	Mag. R.	
Patrick, grocer		DeL.?	St. John	
Samuel			St. A.	
William (1)		Sgt. 2 NJV	Bl. 2	
William (2), painter?		RFA	Mag. R.	St. John?
William (3)			Sch.	
William (4)			P236	Kings Co.
Kelso, Alexander			Char.	
Daniel			Char.	
William		CMG	Char.	
Kelwell, James			Char.	
Kemp, John			Mace's Bay	
Kendall, Solomon		GP	Bl. 3	
Kendel(l), Jesse			Char.	
Joseph		2 NJV	Ken.	
Nathan			Char.	
William			Char.	
Kendrick, James		QR	Mir.	
Thomas			BH/87	Campobello?
Kenne(y) (Kenton), Christopher			Mspc.	
Thomas, hairdresser			Mspc.	
Kennedy, Alexander (1)			Sch.	
Alexander (2)		Sgt. 21st	St. John	
		RRNY		
Allan			Sch.	drowned
Daniel (1), labourer		LAL?	Gr. Bay	
Daniel (2), carpenter			P1353	F'ton
Hugh		pilot	Nash.	Mir.
James		1 NJV?	Bl. 5	
John (1)		pilot?	Char.	
John (2)		KAD	Bl. 4	
John (3), Sr., yeo., 85			P1068	
John (4), Jr.,			P1069	
cordwainer, 85				
John (5)		42nd	Nash.	
Patrick	Ir./Md.	Capt. ML	P83	Nash.	Ir.
William (1)	Md.	PWAR	P1070	Nash.	

297

Kennedy, William (2)		GP	Bl. 3	enl. 57th	
Kenn(e)y, Daniel, tailor		KAD	Bl. 4	F'ton	
Sarah			St. A.		
William			P487		
Kenoll (Knall), Conrad			P364	St. John Co.	
Kent, Rachel	N.J.		P325		
Stephen,	N.J.		P307		
tavernkeeper, 85					
Kenton, see Kenoll, Kenne					
Kepper, John			Mspc.		
Kequick, John			St. John		
Kerby (Kirby), James		RFA			
Kerley, Richard			C429		
Kern, George		RFA			
John Michael	Ger./N.Y.		Queens Co.	U.S.A.	
Mary			St. John		
Ker(r), James (1)	Scot.	Capt. QR	P142	N.S.	
James (2)		PWAR?	York Co.	Sunbury Co.	
John			Ken.		
(Carr?) Robert		dr. ML	Bl. 1		
Kertner (Kestner), George			Rusagonis		
Kervin, James	Mass.		St. A.		
Ketch, John			Bl. 5		
Ketchum, Daniel	Ct.		Kn.	U.S.A.	
Isaac	Ct.		Kn.		
Jedediah, blacksmith	Ct.		Kn.	N.S.	
James	Ct.		P94	Kn.	Carl.
James, Jr.	Ct.		Kn.		
John	Ct.		Wash.	Carl.	
Jonathan	Ct.		Ham. R.		
Samuel	Ct.		Kn.		
Thomas, cordwainer, 85	Ct.				
Kevand, Alexander		Engr.	Queens Co.		
Keys, James		2 NJV			
Keyser, see Kaiser					
Kibler (Kebler), David			Queens Co.		
Kief, David (Keith, Daniel?)			St. John Co.		
Kilberbrack (Kelberbrook), John Godfrey			C372	Ham. R.	
Kilpatrick, Andrew			Ken.		
Robert		2 NJV	Bl. 2		
King, Adam		Sgt. 1 DeL.	Bl. 8		
David			C84, 236		
Daniel, merchant ?					
Francis, 2nd Lt. Co. 50					
George, mariner ?		1 NJV	BH/84		
John (1)		Sgt. QR	Bl. 5	St. George	
John (2)		CMG? 3 NJV?	F'ton		
Luke			C83, 85		
Peter		KAR?	York Co.		
Philip		QR?	Kings Co.		
William	Ct.?		Wash.	F'ton	
Kingsland, Aaron	N.J.		LR		
Kingsley, Zephaniah, merchant, 85	Eng./S.C.		F'ton	Ham. R.	
Zephaniah, Jr.	Eng./S.C.		Ham. R.	N.Y.	
Kingston, Dorothy	S.C.		P844	Bel.	
James			P1058		
William, with schooner			P62		
Kinnear, Andrew	Ir.	CMG	Westm. Co.		
Kinsley, James		RFA	Mag. R.		
Kipp, Isaac		Sgt. 1 DeL.	Bl. 8		
Kirk, John (1), 2nd Lt. Co. 6, tavernkeeper, 85			P1234		
John (2)		PWAR	Nash.		
Kissler, Abraham			BH/84		
Kitchen, Henry		LAR	Kings Co.	New Canaan	
(Keithin?), Thomas, shoemaker	Eng.		Kings Co.	St. John	
William			Rusagonis/02		
Knai (Knaw), Jacob, arr. 89	N.C.		Kes.		

Name	Origin	Regiment/Rank	Code	County	Extra
Knapp, Aaron, mason, 85					
Godfrey, yeoman, 85					
John, carpenter, 85					
Jonathan, 2nd Lt.	Ct.			Kn.	
Co. 1					
Lydia		KOR			
Matthew		LAR?		Kings Co.	
Michael		PWAR		Queensbury	
Moses (1), yeoman, 85	N.Y. U. Co.	ex Sgt. NYV	C258, 9	Kings Co.	
Moses (2)	N.Y. W. Co.	WL	Cumb.		
Thomas, barber, 85					
Titus (1),	N.Y.			St. John	
cordwainer, 85					
Titus (2)		WL		Westm. Co.	
Knepelner, Jasper				St. John	
Kniffen, David		Sgt. KAR	BH/84		
Phiana				Ham. R.	
Robert & Gilbert				Ham. R.	
Knight, Benjamin	Va.?			P182	
John	Pa.	guide		BH	
Joshua	Pa.			BH	Pennfield
Samuel	Scot./S.C.			Gr. Lake	
Knox, Charles		PWAR		Nash.	Queens Co.?
John				Queens Co.	
Thomas				C225	Eng.
Knuo, James				Pass.	
Knutton (Knutting), George,					
tailor, 85					
Jeremiah, saddler, 85					
John, merchant, 85	Eng.			P44	Kn.
(Nutting), Joseph				P562	
Thomas, yeoman, 85					
William,	Mass.			P45	
schoolmaster, 85					
Kollock, Jacob	Del.	Vol. LAR	Mir.		
Joseph	Del.	Vol. LAR	Mir.		
Simon	Del.	Capt. LAR	Mir.		
Kortright, Lawrence				St. John	UC?
Lacey, James				BH/84	St. John Co.
William, gardener, 85				C303	
Lafertie (Lefferty), Daniel		Ord.		Sch.	
Laha, Daniel				Dig.	
Laidler, Robert, brazier				Kemble	St. John
Laird, John		74th		Ken.	Queens Co.
William		1 DeL.		Bl. 8	
Lake, David		2 DeL.			
John		2 DeL.			
Lamb, James H.	N.Y. O. Co.			F'ton	Carl.
Lambert, George	Eng.	Lt. 3 NJV		F'ton	Pr. Wm.	Eng.
John		1 NJV		P1053	Ken.	Deer Is.
Lammey, Hugh				St. A.	
Lamoreaux, Daniel,	N.Y. W. Co.	KAR		C269	Ham. R.
husbandman, 85					
Jesse,				C268	
carpenter, 85					
Joshua	N.Y. D. Co.	WL		P484	Gr. Bay
Lamson, John				Ham. R.	Queens Co.
Lamuel, Allen		KOR			
Lancaster, Christopher				P280	d.
Land, Abel	Pa.	Engr.		P424	UC
Robert, Mrs.	Pa.	guide		P425	UC
Lane, Edward, cordwainer, 85				C78	
Ephraim	Ct.			Kn.	Woodstock
George, mariner, 95				C75	
James		Ord.		C77	Char.
John		84th		Pass.	
Langden, Samuel				P532	Ken.
Langley, John	Mass./N.Y.	Engr.		Queens Co.	
Lantz, John		RFA			
Lapee, Aeneas ?				Kings Co.	
Lapthorne, James				Gn.	
Larman, Charles		PWAR		F'ton	Nash.?
Lattimore, Robert		PWAR?		York Co.	

Leonard, Thomas (1)		Maj. 1 NJV, BH sec.		N.S.	
			P1		
Thomas (2), aet. 12, son of George	Mass.				
Lerong, see Levong					
LeRoy, Simon			Queens Co.	Kings Co.	
Thomas			York Co.		
Leslie (Lesly), Alexander			York Co.		
George		42nd	Nash.		
Richard		Cpl. 2 DeL.	P1166		
Lester, Benjamin, Sr.			P93		
Benjamin, Jr.	N.Y.	Lt. 1 DeL.	P50	N.Y.	
George		RFA			
Jacob, butcher, 95	N.Y. D. Co.		P416	Kn.	
John	N.Y. D. Co.		Queens Co.		
Mary, m. Bernard Manzer?			P1287		
Mordecai, Jr.	N.Y.		P415	N.Y.	
Sarah, wdw of Mordecai, Sr., m. Burling Vincent	N.Y. D. Co.		P904		
Thomas (1), farmer	N.Y. D. Co.		P111		
Thomas (2)		Capt. 2 DeL.	Bl. 9	Queens Co.	
William			Gn.		
Levele, Isaac			Gr. Bay	U.S.A.	
Levick, John Henry		Hess.	Ptld.		
Levong, Peter			P694	N.S.	
Lewis, Cornelius	R.I.?		Ham. R.	N.Y.	
Ichabod	N.Y.	WL	Westm.		
John	Eng./N.J.	Engr.	C32	N.S.	
Richard	N.Y.	Cpl. NYV	Kes.		
Robert		QR	d. '84		
Thomas			C90	Queens Co.	
William, Capt. Co. 50, printer, 85	Eng.		P59		
L(e)ydekker, Samuel B.			P1129	Kings Co.	Q. Co.
Leydick, Godfrey, gentleman, 86; carman, 01?		Sgt. KAD			
Lichton, John (Levick?)			St. John		
Lightensparker, John			St. A.		
Lightfoot, Richard			P1251		
Lights, George			St. A.		
Lilentine, see Lenentine					
Lilley, James			Nash.		
Lillie (Lilly), John	Mass.		St. A.		
Limbeck (Lymbeck), Henry, tailor, 85					
Lincoln, Lemuel, tanner, 85	Mass.		Queens Co.	U.S.A.?	
Lindley, Simon			BH		
Lindop, William			Bl. 6		
Lindsay, Hugh			St. A.		
Ninian		Engr.	St. A.		
Robert (1)		74th	Dig.		
Robert (2)	S.C.		Bel.		
William (1)			St. A.		
William (2)		dr. 3 NJV	Sussex		
Lingley, Joseph			C151	LR	
Link, Henry		NYV	Kes.	York Co.	
Linkletter, Alexander	Mass.		St. A.		
Ebenezer			St. A.		
George, farmer	Ct.		St. A.		
Linkner, Leonard	N.J.		Kn.	St. John	
Linnihan (Lenehan), John		1 DeL.	Bl. 8	St. John?	
Linnekin, Zebedee	Me.		St. A.		
Lint, Abraham		GP	Bl. 3	Carl.	
John		GP	P773	Bl. 3	York Co.
Linthwait, William, currier, 85			P1126	Queens Co.	
Lippincott, Richard	N.J.	AL	BH	UC	
Lips, John			Gr. Bay	UC?	
Lisk, James, gentleman, 85			LR		
Lister, Territ			Mir.		
Little, Benjamin			BH/84		
David		74th			
Samuel			BH	Pass.	

Littlejohn, Peter ?			St. A.	
Thomas ?			St. A.	
Livingstone, George, 2nd Lt.			LR	St. John
Co. 23, house carpenter				
Gilbert Robert	N.Y. D. Co.	Capt. LAL		N.Y.
Philip J.	N.Y.		Sunbury Co.	Ct.
Lloyd, Andrew		RFA	P817	Campobello
David		RFA	Mag. R.	
Loban, Thomas		Cpl. 82nd	Mir.	
Lobdell, Samuel		Cpl. NYV	Kes.	Queensbury
Lock, Joshua		GP	Bl. 3	Pr. Wm.
Samuel		GP	Bl. 3	Penniac
Lockman, David			Pass.	
Lockwood, Abraham	Ct.	WL?	Maug.	
Charles		3 DeL.	BH	
George			P1299	
Gershom	Ct.		Ken.	UC
Jabez, son of Capt. Jabez			Bl. 5	Carl.
Millington	Ct.	a.b.	St. John	dr. '86
Samuel, innholder, 99	Ct.	KAR	P592, 1383	
Solomon, *Hope*				
Lockyer, William Futchen			Kes.	Albert Co.
Loder, Jacob	Ct.		Shef.	
Lodge, James		CMG	Mag. R.	
Logan, John			Kings Co.	
Robert			Kn.	
Lomax, Alexander, shipwright, 85			C5	Kings Co.	Cn.
London, John		trump. LAL?		Queens Co.
Ralph, blacksmith			.Kn.	
Long, Abraham		Cpl. 2 NJV	Bl. 2	
Alexander		RFA	Mag. R.	N.S.?
James		74th BMG?		
John	Mass.		C96	St. A.
Peter			Mir.	N.S.?
Philip		KAR	Bl. 6	LC
William		PWAR	Maug.	
Longmuir, Richard, merchant, 97				Kent Co.
Looby, John			Pass.	
Thomas		RFA	Mag. R.	
Loofbourrow (Lufberry),				
John, blacksmith	Pa.		BH	Eng.
Jonathan			Mir.	
Nathaniel			BH	
Thomas			Mir.	left
Loosely, Charles, innholder			P400, 1284	
Lorraine, William, stonemason, 85	Scot.		P1310	Ptld.
Lord, Henry, yeoman, 85			Lanc.	
Lorton, William, Lt. Co. 22		CMG	P632	
Loshe (Lott?), Sarah	N.J.		Or.	
Losee, Simon, shoemaker			Queens Co.	
William	N.Y. D. Co.	WL		
Lotrum, John			Ken./85	
Lott, Levi			BH/84	
Lounsbury, Daniel		Sgt. LAR	F'ton	York Co.
James		WL	Westm.	
John	N.Y. W. Co.	NYV	P1253	Gn.
Joseph			Gn.	
Sarah			P1285	
William		1 DeL.		UC?
Love, James (1)		ML	P218	Bl. 1
James (2)		Ord.	Norton	
Loveday, Thomas, sailor			C435	Dipper Harbour
Lovell (Lovely?), Jesse & Thomas			Char.	
Lovely, Benjamin		RFA	Mag. R.	Carl.
Lowe, James		PWAR?	LR	N.Y.
John	N.Y.		St. A.	
Lowrey, Thomas			York Co.	

Lowrie, *see* Lawrie						
Lowther, William			St. A.			
Lucas, Clement, Sr.			P319	Queens Co.		
Clement, Jr.			P318	LR	UC	
Richard		Sgt. 2 NJV	Maug.			
Ludlow, Gabriel G., Mayor	N.Y. L.I.	Col. 2 DeL.	C196-8			
85, Esquire, 90						
George Dunean	N.Y. L.I.		F'ton			
Julian, merchant, 85						
Lufbuery, *see* Loofbourrow						
Lufkin, Aaron, Benjamin,			Char.			
Zebulon						
Lugart, Christopher, tanner, 85	QR		P540			
Lugrin, Peter	Hosp.		South Bay		St. John	
Simeon			P808	Kings Co.		
Lukens, Eli, blacksmith	Va.	CMG	Mir.			
Lumsden, George, shoemaker	Ct.		BH/84			
John, 2nd Lt. Co. 36			P509			
Mark, clerk		74th	St. A.			
Lunn, James			St. St.			
John		PWAR	Gr. Lake			
Lunt, John			Queens Co.			
Lutart, Thomas		1 DeL.	Bl. 8			
Lutkins, Harman		3 NJV	Pr. Wm.			
Lyall (Lyle), John			Sch.			
Lycan, Enoch		Lt. WJV	Bl. 2			
Lydne, John		Sgt. QR	York Co.	UC		
Lyman, Daniel	Ct.	Capt. PWAR	F'ton	Eng.		
Lymburner, Matthew	Scot./Mass.	guide	St. A.	UC		
Lynch, John Patrick			P933	Queens Co.	N.Y.	
Mary			Bel.			
Lyon(s), Augustus	Ct.		Kn.	Ct.		
Daniel	Ct. N.Y.		Queens Co.	N.Y.		
Hezekiah,			P1337	Kn.		
carpenter, 85						
Jeremiah		NYV	Kes.			
John	Ct.		P73	Kn.		
Joseph, farmer	Ct.		Kn.			
Peter	Ct.	1 NJV	Kings Co.			
Reuben (1)		NYV	Kes.	Nash.		
Reuben (2), farmer	Ct.		Kn.			
Thomas		NYV	Bl. 3	N.Y.	York Co.	
Mabe(e), Maybee, Elias			BH	Char.	Me.	
Frederick	N.Y.		C401	York Co.	UC	
Gilbert	N.Y. W. Co.		Kings Co.			
Isaac			Kes.			
Jacob, farmer	N.Y. D. Co.	Engr.?	St. J.	St. St.	Me.	
Jeremiah	N.Y. W. Co.		Bel.			
Solomon		a.b.	LR			
William, farmer,	N.Y. D. Co.					
(same?) carpenter, 85						
See also Mawby						
Mac, *see under* Mac or Mc						
Madden, Owen	KAR		Bl. 6	Sunbury Co.		
Maddox, Arthur, Esquire, 85	S.C.	Capt. 4 NJV	P437			
		Capt. RNSV				
John		PL	Bl. 7			
Maden, Michael		RFA	Mag. R.	LR		
Madget(t), Joseph		2 NJV	P1181	Bl. 2	York Co.	
Magee, William			Pass.			
Maghar (Meagher), Edmund			Dig.			
Joseph			St. A.			
Richard, gentleman			St. A.			
Maher, Dennis		PWAR	St. John Co.			
Mahon, Hugh, cordwainer, 87			P917			
Mailer, James			Dig.			
Main (Manes, Mangan),			Ham. R./84			
Michael, yeoman, 85						
same as Maden?						
Mainey, John		1 DeL.	Bl. 8			
Mainwaring James			P467	Kings Co.		
Major, John, tanner			Queens Co.	St. John		
Thomas		KAR	Queens Co.			

Malcolum, Finley			St. A.	
Mallard, Thomas, 2nd Lt.	Eng.		P495	d. '93
Co. 35				
Mallery, Caleb			P999	Burton
Simeon		PWAR	Ken.	
Mallock, Donald		74th		
Mallows, Ambrose		2 NJV		
Samuel	N.H.	wag.	P500	Sussex
Malone(Meloney, Mullowney,				
Manuel?) Anthony		17th	Mispec	
Dennis		KOR		
James	Ir./Pa.	QMG	St. A.	
John (1)		2 NJV	Burton	
John (2)			St. A.	
Mal(l)oy, Charles			BH/84	
Peter		64th	Pass.	
Mance, Mary			C349	
Peter			P328	Dipper Harbour
Manchester, William,			St. John	
shoemaker				
William,				
mariner, 90				
Mandall, Ephraim, cooper			St. John	
Mandeville, Richard			Ken.	LC
Mann, Samuel		Ord.?	BH/84	
Manning, Augustus			St. John	
George, yeoman, 85		RFA	P401	Sussex
William		GP	Bl. 3	
Mansfield, Marks			St. John Co.	
Manuel, Anthony (Malone?)			Bl. 5	
Manzer, Barnet or Bernard		Sgt. 2 DeL.	Queens Co.	St. John
Christopher		Sgt. 2 DeL.	Gr. Lake	
John		2 DeL.	Queens Co.	Queensbury
Martin		2 DeL.	Wash.	
Maphet, see Moffatt				
Marges(t)on, William,			P1110	
tailor, 85				
Marjoribanks, Thomas			St. John	d. '93
Marks, Edward		dr. LAR	LR	
Hezekiah		KAD	Bl. 2	Or.
John			P620	BH/87
Nehemiah	Ct.	a.b.	St. St.	
Marple, Northrup	N.Y.	guide	Char.	Kn.
Marr, Lawrence	Pa.	Cpl. 1 NJV	Queens Co.	UC
Marsh, Cornelius			P344	
George			Maug.?	
John, farmer	Ct./N.Y.		P1371	York Co.
Margaret			Kings Co.	
Richard, blacksmith	N.J.		P1385	Queens Co.
William, blacksmith			P1108	Kn.
Marshall, John			P1345	Gr. Lake
William			St. John	New Canaan?
Marsten (Marston), Abraham		KAR	C14	Bl. 6	Carl.
Benjamin	Mass.		C254	Shel.	Mir.
					Eng.
Jeremiah		KAR	Bl. 6	
See also Masten				
Martin, Adam			Char.	
Andrew			St. A.	
James		KOR	St. A.	
John (1)	Pa.	wag.	St. John Co.	
John (2), physician			P1195	Sussex
Peter	N.Y. W. Co.	GP, NYV	Kes.	
Robert, or Rayen		Engr.	Sch.	
Thomas		Ens. LAR	F'ton	
Marvin, John, farmer	Ct.		Kn.	Woodstock
Mascaline (Maskalyn), Jane			P1202	Kn.
Mason, Andrew, farmer	Pa.			
Samuel, mariner, 85			Queens Co.	Sunbury Co.
Masten, John	N.Y.	Sgt. LAR	St. John	
Masterton, John,		42nd	Nash., absent	
cordwainer, 85				
Masters, William		RFA	Mag. R.	
Mather, Elizabeth			Or.	

Mathe(w)son, Alexander		Sgt. 42nd	Nash.?		
Charles		Ens. QR	P190	Bl. 5	Sussex?
George,		42nd	St. John		
Matthews, Charles			P1237		
David			Ham. R.	St. John	
George, mariner, 95		ML	Bl. 1		
John (1)	N.J.	Cpl. 1 NJV	Wash.		
John (2)			St. A.		
Peter, mariner			St. John Co.		
Richard			Pennfield		U.S.A.
William		74th	Norton?		
Maul, John, tailor, 90		KAR			
Max(s)on, Nathan		Sgt. 3 NJV	Queens Co.		
Maxwell, Andrew	Md.	PWAR?	C607	F'ton	
Enoch, cordwainer, 85		1 DeL.	Bl. 8		
James	Ir.	Ord.	Sch.		
May, Elias		2 NJV	N.S.		
Mawby (Manley?), Silas			St. St.		
Simeon			Sch.		
(Maybee?), Gaspar		KOR	St. John'Co.		
Mayne, Thomas			Mispec		
William		Capt. Lt. QR		UC	
May(e)s, James, farmer	Pa.		Wash.		
Mead, Richard		Ord.	Pennfield		UC
William	N.Y. W. Co.	QR, WL	St. John R.		
Mealye, Patrick			Kent Co.		
Mecaliff (McCaliff), Peter, tailor, 95		3 NJV	P882		
Melick, John, cordwainer, 95	N.J.		St. John		
William, currier, 85	N.J.	Sgt. 1 NJV	P110		
Melody, Martha			St. A./84	aet. 10	
Melville, David, innkeeper, 85			P125		
Thomas			P298	Gn.	
Melvin, Robert, house carpenter				P417	N.Y.
Menzies, Alexander		Ens. LAL	P1336	N.Y.	
Archibald		Lt. 71st	Musq.		
Gilbert Lyster		Ens. 2 DeL.	P170	Eng.	
John, Capt. Co. 24	Ga.	Vol. LAL	P607	d. '86	
Sarah, wdw. Major Alex., 3 DeL.			P1370		
Thomas, Esquire, 85		Maj. LAL	P47	Musq.	
Merarty, Widow, with PL			Bl. 7		
Mercer, Joseph	Scot./N.C.	Ens. NCV	Burton	St. John Co.	
Merchant, Daniel			Mir.		
Jesse, tailor			P127	Queens Co.?	
Meredith, Charles		NCV	Kes.		
Merigan (Marigan), Martin		Ord.	Sch.		
Merigold, Thomas		Sgt. 2 NJV	Bl. 2	UC	
Merrill, Robert		Lt.?	St. St.		
Simon		Sgt. QR		Carl.	
Thomas Hazen			Cumb.		
William			Gr. Lake		
Merrithew, Jonathan			Queens Co.	York Co.	
Roger	Ct.		York Co.		
Merritt, Caleb, tailor, 85			C263		
David, merchant			St. John		
Gilbert			Ken.		
Jesse	N.Y.		Queens Co.		
John, trader		KAR	Ptld.		
Nathaniel	N.Y. W. Co.		Gn.	U.S.A.	
Nathaniel, Jr.	N.Y. W. Co.		Gr. Lake		
Peter		GP	Bl. 3		
Robert	N.Y.		Queens Co.		
Thomas, Sr., Capt. Co. 42?	N.Y. W. Co.			St. John	
Thomas, Jr.	N.Y. W. Co.	Ct. QR		UC	
Merry (Mary), John		1 DeL.	Bl. 8		
Mersereau, Andrew	N.Y. St. Is.		Maug.		
David	N.Y. St. Is.		P498	Or.	
John, Capt. Co. 16	N.Y. St. Is.		P290	Or.	
Lawrence	N.Y. St. Is.				
Paul, Sr., chairmaker, 85			P1102	Queens Co.	

Name	Origin	Service	Location	County	
Mersereau, Paul, Jr., carpenter, 85			P1096	Queens Co.	
Mesier, George		2 NJV	?		
Messicks, Nathan		GP	Bl. 3		
Micheau, Daniel, merchant, 85	N.Y. St. Is.		P51	Kings Co.	
Miles, Elijah	Ct.	Capt. 2 DeL.	Maug.		
Henry			St. John		
Joseph		Cpl. PL	Bl. 7		
Samuel, Lt., Co. 1, yeoman, 85	Ct.				
Thomas, labourer, 90		CMG	Kings Co.		
William		PWAR	St. John Co.		
Millegan (Millican), Jane			P845	Bel.	
Millekin, Benjamin	Mass.		St. A.		
Benjamin, Jr.	Mass.		St. A.	Me.	
Miller (Millar), Alexander, tidesman		54th	Gr. Lake		
Andrew		KAR	P1180	Gr. Lake	
Edward, mariner			Ptld.		
George			Queens Co.		
Henry		Engr.	Queens Co.		
James		74th			
John (1), goldsmith/85					
John (2), blacksmith		PL	Bl. 7	Carl.	
John (3)		a.b.?	Dig.		
John (4)		Engr.?	P1178	Gr. Lake	
		KAR?			
Moses	N.Y. W. Co.		Queens Co.		
Richard		RFA?	LR	West Indies	
Stephen	Mass.		F'ton		
Thomas, Jr.			P1338		
Tobias, gentleman			St. John		
William, cordwainer/85		74th	P825		
Millidge (Milledge), Stephen	N.J.	Ens. 2 NJV	Bl. 2	Albert Co.	
Thomas	N.J.	Maj. 1 NJV		N.S.	
Mills, Bradbury		GP	Bl. 3	Kn.	
Henry	N.Y.	Cpl. KAR	Kings Co.		
Isaac		Cpl. 2 NJV	Bl. 2	York Co.	
James			Mir.		
John, mariner		KAD?	P829		
Nathaniel ?	Mass.		Or.		
Reuben	N.Y. W. Co.	WL	Westm.		
William		2 NJV	P1079	Bl. 2	
Milne, Alexander, 2nd Lt. Co. 38, mason/85			P700		
Colin			St. John Co.		
Milton, Henry		Vol. NYV	N.S.	Albert Co.	
Minchin, Paul	Eng./S.C.	Capt. Navy or 29th ?		Queens Co.	
Ming(o)e, Alexander		2 NJV	?		
Minton, Daniel		PWAR	Mir.		
Mitchell, David		QR ?	Bl. 8		
John (1)	N.Y. L.I.?	Engr.	P1435	Kings Co.	
John (2)	Mass.	Gar.	Bel.		
Jonathan			Ham. R.		
Thomas	Mass.?	Sgt. ?	St. St.		
Moffatt, James	Ir./S.C.	SCL	Bel.		
Moltrup, Enoch, see Northrup	Ct. ?		Or.		
Monger, see Mungar					
Montgomery, Alexander	Ir./N.Y.		P795	Burton	UC
Alexander, Jr.	N.Y.		Queens Co.		
John, turner/85			P640	Navy ?	
Joseph, merchant	N.Y. U. Co.		Musq.		
Sarah			St. A.		
Montross, Peter		LAR	Penniac	UC	
Moody, James		Lt. 1 NJV	N.S.		
John			Or.		
Robert	Ga.	Surg. PWAR		F'ton	
Stephen			P976	Mir.	
Thomas		CMG	Mir.		
Mooney, Edward, butcher	N.Y.		Dipper Harbour		
John, butcher/85	N.Y.		Dipper Harbour	St. John	

Moor(e), Allen			Char.	
Benjamin	N.J. Som. Co.	Vol.	Mir.	left
James (1)	N.Y.	CMG	York Co.	N.Y. ?
James (2)	Scot.		Kn.	
John (1)		KAR	Bl. 6	
John (2)		CMG	Char.	
John (3)		2 NJV	?	
Margaret			Rusagonis	
Robert	N.H.		Char.	
Peter		RFA	Mag. R.	
Samuel	N.J.	Surg. RN	P126	
Moore, Thomas (1)	Pa.		P1085	U.S.A.?
Thomas (2) ?	N.H.		Char.	N.H.
William ?	N.H.		Char.	
Moran, Andrew		KOR	St. John Co.	
Matthias	N.Y. O. Co.	KOR	St. John Co.	
William		KOR	St. John Co.	
Morcan, Thomas			Musq. esch.	
Morden, Moses		2 NJV	Bl. 2, declined.	
Morecraft, James, farmer			St. John Co.	
William		1 DeL.		
Morehouse, Daniel (1)	Ct.	QMR. QR.	Qnsby.	
Daniel (2)	N.Y.	Sgt. NYV	Kes.	
James, carpenter	Ct.		P1078	d.'84
Noah, farmer	Ct.		P1373	Ham. R.
Samuel			Maug.	
Theophilus			Kes.	
Moreland, John, carpenter, 85		N.YV?	Kes.	
Morley, George	Mass.		St. John	
Moroney, James		PWAR	Nash.	
Morrell, Daniel	N.Y. U. Co.	Engr.	P510	Bel.
John, blacksmith, 85	N.Y. U. Co.		Kn.	
Robert			Sch.	
Thomas			Queens Co.	
Morris, Amos		GP	Bl. 3	Pr. Wm.
Enoch	Pa.?		Gn.	
William		ML	Bl. 1	
Morrison, Alexander	Mass.?		St. A.	
Allen		ML	Bl. 1	
David			Char.	
George		Sgt. KAR	Qnsby.	
Henry		KAD	P1183	York Co.
Jacob		Cpl. KAR	Penniac	
James		RFA	Mag. R.	
John, Jr.		LAR	P644	Queens Co.
William			St. A.	
See also Mowerson.				
Morton, Alexander			P1417	St. John Co.
Elkanah	Mass.	lost leg	Sussex	
George			Sussex	
John			St. A.	aet. 10
Mosely, John, shipwright, 85			P1084	
Moss, Amos		2 DeL.	P618	Kn.
Mary, m. Francis Blackburn			Gn.	
Mott, Enoch			Gn.	
John, butcher	N.Y. L.I.		P1377	Queens Co.
Richbell *or* Rigible			Kn.	d. '85
Thomas			Musq.	
Mount, George	N.J.		Queens Co.	
Harry	N.J.		P1024	Musq.
John			Gr. Lake	
Mowat, David		Master *Sally*	St. A.	
James Ryder		Capt. KAR	Eng.	
John		Lt. RN	Char.	
Mowerson, Francis		2 NJV	Bl. 2	
Hartman		2 NJV	Bl. 2?	
Henry, *see* Morrison.				
Mowry, Jonathan		Sgt. LAR	LR	
Muirson, Benjamin Woolsey	N.Y.	ex QR, Em. Ch.	P798, C201	U.S.A.
Mulhardy, Daniel		LAL	Pr. Wm.	
Mulhuish, Thomas		GP	Bl. 3	
Mulkay, David		KOR		

Mulligan, Thomas			P342		
Mullin (Mullen), Barney, yeoman, 85			P1405		
John (1)		GP	Bl. 3	Bel.	
John (2)			P1346	LR	N.Y.
Patrick		LAR	LR		
Thomas (1), innkeeper, 85	Pa.		P403		
Thomas (2), blacksmith	Mass. Worc.		St. John		
Mulock, Francis		Ens. NYV	Kes.	N.S.	
Mumford, Daniel		2 DeL.	Maug.		
Muncure (Muncias), Robert			St. A.		
Munday, Jonathan, labourer, 86	N.J. Msx.				
Joseph	N.J.		St. John Co.		
Nathaniel	N.J.	Ens. QR	R.I.	UC	
Stephen		NYV	Kes.	left	
Mungar, James, carpenter, 85		Sgt. KAR	C187		
Munn, Donald		Cpl. 42nd.	Nash.		
Munro, Daniel			Ham. R.		
Evan			Or.		
John (1)		Capt. KRRNY		Canada	
John (2)		74th	P759	Pennfield	
William, yeoman, 85		42nd	C449		
Munrow, Ephraim			Char.		
Muntush, Lewis			Kes.		
Murchie, William	Scot./N.Y.	CMG	Sch.		
Murdock, William			BH		
Murket, J.	R.I.?		St. John		
Murphy, Alexander			St. A.		
Archibald			St. A.		
James (1)		LAL	Bl. 6		
James (2)		KOR	Pass.		
John (1)		GP	Bl. 3, absent		
John (2)		Cpl. LAL	Kes.		
Luke			P1207		
Michael		1 DeL.			
Patrick			Kes.		
Richard		PWAR	York Co.		
William		3 NJV	P944	Ken.	
Murray, Bartley		1 NJV	Kings Co.		
Daniel, Harvard, '71	Mass.	Maj. KAD	P134, 5, C235	York Co.	U.S.A.
Edward		Ens. QR	P184		
Hugh		NYV?	P442		
James		RFA	Mispec		
Joel			Burton		
John (1), Esquire, 85	Mass.		C440		
John (2), carpenter, 85		Cpl. KAR			
Peter, yeoman, 85			Queens Co.?		
Robert		Capt. Lt. KAD	P123	Bl. 4	d. '86
Thomas		Lt. QR	St. John		
Muzz(e)y, Joseph			Kings Co.		
Myer(s), Abraham	R.I.	2 NJV?	Gn.		
Charles		1 DeL.	Bl. 8		
David	Mass.		St. A.	d. '86	
Edward		LAR	Bl. 3		
Jacob		Engr.	P659		
John	N.J.	CMG	RL		
Rachel			Queens Co.	Kings Co.	
Reuben, yeoman, 85		KAR	C142		
Samuel			P1220	Queens Co.	
William, yeoman, 85		1 NJV?	P1305		
Mac, Mc.					
McAlary (Elroy), William			P242	St. John River	
McAllister, Annanias			Char.		
Daniel			Char.		
John			Char.		
McAlpine, Alexander		PWAR	St. John Co.		
Charles			Queens Co.	Kings Co.	Me.
Cornelius		GP	Bl. 3		

Name	Origin	Service	Grant	Place	Place2
McAlpine, John (1),		CMG	P1444		
labourer, 85					
John (2)	N.Y.	BMG	Wash.	Queens Co.	
Peter, yeoman, 85	N.Y. T. Co.	?	P724	Queens Co.	
Walter			P705	Gn.	St. John
McAnnella, Anna		RFA	Mag. R.		
McArthur, Alexander		74th			
Charles			Sch.		
Robert			Pass.		
McAslong, Humphrey			Pass.		
McAulay (Macaulay),		NYV?	Mir.		
Farquuhar					
James		Surg. mate QR	Or.	UC	
McBean (McBain), Alexander		Ord.	St. St.		
Angus		42nd	C454	Nash.	
John (1)		74th	Sch.?		
John (2), labourer, 86		Ord.	C443		
Neal			Sch.		
McBeath, Francis			F'ton		
McBride, Thomas		GP	Bl. 3	d. '84 or 85.	
McCain, Priscilla			Rusagonis		
McCaleb (McCally), Alexander		KOR	Kings Co.		
McCall, George, merchant, 86	Scot.		P605		
John			P876	UC?	
See also McColl.					
McCallum, Humphrey		74th	St. A.		
John, Sr.		74th	St. A.		
John ,Jr.		74th	St. A.	St. John Co.	
Peter		Sgt. 74th	St. A.		
McCann, Andrew		Lt. QR	P183	UC?	
McCargo, Robert		Cpl. NYV	Kes.		
McCarrick, Peter	N.J.		P381	Queens Co.	
McCart(h)y, Charles		GP	Bl. 3		
Daniel			LR		
Dennis		RFA	Mag. R.		
George		Sgt. KAR?	Bl. 6		
Hugh			Sch.		
Isaiah, carpenter		Engr.	P392	Queens Co.	
John		Sgt. RFA	Mag. R.		
Timothy		KOR			
McCaskill, Finlay		NCR	P368	Kes.	
McCaulay (McAiley), William		42nd	Nash.	Mir.	
McCawley (McCarne?),			Mispec		
Alexander, labourer, 90					
McChain, James (Merchant,		1 DeL.	Bl. 8		
Jesse?)					
McClean, *see* McLean.					
McCloskey, Michael, farmer	Pa.		P1445	Wash.	
Mc(C)Lure, Alexander		QR	Bl. 5		
David, mason, 85			P1261	Gr. Lake	Scot.
McCluskey, William			Sch.		
McColgar (McColgon), Adam		QR	Bl. 5	York Co.	
McColl, Duncan		Engr.	St. St.		
John		74th	Dig.		
McColm, Malcolm, weaver	Ct.		?		
McColone (McConnell?), John	N.Y.?		Bel.		
McCo(o)mb, James (1)		Cpl. ML	Nash.	York Co.	
James (2)		Sgt. QR	Mir.		
McCommiskey, Moses		3 NJV	F'ton		
McConnell, Charles	R.I.		P980	York Co.?	
McCord, Patrick			Queens Co.		
McCormick, Daniel or Donald		74th	Sch.		
Peter, farmer	N.J.		?		
McCorquadale, Mary, 3 ch.		74th			
McCowen, *see* McEwen.					
McCoy, Donald			Mispec.		
Hugh		57th	St. A.		
See also McKay.					
McCra(w), (McRa, McRaw,					
McGraw),					
Alexander (1)	Scot./N.C.	Capt. NCH	St. A.		
Alexander (2)		54th	Nash.		
Donald, yeoman, 85		NCV	Kes.	Mir.	
Duncan		42nd	P201	Nash.	Mir.

Name	Origin	Regiment/Rank	Grant	Place 1	Place 2
McCra(w), Farquahar		42nd		Nash.	Mir.
John (1)		Ord. *or*	P516	Ken. Is.	St. John
John (2)		?		Sch.	
Kenneth				Sch.	
Mark				St. John	
Michael				Mir.	
Neil		42nd		Nash.	Mir.
McCracken, Mary, wdw., 4 ch.				Ken.	UC?
McCraddock, Peter				Maq.	
McCrea, Arthur		KAD		Kn.	
Creighton	N.J.	Ens. QR	P194	Bl. 5	K. Co.
Elizabeth, wdw.	Va.			Bel.	
Isabella (wdw. Henry	S.C.			Halifax	Bel.
Strum, Sgt. SCL, m. Arthur McCrea)					
Robert	N.J.	Capt. QR	P1057	Guernsey	
(McCreigh) Thomas				Maug.	York Co.
McCready, widow, 3 sons,	N.Y. L.I.			Ham. R.	
m. Andrew Sherwood					
William	N.Y. L.I.			Ham. R.	
McCristal, Patrick		64th		Pass.	
McCue, James, labourer, 86				Mir.	
McCullum, James ?				Mir.	
McCulloch, Richard		42nd		St. John	
McCurdy, Lauchlin	Mass.			St. A.	
Neal, shipcarpenter				St. A.	
William, shipcarpenter				Campobello	
McDaniel, *see* McDonald.					
McDavid (McDevitt), William		Cpl. 1 DeL.		Bl. 8	
McDean, James				St. A.	
McDiarmid, Duncan				Char.	
Peter		74th		St. A.	
McDonald, Alexander (1)				Sch.	
Alexander (2)		Lt. But/ Rgrs.		York Co.	
Alexander (3)	N.Y. St. Is.	BMG?		Wash.	
Alexander (4)		Cpl. QR		Mir.	UC
Alexander (5), Sr.		42nd	P245	Mir.	
Alexander (6), Jr.		42nd		Nash.	Mir.
Alexander (7)	Scot./Pa.	Capt. 1 NJV		F'ton	Eng.
Alexander (8)		Cpl. QR *or* NCV?		Mir.	left?
Angus	Scot./N.C.	Capt. NCH	P198	St. A.	
Archibald, physician		Surg. GP		Shef.	
Benjamin		1 NJV		Sunbury Co.	
Daniel *or* Donald		Sgt. NCV		Mir.	
David (1), tailor			P1153	Gr. Lake	
David (2)		GP		Bl. 3	d. '84 *or* 85
Donald (1), yeoman, 85		42nd	C451	Sussex	
Donald (2)		NYV?		Mir.	
Donald (3)		QR?		York Co.	
Duncan		GP		Bl. 3	
Francis		42nd		?	
Hugh		ML		Bl. 1	York Co.
James (1)		ML		Bl. 1	
James (2)		42nd		Nash.	
James (3)		Lt. PWAR	C328, 330	Kings Co.	
John (1)	N.Y. D. Co.			Burton	
John (2)		GP?		Bl. 3	Kes.
John (3)		Sgt. QR?		Mir.	
John (4)	Scot.	2 NJV		Mir.	
John (5)		42nd		Nash.	
John (6)		a. b.?	P1149?	Bel.?	
John (7)		NSV		Char.	
John (8), Jr.?		CMG	P1080		
Joseph				St. A.	
Laughlin		Ens. LAR		Mir.	
Lawrence		1 DeL.		Bl. 8	
Patrick		RFA			
Peter		74th			

Name	Origin	Unit	Grant/Ref	Settlement	Note
McDonald, Richard			Bel.		
Roderick		76th	Mir.		
Sarah			C357		
Stephen		GP	Bl. 3, absent		
Thomas (1)	N.Y. W. Co.	pilot	Wash.		
Thomas (2)			Pass.		
McDougall (McDougald),					
Daniel or Donald		42nd	P243	Nash.	Mir.?
John		74th	St. A.		
Roger		QR	Mir.		
Samuel		Ens. GB	Mag. R.		
McDuffee, Augustus			Or.		
Dudley			Or.		
McEchran (McAchron),					
Duncan, blacksmith		Engr.	St. A.		
Neil		74th			
Robert			St. A.		
McElhatton, Michael,		PL	Bl. 7		
labourer, 86					
McE(I)lroy, Edward, Lt. Co. 44					
John		74th	St. A.		
McEvers, John		GP	Bl. 3		
McEvoy (McAvoy), Daniel		ML	Bl. 1	Carl.?	
McEwen (McCowen), John		1 NJV	Sussex		
McEwen (McGowan), Patrick	N.J./ S.C./N.C.		P813	Bel.	
shoemaker and					
saddler					
McFall, Patrick		2 DeL.	BH		
McFarland (McFarlane,					
McPharlen),					
Alexander		74th	St. A.		
Duncan			St. A.		
Hugh			St. A.		
George, tailor		42nd	Nash.	Mir.	
James		QR	P760	Bl. 5	
John (1)		Sgt. 42nd	C455		
John (2)		GP	Bl. 3		
John (3)		KAR?	Gr. Lake		
McGee, George	Ir.	1 DeL.	Bl. 8	Carl.	
McGeorge, John, merchant, 85					
McGibbon, David		Lt. Flor. Rangers		York Co.	
McGibbins, Henry			P181		
John	Scot./Jam.		P1264	St. George	
McGier (McGear), John		CMG	Sch.		
William			Sch.		
McGill, Ann, wdw. Rowland,			Ken.		
1 DeL.					
John, gentleman, 85	Scot./Va.	Capt. QR	P140	Kings Co.	UC
McGilton, John		2 NJV			
McGilvray, John		42nd	Nash.		
McGinley (McKinley), Charles		ML?	P696		
Hugh		QR	P200		
McGlaskey, George		PL	Bl. 7		
McGloughly, Patrick			Mispec.		
McGonnigal, Edward		84th	Pass.		
McGowan, see McEwen					
McGrath, Dennis			Gr. Lake		
McGraw, see McCra					
McGregor, Daniel	Scot./N.Y.		P507	Gr. Lake	
Donald		42nd	Nash.		
John		42nd	Nash.		
Malcolm		42nd	Nash.		
McGuire, Edward			BH		
Frederick or John?		KAD	Bl. 4	N.Y. or Mir.?	
James, labourer			Mispec.		
Michael		Navy?	St. John		
Theophilus		1 NJV	York Co.		
McHugo(e), Thomas		2 NJV	Bl. 2	Maug.	
McIndoe (McIndue), Robert			St. John	Ken.	
McInnes, Angus		76th	Mir.		
McInish, Donald		74th			
McIntosh, Alexander		71st	P480	Nash.	
Daniel		Sgt. KAR	P1173		
John	Mass.	CMG	St. A.		

Name	Origin	Unit/Rank	Code	Place	Extra
McIntosh, Lochlan		dr. 71st		Nash.	
Malcolm		42nd	C450		
Thomas, carpenter?		74th			
William, yeoman, 85		Sgt. 42nd		York Co.	
McIntyre, Angus		Cpl. 42nd	P842		
Archibald		74th			
Donald		74th			
Duncan				St. A.	
John (1)		74th			
John (2)		74th			
Michael		QR		Bl. 5	
Peter		74th			
Samuel				Dig.	
McIver (McKever), Alexander		42nd		Nash.	
McKachnie, Laughlin				Sch.	
McKain, see McCain					
McKay (McCoy), Angus, tailor, 85		42nd		Ken.	
Daniel (1)			P225		
Daniel (2)			P430	Ken.	
Daniel (3)	Pa.	a. b.		St. A.	
Donald		42nd	P255?	Nash.	
Duncan		42nd	P178		
Elizabeth				St. John Co.	
Francis		42nd	P261		
George, Sr.		42nd		Nash.	
George, Jr.		42nd		Nash.	
Henry		42nd	P258	Nash.	
Hugh	Scot.	Lt. QR	P193, C549, 550	St. George	
John (1)	Scot./Va.	Capt. QR	P192, 1297		Bl. 5
John (2)		RFA	Mag. R.		
John (3)			Nash.		
Joseph		74th			
Murdoch		KAR	F'ton		
Robert, Sr.		42nd	P254		
Robert, Jr.		42nd	Nash.		Mir.
Thomas		KOR			
William (1)		QR	Bl. 5		
William (2)		42nd	P260	Nash.	
McKee, Alexander, 2nd Lt. Co. 11					
Hanford, cooper, 85					
James	Scot.			Ken.	
John, innkeeper, 85	Ir./Ct.		P79		
John, shipmaster	Scot.				
Robert		KAD?	Ham. R.		
William, barber, 85					
McKeel (McKiel), Joseph, carpenter, 85		Em. Ch.	P580	Kings Co.	
McKonellogi (McKennelly?), John		1 NJV	?		
McKenna (McKanna), Hugh		KAD	?		
McKenzie, Alexander		42nd	Nash.		
Caleb		LAR	P229	Ken.	
Donald (1), labourer		Cpl. 42nd	P248	Nash.	
Donald (2)		74th		St. A.	
Hugh		Car.		Nash.	
John (1)		1 NJV		Gr. Lake	
John (2), yeoman, 85		Sgt. 42nd	P249		
(Menzie?) John (3)		Gar.		Nash.	
Kenneth		84th		Pass.	
Lachlan				St. A.	
Malcolm			C6		Bel.
Murdoch		GP		Bl. 3	
Robert				St. John	
Roderick		42nd		Nash.	
Thomas		GP		Bl. 3	d. '84
McKinley, see McGinley					
McKinnon, Gregor		Sgt. NCV	C452	Kes.	Mir.
John		a. b.		St. John	
McKivers, see McEvers					
McLaggan, Peter		Cpl. 42nd	C448	Nash.	
McLancy, James				St. A.	

Name	Origin	Rank/Unit	Code	County	Note
McLannon, *see* McLennan					
McLaughlin (McLachlan),					
Archibald		svd.	Mag. R.		
Donald		74th	St. A.		
John (1)		CMG	Sch.		
John (2)		1 DeL.	Bl. 8		
Nathaniel		1 DeL.	Bl. 8		
Peter		Lt. 74th	Char.		
Thomas ?	N.H.		Char.		
William		QR	Bl. 5		
McLaurin (McLeron), Peter		NYV	Kes.		
McLean (McClean), Alexander		74th	St. A.		
Archibald (1)	Scot./N.Y.	Capt. NYV	P1430	York Co.	
Archibald (2)			Gr. Lake		
Charles (1), mariner, 85			P1352	St. John	
Charles (2)			P567	Gr. Lake	
Donald (1)		Cpl. 42nd	C442, 3?	Sussex	
Donald (2)		Lt. 74th	St. A.		
Duncan ?			Gr. Lake		
Farquar ?			Mir.		
Finlay		74th			
Hugh			Mispec.	UC	
John (1)		74th			
John (2)			Shel.	Mir.	
Lachlan			?		
Peter, cordwainer, 85			P153	Ken.	d. '9-
McLeish, David			P915		
McLellan (McClellan), John		74th			
Peter		74th			
Robert		74th	St. A.		
Rory *or* Roderick			Char.		
McLennan (McLinnon, McClanen),					
Alexander, cordwainer, 85		QR	P199		
William (1)			Sch.		
William (2)		42nd	St. John		
McLeod (McLead, McCloud),					
Alexander			St. A.		
Angus		NCV	Kes.	dr. '88	
Daniel		NCV	P255?	Kes.	
Donald		Cpl. 42nd	P256	Nash.	
Duncan (1)		42nd	P240	Nash.	Mir.
Duncan (2), merchant ?			P245	F'ton?	
Fergus		ML	Bl. 1		
Hugh			St. A.	d. '88	
John (1)		RFA	Mag. R.		
John (2)			Shel.	Mir.	
John (3), grocer, 90 ?			York Co.	St. John	
Malcolm		42nd	Nash.	F'ton	
Mary			Ham. R./84		
Murdock (1)		42nd	Nash.?		
Murdock (2)		QR	Mir.		
Murdock (3)		GP	Bl. 3		
Norman (1)		Capt. 2 NJV	York Co.?		
Norman (2)		KAR	York Co.		
Robert		GB?	Nash.		
Roderick (1), Sr.		GB?	Nash.		
Roderick (2), Jr.		42nd	Nash.		
Roderick (3), merchant, 85		Capt. Lt. KAR			
William (1)		GB?	Nash.	Mir.	
William (2)		Sgt. RFA	Sussex		
McLiesh, *see* McLeish					
McLindon, John (in Co. 36)			St. John		
McLure, *see* McClure					
McMahon, John		PWAR	York Co.		
McMasters, Daniel	Mass.		St. A.		
Hugh			F'ton		
James	Ir./Mass.		Char.		
John (1)		2 NJV	Kn.		
John (2)	Ir./Mass.		Char.		
Patrick	Ir./Mass.		Char.		

Name	Origin	Rank/Unit	Code	Place	Extra
McMichael, Richard,			P104	Kings Co.	
Lt. Co. 39					
William Augustus		Lt. PL	Bl. 7		
McMillan, Alexander		a. b.?	Mir.		
Archibald		74th	St. A.		
James			Sch.		
John, carpenter		Engr.	St. A.		
Miles		42nd	Nash.	Mir.	
McMullen, Francis, tailor, 85		1 NJV	Penniac		
McNab(b), Colin		Ens. NSV	Mag. R.	UC	
James (1)		Lt. RFA	Mag. R.		
James (2)	Scot.	Sgt. 42nd	P250		
McNally, James		KOR	St. John Co.		
Michael		Ens. PWAR	Maug.	Qnsby.	
Patrick (McNamara,					
1 NJV? McFall,					
2 DeL.? McWay,					
Sgt. PWAR?)			Bl. 5		
Thomas		3 NJV	F'ton	Kes.	
McNamara, David		RFA	P643		
Patrick		Sgt. 1 DeL.	P1041	Bl. 8	
McNamee, Charles			Ken.		
McNash, Jacob		dr. 2 NJV	Bl. 2?		
McNeal (McNeil), Archibald	Mass.	Engr.	St. John		
Catherine			Bel.	St. John	
Charles	N.Y.?	pilot?	Bel.		
Daniel		Sgt. NYV	Kes.		
Hugh	Ir./Pa.	Engr.	Burton		
James, tailor, 85					
John		Sgt. 2 DeL.	Burton		
Joseph		NYV	Kes.		
Neil, yeoman, 85			C215	d. '84	
Thomas		LAR	Nash.		
William			Nash.		
McNellis, Charles		PL	Bl. 7		
McNichol(l), John			St. A.	d. '86	
McNiven, Alexander		74th	St. A.		
McOwen, Jonathan		Sgt. 2 DeL.	BH		
McPhadden, Donald		42nd	Nash.		
McPhail, Hugh			St. A.		
John			St. A.		
McPherson, Charles,	Scot.	regt.?	P402		
merchant, 85					
Donald,			P1395		
yeoman, 85					
Evan			Sch.		
Hugh, farmer	N.Y.		?		
James			Char.	St. John	
John		42nd	Char.		
Paul			Char.		
Peter		Capt. GP	P1119	Bl. 3	Brit.
William		42nd	P259	York Co.	
McQuire, Frederick		KOR			
McQuiston, William			Char.		
McRa(w), see McCra					
McRay, Donald, cordwainer, 85					
McRobert, John			P299	Queensbury	
McShaffrey (McSheffrey),					
Daniel		Sgt. 1 DeL.	P982		
McSwain (McSween), Murdoch		42nd	Nash.	Mir.?	
McTavish, Alexander		74th			
McVane (McVean), James		74th	St. A.		
McVicar, Duncan		74th	St. A.		
Niven		74th			
McWay, Patrick		Sgt. PWAR	St. John Co.		
Nairn, William		84th			
Napier, Robert			P1420	Kings Co.	
Narroway, Anthony	Ga.		P68	Gn.	N.Y.
Nase, Henry	N.Y.	Ens. KAR	Nerepis		
Nash, Jedidiah			Kn.		
Joseph		Cpl. RFA	Mag. R.	St. A.	
Samuel, farmer	Ct.		P1375	UC	

Naylor (Nailer), Joshua		Cpl. 1 DeL.	Bl. 8		
William			P366	St. John Co.	
Neal (Niel), Edward (1)		RFA	P1357		
Edward (2)		Sgt. 1 DeL.	Bl. 8	Carl.	
Henry, carpenter, 85			P1407	N.Y.	
John		LAR		UC	
Neal (Neill), Lawrence		QR	Queens Co.		
Nealon, James		Capt. 1 NJV	Maug.?		
Negus, Thomas, labourer			F'ton		
Ne(i)lson, Andrew, baker, 85		GB	P1198		
David		QR	Bl. 5	hanged	
Thomas		2 NJV	Bl. 2?		
Nesbitt, William			Sch.		
Ness, Ann, m. John Simonson			C358, 9		
John, gentleman, 85	Eng.	Lt. PWAR	C329		
Nevil(l), Richard, labourer, 85		PL		Bl. 7	
Newble, James			St. John		
Newman, David	Ct.	Sgt. 1 DeL.	P1276	Bl. 8	
John		2 NJV	Mir.		
Newton, Forbes, tinman, 85			Gr. Bay		
Nice, Cornelius	Pa.	3 NJV	Bel.		
Nichol(l)s, Edward, blacksmith, 90		LAL	Gr. Bay		
John		RFA	Mag. R.		
Samuel			P1196	Kings Co.	
Ruth	R.I.		St. John	2 ch.	
Nicholson, Arthur	Ir.	Ct. KAD	Kes.	Mir.	Carl.
James			St. A.		
John			St. A.		
Nickerson, Joseph			P1450	Gn.	
Eliud (Lloyd)			Bel.		
Thomas			P1451	Queens Co.	
Nicklin, Samuel			P496	Gr. Lake	
Nierly,? William		RFA	Mag. R.		
Niles, James		GP	Bl. 3		
Noble, Francis, labourer, 85	Mass.		P1157		
James, mason, 85					
John (1)		Ord.	Sch.		
John (2)	Va.	Cpl. ML	Bl. 1	Mir.	
Silvanus	Ct.	Sgt. 2 DeL.	Ken.		
Noblet (Knoblit), John	N.Y.		Kn.	Norton	
Nolan, John		RFA	Mag. R.		
Noonan, Timothy		RFA			
Norman, Henry			P456	Mispec	U.S.A.
Norris, Elizabeth, wdw. of Joshua Pike			St. John		
Norstrand, see Van Norstrand					
North, Thomas			Maq.	UC	
Northrup, Benajah	Ct.	Vol. GP	Kn.		
Enoch, joiner, 85					
Zadock			Kn.	Bel.	
Norton, Elias			P836		
Henry			Bel.		
Michael			F'ton		
Norwood, Francis			St. A.		
Gustavas			St. A.		
James			St. A.		
Jonathan, Sr. and Jr.			St. A.		
Samuel			St. A.		
Nostrant, see Van Norstrand					
Nowlan(d), James			Kings Co.		
(Nolan?) John			St. John Co.		
Michael			Digby	Sussex	
Nugent, John		Supt. ?			
Nutt, Silvester			Ken.	U.S.A.	
Nutter, John			Kn.		
William		2 DeL.	Kings Co.		
Nutting (Nutten, Nolten), Joseph, tidewaiter, 85	Eng.	CMG	LR		
Nye, Simon		2 NJV	Bl. 2		
Oachard (Orchard), William			Kings Co.		
Oakley, Joshua	N.Y. W. Co.		Queens Co.		

Obbens (Hobby, Hubbs, Huber), Jacob		Sgt. 2 DeL.?	Or.		
Joseph, shoemaker	N.Y.	2 DeL.	Or.		
O'Blenis (Oblenus), John, carpenter, 85	N.Y.	Engr.	P161	Westm.	
O'Brien (O'Bryan), James	N.J.?	KOR			
John	N.Y. D. Co.	WL	Westm.		
Patrick, tavernkeeper, 95		3 NJV	St. John Co.		
Robert		Adj. 1 DeL.	C136		
O'Conner, Charles		LNE?	St. John	d. '87	
O'Daniels, Hugh			Ken.		
Odell, Daniel	N.Y.	PWAR?	Or.	Bel.	
Jonathan, Rev., Princeton, 54	N.J.	Chap. (Surg.)	F'ton		
Jonathan			C191	Ham. R.	
Odle, (Dondleson?), Thomas		PWAR	St. John Co.		
Ogden, Benjamin	N.Y.	Capt. Em. Ch.?	C312	N. S.	
John	N.Y. W. Co.	WL	Queens Co.		
Jonathan		LAR	Queens Co.		
Michael	N.Y.		Queens Co.	d. '89	
Rachel, m. Timothy Wetmore			C261	St. John	
Robert		KAR	Or.		
O'Hara, Patrick			Gr. Lake		
Old, Nicholas E.		Ens. 1 DeL.	P1042	Bl. 8	
Olden, John		2 NJV	Bl. 2?		
Thomas		QR	Bl. 5		
Oldham, John, mariner (Outen?)			Kn.		
Olds (Oltz?), Pyram			Gn.		
Olive, William, Capt. Co. 30, shipwright, 85	Eng.		C12		
Oliver, Edward			Musquash		
Hampton		Engr.	Gr. Lake/84		
James, Lt. Co. 4	Mass.	recr.	P1241	Queens Co.	d. '84
Robert			LR		
Widow			Dig.		
William Sanford, Sr. Esquire, 85	Mass.	W. Vol.	P27		
William Sanford, Jr.	Mass.		P70		Lt. RN
Olstead, Aaron, blacksmith, 85	Ct.	Cpl. QR	P758		
Eliphalet (Levy)	Ct.		Or.		
Thomas	Ct.	2 DeL.	Gr. Lake		
O'Loghlin, Malachi, mariner			LR		
Patt			St. John Co.		
Oltz, Martin			Burton		
O'Neal (O'Neill), John		Lt. PWAR	York Co.?		
Michael, seaman	N.Y.		?		
Philip	Ir./Pa.	PL	Bl. 7	Carl.	
Oram, James	Pa.	svd.	LR		
O'Reilly, Charles			LR		
Orin, John, labourer, 90			P757		
Ormond, George, St.		Adj. QR	Bl. 5	UC	
Ormsby, Gilbert			BH		
Orr, Thomas		PWAR	St. John Co.		
William, farmer	N.Y. U. Co.		UC		
Orser, William	N.Y.	KAD	Bl. 4	Carl.	
Osborn, Benjamin		guide	Wash.		
Charles			C166	Ken.	U.S.A.
John	N.Y.		P583	Ken.	d. '87
Nathaniel			Ken.	U.S.A.	
Nicholas (or Jacob?)		2 NJV	Bl. 2?		
Samuel, carpenter, 85	N.J.	guide	Kn.	St. John	
Oseman, William		RFA	Mag. R.		
O(u)sterman, Emanuel	N.Y.		Queens Co.	St. John Co.	
Outen (Ostiom, Oldham?), John		RFA	Mag. R.		
Outhouse, Simon	N.Y.	WL	Sackville		
Overton, John		NYV	Kes.		
Owens, John, mariner, 85			P1081		
Jonathan		Sgt. KAD	BH	York Co.	
William	Ir.	Sgt. ML	Bl. 1	Ir.	

Oxford, James ?		Hldrs.	Mir.	
Oxnard, Thomas	Mass.		Gr. Manan	U.S.A.
Pack, George		Ord.	P329	N.Y. '17
Pace (Pase), John			Dig.	Campobello
Paddock, Adino, physician, 85	Mass.	Surg. KAD	P1132	
Josiah, mariner			St. A.	
Pagan, John			St. A.	
Robert	Scot./Mass.		St. A.	
Robert, Jr.			St. A.	Kent Co.?
Thomas			St. A.	
William			St. A.	
Page, William		QR	Musquash	
Paine, William, Esquire, 85	Mass.	Hosp.	Pass.	U.S.A.
Pallers (Pallen?), Archibald			St. A.	
Palmer, Alphaeus	N.Y. W. Co.		Rus.	Shel.	UC
Gideon	N.Y. W. Co.	Lt. WL	Westm.	
Joseph			P557	Wash.	d. '85
Marcus			Queens Co.	
Nathaniel			St. A.	
Pangbourne, Noah		KAR	St. John	
Stephen		2 DeL.	BH/84	
Parent, Daniel	N.Y. W. Co.	CMG	Queens Co.	York Co.
Thomas		1 NJV	BH/84	
Widow of John			Gr. Lake	N.Y.
Parke, John		Wag.	Gr. Lake	
Parker, Asa			Char.	
Benjamin		2 DeL .	BH	
David		KAR	York Co.	
Ebenezer			Char.	
Elijah		GP	Bl. 3	
Isaac			Kings Co.	
John		PWAR	Nash.	
Jonathan, carpenter			P285	
Jonathan, Jr.			C102	Campobello?
Joseph		Em. Ch.?	Pennfield	
Josiah	N.J.	Lt. 2 NJV	Pr. Wm.	
Nathaniel's family		2 NJV	Bl. 2	
Robert	Mass.		St. John	
Timothy, yeoman, 85			P706	
William (1)		Ord.	P676	
William (2)		1 NJV	York Co.	
Park(e)s, John		Ens. GP	Bl. 3	
Joseph		Cpl. 2 NJV		
Nathaniel		Sgt. 2 NJV	Queens Co.	
Parlee, Cornelius				Sussex
Isaac				Sussex
Peter	Pa. B. Co.	2 NJV	Bl. 2	Sussex
Parmelee, Samuel	N.Y.		LR	
Parr, Harriet and William?			Sch.	
Parrity (Paradie), William		Sgt. 1 DeL.	Bl. 8	
Parsons, Esther			Char.	
Levi		GP	Bl. 3	Or.
Nathaniel			Char.	
Tabitha			Char.	
William Norwood		CMG?	St. A.	
Partelow, Amos, shoemaker	N.Y. D. Co.	Sgt. PWAR	St. John	
Amos, Jr., seaman				
Jehiel, cordwainer	Ct.		P1143	
Matthew, tailor, 85	Ct./N.Y.		P1442	
Richard			P187	
Seamor			Queens Co.	
Partlett, Charles			Sch.	
Partridge, Jonas			York Co.	
Passmore, Joel, blacksmith, 90				
Patchen, Andrew	Ct. F. Co.	guide	LR	Carl.?
Patrick, Adam			Gn.	
John		64th	Pass.	
Matthew			Kn.	
Patten (Patton), Andrew, mariner			St. A.	
Thomas		1 NJV	Gr. Lake	
William		KAR?	Sch.	

Pat(t)erson (Pattison), Alexander			Char.	
Archibald, tailor			St. A.	
Catharine			Gr. Lake	
John	Ct.		Sussex	
Jonathan?			Ken.	
Josiah, carpenter, 85			P1100	
Lot Mills	Sgt. QR		Bl. 5	York Co.
Peter			Or.	F'ton
Thomas			Sch.	
Pattullo, Robert, mariner, 95	Scot.			
Paul, Calbe			Pennfield	
John, ordnance cooper	Scot./N.Y.		P1231	
Jonathan			BH	Sch.
William		RFA		
Pauling, John			Char.	
Paulson (Pawlson), William, carpenter, 85				
Payne, Robert, gentleman			York Co.	
Peadley, James			Mispec.	
Peak, Christian	Pa.		Burton	
Peal (Peel, Pell?), James			P1431	
Humphrey, blockmaker, 90			C20	
Margaret			P1086	
Peal (Peel), Robert, 2d. Lt.			C18	St. John
Co. 30				
Pearce, James		svd.	York Co.	
Robert, mariner			Kings Co.	
Pearsall, Henry, shoemaker	N.Y. D. Co.		Gr. Lake	
Mott, farmer	N.Y. D. Co.		?	
Thomas, carpenter	N.Y. D. Co.		Sussex?	
Pearson (Pierson), Jacob			P574	Kings Co.
James, cordwainer		Sgt. 3 NJV		
Richard			Burton	
Peatman, Daniel	N.Y. St. Is.		Kings Co.	
Peck, Henry, shipwright	N.Y.		P1402	N.Y.
James, carpenter	N.Y. Mohawk	Engr.	P1212	Queens Co.
Oliver		Ens. PWAR	Nash.	left
Timothy, farmer	Ct.		P589	Kn.
William, carpenter	Ct.		P1403	Kings Co.
Pecker, Jeremiah, gentleman, 85			N.S.	
Peebles, George	42nd		P253	
John	42nd		P246	Ham. R.
Peel, see Peal				
Peers, (Piers), Ezekiel	N.Y. W. Co.	WL	Kings Co.	Westm.
Samuel, Lt. Co. 41	N.Y. D. Co.		Bel.	
Pegg, Daniel			Ham. R.	
George, carman			St. John Co.	
Pell, Gilbert	N.Y. W. Co.	CMG	P633	
Pellam (Pelham?), John			Maug.	
Pemart, Francis, mariner, 95	N.Y. W. Co.	pilot	C15	
Pendergrass, Edward?			Ken.	
John		KOR	Westm.	
Penn, Michael		1 DeL.	Bl. 8	
Pendleton, Gideon			Deer Is.	
Pennery, Thomas		Cpl. 3 NJV	Queens Co.	
Penny, William			Musquash	
Pennington, James	QR		P695	York Co.
Peply, William		RFA		
Pepper, William		1 NJV		
Percy, Robert		Lt. RN	Queens Co.	
Perkins, Andrew			Kn.	
Azariah	R.I. ?/N.Y.		Kn.	
George		Cpl. KAD	Bl. 4	
Isaac	N.Y./N.J.	WL	Burton	Kings Co.
James		Sgt. KAR	Penniac	York Co.
Robert			Kings Co.	
Perreau, Joseph		RFA	Mag. R.	
Perriman, Joseph			Pass.	
Perrine, William, Capt. Co. 19	N.J.	svd.	P1099	N.Y.
Perry, Isaac, shipwright			Ken.	
Thomas			Kings Co.	
William			LR	New Canaan

Peters, Andrew			St. A.		
Charles		Sgt. 2 DeL.	P1034	UC	
Henry		2 DeL.	St. John		
James	N.Y. O. Co.		P11, 54	Gn.	
Marcus			Queens Co.		
Samuel	N.Y. D. Co.		Queens Co.		
Thomas (1)	N.Y. D. Co.	pris.	Maug.	Gn.	F'ton
Thomas (2)		Engr.	P907	Kn.	
William (1)	N.Y. D. Co.	recr.	P1330	Kings Co.	
William (2)		RFA	Mag. R.		
Peterson (Paterson?), John	N.Y. D. Co.		P536	York Co.	
John Crawford, coachmaker			P1016		
Pettinger, Abraham			P379		
Pettit, John		Sgt. 1 NJV			
Phair, Andrew	N.Y.	Adj. LAL	Pr. Wm.		
Phelps (Phillips), Edward, mason			P215	N.S.	
Phillips, Alexander		2 DeL.			
Frederick, millwright			Westm.		
James			P900	St. A.	Q. Co.
John		Cpl. 2 NJV	Bl. 2	UC?	
Matthew			Sunbury Co.	Carl.	
Nathaniel			St. A.		
Thomas	N.J.		Gn.		
Phipps, James (Phillips?)			Kn.		
Phoenix, Philip, Lt. Co. 24			Ken.?		
Pickel, (Bickle), Nicholas, blacksmith	N.J.		Kn.	Ken.	
Pickens, Andrew	N.J.	Engr.	Ken.		
Picket(t), David, weaver	Ct. F. Co.	wag.	Kn.		
Isaac, mariner, 95					
James, carpenter, 90			P1410	St. John	
John			P1269	Queens Co.	
Lewis, carpenter	Ct.		Kn.		
Medad		Cpl. 2 DeL.	BH		
Pidgeon, George		Br. army	F'ton		
Piercey, James, brickmaker			BH	St. A.	
Pike, Joshua		ex. 1 NJV	P1216	d. '84	
John			Queens Co.		
Thomas			Mir.		
Pilgrim, Francis		1 NJV	BH		
Pindeberry, James, blacksmith		Navy yd.	Sch.		
Pine, Abraham			Sch.		
Alphaeus	N.Y. U. Co.		Queens Co.	Me.	
Henry	N.Y. U. Co.		Gn.		
Ichabod			St. A.		
Samuel			Queens Co.		
Stephen	N.Y. U. Co.		Kings Co.	d. '86	
Pinkney, Charles			Gr. Lake		
David			Gr. Lake		
John			Gr. Lake		
Pipes, William			Char.	Norton	
Pipper, Benjamin			St. A.		
Pit(t)field, George			Sussex		
Pitt, William	N.Y.	dr. 1 DeL.	Bl. 8	Kings Co.	
Place, Aaron, currier	N.Y. L.I.		P1372		
Benjamin, farmer	N.Y. L.I.				
Cornelius			Mir.		
Jacob, carpenter	N.Y. L.I.				
James		Lt. PWAR	C56	LR	U.S.A.
William			P1378	BH/84	
Plantain, John		Engr.	P913		
Player, William		RFA	Char.	UC	
Polley, Alphaeus		DeL.	Westm.	UC	
Pomeroy, Benjamin	Mass.		St. A.		
Richard, mariner	Mass.		St. A.		
Pond, John		2 NJV	Bl. 2	Nash.	
Poole, Henry		KOR			
Solomon ?			BH/84		
Porter, Anna			P534		
Benjamin			Queens Co.		
David, housewright			F'ton		
George			Maq.	Ken.	UC?
John (1), weaver	N.Y. D. Co.		Maq.	d. '85	

Name	Origin	Military	Place	Col5	County
Porter, John (2)		Sgt. 1 NJV	Penniac		
John (3)			wdw. m. John		York Co.
			C. Fox		
John (4)			Queens Co.		
Post, David			Sch.		
Dennis		CMG	Sch.		
John		Sgt. 3 NJV	Sunbury Co.		
Miles		CMG	Sch.		
Pote, Jeremiah, merchant	Mass.		St. A.		
Potter, Isaac			Nash.		
Robert	N.Y. D. Co.		P486	LR	
Stephen (Leven?)			F'ton	Gn.	
Thomas		PWAR	F'ton		
Potts, Stephen	Pa.	Ens. PL	P230	N.S.?	
Powell, Abraham			Gr. Lake	UC	
Amos, carpenter	N.Y. L.I.				
Caleb, farmer	N.Y. D. Co.		Gr. Lake		
Israel			BH		
Jacob			Gn.	Kent Co.	
James, shoemaker	N.Y. D. Co.		Gr. Lake		
Jesse, saddler	N.Y. W. Co.		Gr. Lake		
Lewis			Gr. Lake		
Reuben, shoemaker	N.Y. D. Co.		Gr. Lake	Kent Co.	
Thomas, farmer	N.Y. L.I.		Kent Co.		
Power(s), Charles		2 DeL.	York Co.		
John			Gr. Lake		
Morris		Sgt. RFA	Mag. R.		
Nicholas, mason			Gn.		
Owen ?			Restigouche		
Patrick, mariner ?					
Thomas, carpenter, 85			P1333		
Powly, Stephen			P526	d. '86	
Pratt, Elizabeth			BH/87		
Isaac		1 NJV	BH		
Jacob			BH		
James			BH	St. George	
Nicholas	Ct.	CMG	Rusagonis		
Pray, John			P327		
Preble, Jedidiah			St. A.		
Prentice, David, merchant ?			P1301, 1392		
John			St. John	d. '87	
Prentiss, John Thomas		Lt. Sir J. J.	Gaspe	Bay du Vin	
Prescott, Benjamin			BH		
Joseph, painter	Mass.		F'ton ?		
Preston, Henry			Penniac		
Nathan			Dig.		
Thomas, mason, 90		KAR	C175		
Pretty, Jasper			P492	Rusagonis	
Thomas, carpenter, 85					
Prevost, Augustus		Staff	P119, C387, 8		Eng.
Price, Dennis			Wash.	Carl.	
George		57th	St. John Co.		
Peter	Pa.		BH		
William	Pa.	Sgt. 3 NJV	Ken.		
Pride, Habbakuk		NCV	LR		
Priest, John, brickmaker			Char.	Sunbury Co.	
Priester, Henry		1 NJV	Maug.		
Priestley (Presley), John		GP	Bl. 3		
Prince, John	N.J.	3 NJV	Ken.		
Prindle, John		Sgt. LAR?	Or.		
(Pringle?), Osburne		Engr.	LR		
Pringle, Abraham Marks			Sch.		
Procter (Proctor), Joshua	Pa.	guide	P497		
Nathaniel			P1296	Or.	Mass.
Profit, Daniel and Selby, servants			Sch.		
Profs (?), John		KOR			
Prosser, Benjamin, yeoman, 85		Cpl. 3 NJV	C319		
Jeremiah		2 NJV	Bl. 2	Carl.	
Proud, James			P67	Halifax	
Prout, Thomas (or Proud?)			P1219	Kings Co.	
Pryor, Edward, Capt. Co. 25	N.Y.		P611	Halifax	
Puddington, William, shipcarpenter, 85	Scot.		C35	Kn.	

Pugsley, Gilbert	N.Y. W. Co.		Wash.		
John	N.Y. W. Co.	WL	Ham. R.	USA?	
Pulk, Henry		KOR			
Punt(z)ius, John Philip, tailor, 88	N.Y.			N.Y.	
Purdy, Archelaus	N.Y.		Gr. Lake		
Daniel			LR		
David		Lt. KAR	P839	N.Y.	
Elias, farmer	N.Y. W. Co.		?		
Gilbert	N.Y. W. Co.	WL	P1154	LR	
Jonathan, fisherman, 95	N.Y. W. Co.				
Nehemiah, farmer	N.Y. W. Co.		?		
Stephen			Lanc.		
Thomas, yeoman, 90	N.Y. W. Co.				
Purcell (Parsell), William	N.Y.		P677		
Putnam, Daniel			P339		
Ebenezer			Ham. R.		
James, Esquire, 85	Mass.	BMG	C192		
James, Jr.			C214		
Putney, Samuel		GP	Bl. 3		
Pyke, see Pike					
Quain, Mary			Bel.		
Thomas			Maug.		
Quantum, John			Char.		
Quereau, Elias			York Co.		
Quigg, Hugh	Ir./N.J.	PWAR	P577	Sussex	
Quigley, David			Gr. Manan		
Quill, Thomas	Ir./Va.		P785	Kings Co.	
Quinn, Arthur			St. John Co.		
Charles			Wash./84		
George			Ken.		
John		LAR	F'ton	LC	UC
Quintard, James		1 NJV	Penniac/84		
Racey, Philip		PWAR?	C354	Ken.	
Radan, see Roden					
Rafford, Lewis		PL	Bl. 7	Nash.	
Rainkellor, George		Navy	Mir.		
Rainsford, Andrew	Fla.	svd.	York Co.		
Ramsay, Esther			Char.		
John		PWAR	York Co.	Carl.	
Oris			Musquash		
William		74th			
Ramson (Remson), Jacob		ML	Bl. 1	LR	N.S.?
William			St. John		
See also Rundle					
Randolph, David	Va.		P990		
Ranger, Tartolus			BH/84		
Rankin, Abraham	Pa.		Pennfield		
Angus		74th			
John	Pa. Y. Co.		Pennfield		U.S.A.
Rhoads	Pa.		Pennfield		
Rapelye, John			York Co.		
William, mason			St. John	d. '94	
Rathburn, Joseph	R.I.	BMG	York Co.		
Rattan, Abraham		Sgt. 3 NJV	Bl. 2		
Ray, Donald or Daniel	Scot./N.C.		St. A.		
Rayen, see Raynes					
Raymond, Isaac	Ct.	gar.	Ken.		
Mary	Ct.		Kn.		
Samuel Rice, Sr.			P1249		
Samuel Rice, Jr.		2 DeL.			
Silas, carpenter	Ct.		Kn.		
Stent	Ct.		P1090	Ham. R.	
White, innkeeper, 85	Ct.		Kn.		
Raynes, James, millwright	Pa.		St. St.		
Rea, Jacob John, baker, 85					

Name	Col2	Col3	Col4	Col5	Col6
Read, Reed, Reid, Abraham			Char.		
Alexander, merchant			P404	Eng.	
Arthur, mulatto			St. John Co.		
Duncan	N.Y. Ch. Co.		Albert Co.?		
Frederick			LR		
James (1), carpenter			P1412		
James (2)			St. John	N.S.	
James (3), mariner, 85		pilot	P1347		
John (1)		CMG	Char.		
John (2)		Lt. 1 NJV	Musq.	N.S.	
Reed, Leonard		Lt. KAR	York Co.		
Matthew			Char.		
Robert, mason, 95			P1309		
Robert, gentleman, 90			Char.?		
Stephen			Char.		
Thomas, grocer, 90					
William (1)			Char.		
William (2)	Pa.		P1440		
William (3)		1 NJV?	Or.		
		2 DeL.?			
Reading, Thomas			Or.		
Real, Hannah			St. A./84		
Record, Wightman			Ken.		
Rector, Frederick, tailor			St. John Co.		
Redicker, John		1 NJV	Queensbury		
Reddinton, John		RFA	Maq.		
Re(i)dhead, William			St. A.	U.S.A.	
Redman, Joseph	N.Y.		Que.	St. John	
Rednor (Ridnar), Conrad		3 NJV	F'ton		
Peter		Cpl. 3 NJV	F'ton	UC	
Reece, Alexander			Gr. Lake		
Anthony, 2nd Lt. Co. 8	W.I./Ct.	guide	C315	St. John	
Reeves, John	N.J.	GB?	BH		
Regan, Henry		PWAR	Musq.		
Jeremiah			P409	Kings Co.	
Register, Daniel, miller			BH/87	Sunbury Co.	
Reilly (Riley), Hugh		57th	Sunbury Co.		
James		RFA		wife, 2 ch.	
John (1)		1 DeL.	Bl. 8		
John (2)		Cpl. 3 NJV		UC	
Philip		PWAR	St. John Co.		
Remington, Alexander, smith, 85			York Co.		
Gershom			BH		
James			St. A.		
Jonathan			BH	St. A.	
Samuel			Penniac		
(Reynolds?)					
Remson, John	N.Y.?		Gn.	Kings Co.	
Rennet, Robert, tailor		LAL	F'ton		
Renn(e)y, David, tailor		NYV	Kes.		
Renshaw, Thomas, cordwainer			P1265	Ken.	
William			Ken.		
Retson, Joseph			Sch.		
Revere, Jacob			Gn.		
Rex, George		KOR			
Rexter, William ?			Queens Co.		
Reynolds, Jacob			Gr. Lake		
Jesse			P961		
Samuel	N.Y. D. Co.		Gr. Lake		UC
William		Ct. KAD	BH	Camp.	UC
Rhein, George, miller	Pa.		?		
Jacob		Hess.	Or.	F'ton	
Rheinwald, Frederick, merchant			St. John	N.Y.	
Richards, Charles	N.J.		LR		
John		PL	Bl. 7		
Jonathan	N.J.?		C232	Cn.	
Robert		RFA	Mag. R.		
Stephen, cordwainer, 85		GP	Bl. 3		
Thomas	N.J.?	Sgt. PWAR	Musquash		
Richardson, Thomas		1 NJV	Penniac	Burton	
William		LAL	Pass.		

Ri(t)chie, Charles			Kn.		
James			P555	Musquash	
Robert		Sgt. QR	Mir.		
Ricket, John		2 DeL.	Queensbury	Norton	
Ridnor, see Redner					
Rigby, John			St. A.		
Riger (Rigar, Rigou), John		dr. 2 NJV	Bl. 2	York Co.	
Matthias			BH		
Riggin, Cannon	Md.	Cpl. ML	Bl. 1		
Rikeman (Ryckman), Albert, innkeeper	Pa.		BH	Campobello	
Anthony	Pa.		BH		
Peter	Pa.		BH		
Riley, see Reilly					
Ripley, James			P304		
Riroted, Isaiah			Queens Co.		
Ritner, Catharine			Queens Co.		
Ritter, Frederick, tailor, 85			St. John	d. '03	
Hyronemus		Specht	St. A.		
Rivers, Daniel, cordwainer		1 DeL.	Bl. 8	F'ton	
Rix, Benjamin		BMG	York Co.		
Samuel		70th Drag.	York Co.		
Roach, John		RFA	Mag. R.	Kings Co.	
Roax, John			St. A.		
Timothy			St. A.		
Robb, John, yeoman, 85		Engr.	P1426	Queens Co.	
Robbins, Robert	N.J.?		Pennfield		U.S.A.
Scuder, farmer	N.Y. L.I.			wife, 1 ch.	
(Roblin?), Stephen			Kn.		
Roberts, David, mariner		a. b.		d. '91	
Jonathan		PL	Bl. 7	Norton	
Nathan, millwright	Pa.	BMG		Kings Co.	
Stephen			St. A.		
Zachariah			Gn.		
Robertson, Alexander	Scot.	BMG	St. A.	Shel.	
Daniel or Donald		42nd	P263	Nash.	
Duncan, grocer, 85					
John		42nd	Nash.		
Robie (Robb?), James		CMG?	Char.		
(Roblee?), Thomas	N.Y.?		C31		
Robinson, Beverley	N.Y. D. Co.	Lt.Col.LAR	F'ton		
Christopher		Ens. QR	P163	Bl. 5	UC
John (1)	N.Y.	Lt. LAR	P722	York Co.	
John (2)	Ir./R.I. -	CMG	St. A.		
John (3)		38th	St. John Co.	Queens Co.?	
Joseph	Ga./S.C.	Lt. Col. SCR, sec.	Kings Co.	P.E.I.	
Lawrence, mariner, 85			C423		
Patrick	Ir.	LAR	Gr. Lake		
Robert		Lt. LAR	York Co.		
Thomas	N.Y./Del.	Ens. LAR	Burton	Shel.	
William		CMG?	Kings Co.		
Roden, Henry, baker, 85			C207		
William, Sr., mariner	Pa.		C38, 40, 152		
William, Jr., mariner, 95	Pa.		C39		
Rodney, George Bridges		Surg. asst. LAR	Or.		
Rogers, Andrew, mariner			St. John		
Anna			BH	servant	
Anthony	Ct.		P780	Mir.?	
Anthony, Jr.			Kn.		
Armon			Bl. 2	d.	
Elizabeth	Ct.		P1298		
Fitch, gentleman, 85	Ct.		P143		Ct.
George, yeoman, 85		KOR	P1067	St. John Co.	
Isreal, shoemaker	N.Y. L.I.		Maq.		
Jacob		Sgt. ML	Bl. 1		
James (1)	Eng./N.C.		P857	Bel.	
James (2)			C27	Maug.	
Mary, widow, m. Bartholomew Senior			Bl. 3		
Nehemiah	Ct.	Lt. 1 DeL.	P145	F'ton	N.Y.
Patrick (1)		1 NJV	Penniac		

Rogers, Patrick (2), victualler,	Mass.?	BL	Kings Co.	
innholder				
Richard (1)		Cpl. 1 DeL.	Bl. 8	P1282
Richard (2)		Em. Ch.?	Or.	
Robert			Bl. 3	
Samuel ?	Ct.?		St. A.	
Thomas		3 NJV?	P993	
William (1)			Bl. 3	York Co.
William (2)	N.Y.	LAR?	Burton	
Rooke, Amos (Rourke, James?)			BH	
Matthew, labourer, 90		Vol. NE	St. John	
Roome, Abraham,	N.J.	navy	Ken.	
sailmaker, 90				
Henry, 2nd Lt. Co. 37,	N.J.			N.Y.
painter, 85				
Jacob, saddler, 85		Cpl. 3 NJV?	P1095	
William Henry			P1300	LR
William Lawrence	N.J.		P1092, C430	
Lt. Co. 37				
Rorison, Basil		Lt. KOR	C544?	UC
Rose, Donald		42nd	Nash.	Mir.
John (1)		NCV?	Or.	
		1 NJV?		
John (2)	Scot./S.C.		St. A.	
Timothy			St. A.	
Timothy, Jr.			St. A.	
William		Ord.	Sch.	UC
Rosenell, John,	Eng.		C11	
boatbuilder, 95				
Ross, Alexander (1)		74th	Pass.	
Alexander (2)		QR	Bl. 5	
Andrew		42nd	Nash.	
Charles			Ham. R.	
Daniel or Donald		NCR or V	Mir.	
Daniel			St. A.	
David			P234	Queens Co.
Donald		42nd	P240	Nash.
Edward			St. A.	
Henry			St. A.	
James, Sr.		42nd	P251	Nash.
James, Jr.		42nd	Nash.	
John (1)		Cpl. 42nd	Ken.	
John (2)		Ens. QR?	P191	
John (3)		RFA	Mag. R.	P1237?
Thomas, mariner	Mass.		St. A.	Gr. Manan
Walter	Mass.		Queens Co.	
William Kerr	Scot./S.C.		St. A.	
Roupe (Roop), Christian		Sgt. 2 NJV	Bl. 2	N.S.
Rourke, James		RFA	Mag. R.	
Rouse, David		Sgt. 3 NJV	P214	Sussex
Rowan (Rone), Francis		LAL?	P726	
John, cordwainer, 85			Ken.	
(Rouse?), Samuel				
Rowding (Rawding), Joseph		Sgt. PWAR	St. John Co.	
Ruckle, Jasper, baker, 85	N.Y.		C116?	F'ton
Ruffie, William		GP	Bl. 3	St. John
Ruland, James	N.Y. L.L		P479	d. '84, son
Rulofson, Rulof	N.J.	Ens. 2 NJV	Ken.	
Rumbold, Thomas			C217	
Rundle (Randall), Charles			BH/84	
Jabez	N.Y.	W.L	Westm. Co.	
Rupert (Rubart), Christopher	Ger./S.C.		P770	Ken.
Rush, Martin	N.J.		F'ton	
Ruso, John		1 NJV	Cn.	York Co.
Russell, Alexander	N.J.		LR	Mir.
Jacob	N.Y.		Shef.	York Co.
James		artif.	St. A.	
John		CMG	Ken.	
Joseph (1)	Ct.	a.b.	BH	
Joseph (2), gunmaker		Ord.	St. John	
Lewis		KOR		
Michael		KOR		
Ruel			Char.	
William (Ruttan?)			Char.	
Ruth, George		RFA	Mag. R.	

324

Ruthwell, Donkin, mariner			P680	
Ruttan, *see* Russell				
Ryan, Charles		KAR	York Co.	UC
James		84th	Pass.	
John (1), printer, 85			P59	
John (2)		Ord.	Sch.	
Michael			St. A.	
Miles		PWAR	St. John Co.	
William, cooper, 85		RFA	P393	Musq.
Ryar (Ryer), Edward		GP	Bl. 3	
Michael		GP	Bl. 3	
Ryder, Ebenezer	N.Y.		Maug.	d. '84
Stephen		Ens. 3 NJV	P1386	Pennaic
Ryerse (Ryerson), Joseph	N.J. B. Co.	Lt. 3 NJV	Sunbury Co.	UC
Peter	N.Y. L.I.		Maug.	
Samuel	N.J. B. Co.	Capt. 3 NJV	F'ton	UC
Rynde(r)s, James			Queens Co.	
Sagerburgh (Segerberg),				
Nicholas,	Ger.?		P837	dr. '85
carpenter				
St. Croix, Joshua Temple de			P71	N.S.
Salkeld (Selkeld), John	Flor.	svd.	Char.	
Salter, Thomas	Yar.	pris.	St. John Co.	
Salts, Maurice, shipwright			Sch.	
Sammon (Salmon), James		2 NJV	Sussex	
Sam(p)son, John			Ham. R.	
Peter			Sch.	
Sands, Edward, 2nd Lt. Co.49,	N.Y. L.I.		St. John	
merchant, 85				
Stephen		QR	Gr. Lake	
Sanford, Ephraim		ex. QR	Eng.	St. John
Sanger, Eleazer	N.H.	2 DeL.	BH	
Sappenfield, Jacob, Jr.	N.C.?		York Co.	
S(e)argeant, Andrew			Char.	
David			Char.	
Samuel			Char.	
Solomon			Char.	
Sarles, *see* Searles				
Sarvenier (Servanier), James,	Ger./N.J.	Lt. 3 NJV	P931	
gentleman, 85				
Sattee, *see* Surtee				
Sa(u)nders, Charles			Ken.	
George			Ken.	
Edward			Char.	
John (1)	Va.	Capt. QR	F'ton	
John (2)	N.J.	2 NJV	Ken.	
Sa(u)nderson, Thomas			Bl. 3	UC
Savage, John	S.C.?		Kings Co.	
William, carpenter		ML	Bl. 1	York Co.
Sawyer, Daniel		KAR	York Co.	
Francis			York Co.	
James			York Co.	
Saxton, Isaac, shoemaker			Maug.	Gn.
John		Lt. RGB	Or.	
Zebulon			Or.	
Sayre, Francis	Ct.		Or.	
James (1)	Ct.		Gn.	Westm.
James (2), Rev.		Chap. 2 NJV	Bl. 2	U.S.A.
John, Rev.	N.Y./Ct.		P4	Maug.	d. '84
Scallion, Matthew		Lt. RN	St. A.	
Scarborough, William		PWAR	St. John Co.	
Scheck (Chick), Christian,		KAD	Kn.	
Christopher, carpenter, 85		Sgt. 1 NJV	Sussex	
Johannes	N.Y. L.I.		Kn.	
John	N.Y. L.I.		Kn.	
Jonathan, blacksmith		2 NJV	Ken.	
Schoenewolf, Charles,	Ger.	Hess.	P1170	St. John Co.
labourer, 85				
Schomber (Shampier), Andrew			Kn.	
Ludwig (Lewis),			P384	
carpenter, 85				

Schriver, Baltus		Cpl. NYV	Kes.	
James		Cpl. KAR	Kes.	
Schur(e)man, Jacob	N.Y. W. Co.		Bel.	
Philip,			P1266	
carpenter, 95				
Scobe(y), William, tailor, 85			Or.	
Sc(h)ofield, Ezra,	Ct.	Sgt. 2 DeL.		
cordwainer, 85				
James	Ct.		Or.	UC
John			Bel.	
Jonathan	Ct.		P945	Kn.
Major		NYV	Kes.	
Scoley, Alexander, yeoman, 85				
Scott, Ebenezer	N.J.		Musquash	
Edward			P612	
James (1), baker?		PWAR?	P1433	Queens Co.?
James (2)		74th	St. A.	
John (1)		74th	St. A.	
John (2)		PWAR	St. John Co.	
Robert		CMG	P558	
Samuel			Musquash	
Scovil, Daniel, gentleman, 85				
James, Rev., Yale '57	Ct.		Kn.	
William	Ct.		Kn.	
Scribner, Ebenezer, shoemaker	Ct.	Cpl. QR	Kn.	
Elias, shoemaker	Ct.		Kn.	
Hezekiah	Ct.		Kn.	
Joseph, shoemaker			P310	Kn.
Nehemiah			Kn.	
Philip			Kn.	d.
Thaddeus, shoemaker	Ct.		Kn.	
Scudder, Jesse	N.Y.		Gn.	Burton
Seabrook, Nathaniel		2 DeL.	York Co.	
Seaman, Adam	N.Y. W. Co.		St. John	
Benjamin	N.Y. Rd. Co.		St. John	
Hicks		Sgt. KAR	Bl. 6	Shef.
John, farmer	N.Y. D. Co.		Kn.	left
Richard,	N.Y. Rd. Co.		St. John	N.Y.
gentleman, 85				
Sylvanus	N.Y. W. Co.		St. John	
William			P106	N.S.	N.Y.
Searing, James, mariner, 95	N.Y. L.I.		Kings Co.	
Samuel, farmer	N.Y. L.I.			
Searles, Samuel, Lt. Co. 41				
Stephen	N.Y. Ctldt.	ex. LAR	d. '84	wdw.
William	N.Y. Ctldt.		Queens Co.	
Sears, Henry, hatter, 85				
Joseph	N.Y. W. Co.	WL	Westm.	
Thatcher, carman, 85	Ct./N.Y.		P397	
Sebastian, Magnus, blacksmith			St. John	
Se(a)cord, Elias, blacksmith			Queens Co.	
John		Sgt. NYV	Kes.	UC
William, Lt. Co. 29,	N.Y. O. Co.		P138	Bel.
blacksmith				
Sederquist, John, tailor, 85		QR		
Seedings, Lawrence		guide	Gr. Lake	
Seeds, Dinah, wdw. Jonathan,			Wash.	
2 NJV				
Seeley, Benjamin	Ct.		Shef.	LR
Ebenezer	N.Y. O. Co.		P1332	Wash.
Ephraim		GP	Kes.	Queens Co.
Ezekiel		KAR	Or.	
Gideon		2? 1? DeL.		
Joseph	Ct.		Cn.	
Justus	Ct.	Sgt. KAD	C310	Char.
Michael			Gn.	
Orange			BH	St. George
Seth, farmer	Ct.		P389	Kn.
Segee, Jacob		Cpl. LAR	York Co.	
John		LAR	York Co.	
Joseph		Cpl. LAR	York Co.	
William		LAR	York Co.	
Segerberg, see Sagerburgh				
Segert, Christian			Maq.	Halifax
Sellars, Robert		74th	St. A.	

326

Name	Origin	Regt./Rank	Grant	County	Prov.
Selleck, Thaddeus	Ct.				
Selief (Seluff), Jacob		2 NJV	St. John Bl. 2	Kings Co.	
Senior, Bartholomew, weaver			P513	Maug.	Eng.
Sewell, Jonathan, Jr.			C231	St. John	LC
Stephen			C252	Que.	
Seymour, Thomas			P608		
Shaddock, John		ML	Bl. 1		
Shadwell, see Shotwell					
Shalor, Ephraim			BH	Wash	
Sham, Elizabeth			Ken.		
Shampier, see Schomber					
Shanks, James, carpenter, 85		Capt. Lt. PWAR	C340, 1	Bel.	Ir./N.J.
Shannon, Daniel	N.J.	Ens. 2 NJV	C453	Bl. 2	
David	Pa.	BCV	Kn.		
Sharman, Ambrose		Lt. RFA	Burton		
James			Or.	d. '85	
Sharp, Alexander	Scot.	WL	Kings Co.	Carl.	
Henry (1)	N.J.		Queens Co.		
Henry (2), carpenter		Engr.	F'ton		
James		1 NJV	Bl. 5	Norton	
John, shipwright			P1093	UC?	
Joseph			Ken.		
Robert			Ken.		
Samuel	N.J.		LR	Millstream	
William		QR	Mir.		
Shaw, Aeneas	Scot.	Capt. QR vol.	C154, 5	Bl. 5	UC
George, tanner, 85	N.Y. City		C3		
John (1)		RFA			
John (2)	N.Y. D. Co.		P806	Queens Co.	
Moses, shoemaker	N.Y. D. Co.		P725		
William, shoemaker	N.Y. L.I.				
Shea, Philip, weaver?		LAR	Kes.	F'ton	
William Elihy	Ir.		F'ton	Carl.	
Sheehan, James		Cpl. QR	Norton		
Sheehy (Sheay), Michael		RFA	Mag. R.		
Sheely (Shelley?), John		DeL.?	Bl. 8		
Shefferd, see Sheppard					
Shelcock, John			Mispec.		
Sheldon, John, fisherman, 95		Sgt. KAR	P1056		
Joseph	N.Y.	Engr.	Musq.		
Shelton, Jeremiah		Adj. PWAR	Ken.		
Sheppard (Shepherd, Shefferd),					
Benjamin			Char.		
Jacob		QR	Mir.		
Joseph	Mass.?		St. A.	UC?	
Philip			P363		
Richard		Char.			
Samuel (1)		KAD	F'ton	York Co.	
Samuel (2)			St. A.		
Thomas			Char.		
She(a)rman, Adrien		Engr.	P657		
Andrew	N.Y. W. Co.	2 DeL.	Gn.	Kings Co.	
Sherwood, Adiah	NY. L.I.		P1158	U.S.A.	
Andrew	N.Y. W. Co.		C404	Ham. R.	
John	N.Y. W. Co.	WL	Ham. R.		
Jonathan		Cpl. KAR?	P1199	Kings Co.	
Justus	N.Y. W. Co.	guide	P783	Ham. R.	
Shicklin, Jonathan, blacksmith		2 NJV	St. Martins		
Shields, David			St. A.		
John		BMG			
Samuel			Shel.	Mir.	
Shillfax (Shipman), Jonathan			Norton		
Shippy, Nathan, farmer	N.Y. D. Co.				
Shipton, Francis			Char.		
Shocker, Matthias			P383	Gr. Lake	N.Y.
Shonnard (Shrum, Sholts),					
Frederick, labourer, 85		CMG	P1023	U.S.A.	
Peter			P985	York Co.	UC
Short, John		1 DeL.	Bl. 8	UC	
Shortley, William		RFA	Char.		
Shotwell, Abraham, carpenter, 95	N.Y.		Queens Co.		

Shotwell, Joseph, 2nd Lt. Co. 19			LR	Mir.	
Shropshire, Robert		2 NJV	St. John		
Shrum, see Shonnard					
Shurtliff, Levi		GP	Bl. 3	F'ton	
Sickles, Daniel, cordwainer			P1320	Maug.	York Co
Daniel, Jr.			P1252	York Co.	
Duncan			Ken.	left	
John, tailor, 85	N.J. B. Co.	Engr.	P718		
William			P840		
Zachariah, Lt. Co. 33			Kes.		
Silby, Richard			Gr. Lake		
Sim, see Sims					
Simmons, (Symonds), Israel	N.Y.		St. John		
James	Eng./Mass.	Engr.	St. A.		
John (1)		74th	St. A.		
John (2)		Engr. ?	LR	N.Y.	
Thomas		3 NJV	Bl. 7		
William		QR	Bl. 8	Carl.	
Simonson, John	N.Y. Rd. Co.	Lt. 3 NJV	Maug.		
Simpson, Drummond		navy	P408	BH	N.S.
James, grocer, 85			Mir.		
John, merchant, 85			Mir.		
Michael			Sch.		
Moses			P443	F'ton	
William ?			Queens Co.	Carl.	
Sims (Syms), Caleb			Char.		
David	Scot.		Gr. Lake		
Robert			St. A.		
Sinclair, George, currier	Pa.		Campobello		
Robert			Char.		
Samuel		RFA	Mag. R.	Rusagonis	UC
Sinnott, Moses ?			Musquash		
Sinton, John ?			St. John		
Sipprell, William		1 NJV	Kings Co.	Carl.	
Sise, James		QMR LAL	York Co.	Que.	
Sisson, James		NYV	Kes.		
Jonathan			Kes.		
Skelton, William, mariner			Sch.		
Skene, William			F'ton	Quaco?	
Skidgell (Scetchel), Hendrik		LAR	Bl. 6	F'ton	
Skidmore, Elias			Burton		
Whitehead			Queens Co.		
Skinner, John	N.J.	2 NJV	Bl. 2		
Slacht (Slaight), Henry	N.J.		P334	UC	
Slason, Isaac			LR		
Jedediah, tanner, 96	Ct.		F'ton		
Peter			LR		
Slater, James			Mir.		
Slayman, William		1 DeL.	Bl. 8		
Slip(p), Leonard	Ger./N.Y.		Queens Co.		
Sloan(e), James, labourer, 85	S.C.		St. John		
William, merchant, 85			St. John		
Slobec, John			Ken.		
Slocum, Ebenezer, farmer	R.I.	LNE	Queens Co.		
Elezer, seaman	Mass. H. Co.	intell.	Shef.	Pr. Wm.	
Sloot (Sloat), Benjamin	N.Y.		Wash.		
Ezekiel			F'ton		
Slutt, John, blacksmith			St. John		
Silas	N.Y. W. Co.	2 DeL.	St. John Co.	U.S.A.	
Small, John		RFA	C2	Bel.	P.E.I.
Thomas, labourer, 98 ?			C23		
William			Bel.		
Smart, Andrew, cooper			Queens Co.	·St. John	
Smiler, Christopher, cordwainer, 95			St. John		
Samuel, labourer, 95			St. John		
Smith, Abiel ?			Queens Co.	Mass.	
Abner ?			Queens Co.		
Abraham	Eng./N.J.	Ct. LAL? 3 NJV? Engr.	F'ton	UC	
Adam			Pass.		
Anderson			Ken.		
Andrew			BH	Rusagonis	
Benjamin			York Co.	Halifax	

Name	Col1	Col2	Col3	Col4	Col5
Smith, Bowen	Mass.		Westm.		
Daniel, farmer	Ct. L. Co.		P981	Burton	
Duncan		74th	Pass.		
Ebenezer, shipcarpenter, 85		BMG			
Edward	Mass.?		Mir.		
Elijah	N.Y. W. Co.	WL	Cumb.	Queens Co.	
Eliphalet			Queens Co.		
Elizabeth			Or.	St. John	
Francis			Sch.		
Freeman	N.J.		Pennfield		
George (1), 1st fleet			Kings Co.		
George (2), carpenter, 95		BMG	P591		
Henry, merchant	Mass.		F'ton		
Hezekiah, farmer	Ct.				
Ichabod	R.I.	Capt. Lt. 2 DeL.	P1360	Maug.	
Isaac	N.Y.		Gn.	F'ton	
Isaiah	N.Y. L.I.		Ham. R.		
Israel		2 DeL.	?		
Jacob (1)	Pa. Del.	QR	P764?	Pa.	
Jacob (2)	N.Y. L.I.	Capt. 1 DeL.	P1275	Bl. 8	
James (1), Harvard, C.E.?	N.Y.		Ham. R.		
James (2)			P1043	Queens Co.	
James (3)			Sch.		
Joel			Maug.		
John (1), merchant, Capt. Co. 40	N.Y.		P63	St. John	N.Y.
John (2)			Ham. R.	Norton	
John (3)		1 DeL.	Bl. 8		
John (4)		84th	P713	Pass.	
John (5), son Ichabod	R.I.	2 DeL.	P520?	Gn.	
John Isaiah			P527	Ham. R.	
John Peter		Lt. KAR	Bl. 6	F'ton	UC
Jonathan, farmer	N.Y. L.I.	LNE?	Gn.	d. '86	
Joseph (1), farmer	L.I.? Ct.?	CMG?	P590	Ct.	
Joseph (2)			St. A.		
Joshua			Kn.		
Josiah	N.S.?	Sgt. RFA	Westm.		
Mary, wdw.			Kes.	N.Y.	
Michael	N.Y. L.I.	ex. NJV	Maug.	Woodstock	
Nathan, physician, 85		Surg. 1 DeL.	P517, 1146	St. John	
Nathaniel			Gr. Lake esch.		
Newcomb		GP	Bl. 3		
Nicholas		KAD	Bl. 4		
Peter (1)		KAD	Bl. 4		
Peter (2)		3 NJV?	Char.		
Platt ?			Rusagonis/84		
Priscilla			P1087	Gr. Lake	Ham. R.
Ralph		Ens. 1 DeL.	P1062	St. John Co.	
Reuben			Char.	York Co.?	
Richard (1)	N.Y. L.I.		P529	Musquash	
Richard (2) ?			Char.		
Robert			Wash.		
Rufus			P1061		
Samuel (1)	N.Y. L.I.	Capt. QR	P1130	UC	
Samuel (2)			Bel.		
Samuel Haines Lt. Co. 13, weaver	N.Y.		LR	Queens Co.	
Sarah, widow			Ken.		
Shuba(e)l			P1362		
Silas, carpenter			Maug.	Queens Co.	
Stephen (1)		Sgt. KAR	Queens Co.		
Stephen (2)			Bel.	U.S.A.	
Thomas (1), goldsmith, 85			P1225		
Thomas (2), lawyer, Lt. Co. 6?		W. Vol.?	Burton	St. John	
Thomas (3)		NYV	P786?	Kes.	
Thomas (4)			Rusagonis		
Thomas T., Lt. Co. 40			P1147?		
Weder			Wash.		
William (1)		CMG?	P797		
William (2), yeoman, 85					

Smith, William (3), plumber   P515
    William (4),
      cordwainer, 85
    William (5), Sr.   N.J.?   Maq.   Shef.
    William (6), Jr.   Queens Co.
    William (7), merchant   St. John   Halifax
    William How, physician   St. John   Westm.
Smoose, George   Pass.
Smye, Richard, cooper   CMG   Sch.
Sneeden, Robert   N.Y. O. Co.   P420
Snider (Snyder), Baltus   1 NJV   Maug.   Sussex
    Elias   Pa.   2 NJV   F'ton   Ken.
    Henry   QR? KAD?   Mag. R.
    Jacob, carpenter   Maug.   Sussex
    Martin   C149   Ken.   UC
    Peter   Pa.   2 NJV   F'ton   Ken.
Sniffen, Jonathan   KAD
    Shewbel   N.Y. W. Co.   Em. Ch.   Gr. Bay
Snow, Benjamin, Dartmouth?   2 DeL.   UC?
    schoolmaster, 85
    John   a.b. St. Is.   Gr. Lake/84
Snowden, Joseph   GP   Bl. 3   F'ton
    Randolph, tanner, 85   P1397   Bel.
Solomon, Ezekiel   RFA?
    John   Pass.
    William   Sgt. GP   Bl. 3   d. '84, 5
Sorlie, William   St. John
Soules (Sulis?), Thomas   Sgt. KAR   Gr. Lake   N.S.
South(w)ard, Abell, farmer   N.Y. L.I.   ?
    Ananias, labourer   Gr. Lake   St. John
Southesk, Daniel ?   Pa.   BH
Southick, Daniel   N.Y. D. Co.   KAD   Ken.
Sowers (Sauer), Charles   York Co.
    Christopher, printer, 85 Pa.   transl.   St. John   Ham. R.
    John Andrew   Ger.   St. A.   St. John
    William Banks   Eng.   Queens Co.
Spandoling, Reuben, Sr. and Jr.   Char.
Sparks, Daniel   Queens Co.
    Digory   Cpl. QR   Mag. R.
Speakman, William   Engr.   P556
Spear (Speers), Ebenezer   Char.
    John   Cpl. 3 NJV   P925   Ken.   U.S.A.
                                                  '04
    Robert   QMR. RFA
Speed, William   Gar. Bn.   St. George   Eng.
Spence, James, Capt. Co. 36   Scot.   P490   Sussex
    carpenter, 85
    Robert   Ir./S.C.   militia   P778   Bel.
    William   Scot.   Ken.
Spencer, George   Nash.   Mir.?
    Samuel   CMG   St. A.
    William   St. A.
Spicer, Ebenezer, carpenter   Ct.   P1236   Sussex
Spragg (Sprague), Caleb   N.Y. D. Co.   P851   Bel.
    Elijah   N.Y. D. Co.   Bel.
    Richard   N.Y. D. Co.   LAR   P965   Bel.
    Thomas, Capt. Co. 46   N.Y. D. Co.   recr.   P960   Bel.
Sprague, Moses   St. A.
Sprick, Frederick, baker   N.Y.   P1448
Springer, James   Del.   Queens Co.
    William, blacksmith   Del.   P367   Queens Co.
Springstead, Isaac   KOR   St. John Co.
Sproul (Sprowle), Andrew   Sgt. 42nd   P252
    George   Ir./N.H.   Kings Co.   F'ton
Squier (Squires), Eliakim   BH
    Ichabod   Bel.   UC
    Peter   Cpl. PWAR   York Co.   Mir.
    Richard Burgess, Capt.   P398
      Co. 32, grocer, 85
    Seth, farmer   Ct.   a.b.   Or.
    Seth, Jr., farmer   Ct.   a.b.   Gn.
    Zalmon   Bel.   Kings Co.   St. John
Stackall, Richard, tailor, 85   P1436   St. John Co.
Stackhouse, Charles   BMG   Maug.
    Hastings   BH   Ga.

Stackhouse, Joseph	Pa.	1 NJV	C76	Kings Co.
Robert, house carpenter, 95	Pa.	Sgt. 1 NJV	C97, 98	Cn.
Stac(e)y, Jeremiah		2 NJV	Bl. 2	Gr. Lake
Stafford, William		Surg. mate ML		
Stage, William			Kings Co.	
Stagg, Jacob		Sgt. 2 NJV	Bl. 2	
Standard (Standred, Stannard), John *or* Joseph		RFA	Queens Co.	
Stanford, Abraham, carpenter, 85				
Stanley, John		LAR		Carl.
Thomas		Cpl. 1 DeL.	P1280	Bl. 8
Stannick (Stennick), Conrad		Waldeck	Burton	
Stanton, Benjamin, 2nd Lt. Co. 4, blacksmith, 95	Ct.		P1311	Kings Co.
George, mariner			Ken.	St. John
John		QR	BH	
Joseph		BMG	Musquash	
Stanwood, Jonathan	Mass.?		Char.	
Staples, Francis	Eng./N.Y.	stores	Burton	Kes.
Henry			Burton	Kes.
Thomas			Burton	Kes.
Stark, John	N.H.	Lt. GP	Bl. 3	Mass.
Starkey, Hezekiah, yeoman, 85	N.J.	3 NJV	Wash.	
Jacob, servant			BH	
Mordecai, labourer, 85	N.J.	3 NJV	P878	Wash.
States, Margaret	R.I.		P1434	
William, potter	N.Y.	Engr.		
Stebbings, Cornelius			Gr. Lake	St. John
Josiah	Ct.	recr.	St. John	
Stedham, Amos		2 NJV	Bl. 2	
Steel, John, tailor, 85			d. '94	
Matthew		Sgt. NYV	Kes.	
(Staal?), Patt		64th	Pass.	
Steenberrich (Steensburgh),				
Cornelius		LAR	Penniac	
James			Kes.	
John		dr. NYV	Kes.	
Peter			Kes.	
Widow of John, Eng. dept.?			Kes.	
Steeples, Thomas		ML	Bl. 1	
Steers (Stairs), Richard			Bl. 5	
Stelle, Edward	N.J.	Lt. 2 NJV	Bl. 2	
Steeve, *see* Stivers				
Stephens (Stevens), Andrew, farmer	N.J.		P1379	
Anthony, negro			St. John Co.	
David			P623	Gr. Bay
Elizabeth, wdw. Lt. Richard			York Co.	
John (1)			P1404	St. John Co.
John (2), Harvard '66	Mass.		St. A.	
Joseph, house-carpenter		1 DeL.	F'ton	
Luke		KOR?	St. John Co.	
Samuel, shipwright, 98			Char.	
Shadrach		Sgt. 2 DeL.?	BH	Nash.
Shubal, carpenter, 85	Ct.		P168	
Simon			P189	St. John
Solomon, surveyor, 85			P179	St. John
William			St. A.	
Stephenson (Stevenson),				
Francis	N.C./Va.	ex. QR	Bl. 5	UC
John		Lt. Black Pioneers	Mag. R.	
Solomon		Sgt. QR?	Bl. 5	Queens Co.
William		guide	Sch.	
Sterling, John		Capt. ML	P216	Bl. 1
Sterne, Moses		NCV	Kes.	
Sterrit, John			Kings Co.?	

Stewart (Stuart), Alexander (1)		74th?	Mir.	
Alexander (2)		Lt. KAD	Bl. 4	UC
Allan	Scot/.N.C.	Lt. Col. NCH	St. A.	
Brian Lafferty			Pr. Wm.	N.J.
Charles		2 DeL.?	Mir.	
Duncan (1)		42nd	Nash.	
Duncan (2)	N.C.?	Lt. 74th	St. A.	
Elizabeth, tavernkeeper			St. John	
Hugh			St. A.	
Isaac	Scot./S.C.	troop	P1121	
James (1), labourer		CMG?	St. A.	
James (2), gentleman			Sch.	
James (3), yeoman, 85		Sgt. 3 NJV	P939	Ken.
James (4), merchant, 86			P1237	Eng.?
James (5)		Sgt. LAR	Nash.	
John (1), shopkeeper, 85			P1411?	
John (2), yeoman, 85			Kings Co.?	
John (3), labourer, 90		42nd	Nash.	
John (4), tailor, 90 ?		Ens. ML	Bl. 1	
Malcolm		Cpl. 1 NJV	Queensbury	
Peter (1)		Sgt. 42nd	Nash.	
Peter (2)		BMG	P1432	Mir.
Robert, housecarpenter, 85		42nd?		
Stinson			Char.	
Walter, yeoman, 85	N.Y. D. Co.	Sgt. LAR	P233	Sussex
William (1)	Mass.		St. A.	
William (2)		Capt. KAD	P1419	Bl. 4
Stickel (Stickles), John Frederick			Bel.	
Stiles, Ashbell	Ct.	KAR	P702	U.S.A.
Stilkey, Balthazar			St. A.	
Stil(l)well, Daniel	N.Y. St. Is.	CMG	Gr. Lake	
Jeremiah, mariner	N.J.		Kn.	
John (1)	N.J.		BH	
John (2)	Pa.	KAD?	Gr. Lake	
Mary			P332	
Richard		KAD	Gr. Lake	
Samuel			BH	d. '91
William, weaver			Gr. Lake	
Stinick, see Stannick				
Stinson, David			Char.	
James	Mass.	a.b.	St. A.	
John (1)			St. A.	
John (2)	NH..	WV	P491	Burton
Samuel	N.H.	WV	Burton	
Stivers, Caleb, shoemaker		GP	Bl. 3	Queens Co. UC
Stobe, John, tailor, 85		Cpl. QR		
Stocker, Stephen			P1179	
Stockford, Abraham		2 DeL.	Queens Co.	
Thomas		2 DeL.	Wash.	
Stockley, Paynter			Kings Co.	
Stockton, Andrew Hunter	N.J.	Lt. 1 NJV	P175	Sussex
Charles Witham	N.J.	Ens. Rogers Rangers	Ken.	U.S.A.
Richard Witham	N.J.	Maj. 6 NJV	Sussex	
Stoddart, John, goldsmith, 85			P395	
Stoker, John		Ord.	Kings Co.	
Stone, Benjamin, habitmaker, 85			Queens Co.	
Ebenezer	Ct.		Burton	Gr. Lake
John (1)		RFA	Mag. R.	
John (2)		?	Pr. Wm.	UC
Joshua	Ct.	Sgt. NYV	Kes.	
Josiah			BH	Ken. Is.
William	Ct.	KAD	Pr. Wm.	
Storey, Zachariah		Sgt. NYV	Kes.	Gn.
Storms, Abraham		Sgt. GP	Bl. 3	
John, blacksmith, 90	N.Y. W. Co.		Ptld.	
Samuel, blacksmith, 85			Kings Co.	
Storrow, Thomas, merchant		8th	Campobello	
Stourdy (Sturdee?),			Maug.	

Name	Origin	Service	Place		
Stout, James			St. A.		
John	N.Y.		d. '02		
Peter	N.J.		BH	N.J.	
Stover, Jonathan, mariner			Pass.		
Peter		1 NJV	Sussex		
Stow, Edward, painter, 85	Eng./Mass.	navy	Maug.	St. John	
Straeder (Streightor, Straytor), Christian, merchant, 85	Ger.		P551		
Henry, millwright, Lt. Co. 11			LR		
Straight, Amos	Ct.		Queens Co.		
William	Ct.		Queens Co.		
Strang (L'Estrange), Elizabeth	N.Y. W. Co.				
Gabriel		Sgt. LAR	P1194		
John		KAD	Or.		
Lot(t), mariner, 95	Mass.		Queens Co.	St. John	
Seth			C119, 166, 591,2		
Strat(t), John, labourer, 85					
Stephen		navy	Wash.		
Strawbank, John		1 DeL.	Bl. 8		
Strawberry, Aaron			Musq.	Mir.?	
Straws, Dederick, farmer	N.Y.				
Street, John			P835	UC	
Samuel, cordwainer, 85	Ct.		P831	N.S.	
Samuel Denny	Eng.	Lt. RFA	P22, 65	Burton	
Stretch, John	Pa.?	1 NJV	BH		
Samuel	N.J.	WJV	C54	Ken.	N.Y.
Strickland, Amos	Pa. B. Co.		BH		
Edward			C86		
John	Pa. B. Co.		BH		
Jonathan, *see* Shicklin					
Stringham, William		Engr.	P422		
Studholme, Gilfred	Ir.	Maj. RFA	P40-3	Ken.	
Stultz, Henry		WL	Westm.		
Stump, Michael	Pa.		P1009	Char.	
Sturdivan, Samuel		KAD	Bl. 4		
Sturgis, Jesse	Pa.		Gr. Lake	Westm.	
Stymest, Benjamin	N.Y. L.I.		Mir.		
Jasper, carpenter, 85	N.Y. W. Co.		P810		
Suggit, Christopher, carpenter			Kn.		
Sullivan, Edward		PL	Bl. 7		
James		GP	Bl. 3	d. '84	
Matthew		PWAR	Nash.		
Summers (Somers), Joseph			LR	U.S.A.	
Philip, baker	N.J.	2 NJV	Bl. 2	F'ton	
Sumner, Thomas	N.J. Gloc.	1 NJV	Kn.		
William Augustus			Bel.		
Supplee (Sipprell?), Enoch			P1001	LR	
James		Lt. 1 DeL.	Bl. 8		
Surbitt, George		Ord.	Sch.		
Surtee (Settee), Stephen		RFA	Or.		
Sute (Shudie?), John		1 DeL.	Bl. 8		
Sut(t)er, James			P394	Queens Co.	F'ton
Sutherland, Adam		1 DeL.	Bl. 8		
Alexander		Lt. RFA?	F'ton	Halifax	
George (1)		42nd?	Nash.	Mir.	
George (2)		QR	Mir.		
Hugh		42nd	Nash.		
Jean, m. McKay			Kings Co.		
John (1), brother of Jean		42nd	P265	Nash.	
John (2)		42nd	P262	Nash.	
John (3)		42nd	Nash.		
John (4)			P698	York Co.	
Peter		74th	Pass.		
Robert		42nd	Nash.		
William (1)		42nd	Nash.	Mir.	
William (2)		QR?	Char.		
Sutton, Edward		PWAR	LR		
Joseph, husbandman	Pa. No. Co.	Em. Ch.?	Queens Co.		
Swain, William		Engr.	St. A.		
Swan, John		KAR?	St. A.		

Sweeney, Brian		QR	St. A.		
Francis			St. John Co.		
Miles, mariner, 85		Sgt. QR	P720		
Sweet, George, wheelwright	R.I.		Queens Co.		
Jonathan			Bl. 8		
Sweezy, Aaron	N.Y.? N.J.?		Mir.		
Swift, Joseph	Pa.	Capt. PL	P224	Nash.	Pa.
Swigard, Jonathan	S.C.		St. John	S.C.	
Swim, John		3 NJV	York Co.		
Phoebe			F'ton		
Switzer, Peter, cutler, 85			P1144	N.Y.	
Syms, see Sims					
Sypher (Cypher), John			Gr. Lake		
Lodovick,	N.Y.	P787	Gr. Lake		
gentleman, 85					
William		Engr.	Gr. Lake		
Tabor, Jesse	N.J.	1 NJV	Ham. R.		
Thomas			Burton		
Tucker		1 NJV	St. John		
Tacks, Andrew ?			Char.		
Talbert (Tolbut), Osbourn		Cpl. 3 NJV	P937		
Tallent, Joseph		ML	Bl. 1	Kn.	
Talley, John			Gr. Lake		
Tappan, William		2 DeL.	Carl.?		
Tarbell, Samuel	Mass.	Vol. KAD	St. John	LC	
Tarrant, Leonard	Va.		Burton	Wash.	
Tater, George	N.Y. D. Co.		Sunbury Co.		
Taylor, Abel			C88		
Amos, cooper, 85			Cn.		
Archibald Pattison	Scot./N.C.		St. A.	Bahamas	
Edward	N.J.?		P289, C25		
George	N.J.	1 NJV	St. John		
Gillam		CMG	St. A.		
Henry		3 NJV	Queens Co.		
Isaac		BCV	P1246		
James (1)		KAD?	Bl. 2, pur.		Carl.
James (2), merchant	Scot.	Sgt. 3 NJV	P926	F'ton	
James (3)			Ham. R.		
John (1)		QR	Mag. R.		
John 2), yeoman, 85	Pa.?	QMR.GP	P692	Bl. 3	F'ton
John (3)		CMG?	St. A.		
John (4)		Sgt. KAR	St. John	d. '02	
Lawrence		PL	Bl. 7		
Matthew, shipcarpenter, 85			P1306		
Oliver, Lt. Co. 43			P308		
Ralph			St. A.		
Samuel			St. John Co.	Sussex	
Thomas D. (Joseph)?		KAR	Bl. 6		
Walter		74th			
William (1), carpenter		Ord.?	Kings Co.		
William (2), son of James (2)			Maug.		
Teed (Tidd), Daniel, carman			Woodstock		
Elias	N.Y.	dr. KAR	Bl. 6	Carl.	
Joseph	N.Y. W. Co.	WL	P1205	Bel.	
Nathaniel			Bel.	St. John	
Philip		Cpl. KAR	Bl. 5		
Silvanus	N.Y.	dr. KAR	Bl. 6	Carl.	
Solomon		KAR	Bl. 6	Carl.	
Teeple, Peter		Sgt. KAD	York Co.	UC	
Temple, Joseph	Mass.?	1 DeL.	Bl. 8		
Tennant		a.b. St. Is.		Bel.	
Tenny, Asa	Mass.		Char.		
Jonathan	Mass.		Char.		
Terrill, Anthony	N.Y. D. Co.	guide	Queens Co.	Bahamas	
William	N.J.	guide	Bl. 7	d. '90	
Terry, Daniel	Ct.	KAD	Bl. 4		
Zebedee, Sr.	Mass.	Capt. LNE	C58	U.S.A.	
Zebedee, Jr.	Mass.		C128	Ham. R.	
Tetley, Jonathan		Cpl. 3 NJV	Gr. Lake		
Thain, James			P489	St. John	
William, mason, 95					

Thames, Thomas		1 DeL.	Bl. 8		
Thatcher, Abel			BH	York Co.	
Bartholomew	N.Y. H. Co.	Capt. 2 NJV	Bl. 2	N.J.	
Jonathan		Sgt. 2 NJV			
Theal(l), Charles	N.Y. D. Co.		P176	LR	
Gilbert	N.Y. W. Co.		P1029		
Samuel, cordwainer, 85					
Samuel, Jr., labourer, 96					
Tertullus			St. John Co.		
Thom, John			Pr. Wm.		
Thomas, Charles, mariner	Ct.	mar.	P20		
Dugal			St. A.		
Evan	Pa.	BCV	BH	Pennfield	
Henry, Capt. Co. 3	N.Y.	BMG	P9, 616		
Jacob		Cpl. PL	Bl. 7	Kn.	
John		QR	Bl. 5	Shef.	
Jonathan	Mass.		St. John	U.S.A.	
Joshua	Pa. No. Co.	BCV, QR	Burton		
Mary			Or.		
Samuel, mariner		QR?	P587		
Stephen		Adj. KOR?	P793		
Thomas, boatbuilder, 85	Ct.		P804		
Walter	N.Y.		P615	Bel.	
William, labourer, 87	Pa.	Capt. BCV	P627		
Thom(p)son, Alexander		KAR	Bl. 6		
Charles		dr. 2 NJV	Bl. 2		
Cornelius	N.J.	Lt. 2 NJV	Bl. 2	UC	
David, joiner, 85	N.Y.?	guide		UC	
Dugal			St. A.		
James (1), merchant	N.Y.		St. A.		
James (2)		RFA	Mag. R.		
James (3)	N.J.	2 NJV	Bl. 2		
John (1)	N.J.	Lt. 1 NJV	Maug.	U.S.A.	
John (2)		Sgt. 42nd	Nash.		
John (3)	Scot.		P1325		
Lewis	N.J.	Ens. 2 NJV	Bl. 2	U.S.A.	
Mary	Pa.		P1107	Ken.	
Peter, free negro		1 DeL.	Bl. 8		
Richard			Mag. R.		
Robert (1)		3 NJV	P736	Bel.	
Robert (2)		74th			
William, merchant, 95		KAR? 3 NJV?			
Thorn(e), James, farmer, Lt. Co. 36	N.Y. D. Co.				
Joseph, mason, Capt. Co. 44	N.J. Mx. Co.	CMG	P630	BH	
Melancthon	N.Y.		P1186	Kings Co.	New Canaan
Robert, carpenter	N.Y. D. Co.		Wash.		
Samuel	N.Y. D. Co.		Wash.	UC	
Stephen		Sgt. NYV	Queens Co.		
Thomas		Engr.	Gr. Lake	York Co.	
William, Lt. Co. 44	N.Y.		P631	BH	
Thornton, James			Maug.		
John	N.C./S.C.		P779	Pr. Wm.	left
Luke D.			P1111	LR	
Matthew	NH	pris.	St. A.		
Peter, barber		KAD	P331		
Thomas		QR	Bl. 5		
Thorp, Abner		2 NJV	Bl. 2	Ken.	
Elisha, innkeeper, 85			LR		
Jabez		Sgt. PWAR	St. John Co.		
James			Kes.		
John, blacksmith, 85			P821		
Thrasher, George		CMG	Musquash		
Thringe, James			St. A.		
Thumb, James		KOR?			
Thurston, John	N.Y. D. Co.		Gr. Lake		
Tilby (Tealby), John		QR	Bl. 5		
Till, Jacob		Engr.	P380	Gn.	Mir.
Tillen, John			Mispec		

Name	Origin	Military	Grant	Location	Extra
Tilley, James			P345		
Samuel, joiner, 85	N.J./N.Y.	WL	P1201	Queens Co.	Shef.
(Tillage), Samuel			PL	Mir.	
Tilton, Clayton	N.J.		Musquash		
John, mariner	N.J.		Lepreau		
Thomas			P302		
William			Musquash	U.S.A.	
Timison, Casper, carpenter	N.Y. L.I.		?		
Tindal, James, carpenter			Bl. 1		
Tingle, William		1 DeL.	Bl. 8		
Tippets (Tipping), Francis			Sch.		
Tisdale, Ephraim	Ct.		P998	Gr. Lake	UC
Henry, blacksmith			P594	U.S.A.	
Titus, Benjamin	N.Y.		Wash.		
John	N.Y.		Wash.	UC	
Silas			Wash.		
Todd, Mix	Ct.	PWAR	York Co.		
Tokeley, Richard		KAR	Sussex		
Tomlinson, Isaac	Ct.	Lt. KAD	C248		
John, tailor, 85	Ct.		P822		
Joseph	Pa. B. Co.		P466	BH	
Samuel	Pa.		BH		
Toner, Peter	Pa.	BCV			
Tooker, Abiah			Maug.		
Toole, John, victualler, 85		Sgt. KAD			
Topham, John		54th	Or.	Queens Co.	
Tower, William (1)			St. A.		
William (2)		2 DeL.?	Gr. Lake		
Towne, Archelaus and Samuel			Char.		
Townsend, George			C282		
Job			P1227	BH	York Co.
John	N.Y. W. Co. wag.		Gn.		
Leven		Capt. Lt. ML	P222	Bl. 1	
Trafford, Robert			BH		
Trafton, Thomas, baker. 85		PWAR	Penniac		
Trainer (Traynor), James			Bl. 5		
Traphager, Henry, cordwainer, 85			P1268		
John			St. John Co.		
Travis (Travers), Anne			Ken.		
Elizabeth	N.Y. W. Co.		Ken.		
Francis, tailor, 95			Nash.		
James	N.Y. W. Co.	NYV	P814	UC	
Jeremiah	N.Y. W. Co.	dr. LAR	Kings Co.		
John, labourer, 90		RFA	Mag. R.		
Nathan	N.Y.		Cumb.		
Treadwell, Ephraim	Ct.		Maug.	d. '84	
Nathaniel, yeoman, 85	Ct./N.H.?		Wash.	UC	
Samuel	Ct.		Wash.		
Thomas, farmer	N.Y. L.I.				
Trebblecock, Thomas		42nd	C306	St. John Co.	
Trecartin, Martin, carpenter	N.Y. D. Co.		P1112	LR	
Trendle, Hester			Ken.		
Triglith, Peter			P1409	Kings Co.	
Tripp, Peleg			Queens Co.	York Co.	
Troak, James		RFA	Mag. R.		
Troop (Troup), Esther, wdw.				UC	
Lt. John, 3 NJV,					
m. George Ross					
William		Cpl. PWAR	Nash.		
Trott, Thomas	Mass.		Kings Co.		
Trotter, Peter			Ken.		
Trowbridge, Joseph Easton			BH		
Samuel			BH	Or.	UC
Trumpour, Paul		Ens. DeL.		UC	
Zachariah, cordwainer			F'ton		
Tucker, George		Engr.	P704	York Co.	
Solomon		a.b.	Burton		
Thomas		KAD	Bl. 4		
Tully (Tillen?), John			St. John		
William, labourer			Lanc.		
Tupper, Eldad	Mass.	Lt. GP., sec.			
Turch, Gregory			Wash.	St. John	

Turnbull, James, shipcarpenter		Capt. N.J.			
Turner, Calvin		BMG	Or.		
Holden			York Co.		
James		NYV?	St. A.		
Joel Spencer		QR	Bl. 5	Mir.	
John (1)		Engr.	P959	Kings Co.	
John (2)			Maq.	F'ton	
Miller	Ct.	gar.			
Nicholas	Mass.		St. A.		
Samuel B.	Mass.		St. A.		
Thomas	Mass.		St. A.		
William (1)		QR	Mir.		
William (2)	N.J.	Lt. 2 NJV	Nash.	Carl.	
Turney, Thomas		Sgt. NYV	Kes.		
Tuttle, Amos			P701		
Daniel	Ct.		Or.	UC	
Twaddle, James			Gr. Lake		
Tyler, John	N.J.?		Spry's	St. John	
William	N.Y. Char. Co.	Lt. KR PWAR?	Nash.	Rest.	LC
Tyng, William	Mass.	CMG	P595-604	Gn.	U.S.A.
Tyrer, Benjamin		2 NJV	Bl. 2		
Uhart, *see* Yourt					
Uhthoff, Henry			St. John		
Uins, Timothy		2 NJV	Bl. 2		
Ull, Mary			P627		
Umphries (Humphry), Adolf			Gn.		
Underhill, Bartow	N.Y.		Queens Co.		
Elnathan	N.Y.		Kes.		
John, Lt. Co. 46			Ken.	U.S.A.	
Nathaniel, Lt. Co. 21	N.Y. W. Co.	Sgt. BL	Maug.		
William	N.Y. W. Co.	ex. QR	P173	Queens Co.	
Underwood, Benjamin			Mag. R.	York Co.	
Duty	R.I.	LNE	Kn.	UC	
Henry, blacksmith	N.C.	NCV	Gr. Lake		
John, farmer	R.I.	BMG	Kn.		
Peleg		KAD	Kings Co.	UC	
Upham, Edward, auctioneer, 90			Burton	St. John	
Jabez	Mass./Vt.		Kings Co.		
Joshua, Harvard '63	Mass.	Maj. KAD	C240	Maug.	Ham. R.
Urion, Miles, mariner	N.J.		P1127		
Urquhart, Donald		42nd	Nash.		
John		ML	Bl. 1	Bel.	
Utley, Joseph, trader, 85					
Vail (Veale), Asher	N.J.		Gn.		
Benjamin			So. Bay		
Daniel			Bel.		
Isaac		Sgt. NYV	Kes.	Queens Co.	
John			Bel.		
Jonathan		Sgt. 2 NJV	Bl. 2	York Co.	
Joseph			Gr. Bay		
Lewis	N.J.		Spry's	UC	
Moses			Bel.		
Nathaniel	N.J.		P1105	d. '83	
Peter		PWAR	York Co.		
Robert	N.J.		C73	Sussex	
Wilmot		KAD	P174	Bl. 4	
Valentine, George			BH		
Valleau, Fauconnier, "sadler"	N.Y.	Engr.	Queens Co.		
John	N.Y. W. Co.	Surg. mate GP	Bel.		U.S.A.
Peter	N.Y. D. Co.		St. A.	UC	
Theodore	N.J.	QMR. 1 NJV			U.S.A.
William			Sunbury Co. left		
Van, Patrick, black			York Co.		
Van Allen, Henry	N.J.	Ens. 3 NJV	P888	Burton	UC
William, Sr.	N.J.	Lt. Col. PL	P889	Burton	UC
William, Jr.	N.J.	Capt. NJV	Gr. Lake		

Van Amburgh, Abraham, cordwainer, 85	N.J.		P539		
William			Queens Co.		
Vanater, Aaron			Or.		
VanBuskirk, Abraham		Lt. KOR	St. John Co.		
Lawrence	N.J.	Engr.	Maug.		
Vance, John	N.Y.?		Bl. 8	York Co.	
William	N.H.		St. A.	Maug.	
Vanclief, Daniel			BH		
Vanderbeck, Abraham	N.J.	Sgt. 3 NJV	F'ton		
Vanderbilt, Fanny			P891		
Vanderburg, Henry, Sr.	N.Y. D. Co.		Burton		
Henry, Jr.	N.Y. D. Co.		Burton		
Peter	N.Y. D. Co.		Or.	UC	
Richard	N.Y. D. Co.	Capt. Em. Ch.	Burton	UC	
Vanderfield, William			Bl. 8		
Vandewater, Francis	N.Y.		P582		
Vandine, Arthur			Gr. Lake		
Cornelius			Gr. Lake	U.S.A.	
Dow	N.Y. L.I.	Capt. LAR, sec.	Gr. Lake		
Van Dumond, see Dymond					
Vanfelt, Francis			St. John		
VanHoozen, Ephraim		3 NJV	York Co.		
VanHorn, Cornelius, merchant, 85	N.J.	CMG		UC	
Gabriel, innkeeper	N.J.		F'ton		
VanHorsten, Hendrick		Cpl. GP	Kes.		
VanMaple, Mary	N.Y.		Burton		
Van Mater, Chrinyonce	N.J.	pris.	Shel.	St. John	N.J.
VanNorstrand, Albert, 2nd Lt. Co. 40, farmer	N.Y. L.I.				
Daniel, Lt. Co. 47, farmer	N.Y. L.I.		Ham. R.		
John, farmer	N.Y. L.I.		Ham. R.	U.S.A.	
Peter, weaver	N.Y. L.I.			UC?	
Van Pelt, Catherine			Or.	Wash.	
Samuel		KAR	C307	Sussex	
Tunis			P287	Ken.	
Van Scriver, John		NYV	P897	Kes.	U.S.A. UC?
Van Tassel, Isaac	N.Y.	WL	Maug.		
Vanwart, Abraham	N.Y. W. Co.	GP	Bl. 3	Gn.	
Garret	N.Y. W. Co.	GP	Queens Co.		
Isaac	N.Y. W. Co.		Queens Co.		
Jacob	N.Y. W. Co.		Queens Co.		
William	N.Y. W. Co.		Queens Co.		
Van Winkle, John, Lt. Co. 52, saddler, 85			P996		
Nathaniel			St. John		
Van Wyck	N.Y. L.I.		St. John		
Vaux, Joseph Richmond			Musquash		
Veal(e), see Vail					
Venner, John Lauder, merchant, 85			St. John	England	
Vermilyea, Peter, carpenter, 85	N.Y.?	Cpl. LAR	LR		
William, carpenter	N.Y.		P622		
Verner (Vernon), Edward, schoolmaster	Pa.?		Shef.		
Gideon	Pa.	guide	Mag. R.	UC	
Viall, William	Mass.		St. A.		
Vincent, Burling	N.Y. D. Co.		Ken.		
Charles	N.Y. D. Co.	WL	Ken.		
Elijah		Ens. GP	Bl. 3	UC	
Isaac			Queens Co.		
Vroom, Peter	N.J.		St. John	N.S.	
Waddington, Burrows	N.J.?		P1040	Sussex	
Wade (Wead), Thomas, farmer	R.I.		Gn.		
Wadlow, John			Ken.		
Wager, Allen		1 NJV	Sussex		

338

Wagstaff, Thomas Howard, silversmith, 85			P984		
Wainwright, James, merchant			St. John		
Waldman, *see* Waltman					
Waldron, Peter G., mason, 85			Musquash		
Walker, Benjamin	Mass.	Cpl. QR	P1294	Bel.	
John	N.Y.?	Engr.	Bel.		
Joseph		RFA	St. A.		
Matthew			Sch.		
Moses		QR	Bl. 5	Spry's	U.S.A.
Richard, Capt. Co. 35 Eng.			P155	d. '85	
Silas			Char.		
Thomas (1)	Ir./S.C.		P846	Bel.	
Thomas (2)		RFA?	Mag. R.		
Thomas (3), cooper	Eng./N.Y.	Ord.	P1208		
Thomas (4)		Lt. NYV	Kes.	N.S.	
Wall, Frederick		NYV	Kes.		
James, mariner	Ct.?	a.b.	Sch.		
John, mariner	Ct.?	a.b.	Sch.		
Patrick		Sgt. GP	Bl. 3		
Wallace, Jacob	N.Y.W. Co.		BH		
John	N.J.	1 NJV	C389		
Jonathan	N.Y.W. Co.	Sgt. NYV	BH	Char.	
Wallbridge, Asa	N.Y. D. Co.		Queens Co.		
Waller, James, *same as* Wall?			Sch.		
Walls, James, cooper			Mir.		
Wally, Jacob		PWAR	Kes.		
Walsh (Welch), Edward		KAR/a. b.?	Kn.		
Francis, Capt. Co. 11	Pa.	sea	St. A.	Eng.	
George		RFA	Mag. R.		
John (1), carpenter		2 DeL.?	St. John		
John (2)			Deer Is.		
Roger		KOR	St. John Co.		
Thomas		QMR. ML	Nash.	Md.	UC
William		3 NJV	F'ton	Carl.	
Walter(s), Cornelius		LAR	Mir.		
Daniel	N.Y. D. Co.	WL	Gr. Lake		
Robert	N.C.	NCV	Gr. Lake		
William		NCV	LR	Sunbury Co.	
Waltman (Woltma), Peter	Pa.	BCV	BH	Mace's Bay	
Walton, Benjamin, shipwright			St. A.		
David			Sch.		
Jesse	Ir./N.Y.		BH		
Thomas	Pa.	BCV	Kings Co.		
Wanamaker, Elizabeth, m.	N.J.		Maug.		
John Post					
Henry		3 NJV	Ken.		
John		3 NJV	Ken.		
Peter		Cpl. 3 NJV	F'ton	UC	
Wangy (Wansay), Nathaniel			Kings Co.		
Wanser, Henry, blacksmith	N.Y. L.I.		?		
Wanton, William	R.I.		St. John		
Ward, Benjamin		Lt. LAR	Sunbury Co.	U.S.A.	
Billias, farmer	Ct.		Kings Co.		
Daniel, 2nd Lt. Co. 34, cartman, 85			P1162		
Dollen		70th	Pass.		
Elisha			Ken.		
Jacob			C313		
James		2 NJV	Burton		
John, gentleman, 85		Lt. LAR	P412, C314		
Joshua		Ens. PWAR	Burton	Eng.	
Robert		Sgt. LAR	Kings Co.		
Shadrach		Sgt. PWAR	Nash.		
Uzal, 2nd Lt. Co. 16, hatter, 85	N.J.		P1364		
William, silversmith			Burton	F'ton	
William, merchant, 85 *same?*					
Wardell, Cornelius (Walter?)			Ham. R./84		
James			St. A.		
Michael, carpenter, 85		Sgt. NJV	UC		
Warden, Robert			St. A.		
Ware (Wier), David			Queens Co.		

339

Name	Origin	Regiment/Rank	Grant	Location	Location 2
Warner (Werner,) Charistian, baker, 85			P1120		
Edmund (Edward?)		1 NJV?	Ken.		
John		Engr.	P1302, 1428		
Warren, Nathaniel	Mass.	LAR	Queens Co.	Kings Co.	
Warwick, Anthony	S.C.	Cpl. QR	Bl. 5		
Frederick			P560		
Washburn, Joseph			Queens Co.		
Samuel, 2nd Lt. Co. 45					
Zephaniah			Ken.		
Waterbury, David, cooper, 95	Ct.		LR		
John, schoolmaster, 85	Ct.	gar.	P621		
Peter Cook, gentleman, 85	Ct.	Ct. LAL	P114	Pr. Wm.	
Silvanus	Ct.	pilot	Gn.		
William, labourer			F'ton		
Waters, Abijah, cordwainer, 85			P832		
Abraham, joiner, 85	Ct.		P585		
Waterson, John			Sch.		
Watkeys (Watkins), Hezekiah			BH		
Samuel	Ct.		BH		
Wat(t)leworth, William			Kings Co.	WI	
Watson, Christopher, labourer, 95			Kn.		
Francis, carpneter, 85			St. John		
James, carpenter, 96			P1223	Westm.	
John (1)	Mass.	Hosp.	St. John		
John (2), blacksmith, 85	Scot./Pa.	PWAR	C278	Queens Co.	
Martin			Queens Co.		
Peter			Kings Co.	York Co.	
Robert, cooper		a.b.	St. A.		
Thomas		1 NJV	LR		
Watt(s), Henry		KOR			
John (1)		74th	Pass.		
John (2)	N.Y. City	NYV?	P1197	Kn.	
Robert		74th	Pass.		
William, carpenter		2 NJV	Bl. 2	F'ton	
Watty, Philip			P928		
Way, Cornelius		Sgt. LAR	LR		
Joseph			BH		
Titus		KAR	Bl. 6	Carl.	
Wayhop, William		KAD	Bl. 4		
Wayman, see Weyman					
Wead, see Wade					
Weatherhold, Francis		Cpl. RFA	Mag. R.		
Weaver, Frederick		2 NJV	Bl. 2	Mir.	
George		2 NJV	C419	Bl. 2	
Webb, Richardson	N.Y.	KAD	Or.		
Sarah			P645		
Susannah			Sch.		
William, labourer, 85	N.Y.	BMG	P1206		
Webber, James			Burton		
Jeremiah			Burton		
William, carpenter			BH	Wash.	
Webster, Elizabeth			P503	Bel.	
Weed, Isabella			Mag. R.		
Jonas			BH		
Weeks, Alexander			Gr. Lake	Burton	
Nathaniel, farmer	N.Y. D. Co.				
Zophar, cooper	N.Y.		P528		
Weir (Wear), John		42nd	P264	Nash.?	
Weldon, Patrick, yeoman, 85		PWAR	P31	left	
Welling, John			St. John	P.E.I.	Westm.
Peter, carpenter, 85	N.Y. U. Co.	Engr.	C394		
William		LAR	C393	York Co.	U.S.A.
Wells, Gad	Ct.	AL	Ken.	U.S.A.	
James or Jane			Kn.	U.S.A.	
Nathaniel, millwright	Md.		?		
Nathaniel, Jr., miller	Md.		?		
William		ML	BH		

Wentworth, Joseph			P205	St. John	
William			Kes.		
Wert (Wort), Conrad,			C21	Cn.	
shipcarpenter					
Godfrey		2 NJV	Macnaquac		
West, Israel	N.J.	2 NJV	Bl. 2		
James		CMG	St. John Co.		
John		17th	Ham. R.		
William (1)		1 NJV	P429	York Co.	
William (2)		Sgt. 17th	St. John Co.		
Westall, William			Sunbury Co.		
Weston, Ebenezer ?			Char.		
John		1 DeL.	Bl. 8		
Westrope, John		Ens. PWAR	?		
Wetmore, Caleb	N.Y.W.Co.		Ken.	Cn.	
David Brown	N.Y.W.Co.		C265	Ken.	
James, school-	N.Y.W.Co.		St. John		
master, 93					
John, Capt. Co. 52	N.Y.W.Co.		C368	N.S.	
Josiah, cordwainer			St. John		
Luther,	N.Y.W.Co.		C295		
gentleman, 95					
Robert G.	N.Y.W.Co.		Ham. R.	U.S.A.	
Theodore,	N.Y.W.Co.				
yeoman, 96					
Thomas,	N.Y.W.Co.		C311	Gn.	
2nd Lt. Co. 7					
Timothy, Lt. Co. 7,	N.Y.W.Co.		C267		
Esquire, 85					
Timothy Fletcher,	N.Y.W.Co.		C269	U.S.A.	
physician					
William,	N.Y.W.Co.		C367		
labourer, 96					
Weyman, Edward		1 NJV	Ken.		
Margaret, wdw. of	N.Y.W.Co.		Maug.		
Moses					
Whaley (Waily, Weakley ?),					
Thomas		Cpl. LAL	P684		
Wheaton, Daniel		GP	Bl. 3	d. '84	
David		GP	Bl. 3	Maug.	Westm.
Ephraim, cartman	N.J./Ct.		Bel.	St. John	
James		KAD	P775	Bl. 4	
Wheeler, Edward	N.Y. A. Co.		Maug.	York Co.	
George	N.Y. A. Co.		Or.	d. '86	
Henry		LAR	Mir.		
John, farmer	N.J.	svd.	Swan Cr.	Sussex	
Nicholas, mason, 85	N.Y. A. Co.		York Co.		
Reinhard (Reynard)		KAR	P989	York Co.	Carl.
Sarah, wdw. Lt.			C260		
Josiah, m. Thomas					
Hanford, 1784					
Whelan, Francis (also James)		2 DeL.	Carl. ?		
Whelpley, Darling	Ct.		Kn.		
Jonathan,		nco. LAR	Kn.		
cartman, 96					
Oliver	Ct.		Kn.		
Whinom, Thomas ?			Mir.		
Whittaker, George			St. John		
White, Amos	N.J.?		BH/87		
Andrew, butcher			P559		
Dominick			St. John Co.		
Elizabeth, wdw. of			Or.		
William, d. en route					
Henry		ML	P220	Nash.	
Isaac			Kes.		
James		CMG	Kn.		
Jane			Gn.		
John (1)		2 NJV	Bl. 2		
John (2), pilot, 85	Ct.	pilot	P1010, 1182, 1240		
John (3)		74th	Pass.		
Joseph		ML	Bl. 1	Gn.	
Peleg or Peregrine			P1331	Bel.	
Peter		RFA	P238		
Rufus			St. A.		

White, Thomas (1)		Cpl. NYV	P385	Kes.	
Thomas (2). tailor, 86	N.J.	Ord.?	P956		
Vincent, weaver	N.J.	ex. NJV	P954	Gr. Lake	
William (1)	N.J.	Vol. 1 NJV	P570	Gr. Lake	
William (2)		a.b.	P665	St. John Co.	
Whitehead, Benjamin		2 DeL.	York Co.	U.S.A.	
James		NYV	P494	Kes.	
John		navy	Ken.		
Whit(e)ley, Moses	Va./S.C.	Lt. SCR	St. John Co.	U.S.A.	
William		Sgt. QR	York Co.		
White(k)nact, John		1 NJV	Sussex		
Whiting, Leonard			Char.		
Sylvanus	Ct.		St. John		
William			P769	Kn.	
Whitlock, John		Capt. QR	C509, 510	Bl. 5	LC
Jonathan			C508		
Solomon		Cpl. PWAR	Penniac		
Thomas, merchant, 85			P10, 158		
William,			C7	Sussex	
merchant, 85					
Whitney, Josiah			BH		
Nathan, 2nd Lt.	N.Y. W. Co.		P675	N.S.	
Co. 48					
Nathan, Jr.	N.Y. W. Co.		P666		
Samuel (1)		LAL	Bl. 6		
Samuel (2),	Ct.		St. John		
hatter, 85					
Sylvanus, Capt.	Ct.		Kn.	St. John	
Co. 1, labourer, 95?					
Whitworth, Nathaniel			Kings Co.	Eng.	
William		NCV	Kes.		
Wicke, see Weeks					
Wiederholt, see Weatherhold					
Wideman (Weedeman),					
Bernard, yeoman, 85			P1176?		
Wier, see Ware					
Wiggins, Charlotte	N.Y.		P374	Sussex	
m. (1) Stephen Hustice,					
(2) Oliver Arnold					
Daniel			P1145		
Isabella			P1244	Kn.	
Jacob			Gr. Lake		
John	N.Y. U. Co.	2 DeL.	P634	Ptld.	
Samuel, merchant			St. John		
Stephen	Eng./N.Y.		Queens Co.	St. John	
Wightman, John,	R.I.	Lt. LNE	St. John		
gentleman, 95					
Wilbour, William, cabinet		QMR. KAD	C167		
maker					
Wil(l)cox, Robert			Sussex		
Wilds (Wiles), Solomon	PL		Bl. 7	Bl. 3	
Wiley, William, carpenter, 85					
Wilkie, Joseph		LAL	Or.		
Wilkins, Andrew			Char.		
John, labourer			F'ton		
Thomas		3 NJV	Wash.		
Wilkinson, Francis		RFA	Mag. R.		
Robert	N.Y.	Engr.	Kings Co.		
Willard, Abijah, merchant, 85	Mass.	CMG	C345		
Solomon	N.H.	WV	P108	U.S.A.	
Willery, Henry		KOR	St. John Co.		
Williams, Benjamin	N.Y. City?		Gr. Lake		
Charles Perry			P241		
David	N.H.?		LR		
Elijah, merchant, 86	N.H.	WV		U.S.A.	
Gilbert		Sgt. GP	Bl. 3	NY	
Jacob		NYV	Kes.		
James			BH	LR	
John (1), Sr.		BMG	P1227	Sunbury Co.	
John (2), Jr.		BMG	P1228		
John (3)	N.J.		Kings Co.		
John (4)			Queens Co.		
Jonathan,		Capt. GP	P172	Bl. 3	UC
yeoman, 85					
Joseph	N.J.	AL	BH		

Williams, Nehemiah		KOR	St. John Co.		
Nicholas, labourer, 95		1 NJV			
Oliver		Engr.	Gr. Lake		
Philip	N.Y.		Maug.	York Co.	
Reuben (1)	N.Y. W. Co.	WL	Queens Co.		
Reuben (2)		Cpl. PWAR	St. John river		
Richard		QR	F'ton		
Samuel	N.C.	BMG	LR	UC	
Thomas		CMG	P353		
William	N.Y. U. Co?	PWAR?	P1089	LR	
Wynant	N.Y. D. Co.	guide	Or.	UC	
Williamson, Archibald	Scot.		Dig.		
(Williams?), George			C279		
John	Ct.? N.Y.?	navy?	Gn.		
Robert		Ens. PWAR?			
Willis, John	N.J.	Lt. 2 NJV	Bl. 2	Mir.	
Williston, John Bayley	N.Y.?		Bl. 6	Mir.	
Willega (Willowgee), Christopher			Kn.		
Wilmot, Lemuel	N.Y. L.I.	Capt. LAR	F'ton	Lincoln	
Malcolm	R.I.?	Ens. 3 NJV	Sunbury Co.	Westm.	
Wilsey, Lawrence		KAR	F'ton	Carl.	
Wilson, Adam		42nd	Nash.		
Alexander		QR	Bl. 5	Queens Co.?	
Daniel	Ct.?		Rusagonis/84		
David			BH		
Ezekiel			BH		
George, merchant, 85	Scot./N.Y.		P1254	Gr. Lake	
(Willson), John (1)	N.J.	CMG?	Maug.	Mir.	UC
John (2), mariner		a.b.	LR		
John (3)			Carl.		
Joshua			BH	Maine	
Mary			Sch.		
Nathaniel	Ir./S.C.		Ken.	St. John	
(Samuel) Richard	Ir./N.C.	Lt. GB	Nash.		
Robert (1), merchant			P118	d. '85	
Robert (2)			P1308		
Robert (3)		a.b.	Char.		
Thomas	N.J.		Sch.		
Widow			Dig.		
Winant (Winient), Cornelius			P303		
Daniel			Dip. Har.	U.S.A.	
Winder, Edmund, merchant, 85					
Moses, labourer			BH		
Windsor, John, silk dyer			St. John		
Wingfield, James		GP	Bl. 3		
Wingood, Matthew		a.b.	Sch.		
Winn, William		NYV?	St. John Co.		
Winnard, Bartholomew		PWAR	St. John Co.		
Winslow, Edward	Mass.	Mus. Mas. Gen.	P80, C202		F'ton
Hannah			C226		
Penelope			C227		
Sarah			C230		
Winter, John, son of John Windsor?			St. A.	minor	
Wintzer, Constantinus or Christian		Hess.	Kn.		
Wise (Wyse), John		2 NJV	Bl. 2	St. John	
Nicholas, labourer, 95			St. John Co.		
William, tavernkeeper, 95			St. John Co.		
Wisely, George, tailor			St. A.		
Wiser, Frederick, Lt. Co. 31		Engr.	N.S.		
Wiswal, Peleg			Sussex	N.S.	
Witham (Whithom), Stover			Dig.	St. John?	
Wittinton, John			Char.		
Wolf, Conrad		dr. 1 NJV	Queens Co.		
Wolhaupter, John ?			St. John	F'ton	
Wolverton, Henry			Maug.		
Thomas			Maug.	Carl.	
Wood, Caleb	N.Y. L.I.		Gr. Lake		
Daniel			Rusagonis		
George			Char.		
Israel	N.Y. U. Co.		Ken.	UC	

Wood, Jacob		3 NJV	Nash.		
James			Queens Co.		
John	N.Y.? Pa.?		Kn.		
Joseph, blacksmith			C346		
Peter			?		
Platt			Ken.	UC?	
Robert, tobacconist	Pa.		P391		
Samuel		KAR	Or.	Shef.	
Solomon		Sgt. 1 DeL.	Bl. 8	Nash.	
Stephen		1 NJV	Penniac	Queens Co.	
Thomas (1)		LAL?	Or.		
Thomas (2)	N.J.		BH		
Timothy			Ken.	Queens Co.	
Woodland, Anthony		KAR	Bl. 6	York Co.	
Woodl(e)y, George	Ger./N.J.	1 NJV	P575	UC	
Matthias	Ger./N.J.		Queens Co.	UC?	
Woodsworth, Giles, *see* Woodward *or* Woodworth					
Woodward (Woodworth),					
Abraham	N.C.?		BH		
Anthony	N.J.		BH		
Anthony, Jr.	N.J.		BH		
Giles	N.J.		P979	Gn.	St. J.?
Isaac	N.J.		BH	St. John	
Jacob	N.J.		BH		
Jesse, merchant, 95	N.J.		BH		
Jesse, Jr.	N.J.		St. John	Halifax	
John, merchant	N.J.	Ens. 1 NJV	BH	St. John	
Nimrod			BH		
Robert		Ens. 3 NJV	BH	Carl.	
Samuel (1)	N.J.	guide		Carl.	
Samuel (2)		ML	P221	Bl. 1	
Simeon?			Dig.		
William		RFA	Mag. R.		
Wooley, Elihu		Cpl. 1 NJV	P683	U.S.A.	
Henry			Ham. R.		
John			Ham. R.		
Thomas, Capt. Co. 47		ex. 1 NJV	Ham. R.		
Woolton (Whooton), Morris, cooper, 85		Cpl. LAL	P689		
Woolsey, Benjamin Muirson, *see* Muirson					
Jacob (Wilsey?)		GP	Bl. 3	d. '84	
Wooster, Henry		KAD	Bl. 4	left	
Worden, Anderson			Kings Co.		
Gabriel, mason	N.Y.W. Co.		Queens Co.		
Isaac	N.J.		Wash.		
Jarvis, mason, 85		Sgt. KAR	P1072		
Jeremiah, bricklayer, 85			P1270	Gr. Bay	
John (1), cordwainer		KAD	C147	Cn.	
John (2)			Queens Co.		
Wort, *see* Wert					
Worth, Benjamin	N.J.		BH		
John		3 NJV	Rus.		
Wray, John		nco. 38th	P433	St. John Co.	
Wright, Alexander		1 NJV	C321	Penniac	Kn.
Archibald	Scot.		Gr. Lake	UC	
Corvad, shipwright, 85					
Daniel		Sgt. KAR	Bl. 6		
Elias	N.Y. Q. Co.		P986	Pennfield	
Elizabeth, m. Solomon Powell			Ken.		
Gilbert, mason	N.Y. L.I.				
Jacob	N.Y.?		Ken.		
James		3 NJV	Carl.		
John Watson, shipwright			P166	Kn.	
Jonathan		PWAR	St. John Co.		
Malcolm		KAR	LR	Mir.	UC
Musco		Cpl. PL	Bl. 7	Nash.	Carl.
Nathaniel			Gr. Lake	York Co.	
Phoebe, m. John Porter			Bel.		

Wright, Richard		2 NJV	Bl. 2		
Samuel			Or.		
Solomon	N.Y./Ct.	WL	Maq.		
Susanna, wdw.			Gr. Bay	Queens Co.	
William, m. John Lawson					
Thomas		54th	C283	Mir.	
Uriah	N.Y. D. Co.		P790	Queens Co.	
William (1), Capt. Co. 15	N.Y./N.J.		P1000		
William (2), Jr.	N.Y.		P1002		
William (3), brother of Samuel				Kings Co.	
Wyatt, Hezekiah		Sgt. KAR	Or.		
Wyer, David			Pass.	d. '85	
James		74th	Pass.		
John			Char.	St. John?	
Thomas, merchant	Mass.		St. A.		
Wylie (Wiley), George			Sch.		
Wylly, William	Ga.	Capt. KCR	St. John	Bahamas	
Wynant, *see* Winant					
Yearsley, Thomas, 2nd Lt. Co. 17, silk dyer, 85			C103	St. John	
Yeaston, John ?			Pass.		
Yelden, Alexander		Sgt. 42nd	Nash.	Mir.	
Yeamans (Yeomans, Youmans),					
Benjamin		svd.	Queens Co.		
Eli			C327	Kings Co.	
John, Lt. Co. 45	N.Y. D. Co.	pris.	Gr. Lake		
William	Eng.		Wash.		
Yerxa, John	N.Y. W. Co.	WL	Burton	Kes.	
Yorke, James	R.I.	ves.	Or.	Carl.	
Young, Abraham	N.Y.		C79	Gr. Lake	UC
Ephraim	Mass.		Dig.		
Francis, clockmaker, 85	Pa.		P1124		
George			P637	Kings Co.	
Henry		Sgt. 2 NJV	C33	Bl. 2	Q. Co.
Isaac		CMG	Gr. Lake		
Jacob	Mass.	KOR	St. A.		
James		74th	St. A.		
Jeremiah			Dig.		
John		LAR?	Nash.		
Joseph		KAD	Bl. 4	Carl.	
Peter, blacksmith, 85		ex. NJV	C34, 80	Burton	ref. from N.E.
Stephen			Burton		
Thomas		ML	P221	Bl. 1	
William (1)		Sgt. PWAR	Ken.		
William (2), Lt. Co. 30, Pa. shipwright, 85		Hosp.?	C9	St. John	
William (3)		2 NJV	Bl. 2		
William (4)		Sgt.? NYV	dr. '84		
Youngshusband, George, mariner, Lt. Co. 12, merchant, 95			P1117		
Robert, mariner			P1136		
Yourt (Uhart, Heward), John yeoman, 85		2 NJV	Bl. 2		

ADDENDUM

Dunmead, William		NJV	UC
Keithland, Cathline, Philip	N.J.	NJV	
Ken			
Tompkins, Edmund		LAR Bl. 6	
Edward		Sgt. LAR Penniac	
Elijah		LAR	
Jacob		Sgt. PWAR Salmon R.	Carl. Co.
John		Sgt. LAR	
Obidiah		Sgt. LAR	,, ,,
Roger	N. Y.	LAR dr.	
Thomas		KAD Schoodic	

BIBLIOGRAPHY

The unprinted sources upon which this study of the
Loyalists of New Brunswick is based are:

New Brunswick Crown Land Office, Memorials,
Grant Books, Maps. (There are about 10,000 Memorials
covering the years from 1784 to 1830. They are supposed
to be sorted chronologically by counties, but the
arranging was hastily done. For some of the counties
there are indexes.)

New Brunswick Legislative Library, additional
Memorials.

New Brunswick Council, Journals, 1785.

New Brunswick Museum, Archives Department,
Saint John:
A. S. Beyea, *History of French Village.*
Florence Estabrooks, *The Estabrooks Family.*
Additional Memorials, MSS.

Saint John Public Library.
Family histories.
Gagetown Church Records (copy).

Saint John City Hall.
Roll of Freemen.

Acadia University Library.
Church Records and Minute Books.

Public Archives of Nova Scotia.
Grants, Memorials, Accounts, particularly of
Studholme.

347

Public Archives of Canada.
  Muster Rolls of the Loyalist Regiments.
  Raymond Collection.
  Various MSS.

Public Record Office, London.
  Loyalist petitions in AO 13.
  Admiralty Papers.
  Colonial Office Papers.
  Foreign Office Papers.
  War Office Papers.

Historical Society of Pennsylvania, Manuscripts Department.
  Hughes Papers.
  Jacobs Papers.

American Philosophical Society, Philadelphia.
  Franklin Papers.

Colonial Williamsburg, Inc.
  British Headquarters or Carleton Papers.

Clements Library, University of Michigan.
  Clinton Papers.

In addition, the list of New Brunswick Loyalists has been checked with the Records of Deeds in St. John, Kings, Queens, Sunbury, York, Charlotte, Westmorland, and Northumberland counties, and with Probate records.

My thanks are due to the curators of all these Libraries and Offices.

Periodicals

The New Brunswick Magazine.
Acadiensis.

The Royal Gazette and the New Brunswick Advertiser.
Collections of the New Brunswick Historical Society.
Bulletins of the New Brunswick Historical Society.
Collections of the Nova Scotia Historical Society.
New England Historical and Genealogical Register.
New York Genealogical and Biographical Record.
Collections of the New York Historical Society.
Collections of the New Jersey Historical Society.
Journals and Sessional Papers of the Legislature of New Brunswick.
New Brunswick Almanacs.
Publications of the Champlain Society.

Printed Works

Brebner, J. B., *The Neutral Yankees of Nova Scotia: a Marginal Colony during the Revolutionary Years.* (New York, 1937).

Davidson, W. H., *William Davidson,* 1740-1790. (Saint John, 1947.)

Ganong, W. F., Papers in the *Transactions of the Royal Society of Canada,* and elsewhere.

Gilroy, Marion, *Loyalists and Land Settlement in Nova Scotia.* (Halifax, 1937.)

Lawrence, J. W., *Foot-Prints; or Incidents in Early History of New Brunswick.* (Saint John, 1883.)

The Judges of New Brunswick and their Times. (Saint John, 1907.)

Loyalists' Centennial Souvenir. (Saint John, 1887.)

Maxwell, L. M. B., *The History of Central New Brunswick.* (Sackville, 1937.)

Raymond, W. O., *The River St. John*. (1st ed. 1905, 2nd ed., Saint John, 1910, 3rd ed., with notes by J. C. Webster, Sackville, 1943.)

The Winslow Papers. (Saint John, 1901.)

Kingston and the Loyalists of 1783.

Sabine, L., *Biographical Sketches of Loyalists of the American Revolution*. (Boston, 1864.)

Second Report of the Bureau of Archives, Ontario, 1905. (United Empire Loyalists: Enquiry into the Losses and Services in Consequence of their Loyalty. Evidence in Canadian Claims.)

(These are only the few with direct bearing on the Loyalists of New Brunswick.)

INDEX

351

352

353

354

Fencible Americans, 5, 75, 119, 120, 130, 141, 167, 202, 203, 211, 215, 248.
Ferguson's Corps, 5.
Fifty-five, the, 60, 175-177, 183, 250, 251.
Finney, Caleb, 228.
Finucane, Bryan, 76, 138.
Fisher family, 158.
Fisher, Mrs. Lewis, 87, 90, 96, 97, 103, 106, 108.
Fisher, Peter, 218.
Fishing, 34, 35, 109, 118, 120, 121, 193, 197, 200, 203.
Fitzgerald, Lord Edward, 219, 220, 222.
Flewelling family, 158, 160.
Flewelling, Guilford, 155.
Flewelling, John, 245.
Florida, 7, 28, 59.
Folkins family, 158.
Ford, John, 247.
Forrester, James, 78, 246.
Forrester, John, 58, 78, 245.
Forrester, Joseph, 58.
Fort Beauséjour, 110, 111, 112, 114.
Fort Cumberland, 59, 69, 78, 118, 119, 190, 198, 200, 211.
Fort Frederick, 119.
Fort George, 200.
Fort Howe, 36, 37, 68, 75, 77, 95, 98, 99, 105, 116, 119, 120, 129, 141, 167, 189, 195, 249.
Fort Lawrence, 111.
Foster family, 159.
Foster, Benning and Ezekiel, 228.
Foster, Ebenezer, 116, 171.
Fowler family, 158, 209.
Fowler, Daniel, 246.
Fowler, Gabriel, 154.
Fowler, Henry, 245, 247.
Fowler, Weeden, 247.
Fox, Charles James, 89, 136.
Fox, Henry E. 64, 89, 97, 101, 127, 128, 129, 130, 131, 134, 136, 139.
Francfort Township, N.B., 168.
Francklin, Michael, 121.
Franklin, Benjamin, 19.
Franklin, William, 18, 19, 23, 25, 134.
Frederick, son of George III., 146, 186.
Fredericton, N.B., 146, 162, 168, 179, 185-188, 190, 193, 196, 206, 207, 208, 218, 235, 237.
Free Briton, 58, 77.
Freeman of Saint John, 160-163.
Freetown, Mass., 3.
French, (see also Acadians), 97, 184.

French Lake, N.B., 194.
French Revolution, 143.
French, James, 98.
Frink family, 158.
Frost, Jeremiah, 228.
Frost, Sarah, 77.
Fukes, Daniel, 179.
Fundy, Bay of, 36, 38, 51, 68, 69, 85, 88, 92, 95, 105, 106, 109-123, 125, 126, 137, 138, 163, 164, 166, 167, 170, 182, 191, 198, 209, 211, 215, 219.

Gage, General, 3, 118.
Gagetown, N.B., 1, 38, 74, 75, 97, 116, 146, 168, 170, 189, 190, 220.
Gal(l)ilee, Samuel, 94, 95.
Ganong family, 158.
Gardiner family, 159.
Gardiner, Alexander, 247.
Garrison Battalion, 65, 86, 98, 185, 248.
Gaspé, Que., 110.
Generous Friends, 59, 78.
George III., 146, 180, 186.
Georgia, 7, 155.
Germaine, Lord George, 9, 17, 18, 132.
German, 113, 117, 154, 159, 205.
Germany, 59, 171.
Gerow family, 158.
Giberson family, 158.
Gibson, Robert, 51, 72.
Gidney family, 158, 209.
Gidney, Joshua, 246.
Gilbert family, 49, 156, 158.
Gilbert, Samuel, 3.
Gilbert, Thomas, 1, 3, 49.
Gill, Robert, 74, 86.
Gillies family, 159.
Gillies, Jesse, 208.
Glasier, Beamsley, 171.
Glenie, James, 233.
Gloucester, Virginia, 24.
Golding family, 158.
Goldsbury, Samuel, 14, 251.
Goold, Arthur, 119.
Gordon, Hugh Mackay, 100.
Gordon, Robert, 78.
Gor(e)ham family, 158.
Gor(e)ham, Joseph, 58, 78, 119, 245.
Goudge, Thomas, 246.
Governor of New Brunswick, 139-150, 177, 178, 186-188.
Governor of Nova Scotia, (see also Parr, John), 32.
Grand Bay, N.B., 193.
Grand Duchess of Russia, 70, 71, 80.

356

357

358

360

Pickel family, 158.
Pitcher, Moses, 58.
Pitt, William, 134.
Plymouth, Mass., 9, 13, 29, 141.
Portland, Me., 97.
Portland Point, N.B., 145, 151.
Port Matoon Association, 167, 201.
Port Mouton, N.S., 167, 201, 211.
Port Roseway, N.S., 35, 46, 47, 49, 50, 59, 60, 71, 77, 79, 84, 92, 127.
Port Royal, N.S., 112.
Post-Loyalists, 200, 226, 230.
Potts, John, 250.
Poughkeepsie, N.Y., 55.
Powell family, 158.
Pre-Loyalists, 70, 75, 105, 109-123, 166, 184, 192, 195, 196, 197, 200, 205, 206, 208, 215, 223, 226-229.
Presbyterians, 133, 237.
Prescot(t), General, 11, 12, 13.
Prevost, Major, 85, 105, 129.
Price family, 195.
Prince Edward Island, 99, 135, 156.
Prince of Wales' American Regiment, 5, 41, 66, 86, 98, 130, 152, 180, 185, 207, 210, 215, 249.
Prince William, N.B., 180, 207, 210.
Prisoners, 14, 20-23.
Privateers, rebel, 68, 115, 118, 119, 197.
Providence, 73.
Provincial Light Infantry, 88.
Provincial Normal School, N.B., 225.
Provincials, 13, 23, 41-45, 52, 53, 61-67, 85-91, 103-106, 108, 120, 126, 128, 129, 130, 145, 151, 152, 153, 173, 178, 179, 197, 216, 249.
Provisions, (Royal Bounty of), 6, 7, 10, 14, 30, 44, 47, 51, 63, 91, 94-108, 188, 189, 192, 210, 223.
Pryor, Edward, 246.
Pugsley family, 158.
Purdy family, 158.
Putnam family, 158.
Putnam, James, 9, 141.
Pynchon, Joseph, 35.

Quakers, 92, 191, 202, 211, 216, 237, 245.
Quebec (see also Canada), 24, 36, 139, 157, 198, 227, 232.
Queensbury, N.B., 180, 194.
Queens Co., N.B., 105, 107, 146, 147, 149, 151, 182, 189, 204.
Queens Co., N.Y., 29.
Queen's Rangers, 5, 65, 98, 105, 180, 198, 203, 207, 213, 214, 249.

Quereau, Elias, 98.
Quit rents, 32, 44, 132, 172.

Ramsheg, N.S., 199.
Ranger, 86.
Rations, see Provisions.
Raymond, Samuel, 193.
Raymond, W. O., 81, 151.
Reece, Anthony, 245.
Reed family, 159.
Reed, James, 91, 245.
Reed, Leonard, 98.
Reed, Thomas, 77.
Refugees, 3, 4, 5, 7, 8, 9, 13, 14, 25, 47, 58, 64, 67, 84, 88, 91, 103, 104, 105, 126, 127, 128, 145, 151, 152, 153, 167, 197, 205, 208, 209, 215, 216, 220, 249.
Regiments, British American, see Provincials.
Regiments, British of the Line:
20th, 33.
33d, 99.
42d, 98, 196, 201, 208.
54th, 219.
57th, 99
60th, 65, 66, 131, 168.
64th, 70th, 74th, 84th, 201.
Reid, Alexander, 148, 149, 209.
Restigouche River, N.B., 115, 198.
Rhode Island, 4, 7, 9, 10, 11, 12, 13, 18, 29, 77, 99, 110, 111, 117, 131, 251.
Richards, Mark, 78, 92.
Ritchie, John, 73.
Roberts family, 158.
Robinson family, 159, 163.
Robinson, Beverley, 41, 130, 141, 142, 152.
Robishaux, Mrs., 228.
Rogers family, 159.
Rolf or Ralph, Daniel, 228.
Roman Catholics, see Catholics.
Rombouts (Rumbout), N.Y., 56.
Ro(o)me, George, 18, 19.
Ro(o)me, Henry, William L., 247.
Ro(o)me, John Chevalier, 251.
Rose, 3.
Ross family, 159.
Rowbotham, Francis, 92.
Roxby, John, 73.
Royal Fencible Americans, see Fencible Americans.
Royal Highland Regiment, 5.
Royal North Carolina Regiment, 157.
Royalton, Vt., 153.
Ruggles, Timothy, 9, 15, 18, 19.